高级实用英语系列教材

美国总统演讲名篇赏析

Appreciating Excellent Speeches by the US Presidents

主　编　徐中川（中国海洋大学）
编　委　邹姗姗（中国海洋大学）
孙广峰（中国海洋大学）
乔发光（山东大学）
冯延群（上海海洋大学）
李玉香（同济大学）

中国人民大学出版社
·北京·

序言

我和中川2005年相识于海大校园。课暇相见，多有切磋。他主编这部《美国总统演讲名篇赏析》期间，同我频频交流。他的教学认真和为学勤勉给我印象深刻。如今，他们的辛勤汗水凝成著作，我应命写序，诚惶却欣然。

美国的建国历史迄今还不到250年，但美国的治国理念影响、制度文明辐射乃至信仰和价值观输出，却是其他任何国家和地区无法比拟的，因而也是不容回避和忽略的。而所有的这一切都体现在美国总统的各类演讲中。众所周知，美国总统个个都是经历了无数选战历练、辩才非凡的政治家。他们的演讲几乎篇篇都称得上语言与政治相结合的文学精品，有些甚至被公认为全球文学宝库中的不朽之作。

这部教材的编著者们基于多年的研读积累和丰富的教学经验，从美国总统各种公开演讲中精选出13位总统的16篇演讲：从立国初期奠定共和政体的华盛顿、杰斐逊，到南北战争时期维护国家统一的林肯；从20世纪初期充满理想主义的威尔逊，到30、40年代带领美国人民战胜大萧条与法西斯暴政的小罗斯福；从冷战时期同苏联对抗的杜鲁门、肯尼迪，到坚信“政府不是问题的解决办法，政府本身才是问题所在”的里根，直至后冷战时期经历了“9·11”恐怖袭击事件的小布什和首位黑人总统奥巴马。总统、演讲与当下的时政相关联，语言、文化与当今的时局相映照，这等于凝练出一部微型但较为系统的美国发展史。赏读这些原汁原味的美国总统经典演讲，读者不仅能够体会演讲的语言魅力、修辞力度和思想深度，还能洞悉美国政治文化和社会发展的非凡进程，比较全面地了解美国核心文化、价值观念和思维方式，从而在提高学生语言综合技能（特别是修辞和口语表达技能）的同时，培养包容的人文精神和开阔的国际视野。

大学英语教学改革的方向在哪里？这一点在新颁布的《大学英语课程教学要求》中已明确指出，那就是要将语言教学、技能训练和文化导入三者有机地融合起来。中川等编著者紧扣当前大学英语教学改革方向，采撷颇能体现美国历史发展进程和核心文化观念的美国总统演讲名篇，将其编写成一部集语言教学、技能培养和文化导入三者为一体，既富知识性、又富人文性和思想性的创新性美国总统演讲教材，体现了中国海洋大学、山东大学、同济大学等国内知名高校教学与科研一线的中青年骨干教师探索大学英语教学改革的勇气和成绩。加之编排科学、合理、新颖，符合教学实际，因而是一部值得推荐的优秀教材。

中国海洋大学教授、翻译研究所所长

前言

亲爱的读者，你想有效提高自己的英语阅读理解能力吗？你想迅速提高英语口语表达能力吗？你想了解美国的历史、政治、文化与价值观吗？那么，选择使用本书一定不会使你失望。

本书秉承"阅读中外经典，通识人类文化"的大学通识教育指导思想，以几个权威的美国演讲修辞网站中给出的美国总统最佳演讲和国内十余本美国总统演讲精选集、美国总统就职演讲全集等资料为基本依据，并参考笔者本人对美国总统演讲的阅读、研究与教学经验，精选美国总统演讲 16 篇（其中就职演讲 10 篇，就重大问题发表的其他演讲 6 篇）。这些演讲都曾在美国历史上产生过重大而深远的影响，堪称世界文学与思想殿堂中璀璨的明珠。学习它们，不仅可以有效地提高你的英语阅读能力和审美情趣，而且可以帮助你了解在短短的 200 多年中造就自由、民主、富强的世界第一大国美国的宪政制度和价值观，同时也串起了美国从开国奠基时期、南北战争时期、两次世界大战时期、冷战时期直至冷战后时期的诞生、成长到强大的发展史。读者可在提高自己阅读与表达能力的同时，领略到语言文字的巨大魅力，丰富自己的政治、历史和文化知识，并得到一种精神上的享受。

不同于坊间名目繁多的各种美国总统演讲集的是，本书不仅对收录的每篇演讲提供演讲的原文与中文译文、作者简介 (About the Author)、演讲背景 (About the Speech)、生词解释 (Notes to the Speech)、名句摘引 (Famous Remarks)（注：名句摘引以粗黑体标在演讲原文中）等内容，同时我们还提供了以下特色板块：

1. 演讲赏析 (Appreciating the Speech)：通过对演讲内容、结构和语言特色等的分析，帮助读者从宏观和微观这两个层面上理解和欣赏演讲，有效提高阅读理解和英文写作能力。

2. 文化知识链接 (Culture Links)：该板块是本书最大特色，涉及美国历史、政治、教育、宗教、法律、军事、成功观、家庭观等方方面面，帮助读者广泛、深入地了解美国社会与文化，提高跨文化交际能力。

3. 相关练习题 (Relevant Exercises)：不仅包括检测对演讲理解方面的问题，同时设计了相关的思考、讨论题，目的是引导学生勤于思考和分析、判断，以有效培养、提高他们的思辨能力。

此外，本书还收录包含了美国历史上最重要的三大政治文献（《五月花号公约》、《独立宣言》、美国《宪法》及《修正案》）等的实用附录，并配备光盘，为大部分演讲提供了音频或视频资料。这样就便于读者更有效地理解、欣赏、模仿每篇演讲，并运用其中的精彩词句于实际口语活动之中。

美国总统演讲是一座丰富的语言文化宝库，它对各层次的英语学习者（尤其是中高级英语学习者）都是取之不尽的优质学习资源。我们希望并相信，在本书的帮助下，读者们经过认真研读，能够获得英语语言技能和文化修养上的双丰收。

本书内容丰富、生动、实用，它集语言知识、修辞知识和美国历史文化知识于一身，不仅可作为大学英语通识课、选修课的教材（任课教师可根据课时、学生等具体情况，在一学期中教授完全部演讲，或选择其中的 8 ～ 10 篇），也是广大中高级英语学习者提高英语水平、了解美国文化的良好读本。

需要提请读者注意的是，美国总统都是能言善辩的政治家，是美国政府的代言人，因而有的演讲中不可避免地反映了演讲者的个人观点或带有时代的烙印，请大家在阅读时作出正确的分析和判断。

本人统筹、设计了全书的宏观和微观结构，完成了演讲及附录的选取、译文的整理、视频和音频材料的搜集整理等工作。各篇演讲的具体赏析由本人和来自我校及山东大学、同济大学、上海海洋大学的几位同事、同仁合作完成，并由本人对全稿进行了终审、统稿。

在本书的编写过程中，承蒙中国海洋大学外语学院副院长赵德玉教授、翻译研究所所长任东升教授提出宝贵意见，在此向他们深表谢意。本书的编写和出版过程中，一直得到中国人民大学出版社外语分社领导和编辑们的热情支持和帮助，在此谨表谢忱。

虽然我们本着对读者负责的态度以一丝不苟的精神完成了全书的编写和校对工作，但书中仍难免存在疏漏、不足之处，还望同行专家和广大读者不吝批评指正，以便于我们在再版时作出改进。

本人电子邮箱：xzc_ouqd@yahoo.com.cn

徐中川

2012 年 12 月于中国海洋大学外语学院

目录一
（总目录）

* 表示有视频及音频

⁺ 表示有视频

目录二
（文化知识链接目录）

演讲中的修辞运用

演讲中的修辞运用

美国总统演讲是美国总统为了阐述政府的大政方针及对国内外重大问题的主张而做的，几乎每篇都经过了反复修改和精心润色，表现出了娴熟的驾驭语言的技巧，其中的许多篇章被公认为演讲中的传世之作。在这些精彩演说中，丰富的修辞手段的运用无疑起到了重要的作用。在此，我们简要介绍一下美国总统演讲中的常用修辞技巧。实际上，这些修辞手段（或叫修辞手法）常常用于各类演讲及散文、小说、诗歌等其他文体中。

1. 头韵（alliteration）：是一种常用的语音修辞手法，指在相邻或相近的一串词语中重复出现开头的音素，以增强语言的节奏感和表现力。

例如，小布什总统在 2001 年的就职演说中说："Today, we affirm a new commitment to live out our nation's promise through **civility, courage, compassion and character**." 在这句话中，courage, compassion 和 character 三个词都以辅音 / **k** / 开头。

又如，谚语"**Spare** the rod, and **spoil** the child"中的 spare 和 spoil 都以辅音 / s / 开头，也是运用了头韵的修辞手法。

2. 反复（repetition）：指通过重复同一个词、短语或句子来加强语气，起到加深听众印象的效果。

例如，富兰克林·罗斯福总统在日本偷袭珍珠港后在国会的演说中的：

"**Last night Japanese forces attacked** Hongkong.
Last night Japanese forces attacked Guan.
Last night Japanese forces attacked the Philippine Islands.
Last night Japanese forces attacked Wake Islands."

在这里，罗斯福通过重复运用"Last night Japanese forces attacked ..."这一句式，加深了听众（即美国国会议员）对日本疯狂侵略行径的印象，给予他们以震惊和警醒的作用。罗斯福这篇演说促成了美国国会当天就作出决定，对日本宣战。

又如，英国著名诗人塞缪尔·泰勒·柯勒律治（Samuel Taylor Coleridge），在 *The Ancient Mariner* 中将 alone 一词重复了 4 遍，起到了强调其时之孤独心境的强烈效果：

Alone, alone, all, all **alone,**

Alone on a wide, wide sea!

3. 排比（parallelism）：指将一串相关的词、短语或句子做相似的安排，从而形成一个结构平衡、语义紧凑的整体，起到节奏鲜明、增强语势的效果。与反复不同的是，排比主要是重复句型结构。

例如，林肯总统1863年在葛底斯堡演说中的名句："... and that government **of the people, by the people, for the people**, shall not perish from the earth."

又如，法国思想家，文学家罗曼·罗兰（Roman Rolland）在"Mohandas Gandhi"一文中写道："This is the man **who has stirred three hundred million people to revolt, who has shaken the foundations of the British Empire, and who has introduced into human politics the strongest religious impetus of the last two thousand years**."

4. 对照（antithesis）：指把意义相反或相对的词、短语或从句排列在平行或对称的结构中，来表达相反或相对的概念。这种修辞方法可以深刻地揭示和突出事物的对立和矛盾，并且由于句式平行对称，读起来朗朗上口，从而起到鲜明的对照效果。与排比不同的是，对照一般仅由结构相同或相近的两项构成（且两项表达相反或相对的概念），而排比由结构相同或相近的两项或两项以上构成（各项之间的意义一般是相关或相近）。

例如，肯尼迪总统1961年就职演说中的："**United**, there is **little we cannot do** in a host of cooperative ventures. **Divided**, there is **little we can do**—for we dare not meet a powerful challenge at odds and split asunder." 其中的United与Divided形成对照，little we cannot do与little we can do形成对照，从而形象而生动地阐明了团结和分裂将会带来的截然不同的后果。

又如，19世纪英国批判现实主义小说家狄更斯（Charles Dickens）在*A Tale of Two Cities*中被广泛传诵的名句："It was **the best of times**, it was **the worst of times**; it was **the age of wisdom**, it was **the age of foolishness**; it was **the epoch of belief**, it was **the epoch of incredulity**; it was **the season of Light**, it was **the season of Darkness**..."这里连续运用多个对照，节奏铿锵、对比分明、引人深思。

5. 明喻（simile）：也叫打比方，指把所要说明的事物用比喻词同另一种具有鲜明的同一特征的事物联系起来，以作比拟，从而更加形象、生动地说明事物。英语中常用的比喻词有like, as, seem, as if, as though等。

例如，老布什总统在1989年的就职演讲中把极权主义思想形象地比做没有生机的树叶："The totalitarian era is passing, its old ideas blown away **like leaves from an ancient, lifeless tree**."

又如，美国小说家欧内斯特·海明威（Ernest Hemingway）在 *For Whom the Bell Tolls* 中对一匹马的描述："He was a beautiful horse that looked as if he had come out of a painting by Velasquez." 使读者在脑海中联想到了著名西班牙画家维拉斯凯兹笔下的骏马形象，起到了栩栩如生的效果。

6. 暗喻（**metaphor**）：也叫隐喻，它不用比喻词，直接把一事物当做另一事物来描述，两事物之间的联系和相似之处隐含在句意中，从而起到了使语言生动形象、增强语言表现力的作用。

例如，托马斯·杰斐逊总统的名句："The **tree** of liberty must be refreshed from time to time with the blood of patriots and tyrants. It is its natural **manure**." 在本句中，杰斐逊总统把自由比做大树，把鲜血比做用来浇灌自由之树的肥料，比喻形象深刻，表达了以鲜血和生命捍卫自由的坚定主张。

又如，美国人权运动领袖马丁·路德·金博士在其著名演讲 *I Have a Dream* 中说，"Instead of honoring this sacred obligation, America has given the Negro people a bad **check**, a check which has come back marked 'insufficient funds.' But we refuse to believe that the bank of justice is bankrupt." 本句中，马丁·路德·金把美国政府在 1863 年的《解放黑奴宣言》中给予美国黑人平等权利的承诺比做一张支票，一张打上了"现金不足"记号的支票，给美国政府以无穷的嘲讽和揭露，给听众留下了深刻的印象。

7. 拟人（**personification**）：是把物（包括动物、植物和抽象的概念等）当做人来描述的一种修辞手法。这种手法能够起到使所讲述的对象栩栩如生、活灵活现的效果，增强了语言的感染力和生动性。

例如，里根总统在其首任就职演讲中说："By your gracious cooperation in the transition process, you have shown **a watching world** that we are a united people pledged to maintaining a political system which guarantees individual liberty to a greater degree than any other, and I thank you and your people for all your help in maintaining the continuity which is the bulwark of our Republic." 本句中，里根总统把世界拟人化了，把它看做正在注视着美国的生命个体，激励美国人民团结一心维护美国的政治制度。

又如，美国著名批判现实主义作家欧·亨利的 *The Last Leaf* 中的一句话："In November a cold, unseen stranger, whom the doctor called Pneumonia, **stalked about the colony, touching one here and there with his icy fingers.** Over on the east side the ravager **strode boldly, smiting**

its victims by scores."在本句中，作者用几个表示动作的词（stalked，touching，strode，smiting）把肺炎（Pneumonia）拟人化了，使读者眼前浮现出一个到处肆虐、摧残生命的恶魔形象。

8. 夸张（hyperbole）：是为了达到某一目的而故意夸大（或缩小）事实的修辞手法，用以强调某一观点或抒发作者的强烈感情，从而给听众以鲜明、深刻的印象。需要注意的是，夸张是以事实为基础进行夸大，是一种艺术的修辞手法，而不是欺骗手段。运用这种修辞手法必须使人一听就知是夸张，能够引起人们的想象，但不能使人误以为真。

例如，肯尼迪总统在 1961 年的就职演讲中就用了夸张的手法。在谈到保卫自由制度时，他说："In the long history of the world, **only a few generations** have been granted the role of defending freedom in its hour of maximum danger."此句中，肯尼迪用夸张的手法激励并号召美国人民肩负起自己的神圣历史使命，献身于捍卫自由和人权的伟大事业。

又如，英国戏剧大师莎士比亚（William Shakespeare）的名作 *Hamlet* 中哈姆雷特的一句话，"I loved Ophelia: **forty thousand brothers could not, with all their quantity of love**, make up my sum."本句中，莎士比亚以艺术夸张的手法描写了哈姆雷特对奥菲利亚的爱，"四万个兄弟的爱合起来，还抵不过我对她的爱"，形象地说明了这爱情的炽烈程度。

9. 层进（climax）：是指在阐述论点时，根据由浅入深、由小到大、由低到高的原则，像上楼梯一样拾级而上的逐层深入、步步推进的修辞手法。这种修辞手法可加强感情色彩、增强气势，使听众易于对演讲者论点产生认同感。

例如，肯尼迪在 1961 年的就职演讲中谈到对一个和平、安全、正义的世界到来的期盼时说："All this will not be finished **in the first 100 days**. Nor will it be finished **in the first 1,000 days**, nor **in the life of this Administration**, nor even perhaps **in our lifetime on this planet**. But let us begin."此句以层进的手法，生动地表达了肯尼迪的坚定主张，即美国人民要从我做起，从现在做起，经过不懈努力，促成这样一个世界的早日到来。

又如，英国散文家、哲学家弗朗西斯·培根（Francis Bacon）在 *Of Studies* 中的名句，"Some books are to be **tasted**, others to be **swallowed**, and some few to be **chewed and digested**."本句中，培根用"品尝"、"吞咽"、"细嚼并消化"，层层推进，形象地向我们道出了对于不同书籍的不同阅读方法，给我们以非常深刻的印象。

10. 反问（rhetorical question）：指用疑问的形式表达确定的意义，不必回答，因其答案已寓于问题的反面。这种修辞手法可加强语言效果和听众印象，引起他们的深思和共鸣。

例如，亚当斯总统在1797年的就职演讲中用“What other form of government, indeed, can so well deserve our esteem and love?”一句反问，表达了对美国政体由衷的崇敬和信心。

又如，美国独立战争时期的著名政治家、演说家帕特里克·亨利(Patrick Henry)在1775年弗吉尼亚州大会的演讲中的铿锵之语，即运用了一连串的反问：“But when shall we be stronger? Will it be the next week, or the next year? Will it be when we are totally disarmed, and when a British guard shall be stationed in every house? Shall we gather strength by irresolution and inaction? Shall we acquire the means of effectual resistance, by lying supinely on our backs, and hugging the delusive phantom of hope, until our enemies shall have bound us hand and foot?”表达了他要美国人民立刻行动起来、坚决反抗英国殖民统治的坚定主张。

除以上列出的以外，美国总统演说中还常常运用大词（即含有6个字母以上或3个音节以上的较正式用词）、引用（如《圣经》中的话、名人先贤的话、警句、谚语等）、设问（即自问自答）和倒装句式等修辞手法。所有这些修辞手法的灵活使用，增加了美国总统演说的正式性、庄重感，加强了语言的感染力和鼓动性，易于给听众留下非常深刻的印象，并赢得他们的信任和支持。

主要参考书目：

1. 李树德，冯奇．英语修辞简明教程（第二版）．上海：复旦大学出版社，2011, 1
2. 肖福寿．美国总统就职演说赏析．上海：上海大学出版社，2009, 2
3. 冯景照，蔡宇茗．朗文名人演讲精选和技巧解析．南京：译林出版社，2007, 4
4. 冯翠华．英语修辞大全．北京：外语教学与研究出版社，2005, 1
5. 杨霞华．英文写作与修辞．合肥：安徽教育出版社，1984, 11

《美国总统演讲名篇赏析》

正　文

George Washington

(1732—1799)

乔治·华盛顿

1

George Washington's First Inaugural Address

Delivered 30 April, 1789, in New York

❑ About the Author

乔治·华盛顿（George Washington, 1732—1799），出生于弗吉尼亚州一个种植园主家庭，美国独立战争时大陆军（Continental Army）总司令，1789年成为美国第一任总统，在接连两次选举中他都获得了全体选举团无异议支持，担任了两届美国总统（1789—1797）。他在北美13个殖民地的独立和随后统一为美利坚合众国的过程中起到了十分关键的作用，因而被称为美国国父。学者们则将他和亚伯拉罕·林肯并列为美国历史上最伟大的总统。

在美国独立战争中，他运筹帷幄，身先士卒，率领大陆军团经过8年的艰苦奋战（1775—1783）赢得美国独立。那时，他的威望如日中天，他的一些同僚怂恿他黄袍加身，被他严词拒绝。他毅然辞去军职，回到了他在维农山（Mount Vernon）的庄园继续平民生活。

1787年他主持制宪会议，制定了现在的美国宪法，为美国的宪政制度打下坚实的基础。他在两届的任期中创立了许多持续到今天的政策和传统。1796年9月17日，在两届任期即将结束之际，他发表告别演讲，自愿放弃权力，坚决不再续任，以其实际而坚定的行动，在当时仍是皇权统治的世界上，开创了神话般的自愿"放权"、和平转移权力的先例，从而使美国总统任期绝不超过两届成为惯例（罗斯福总统因第二次世界大战的原因，任期超过了两届，属例外。但在罗斯福去世后这个惯例正式地被写进宪法第22号修正案里）。华盛顿以其杰出的贡献、超凡的人格魅力和不贪恋权位的高风亮节成为美国总统中永远的楷模，世代受到全体美国人民的敬仰和世界人民的尊敬。

❑ About the Speech

虽然多年的征战使华盛顿的身心疲累交加，但对祖国前途的神圣的责任感还是让华盛顿不甚情愿地接下担任第一任总统这一重担。或许在当时，对于巩固新生的共和国来说，没有任何其他人能够比他更能胜任了。华盛顿对身为第一任总统的意义有着深刻的理解。他说："我走上了前人未走过的路，我的一举一动都会被后任者作为先例来遵循。"在他任总统的 8 年中，他为未来的总统们立下了传统，做出了表率，确立了大政方针。

在华盛顿就任总统时，经过 8 年独立战争的美国问题成山、内忧外患交困。首先，美国国内财政状况岌岌可危、债台高筑，政府信用扫地。其次，在边远地区，英国和西班牙还在制造矛盾，挑起事端。另外，华盛顿虽然久经沙场，战功赫赫，但对民政事务缺乏经验，特别是要把一种崭新的、前人没有试验过的政治体制付诸实践，对他来说确实是一个挑战。华盛顿就是在这样的一种背景下，于 1789 年 4 月 30 日，在纽约的联邦会议厅（Federal Hall）的阳台，手按《圣经》，在联邦大法官的主持下进行了庄严的宣誓后，发表了这篇流芳百世的就职演说。

怀着诚惶诚恐的心情走上总统岗位的华盛顿深知其责任重大。在演说中，华盛顿充分估计到了前进征程中所会遇到的困难，但同时相信在上帝的护佑下，美国人民有责任和信心守护好这个新生国家的民主和自由的制度，他说："因为人们理所当然地、满怀深情地、也许是最后一次把维护神圣的自由之火和共和制政府的命运，系于美国人所遵命进行的实验上。"他把建立和维护宪法的尊严，实现宪法确立的目标，并使全体美国人民树立牢固的国家认同感作为他施政的重要内容。

❑ The Speech in Full

Fellow-Citizens of the Senate and of the House of Representatives:

1. Among the vicissitudes incident to life[1] no event could have filled me with greater anxieties than that of which the notification was transmitted by your order, and received on the 14th day of the present month[2]. On the one hand, I was summoned by my country, whose voice I can never hear but with veneration[3] and love, from a retreat which I had chosen with the fondest predilection[4], and, in my flattering hopes, with an immutable[5] decision, as the asylum of my declining years[6]—a retreat which was rendered every day more necessary as well as more dear to me by the addition of habit to inclination, and of frequent interruptions in my health to the gradual waste committed on it by time. On the other hand, the magnitude and difficulty of the trust to which the voice of my country called me, being sufficient to awaken in the wisest and most experienced of her citizens a distrustful scrutiny[7] into his qualifications, could not but

overwhelm with despondence[8] one who (inheriting inferior endowments from nature and unpracticed in the duties of civil administration) ought to be peculiarly conscious of his own deficiencies. In this conflict of emotions[9] all I dare aver[10] is that it has been my faithful study[11] to collect my duty[12] from a just appreciation of every circumstance by which it might be affected. All I dare hope is that if, in executing this task, I have been too much swayed by a grateful remembrance of former instances, or by an affectionate sensibility to this transcendent[13] proof of the confidence of my fellow-citizens, and have thence too little consulted my incapacity as well as disinclination for the weighty and untried cares[14] before me, my error will be palliated[15] by the motives which mislead me, and its consequences be judged by my country with some share of the partiality in which they originated.

2. Such being the impressions under which I have, in obedience to the public summons, repaired to[16] the present station, it would be peculiarly improper to omit in this first official act my fervent supplications[17] to that Almighty Being[18] who rules over the universe, who presides in the councils of nations, and whose providential[19] aids can supply every human defect, that His benediction may consecrate to[20] the liberties and happiness of the people of the United States a Government instituted by themselves for these essential purposes, and may enable every instrument employed in its administration to execute with success the functions allotted to his charge. In tendering this homage[21] to the Great Author[22] of every public and private good, I assure myself that it expresses your sentiments not less than my own, nor those of my fellow-citizens at large[23] less than either. **No people can be bound to acknowledge and adore the Invisible Hand[24] which conducts the affairs of men more than those of the United States.** Every step by which they have advanced to the character of an independent nation seems to have been distinguished by some token[25] of providential agency; and in the important revolution just accomplished in the system of their united government the tranquil deliberations[26] and voluntary consent of so many distinct communities from which the event has resulted can not be compared with the means by which most governments have been established without some return of pious[27] gratitude, along with an humble anticipation of the future blessings which the past seem to presage[28]. These reflections, arising out of the present crisis, have forced themselves too strongly on my mind to be suppressed. You will join with me, I trust, in thinking that there are none under the influence of which the proceedings of a new and free government can more auspiciously commence[29].

3. By the article establishing the executive department it is made the duty of the President "to recommend to your consideration such measures as he shall judge necessary and expedient[30]." The circumstances under which I now meet you will acquit me from entering into that subject further than to refer to the great constitutional charter under which you are assembled, and which, in defining your powers, designates[31] the objects to which your attention is to be given. It will be more consistent with those circumstances, and far more congenial with the feelings which actuate me[32], to substitute, in place of a recommendation of particular measures, the tribute that is due to the talents, the rectitude, and the patriotism which adorn the characters selected to devise and adopt them[33]. **In these honorable qualifications I behold the surest pledges that as on one side no local prejudices or attachments, no separate views nor party animosities[34], will misdirect the comprehensive and equal eye which ought to watch over this great assemblage of communities and interests, so, on another, that the foundation of our national policy will be laid in the pure and immutable principles of private morality, and the preeminence of free government be exemplified by all the attributes[35] which can win the affections of its citizens and command the respect of the world.** I dwell on this prospect with every satisfaction which an ardent love for my country can inspire, since there is no truth more thoroughly established than that **there exists in the economy and course of nature an indissoluble[36] union between virtue and happiness; between duty and advantage; between the genuine maxims of an honest and magnanimous[37] policy and the solid rewards of public prosperity and felicity[38]; since we ought to be no less persuaded that the propitious[39] smiles of Heaven can never be expected on a nation that disregards the eternal rules of order and right which Heaven itself has ordained; and since the preservation of the sacred fire of liberty and the destiny of the republican model of government are justly considered, perhaps, as deeply, as finally, staked on[40] the experiment entrusted to the hands of the American people.**

4. Besides the ordinary objects submitted to your care, it will remain with your judgment to decide how far an exercise of the occasional power delegated by the fifth article of the Constitution[41] is rendered expedient at the present juncture by the nature of objections which have been urged against the system, or by the degree of inquietude[42] which has given birth to them. Instead of undertaking particular recommendations on this subject, in which I could be guided by no lights derived from official opportunities, I shall again give way to my entire confidence in your discernment[43] and pursuit of the public good; for I assure myself that whilst you carefully avoid every alteration

which might endanger the benefits of an united and effective government, or which ought to await the future lessons of experience, a reverence[44] for the characteristic rights of freemen and a regard for the public harmony will sufficiently influence your deliberations on the question how far the former can be impregnably[45] fortified or the latter be safely and advantageously promoted.

5. To the foregoing observations[46] I have one to add, which will be most properly addressed[47] to the House of Representatives. It concerns myself, and will therefore be as brief as possible. When I was first honored with a call into the service of my country, then on the eve of an arduous struggle for its liberties, the light in which I contemplated my duty required that I should renounce every pecuniary[48] compensation. **From this resolution I have in no instance departed;** and being still under the impressions which produced it, I must decline as inapplicable to myself any share in the personal emoluments[49] which may be indispensably included in a permanent provision for the executive department, and must accordingly pray that the pecuniary estimates for the station[50] in which I am placed may during my continuance in it be limited to such actual expenditures as the public good may be thought to require.

6. Having thus imparted to you my sentiments as they have been awakened by the occasion which brings us together, I shall take my present leave[51]; but not without resorting once more to the benign Parent of the Human Race[52] in humble supplication that, since He has been pleased to favor the American people with opportunities[53] for deliberating in perfect tranquillity, and dispositions for deciding with unparalleled unanimity on a form of government for the security of their union and the advancement of their happiness, so His divine blessing may be equally conspicuous in the enlarged views[54], the temperate consultations, and the wise measures on which the success of this Government must depend. (1,433 words)

❑ Notes to the Speech

1. Among the vicissitudes incident to life: 在人生沉浮中

   vicissitudes [vi'sisitju:dz] *n.* the ups and downs and changes in your life（人生的）多变，变化无常

   incident to sb./sth. 伴随某人 / 某物而来的

2. 本句中包含 no… than… 句式，对 no 后的成分（即 event 一词）起强调作用，加强了行文的感情色彩。

transmit [trænz'mit] *vt.* cause to pass from one place or person to another 传输；传递；传播

3. veneration [ˌvenə'reiʃən] *n.* a feeling of great respect 尊敬，敬重
4. predilection [ˌpri:di'lekʃən] *n.* <formal> a particular liking or preference for sth. 偏爱，偏好
5. immutable [i'mjutəbl] *adj.* not changing or able to be changed 不变的；不可改变的
6. asylum of my declining years: 我暮年的归宿
   asylum [ə'sailəm] *n.* place of safety or refuge 庇护所；避难所
   somebody's declining years: the last years of someone's life 迟暮之年
7. scrutiny ['skru:tini] *n.* close and critical examination 仔细审查，仔细审视
8. despondence [di'spɔndəns] *n.* loss of hope; misery 沮丧；失望；苦恼
9. in this conflict of emotions: 怀着这种矛盾的心情
10. aver [ə'və:] *vt.* <formal>declare that something is the case 断言；坚称
11. faithful study: 忠贞不渝的努力目标
    study ['stʌdi] *n.* subject that is investigated 研究科目；课题
12. collect my duty: 恪尽职守
13. transcendent [træn'sendənt] *adj.* going far beyond ordinary limits 超凡的；卓越的
14. disinclination for the weighty and untried cares：消极对待未曾经历过的大事
    disinclination [ˌdisinkli'neiʃən] *n.* <formal> unwillingness 不情愿；勉强
15. palliate ['pælieit] *vt.* <formal> reduce the effects of illness, pain, etc. without curing them 减轻，缓解（症状）
16. repair to: go to (a place) 去，赴，前往
17. fervent supplications: 热忱的祈求
    supplication [ˌsʌpli'keiʃən] *n.* a supplication is a prayer to God or a respectful request to someone in authority for help 祈求；祈愿
18. Almighty Being: 上帝
    almighty [ɔ:l'maiti] *adj.* having unlimited or very great power 全能的；万能的
19. providential [ˌprɔvi'denʃəl] *adj.* happening at a favorable time 适时的，及时的
20. consecrate ['kɔnsikreit] to: 献身于
21. tendering this homage: 献上这份敬意
    tender ['tendə] *vt.* offer or present sth. formally 正式提供或提出某事
22. the Great Author: 造物主，上帝
23. my fellow-citizens at large: 我广大的同胞们
    at large：as a whole 整个的

24. the Invisible Hand：看不见的手，指上帝之手
25. token ['təukən] *n.* sign, symbol or evidence of sth. 表征；标志；证据
26. tranquil deliberations: 平静的思考
27. pious ['paiəs] *adj.* showing and feeling deep respect for God and religion 虔诚的；敬神的
28. presage ['presidʒ] *vt.* be a sign or warning of 预示；预兆；预知
29. auspiciously commence: 一开始就事事如意
    auspicious [ɔːs'piʃəs] *adj.* suggesting that there is a good chance of success 吉利的；吉祥的
30. expedient [iks'piːdiənt] *adj.* useful or helpful for a particular purpose 有用的，有益的
31. designate ['dezigneit] *vt.* mark or point out (sth.) clearly 清楚地标出或指出，明确
32. congenial with the feelings which actuate me: 适合我此时的心情
    congenial [kən'dʒiːnjəl] *adj.* suited or pleasing to your tastes 适宜的；合意的
33. the tribute that is due to the talents, the rectitude, and the patriotism which adorn the characters selected to devise and adopt them：对那些被选中去规划和采纳这些措施的人的才能、正直和爱国心的赞颂
    tribute ['tribjuːt] *n.* something done, said, or given to show respect or admiration for someone 颂词，称赞；献礼
    rectitude ['rektitjuːd] *n.* morally correct behavior 操行端正；正直
34. animosity [ˌæni'mɔsiti] *n.* hatred or strong dislike 仇恨；憎恶；敌意
35. attribute ['ætribjuːt] *n.* a quality or feature 属性；特性；特征
36. indissoluble [ˌindi'sɔljubl] *adj.* unable to be destroyed 无法摧毁的；牢不可破的
37. magnanimous [mæg'næniməs] *adj.* generous or forgiving towards a rival or enemy 宽宏的；气量大的
38. felicity [fi'lisiti] *n.* great happiness（极大的）幸福，快乐
39. propitious [prə'piʃəs] *adj.* indicating a good chance of success; favorable 吉利的；有利的
40. stake sth. (on sth.): 拿（金钱、生命等）就某事物打赌。此处 stake on 意为“系于”。
41. an exercise of the occasional power delegated by the fifth article of the Constitution: 行使宪法第 5 条所授予的临时权力
    delegate sth. to sb.: entrust (duties, rights, etc.) to sb. in a lower position or grade 将（职责、权利等）委派给下级；授权给
42. inquietude [in'kwaiətjuːd] *n.* <formal> uneasiness of mind; anxiety 不安；忧虑
43. discernment [di'səːnment] *n.* ability to judge well; insight 识别力；洞察力
44. reverence ['revərəns] *n.* deep respect 尊敬；崇敬

45. impregnably [im'pregnəbli] *adv.* 坚不可摧地；牢不可破地
46. foregoing observations: 上述意见
    observation [ˌɔbzəː'veiʃən] *n.* remark or comment 言语；评论
47. address [ə'dres] *vt.* make a speech or remark to 对……讲话；对……发表演说
48. pecuniary [pi'kjuːnjəri] *adj.* <formal> relating to money 与金钱有关的
49. emolument [i'mɔljumənt] *n.* <formal> a salary or fee 薪水；报酬
50. the pecuniary estimates for the station: 这个职务所需的经费预算
    estimate ['estimeit] *n.* a rough calculation 估计；估算
51. take my present leave：现在我就要向大家告辞
    take one's leave：<formal> say goodbye 告别
52. resorting once more to the benign Parent of the Human Race: 再次向仁慈的上帝寻求帮助
    Parent of the Human Race: 人类的父，指上帝
53. favor the American people with opportunities: 赐予美国人民以机会
    favor sb. with: give sb. something they wish for 赐予，给予
54. enlarged views: 扩大了的眼界

❑ Appreciating the Speech

从内容上看，华盛顿的就职演说主要包括3部分：首先，他表达了自己对肩负总统重任的忐忑心情和感受。他说："国家召唤我担负的责任如此重大和艰巨，足以使国内最有才智和经验的人度德量力，而我天资愚钝，又无民政管理实践，理应倍觉自己能力之不足，因而必然感到难以肩此重任。"这句谦恭的话语使一位谦谦君子（a modest, self-disciplined gentleman）的儒雅形象立于听众面前，易于赢得他们的好感，获得他们的信任。接下来，他向"全能的上帝"（Almighty Being）表达自己的无比崇敬之情。他祈求上帝赐福于年轻的美利坚合众国，并申明："除了仰仗上帝的力量，一个新生的自由政府别无他法能一开始就事事顺利"（ there are none under the influence of which the proceedings of a new and free government can more auspiciously commence）。最后，他对重大问题表明了基本立场（fundamental standpoint）。当时，宪法是人们关注的主要问题，因此他在演说中特别提到了"我国伟大的宪法"，他用充满激情的语言指出："上帝亲自规定了永恒的秩序和权利法则，他绝不可能对无视这些法则的国家慈祥地加以赞许"（ the propitious smiles of Heaven can never be expected on a nation that disregards the eternal rules of order and right which Heaven itself has ordained），并着重称颂维护宪法利益之人。同时，他还要求国会成员"避免做出任何可能危及团结和政府利益的修订，或避免做出尚需实践检验的修订"。他巧妙地借用了信仰的力量（the power of beliefs），向

危及国家团结、藐视宪法的人群施加压力 (exerted pressure on those who endangered the Union and disregarded the Constitution)，从另一角度提出了对国民的期望和维护宪法的重要意义，措辞非常独特。他还宣布，“我必须拒绝对我不相适用的任何个人津贴”，显示出其高洁的人格风范 (noble character)，为美国后来的政治家廉洁从政起到了榜样作用。

从语言上讲，这篇演说主要有三个特色。一是大词（正式词）的使用（the use of big words），如 vicissitudes, predilection, despondence, transcendent, providential, inquietude 等等，这类词的大量使用增加了演说的正式性和庄重感（make the speech more formal and solemn）。二是长句多，句式结构复杂（the use of long sentences with complex sentence patterns）。这样的例子在本演讲中比比皆是，如第一段的第二句（On the one hand,...committed on it by time.），其中包含多个定语从句、介词短语和同位语成分。这些长句虽长，但结构严谨、含意丰富，给人以庄重严肃之感。另外，在本篇演讲中，还多次使用了平行结构（frequent use of parallelism），如 “since there is no truth more thoroughly established than that there exists in the economy and course of nature an indissoluble union <u>between</u> virtue and happiness; <u>between</u> duty and advantage; <u>between</u> the genuine maxims of an honest and magnanimous policy and the solid rewards of public prosperity and felicity, ...” 这里，华盛顿一连用了 3 个平行的从句，有效地加强了语言的节奏感（more rhythmic），增加了演讲的感染力（appealing）和感召力（inspiring），把他的观点表达得淋漓尽致。

❑ Culture Links

（1）华盛顿与美国宪法的制定

美国宪法是世界上第一部成文宪法，它制定于 1787 年，距今已二百多年了，但这部宪法跨越了两个多世纪仍然历久弥新，其基本体系仍然运转良好，堪称一个奇迹。根据这部宪法，美国成为一个由各自拥有主权的州所组成的联邦国家，同时也有一个联邦政府来为联邦的运作而服务。从此联邦体制取代了基于邦联条例而存在的较为松散的邦联体制。1789 年，美国宪法正式生效。该部宪法为日后许多国家成文宪法的制定提供了成功的典范。

1787 年华盛顿主持了在费城举行的制宪会议。他虽没有参与讨论，但他的宪政思想（包括天赋人权思想、共和联邦思想、分权制衡思想等）深刻地影响着制宪会议的走向，他的威望维持了会议的秩序，并让代表团能专注于讨论。在会议后他的威望使得包括弗吉尼亚州议会在内的许多人相信这个会议的成果，并支持美国宪法。

美国宪法实施后，以修正案的方式进行过多次补充、修改，但是 1787 年宪法的基本原则至今依然发挥着重要的作用。这些原则（三权分立、联邦体制、宪法至上、人人平等）对国家的繁荣、进步，为人民的自由、幸福起到了保障作用。

在华盛顿的主导下，美国制定和实施了宪法；在实践中，华盛顿始终一丝不苟地遵循宪法、维护宪法的尊严，这在本篇演讲中也多有体现。如他在演讲中说："根据设立行政部门的条款，总统有责任'将他认为必要而妥善的措施提请国会审议'。但在目前与各位见面的这个场合，恕我不进一步讨论这个问题，而只提一下伟大的宪法，它使各位今天聚集一堂，它规定了各位的权限，指出了各位应该注意的目标。"

（2）分权制衡的政府形式

"权力导致腐败，绝对的权力导致绝对的腐败。"熟知这一定律的美国的国父们，为了对联邦政府的权力进行有效的制约，以避免政府权力滥用，在 1787 年制定美国宪法的过程中，对联邦政府的权力进行了分割，目的是在分权的基础上使各权力部门之间相互制约，从而建立一个三权（立法、司法、行政）分别独立、互相制衡的体制。

美国宪法中规定的分权与制衡 (checks and balances) 体制实际上包括"水平方向的分权制衡"和"垂直方向的分权制衡"两个方面。关于水平方向上的分权，美国宪法的第一条、第二条和第三条分别对联邦政府的立法权、行政权和司法权作了规定，并将这三种权力分别赋予国会、总统和法院。在分权体制下，立法、行政和司法的权力是分立的，并不互相从属；同时，三种权力又互相制约。例如，立法权属于国会，但总统有权批准或否决国会的立法，国会还可以以 2/3 多数推翻总统的否决；行政权力属于总统，但行政机构的设置、行政官员的任命以及所需要的经费需经国会以法律的形式批准；司法权属于各级联邦法院，但法官须由总统提名并经过参议院批准，而法官一经任命则任职终生（除由于身体原因不能履职外），因而不必对总统或参议院俯首听命，最高法院可以判决国会的法律或总统的行政命令是否合乎宪法，等等。关于垂直方向上的分权，主要是通过联邦制实现的。在美国宪法规定的联邦制的体制下，州与联邦的权力都被认为是来自人民，因而州和联邦并不是一种从属的关系，而是具有一定的相互独立性。既然州并不从属于联邦，州就可以享有自己的权力。宪法中规定，联邦政府只拥有在宪法中列出的如立法、征税、统领全国军队、管理州际和国际贸易、发行货币、对外宣战和缔约等权力，而其余未列明的权力都属于各州及其人民，在属于州的权力范围内，联邦政府不能干涉。因此，州与联邦之间也存在分权，基于这种纵向的分权，州也可以对联邦政府的权力构成一种制约。

美国的国父们深知，防止营私舞弊的唯一有效办法不是去进行道德上的说教，不是去进行思想上的教育，而是利用他们相互之间的利益来进行制衡。他们所创造的分权与制衡的体制，就是要通过利益牵制的机制，来达成权力之间的制约。那就是用私利来制约私利，用权力来制衡权力。

美国建国两百多年来，其社会已发生了天翻地覆的变化，美国的内外政策也在随着时代与时势的变化而不断变化，但美国始终不变的是他们对"分权制衡"这一政府组织原则的坚守。这一原则至今行之有效，保证了美国社会的长治久安，促进了美国社会、经济的健康发展，并为越来越多的国家所接受。

（3）美国人的“选民”意识

1620年，当一批英国清教徒乘坐“五月花号”在美洲新大陆马萨诸塞的普利茅斯登陆时，他们真诚地相信是上帝把自己从欧洲压迫者的重轭下拯救出来的。作为最后的新教改革者，这些流亡者把自己视为古代犹太人的继承人，而他们多舛的旅途就好比古代犹太人逃离他们的埃及监工，在沙漠里漫无目的地流浪了40年后，被耶和华拯救，送往应许之地（出自旧约圣经《出埃及记》）迦南。带领这些清教徒来到普利茅斯的布雷福德这样来形容他们的使命：“我们将建成山巅之城，世界上所有人的眼睛都在瞧着我们。”

华盛顿在本篇演讲中也毫不掩饰地流露出这种选民意识和使命感，如，他说：“没有人能比美国人更坚定不移地承认和崇拜掌管人间事务的上帝。他们在迈向独立国家的进程中，似乎每走一步都有某种天佑的迹象……在目前转折关头，我产生这些想法确实是深有所感而不能自已，我相信大家会和我怀有同感，即除了仰仗上帝的力量，一个新生的自由政府别无他法能一开始就事事顺利。”在演讲接近结尾处，他说道：“因为我们应该同样相信，上帝亲自规定了永恒的秩序和权利法则，它绝不可能对无视这些法则的国家慈祥地加以赞许；因为人们理所当然地、满怀深情地、也许是最后一次把维护神圣的自由之火和共和制政府的命运，系于美国人所遵命进行的实验上。”表达了一种强烈的责任感和使命感。

许多美国人至今仍把自己看做是“上帝的选民”，而美国则是应许之地。他们相信美国注定要走向伟大，走向辉煌，美国之道就是上帝之道，就是正义之道。他们的成功似乎就是他们被选择这一事实的肯定性证明。上帝的确已经回报了他们的信仰和侍奉，使他们成为地球上最繁荣强大的国家。“选民”意识给他们带来的使命感，使他们认为，他们作为上帝的选民，受“上帝的委托”，对人类的发展和命运承担一种特殊的责任，传播和推行他们的民主制度和价值观是他们的神圣使命。

2001年9月11日美国遭遇恐怖袭击，小布什总统因此发动了以美国为首的一连串所谓的“反恐战争”。在2001年10月他发动了阿富汗战争，推翻了塔利班独裁政权并铲除基地组织势力，接着他在2003年3月发动了以建立一个民主政权为目标的伊拉克战争，推翻了萨达姆政权。这两场战争，特别是后者，在美国国内和国际上都不乏反对者，美国也因此付出了人力、物力和财力上的巨大代价。他们愿意做这种“世界警察”、“世界宪兵”的主要原因，恐怕都与他们的“选民”意识有关。

❑ Questions Concerning the Speech

1. Why does Washington feel extremely anxious over being elected President of the United States of America?
2. What supplications does Washington make to that Almighty Being?
3. What subject does he refrain from entering into?

4. What virtues of the people's elected representatives does he speak of and why does he dwell on these virtues?
5. What does Washington say about the American "experiment" and "the sacred fire of liberty"?
6. What do the external "rules of order and right" refer to in this inaugural address and what will government acting in accordance with these objective laws do?
7. How does Washington manage to inspire in his audience a sense of equality and cordiality?

❑ Paraphrase the Following Sentences

1. I was summoned by my country, whose voice I can never hear but with veneration and love, from a retreat which I had chosen with the fondest predilection, and, in my flattering hopes, with an immutable decision, as the asylum of my declining years.
2. No people can be bound to acknowledge and adore the Invisible Hand which conducts the affairs of men more than those of the United States.
3. By the article establishing the executive department it is made the duty of the President to recommend to your consideration such measures as he shall judge necessary and expedient.
4. there exists in the economy and course of nature an indissoluble union between virtue and happiness; between duty and advantage.
5. Heaven can never be expected on a nation that disregards the eternal rules of order and right which Heaven itself has ordained.
6. I must decline as inapplicable to myself any share in the personal emoluments.
7. I shall take my present leave; but not without resorting once more to the benign Parent of the Human Race in humble supplication.
8. His divine blessing may be equally conspicuous in the enlarged views, the temperate consultations, and the wise measures on which the success of this Government must depend.

❑ Questions for Discussion

1. 试论华盛顿两次主动放权的个人因素和历史、文化因素。
2. 华盛顿就任美国首任总统时，中国处于哪个朝代、哪个皇帝的统治下？当时的治国方式与那时的美国相比有何特点？

3. 请阅读附录中美国宪法中的《权利法案》(即前 10 个修正案)，并说明他们在保障美国人民基本权利方面的重要意义。

❑ Translation

乔治·华盛顿：首任就职演讲

1789 年 4 月 30 日，纽约

参议院和众议院的同胞们：

1. 在人生沉浮中，没有一件事能比本月 14 日收到根据你们的命令送达的通知更使我焦虑不安。一方面，国家召唤我出任此职，对于她的召唤，我永远只能肃然敬从；而隐退是我以挚爱之情、满腔希望和坚定的决心选择的暮年归宿，由于爱好和习惯，且时光流逝、健康渐衰、时感体力不济，愈觉隐退之必要和可贵。另一方面，国家召唤我担负的责任如此重大和艰巨，足以使国内最有才智和经验的人度德量力，而我天资愚钝，又无民政管理实践，理应倍觉自己能力之不足，因而必然感到难以肩此重任。怀着这种矛盾心情，我唯一敢断言的是，通过正确估计可能产生影响的各种情况来恪尽职守，乃是我忠贞不渝的努力目标。我唯一敢祈望的是，如果我在执行这项任务时因陶醉于往事，或因由衷感激公民们对我的高度信赖，因而受到过多影响，以致在处理从未经历过的大事时，忽视了自己的无能和消极，我的错误将会由于使我误入歧途的各种动机而减轻；而大家在评判错误的后果时，也会适当包涵产生这些动机的偏见。
2. 既然这就是我在遵奉公众召唤就任现职时的感想，那么，在此宣誓就职之际，如不热忱地祈求全能的上帝就极其失当，因为上帝统治着宇宙，主宰着各国政府，他的神助能弥补人类的任何不足，愿上帝赐福，保佑一个为美国人民的自由和幸福而组成的政府，保佑它为这些基本目的而做出奉献，保佑政府的各项行政措施在我负责之下都能成功地发挥作用。我相信，在向公众利益和私人利益的伟大缔造者献上这份崇敬时，这些话也同样表达了各位和广大公民的心意。没有人能比美国人更坚定不移地承认和崇拜掌管人间事务的上帝。他们在迈向独立国家的进程中，似乎每走一步都有某种天佑的迹象；他们在刚刚完成的联邦政府体制的重大改革中，如果不是因虔诚的感恩而得到某种回报，如果不是谦卑地期待着过去有所预示的赐福的到来，那么，通过众多截然不同的集团的平静思考和自愿赞同来完成改革，这种方式是不能与大多数政府的组建方式同日而语的。在目前转折关头，我产生这些想法确实是深有所感而不能自已，我相信大家会和我怀有同感，即除了仰仗上帝的力量，一个新生的自由政府别无他法能一开始就事事顺利。
3. 根据设立行政部门的条款，总统有责任“将他认为必要而妥善的措施提请国会审议”。

但在目前与各位见面的这个场合，恕我不进一步讨论这个问题，而只提一下伟大的宪法，它使各位今天聚集一堂，它规定了各位的权限，指出了各位应该注意的目标。在这样的场合，更恰当也更能反映我内心激情的做法是不提出具体措施，而是称颂将要规划和采纳这些措施的当选者的才能、正直和爱国心。我从这些高贵品格中看到了最可靠的保证：一方面，任何地方偏见或地方感情，任何意见分歧或党派敌视，都不能使我们偏离全局观点和公平观点，即必须维护这个由不同地区和利益所组成的大联合；因此，在另一方面，我国的政策将会以纯洁而坚定的个人道德原则为基础，而自由政府将会以那赢得民心和全世界尊敬的一切特点而显示其优越性。我对国家的一片热爱之心激励着我满怀喜悦地展望这幅远景，因为根据自然界的构成和发展趋势，在美德与幸福之间，责任与利益之间，恪守诚实宽厚的政策与获得社会繁荣幸福的硕果之间，有着密不可分的统一；因为我们应该同样相信，上帝亲自规定了永恒的秩序和权利法则，他绝不可能对无视这些法则的国家慈祥地加以赞许；因为人们理所当然地、满怀深情地、也许是最后一次把维护神圣的自由之火和共和制政府的命运，系于美国人所遵命进行的实验上。

4. 除了提请各位注意的一般事务外，在当前时刻，根据激烈反对共和制的各种意见的性质，或根据引起这些意见的不同程度，在必要时行使宪法第 5 条授予的权利究竟有多大益处，将依靠你们来加以判断和决定。在这个问题上，我无法从过去担任过的职务中找到借鉴，因此我不提具体建议，而是再一次完全信任各位对公众利益的辨别和追求；因为我相信，各位只要谨慎避免做出任何可能危及团结和政府利益的修订，或避免做出尚需检验的修订，那么，各位对自由人特有权利的尊重和对社会安定的关注，就足以影响大家慎重考虑在何种程度上坚定不移地加强前者，并有利无弊地促进后者。

5. 除上述意见外，我还要补充一点，而且觉得向众议院提出最恰当。这条意见与我有关，因此应当尽量讲得简短一些。我第一次荣幸地奉召为国家效劳时，正值我国为自由而艰苦奋斗之际，我对我的职责的看法要求我必须放弃任何俸禄。我从未违背过这一决定。如今，促使我做出这一同样决定的想法仍然支配着我，因此，我必须拒绝对我不相适应的任何个人津贴，因为这些津贴可能是列入并成为政府部门常设基金不可分割的一部分。同样，我必须恳求各位，在估算我就任的这个职位所需要的费用时，可以根据我的任期以公共利益所需的实际费用为限。

6. 我已将有感于这一聚会场合的想法奉告各位，现在我就要向大家告辞；但在此以前，我要再一次以谦卑的心情祈求仁慈的上帝给予帮助。因为承蒙上帝的恩赐，美国人有了深思熟虑的机会，以及为确保联邦的安全和促进幸福，用前所未有的一致意见来决定政府体制的意向；因而，同样明显的是，上帝将保佑我们扩大眼界，心平气和地进行协商，并采取明智的措施，而这些都是本届政府取得成功所必不可少的依靠。

2

George Washington's Farewell Address

Published 17 September, 1796, in newspapers in Philadelphia

❑ About the Speech

乔治·华盛顿（George Washington, 1732—1799）因在美国独立战争和建国中扮演了最重要的角色，毫无异议地被选为这个新国家的第一任总统。尽管华盛顿相当不情愿，他还是被推选为第二届总统。两届总统任期届满后，美国人民挽留华盛顿继续竞选连任，华盛顿拒绝了："我走在尚未踏实的土地上，我的所作所为将可能成为以后历届总统的先例。"他向美国人民解释，"你们再继续选我做总统，美国就没有真正的民主制度了"。他平静地离开了政坛，回到他向往已久的家园——维农山庄。他的退隐为美国总统的任期立下了不超过两届的先例。

1796年9月17日，华盛顿在费城的报纸上刊登了他的告别演说。演说中充分表达了他对美国国民父亲般的殷切之情，不愧人们对他的"美国国父"的称号。他在演说中以博大的胸怀、谦和的态度、真挚的感情和恳切的语言，语重心长地谆谆告诫他的国民统一在政府领导下，同心同德、团结一致，放弃过激的党派情绪，排除地理上的差异造成的影响。他坚定地指出，我们的"真正的政策是避免与国外世界的任何一部分永久结盟，只能信托暂时的结盟以应付特别紧急的情况"。

华盛顿提出的避免卷入国外争端的警告被称做是"华盛顿的伟大法规"，而他的这些告诫，后来也成为美国历代执政者在对外政策上所奉行的圭臬，对美国后来的政治生活有着重大深远的影响。

❑ The Speech *(abridged)*

Friends and Fellow Citizens:

1. The period for a new election of a citizen to administer the executive government of the United States being not far distant, and the time actually arrived when your thoughts must be employed in designating[1] the person who is to be clothed with that important trust, it appears to me proper, especially as it may conduce[2] to a more distinct expression of the public voice, that I should now apprise[3] you of the resolution I have formed, to decline being considered among the number of those out of whom a choice is to be made.

...

2. **The unity of government which constitutes you one people is also now dear to you. It is justly so, for it is a main pillar in the edifice[4] of your real independence, the support of your tranquility[5] at home, your peace abroad; of your safety; of your prosperity; of that very liberty which you so highly prize.** But as it is easy to foresee that, from different causes and from different quarters, much pains will be taken, many artifices[6] employed to weaken in your minds the conviction of this truth; as this is the point in your political fortress[7] against which the batteries of internal and external enemies will be most constantly and actively (though often covertly[8] and insidiously[9]) directed, it is of infinite moment that you should properly estimate the immense value of your national union to your collective and individual happiness; that you should cherish a cordial, habitual, and immovable attachment[10] to it; accustoming yourselves to think and speak of it as of the palladium[11] of your political safety and prosperity; watching for its preservation with jealous anxiety; discountenancing[12] whatever may suggest even a suspicion that it can in any event be abandoned; and indignantly frowning upon the first dawning of every attempt[13] to alienate[14] any portion of our country from the rest, or to enfeeble[15] the sacred ties which now link together the various parts.

...

3. In contemplating the causes which may disturb our Union, it occurs as matter of serious concern that any ground should have been furnished for characterizing parties by geographical discriminations, Northern and Southern, Atlantic and Western; whence[16] designing men may endeavor to excite a belief that there is a real difference of local interests and views. One of the expedients[17] of party to acquire influence within particular districts is to misrepresent the opinions and aims of other districts. You

cannot shield[18] yourselves too much against the jealousies and heartburnings which spring from these misrepresentations[19]; they tend to render alien to each other[20] those who ought to be bound together by fraternal affection[21].

…

4. I have already intimated[22] to you the danger of parties in the State, with particular reference to the founding of them on geographical discriminations. Let me now take a more comprehensive[23] view, and warn you in the most solemn manner against the baneful effects of the spirit of party generally.

5. This spirit, unfortunately, is inseparable from our nature, having its root in the strongest passions of the human mind. It exists under different shapes in all governments, more or less stifled[24], controlled, or repressed[25]; but, in those of the popular form, it is seen in its greatest rankness[26], and is truly their worst enemy.

6. The alternate domination of one faction[27] over another, sharpened by the spirit of revenge, natural to party dissension[28], which in different ages and countries has perpetrated the most horrid enormities[29], is itself a frightful despotism[30]. But this leads at length to a more formal and permanent despotism. The disorders and miseries which result gradually incline the minds of men to seek security[31] and repose in the absolute power of an individual; and sooner or later the chief of some prevailing faction, more able or more fortunate than his competitors, turns this disposition[32] to the purposes of his own elevation, on the ruins of public liberty.

7. Without looking forward to an extremity of this kind (which nevertheless ought not to be entirely out of sight), the common and continual mischiefs of the spirit of party are sufficient to make it the interest and duty of a wise people to discourage and restrain it.

8. It serves always to distract the public councils and enfeeble the public administration. It agitates[33] the community with ill-founded jealousies and false alarms, kindles the animosity[34] of one part against another, foments[35] occasionally riot and insurrection[36]. It opens the door to foreign influence and corruption, which finds a facilitated access to the government itself through the channels of party passions. Thus the policy and the will of one country are subjected to[37] the policy and will of another.

9. There is an opinion that parties in free countries are useful checks upon the administration of the government and serve to keep alive the spirit of liberty. This within certain limits is probably true; and in governments of a monarchical[38] cast, patriotism may look with indulgence[39], if not with favor, upon the spirit of party. But in those of the popular character, in governments purely elective, it is a spirit not to be encouraged. From their natural tendency, it is certain there will always be enough of that spirit for every salutary[40] purpose. And there being constant danger of excess, the effort ought to be by force of public opinion, to mitigate[41] and assuage[42] it. A fire not to be quenched[43], it demands a uniform vigilance[44] to prevent its bursting into a flame, lest, instead of warming, it should consume.

…

10. As a very important source of strength and security, cherish public credit. One method of preserving it is to use it as sparingly[45] as possible, avoiding occasions of expense by cultivating peace, but remembering also that timely disbursements[46] to prepare for danger frequently prevent much greater disbursements to repel it, avoiding likewise the accumulation of debt, not only by shunning[47] occasions of expense, but by vigorous exertion[48] in time of peace to discharge the debts which unavoidable wars may have occasioned, not ungenerously throwing upon posterity[49] the burden which we ourselves ought to bear.

…

11. Against the insidious wiles of foreign influence[50] (I conjure[51] you to believe me, fellow-citizens) the jealousy of a free people ought to be constantly awake, since history and experience prove that foreign influence is one of the most baneful[52] foes of republican government. But that jealousy to be useful must be impartial[53]; else it becomes the instrument of the very influence to be avoided, instead of a defense against it. Excessive partiality for one foreign nation and excessive dislike of another cause those whom they actuate[54] to see danger only on one side, and serve to veil and even second the arts of influence on the other. Real patriots who may resist the intrigues[55] of the favorite are liable to become suspected and odious[56], while its tools and dupes[57] usurp[58] the applause and confidence of the people, to surrender[59] their interests.

12. The great rule of conduct for us in regard to foreign nations is in extending our commercial relations, to have with them as little political connection as possible. So far as we have already formed engagements, let them be fulfilled with perfect good faith. Here let us stop. Europe has a set of primary interests which to us have none; or a very

remote relation. Hence she must be engaged in frequent controversies, the causes of which are essentially foreign to our concerns. Hence, therefore, it must be unwise in us to implicate ourselves by artificial ties in the ordinary vicissitudes[60] of her politics, or the ordinary combinations and collisions of her friendships or enmities[61].

13. Our detached[62] and distant situation invites and enables us to pursue a different course. If we remain one people under an efficient government. the period is not far off when we may defy[63] material injury from external annoyance; when we may take such an attitude as will cause the neutrality[64] we may at any time resolve upon to be scrupulously[65] respected; when belligerent[66] nations, under the impossibility of making acquisitions upon us, will not lightly hazard the giving us provocation[67]; when we may choose peace or war, as our interest, guided by justice, shall counsel.

14. Why forego the advantages of so peculiar a situation? Why quit our own to stand upon foreign ground? Why, by interweaving our destiny with that of any part of Europe, entangle[68] our peace and prosperity in the toils of European ambition, rivalship, interest, humor or caprice?

15. It is our true policy to steer clear of permanent alliances with any portion of the foreign world[69]; so far, I mean, as we are now at liberty to do it; for let me not be understood as capable of patronizing infidelity[70] to existing engagements. I hold the maxim[71] no less applicable to public than to private affairs, that honesty is always the best policy. I repeat it, therefore, let those engagements be observed in their genuine sense. But, in my opinion, it is unnecessary and would be unwise to extend them.

...

16. Though, in reviewing the incidents of my administration, I am unconscious of intentional error, I am nevertheless too sensible of my defects not to think it probable that I may have committed many errors. Whatever they may be, I fervently[72] beseech[73] the Almighty to avert or mitigate[74] the evils to which they may tend. I shall also carry with me the hope that my country will never cease to view them with indulgence; and that, after forty five years of my life dedicated to its service with an upright zeal[75], the faults of incompetent abilities will be consigned[76] to oblivion[77], as myself must soon be to the mansions of rest.

17. Relying on its kindness in this as in other things, and actuated by that fervent

love towards it, which is so natural to a man who views in it the native soil of himself and his progenitors[78] for several generations, I anticipate with pleasing expectation that retreat in which I promise myself to realize, without alloy[79], the sweet enjoyment of partaking[80], in the midst of my fellow-citizens, the benign[81] influence of good laws under a free government, the ever-favorite object of my heart, and the happy reward, as I trust, of our mutual cares, labors, and dangers. (1,725 words)

❑ Notes to the Speech

1. designate ['dezigneit] *v.* choose or name for a particular job or purpose 选派，任命；<formal> point out or call by a special name 表明；指出
2. conduce [kən'dju:s] *v.* <formal>help to produce; be conducive to 导致；有益于，有贡献于
3. apprise [ə'praiz] *v.* <formal> inform; tell 通知；报告
4. a main pillar in the edifice：大厦的主要支柱
   edifice ['edifis] *n.* <formal or pomp> a large fine building, such as a palace or church 大厦；大建筑物
5. tranquility [træŋ'kwiliti] *n.* 宁静；平静
6. artifice ['ɑ:tifis] *n.* 轨迹；欺骗；巧妙的办法
7. fortress ['fɔ:tris] *n.* 堡垒，要塞 *vt.* 设置要塞；用要塞防守
8. covertly ['kʌvətli] *adv.* 暗中地，偷偷摸摸地
9. insidiously [in'sidiəsli] *adv.* 阴险地；隐伏地；暗中为害地
10. attachment [ə'tætʃmənt] *n.*（用电子邮件发送的）附件，附属物；依恋，依附
11. palladium [pə'leidiəm] *n.* [化学] 钯；守护神
12. discountenance [dis'kauntinəns] *n.* <formal> look with disfavor on behavior and try to prevent it 不赞成 *v.* 使丢脸；不赞成；使慌张
13. frown upon the first dawning of every attempt：不赞成每个企图的最初出现
    frown upon：蹙眉而露出不悦之色，表示不赞成；看不惯
    dawn [dɔ:n] *n.* 黎明，拂晓；开端；醒悟 *v.* 破晓，（天）刚亮；开始
14. alienate ['eiljəneit] *v.* make someone become unfriendly, unsympathetic, or unwilling to give support 使疏远，离间；让与
15. enfeeble [in'fi:bl] *v.*<formal> make weak; cause to lose strength completely 使衰弱；使无力
16. whence [wens] *n.* 根源 *adv.* 从何处 *pron.* 何处 *conj.* 由此
17. expedient [iks'pi:diənt] *adj.* useful or helpful for a purpose, esp. one's own purpose,

although not necessarily morally correct 权宜的；方便的；有利的 *n.* 权宜之计；应急手段

18. shield [ʃi:ld] *n.* 盾；保护罩 *v.* protect from 保护，庇护；给……加防护罩
19. spring from these misrepresentations：来自这些误解
    spring from：起源于；来自
20. render alien to each other： 使对方互不相容
    render ['rendə] *v.* 致使，造成；给予，提供
    alien ['eiljən] *adj.* belonging to another country or race, foreign; very different in nature or character, esp. so different as to cause dislike or opposition 外国的；相异的；异己的；不相容的
21. fraternal affection：兄弟般的感情
    fraternal [frə'tə:nl] *adj.* of, belonging to, or like brothers; friendly, brotherly 兄弟般的；友善的，亲如手足的
22. intimidate [in'timideit] *v.* frighten, esp. by making threats 恐吓，威胁；胁迫
23. comprehensive [ˌkɔmpri'hensiv] *adj.* thorough; broad; including a lot or everything 综合的；广泛的；有理解力的
24. stifle ['staifl] *v.* prevent from continuing 扼杀；使窒息；藏匿
25. repress [ri'pres] *v.* make a deliberate effort not to show or have this feeling 抑制，镇压；约束
26. rankness ['ræŋknis] *n.* the attribute of having a strong offensive smell 繁茂；恶臭
27. faction ['fækʃən] *n.* an organized group of people within a larger group, which opposes some of the ideas of the larger group and fights for its own ideas 小集团，宗派；派系间斗争，内讧
28. dissension [di'senʃən] *n.* disagreement; argument 意见分歧；争论，不和
29. perpetrated the most horrid enormities：犯下最恐怖的罪行
    perpetrate ['pə:pitreit] *v.* <formal> do sth. wrong or criminal; be guilty of 做（错事）；犯（罪）
    horrid ['hɔrid] *adj.* very unpleasant 极讨厌的，极糟的
    enormity [i'nɔ:miti] *n.* <formal> (an act of) great wickedness 暴行；极恶；凶暴
30. frightful despotism：可怕的暴政
    despotism ['despətizəm] *n.* cruel and unfair government by a ruler or rulers who have a lot of power 专制；暴政
31. incline the minds of men to seek security：使人倾向于寻求安全
    incline to：具有……倾向；易……

32. disposition [ˌdispəˈziʃən] *n.* the way people tend to behave or feel; willingness; tendency 性情，性格；意向；倾向
33. agitate [ˈædʒiteit] *v.* make someone feel anxious and nervous; argue strongly in public for or against some political or social change 使焦虑；鼓动，煽动，宣传
34. animosity [ˌæniˈmɔsiti] *n.* 敌意；怨恨；憎恶
35. foment [fəuˈment] *vt.* cause to develop 激起；煽动（麻烦）等
36. insurrection [ˌinsəˈrekʃən] *n.* violent action that is taken by a large group of people against the rulers of their country, usually in order to remove them from office 造反；暴动；叛乱
37. be subjected to：遭受，使经受；受……的控制
38. monarchical [mɔˈnɑ:kikəl] *adj.* 国王的，帝王的
39. indulgence [inˈdʌldʒ(ə)ns] *n.* treating someone with special kindness, often when it is not a good thing 沉溺，迁就；溺爱，放纵
40. salutary [ˈsæljutəri] *adj.* causing or likely to cause an improvement in character, future behavior, health, etc. 有益的，有帮助的
41. mitigate [ˈmitigeit] *v.* make sth. less unpleasant, serious, or painful 使缓和，使减轻；使平息
42. assuage [əˈsweidʒ] *v.* 减轻，缓和；平息；使安静
43. quench [kwentʃ] *v.* 熄灭；扑灭；抑制（欲望）
44. vigilance [ˈvidʒiləns] *n.* <formal> 警觉，警惕，警戒；失眠症
45. sparingly [ˈspεəriŋli] *adv.* 节约地；保守地；仁慈地；缺少地
46. disbursement [disˈbə:smənt] *n.* 支付，支出；支付款
47. shun [ʃʌn] *v.* deliberately avoid or keep away from sb. or sth. 避开，回避；避免
48. exertion [igˈzə:ʃən] *n.* 努力，费力；（能力、权利等的）运用，行使
49. posterity [pɔsˈteriti] *n.* everyone who will be alive in the future 后代，后世；子孙，后裔
50. the insidious wiles of foreign influence：外国势力的阴谋诡计
    insidious [inˈsidiəs] *adj.* unpleasant or dangerous and develops gradually without being noticed 隐伏的，潜在的；阴险的，狡猾的
    wile [wail] *n.* 诡计，阴谋
51. conjure [ˈkʌndʒə] *v.* <old use> ask someone solemnly to do sth.; do clever tricks which seem magical 祈求，恳求；变戏法，变魔术
52. baneful [ˈbeinful] *adj.* harmful; poisonous 有害的，有毒的
53. impartial [imˈpɑ:ʃəl] *adj.* fair; not giving special favor or support to any one side 公正的，不偏不倚的；无偏见的
54. actuate [ˈæktjueit] *v.* <formal> cause to act; activate or motivate 使活动；驱使，激励

55. intrigue [in'tri:g] *n.* 阴谋，诡计；私通，奸情　*v.* 迷住，激起好奇心
56. odious ['əudjəs, -diəs] *adj.* <formal> hateful; very unpleasant 可憎的，讨厌的，丑恶的
57. dupe [dju:p] *v.* 愚弄；欺骗　*n.* 易受骗的人，上当者
58. usurp [ju(:)'zə:p] *v.* <formal> take (power or position) for oneself illegally or without having the right to do so 篡夺，夺取；侵占
59. surrender [sə'rendə] *v.* give up or give in to the power (esp. of an enemy), as a sign of defeat 投降，屈服于
60. vicissitude [vi'sisitju:d] *n.* <formal> continual change, esp. from good to bad, in one's nature, condition of life, etc. 变迁；兴衰
61. enmity ['enmiti] *n.* a feeling of hatred towards someone that lasts for a long time 敌意，仇恨，愤恨
62. detached [di'tætʃt] *adj.* (of a house) not connected on any side with any other building 独栋的；分离的；not showing much personal feeling 超然的，客观的，公正的
63. defy [di'fai] *v.* show no fear of nor respect for; openly disobey; refuse to obey; ask someone, very strongly, to do sth. considered impossible 蔑视；公然违抗；不服从；向某人挑战；刺激某人做某事
64. neutrality [nju:'træliti] *n.* 中性，中立；中立立场
65. scrupulously ['skru:pjuləsli] *adv.* 严谨地，小心翼翼地；多顾虑地
66. belligerent [bi'lidʒərənt] *adj.* 交战的；好战的；交战国的　*n.* 交战国；参加斗殴的人或集团
67. provocation [prɔvə'keiʃən] *n.* 挑衅；激怒；挑拨
68. entangle [in'tæŋgl] *v.* cause to become twisted or mixed with sth. else 使纠缠，卷入；使混乱
69. steer clear of permanent alliances with any portion of the foreign world：避免同任何外国订立永久的同盟

    steer clear of：avoid, shun 避开，绕开

    alliance [ə'laiəns] *n.* a group of countries or political parties that are formally united and working together because they have similar aims; a relationship in which two countries, political parties, or organizations work together for some purpose（国家或政党的）联盟，同盟；联合，结盟
70. infidelity [ˌinfi'deliti] *n.* (an example or act of) not being faithful 无宗教信仰；背信；不忠诚
71. maxim ['mæksim] *n.* 格言，准则，座右铭
72. fervently ['fə:vəntli] *adv.* sincerely, enthusiastically 热心地，热诚地

73. beseech [bi'siːtʃ] *v.* <formal or literary> ask eagerly and anxiously（正式或文）祈求，恳求，哀求
74. mitigate ['mitigeit] *v.* lessen the seriousness of (evil, harm, pain, etc.) 减轻，缓和
75. upright zeal：正直的热忱
    upright ['ʌprait] *adj.* straight 垂直的，直挺挺的；honest, fair, responsible, etc. 诚实的，正直的，规矩的
    zeal [ziːl] *n.* great enthusiasm, especially in connection with work, religion, or politics 热情，热忱
76. consign [kən'sain] *v.* send to a person or place for sale 寄售，托运；to put into the care or control of someone else 把……托付给
77. oblivion [ə'bliviən] *n.* the state of bing completely forgotten 被完全忘却的状态；遗忘；the state of being unconscious or not noticing one's surroundings 无知觉的状态；漠视，不在意
78. progenitor [prə'dʒenitə] *n.* <tech or formal> a person or thing from the distant past, from which someone or sth. is descended; ancestor 起源；先驱，祖先
79. alloy ['æləi] *v.* 使成合金；使减低成色　*n.* 合金
80. partake [pɑː'teik] <old use or formal> take part (in an activity), participate 参加，参与
81. benign [bi'nain] *adj.* <rather formal> kind and gentle 慈祥的，和蔼的，亲切的；(of a disease) not dangerous to life 非恶性的，良性的

❑ Appreciating the Speech

华盛顿的告别演讲成为美国历史上最富影响力 (influential) 的政治演说之一。**从内容上看，**在演说中华盛顿阐述了过分的党派偏见 (undue partisanship) 可能对国家造成的不良影响 (baneful effects)，他呼吁人们抛弃党派之争，团结起来为增进公众利益 (enhance the public interest) 而努力。他还主张美国应该避免受到他国的干涉 (interference)，因为美国应该只专注于 (concentrate on) 美国人的利益。他建议与世界上其他国家保持友谊和贸易关系 (maintain friendship and trade relations)，并应该避免牵扯进欧洲的战争 (get involved into the European war)。他认为应该避免与某国家保持长期的同盟关系 (to steer clear of permanent alliances with any portion of the foreign world)，并指出应该注意当时美法间的结盟。

从语言上看，这篇演说比较突出的特点 (outstanding feature) 是排比 (parallelism) 和比喻 (simile and metaphor) 的运用。排比的使用起到了节奏鲜明、增强语势 (enhance language force) 的效果，例如第 2 段中提到政府的统一对美国人民的重要性 (the importance of the unity of the government to American people) 时，华盛顿用四个"of

结构”列举了政府统一的种种益处 (various benefits of a united government)；在第 8 段中，华盛顿通过“It serves...It agitates...It opens...”这一结构历数了党派风气的弊端 (enumerate the drawbacks of the partisanship)；华盛顿在第 13 段中用 4 个“when 结构”，在第 14 段中 3 个“why 结构”述说了在一个称职的政府领导下保持团结的重要性。而比喻的使用使语言生动形象 (vivid and lively)，增强了语言的表现力 (enhance the expressive force of the language)。比如文中两处暗喻 (metaphor) 的使用，第 2 段中“政府的统一 (the unity of government)”被喻为“大厦的主要支柱 (a main pillar in the edifice)”；第 9 段中“党派风气”被比做“不能熄灭的火 (A fire not to be quenched)”，以提醒大家始终小心戒备 (uniform vigilance)，防止它“燃成熊熊烈焰，否则，它不仅不能给人取暖，反而会烧毁一切 (prevent its bursting into a flame, lest, instead of warming, it should consume)”。另外，这篇演说中还有个特点是大词长词的运用，如 insidiously, perpetrate, discountenance, dissension, animosity, vicissitude, scrupulously, progenitor, partake 等，使语言更为正式庄重 (formal and serious)。

❑ Culture Links

(1) 华盛顿精神

在岁月的长河中，确有一些真正的伟人。他们高贵的品质、伟大的功绩、深刻而崇高的思想与人格风范，达到常人难以企及的高度，他们的名字将永远为全人类所铭记。乔治·华盛顿无疑就是这样一位伟人。

众所周知，华盛顿临危受命，作为大陆军总司令，率领这支经验不足、给养匮乏的军队，经过 8 年的浴血奋战，打败了强大的英国殖民军，使美国真正赢得了独立。这时的华盛顿声望如日中天，深受全国军民的拥戴，他若想成为首任国家元首，那是唾手可得的事。但此时的华盛顿所思考的不是个人的权力，而是一个新生国家的政治走向。为了国家的长治久安，为了人民的永久幸福和尊严，他毅然主动辞去军职。在仪式上，华盛顿用一种庄严、感人的方式发表一篇简短的讲话：“现在，我已完成了战争所赋予的使命，我将退出这个伟大的舞台，并且向尊严的国会告别。在它的命令之下，我奋战已久，谨在此交出委任并辞去所有公职。”他昔日的下属，时任国会议长答道：“您在这块土地上捍卫了自由的理念，为受伤害和被压迫的人树立了典范。您将带着全体同胞的祝福退出这个伟大的舞台，但是您的道德力量并没随您的军职一起消失，它将永远激励子孙后代。”辞职的他回到了家，回到了自己的农场，过上了平静的生活。在那到处都还是皇帝和国王的世界上，在那打了江山坐江山的时代里，华盛顿主动放弃军权，实乃石破天惊之壮举，他给这个新生的国家，也给世界树立了一个影响深远的先例和榜样。

几年以后，美国宪法通过，合众国需要一位总统。那时人们都认为，鉴于当时的情况，美国第一位总统非他莫属。于是，他听从国家召唤，再次献身于国家，于 1789 年成为美国历史上的第一位总统，也是第一位全票当选的总统、第一位没有任何党派身份的总统。8年的总统任期，正值国家最艰难的岁月，他以对国家、对人民的朴素感情，殚精竭虑，为美利坚的未来奠定了坚实的基础。但连任两届总统后，他坚决地拒绝继续连任，他说，"我走在尚未踏实的土地上，我的所作所为将可能成为以后历届总统的先例。"他向美国人民解释，"你们再继续选我做总统，美国就没有真正的民主制度了"，就这样，他为美国总统任期立下了不超过两届的先例。1799年12月13日，征战一生、功勋卓著的华盛顿平静地去世了，没有痛苦，没有叹息。他去世的消息传出后，举国哀痛。昔日的敌人英国也为他的逝世鸣礼炮20响致哀。

伟人逝去了，但是他毕生奋斗、培植、呵护建立的美利坚合众国却稳固长存，他所建立的民主、自由、独立的国家理念从此深入人心，成为世界政治的前进方向。他那无与伦比的军人勇气、政治家的风范、至高的荣誉感和人格魅力将永放光彩。华盛顿不仅属于美国，他也属于世界；他不仅是美国的骄傲，也是全人类的骄傲。

华盛顿的不贪恋权力的主动放权精神，他的人民利益至上、宪法至上的精神，被称为华盛顿精神。

（2）美国政党制度

① 美国政党制度的形成

美国是世界上最早出现政党的国家之一，也是典型的两党制国家之一。民主党与共和党在国家政治生活中占据重要位置。美国的选举制度、议会制度、行政管理制度以及司法制度，都与两党制有着密切联系。

1787年，美利坚合众国的开国元勋们起草《美国宪法》时并未预见政党在政府管理制度中的作用。实际上，他们通过分权、制约和平衡原则和由选举团间接选举总统等各项宪法规定，力图将政党及政治派别排除在政府管理制度之外。尽管美国的开国元勋们用心良苦，美国仍开全国性政党执政之先河，并于1800年通过一次选举，将行政权力从一个党派转移到另一个党派手中。19世纪初，选民必须拥有一定财产的规定被取消后，更多的人有了选举权，美国政党的发展与此密切相关。由于选民人数大量增加，需要一种手段来动员广大选民。为完成这一至关重要的任务，政党应运而生。

18世纪北美资产阶级革命胜利后，当时美国统治阶级内部在批准1787年宪法运动中，形成了联邦主义者（或称联邦党人）和反联邦主义者（或称反联邦党人）两大政派。1789年联邦政府成立后，两派在宪法解释、联邦与各州权限，以及公债、设立国家银行等问题上发生严重分歧，以A.汉密尔顿为首的联邦党人代表东北部大资产阶级、大商人等利益，主张对宪法从宽解释，建立一个中央集权政府；以T.杰斐逊为首的反联邦党人代表资产阶级民主派、州权派等利益，主张对宪法从严解释，要求扩大州权，保障自由。两派在国会内外进行活动，逐步由国会内的政治派别发展为全国性政党。反联邦党人于1791年开始组织共和党，由国务卿杰斐逊任领袖，故又称杰斐逊共和党。联邦党人于1795年正式成立联邦党，并于 1797—1801 年执政。1801 年以后，联邦党一蹶不振，至 1817 年已名存实亡。共和党在 1792 年欧洲战争爆发后，势力迅速扩大，在 1800 年的竞选中获胜，杰斐逊当选总统。到 19 世纪 20 年代，共和党分裂为两派：国民共和党和民主共和党。国民共和党在 1828 年和 1832 年的两次总统竞选中失败，以后逐渐湮没无闻。民主共和党在 1828 年选举中简称民主党，大选获胜后，杰克逊当选总统，后正式定名为民主党。1834 年，辉格党成立，它是反对杰克逊政权的松散的党派联盟，后成为全国性的主要政党。19 世纪 40 年代末，辉格党联盟开始瓦解。1854 年 7 月，共和党成立，在以后的 4 年中，共和党在北方各州取代辉格党，成了民主党的主要对手。至此，美国两大政党形成，两党制开始确立。

在当今的美国，除了民主党和共和党外，还有美国社会党、美国共产党、绿党等党派，但由于这些党派人数少，影响小，因而从未对上述两大主要政党形成真正的威胁。

② 美国政党制度的特点

美国是现代政党制度发育最早的国家之一，在其长期的发展演变过程中形成了自己鲜明的特色，其中以下两特色尤为显著：

A. 两党制。美国是两党制国家，两大主要政党民主党和共和党轮流执政，互相监督和制约，垄断了联邦和州的政治权力，并使这一体制具有极强的稳定性。自两大政党出现至今，这一状况从未受到有力的挑战，在可以预见的未来，也看不到有第三党能够威胁两大政党的迹象。鲜明而稳定的两党制是美国政党政治的一大特色，对美国的政治制度和政治生活产生了重大影响。

B. 组织的松散和权力的分散。在美国，联邦制和分权制原则充分地体现在政党制度之中。表面上看，两党都各有自己的全国委员会，委员会形式上是党的最高机构，但实际上，两党全国委员会的权力和作用却有很大的局限，拥有的资源也很贫乏，特别是在非大选年，其作用和影响就更小了。

政党纪律的相对松弛在美国表现得尤为突出。与议会制国家不同，在总统制的美国，总统和国会的权力各有其宪法依据。因此，尽管两党在国会中都有自己的议会党团，但作为党的名义领袖的总统对本党在国会中的组织和普通议员都缺乏有效的制约手段，国会中的两党组织对本党议员也没有直接控制的权力。就党的普通成员而言，党的纪律就更为松弛了。除了少数职业党员外，普通公民拥有参加某政党和退出某政党的充分自由，他们的行为也不受党籍的任何约束。实际上，所谓党员只是在选举登记时声称自己支持某党而已，并无任何入党的组织程序。而且，在实际投票中，他也不必一定按照其在选民登记时的党派立场投票。

在美国人的观念中，政党（即政治团体）与学术团体、体育团体、宗教团体等一样，只是因为有相同的观点、兴趣、信仰等而凑在一起的一帮人而已。合则聚，不合则离。在层次上，一个党员（包括执政党党员）并不比一个“诗歌爱好者协会”或“桥牌协会”会员显得更"高级"。所以，在美国参加一个政党（当然包括参加一个执政党），没有什么人会觉得这是一件特别"光荣"的事，更不会有什么特权。

❑ Questions Concerning the Speech

1. Why is the unity of government very dear to American people?
2. What may cause the disturbance to America?
3. What are the baneful effects of the spirit of party Washington warned the American people?
4. Why did Washington say the spirit of party is a spirit not to be encouraged?
5. What is the method of preserving public credit?
6. Why should people beware of the insidious wiles of foreign influence? And how?
7. What is the great rule of conduct for us concerning foreign nations?
8. What kind of circumstances will we meet if we pursue a different course—remain one people under an efficient government?

❑ Paraphrase the Following Sentences

1. ... it is of infinite moment that you should properly estimate the immense value of your national union to your collective and individual happiness; that you should cherish a cordial, habitual, and immovable attachment to it ...
2. In contemplating the causes which may disturb our Union, it occurs as matter of serious concern that any ground should have been furnished for characterizing parties by geographical discriminations, Northern and Southern, Atlantic and Western; whence designing men may endeavor to excite a belief that there is a real difference of local interests and views.
3. The alternate domination of one faction over another, sharpened by the spirit of revenge, natural to party dissension, which in different ages and countries has perpetrated the most horrid enormities, is itself a frightful despotism.
4. And there being constant danger of excess, the effort ought to be by force of public opinion, to mitigate and assuage it. A fire not to be quenched, it demands a uniform vigilance to prevent its bursting into a flame, lest, instead of warming, it should consume.
5. Real patriots who may resist the intrigues of the favorite are liable to become suspected and odious, while its tools and dupes usurp the applause and confidence of the people, to surrender their interests.

6. I shall also carry with me the hope that my country will never cease to view them with indulgence; and that, after forty five years of my life dedicated to its service with an upright zeal, the faults of incompetent abilities will be consigned to oblivion, as myself must soon be to the mansions of rest.

❑ Questions for Discussion

1. 华盛顿在告别演讲中历数了党派纷争的种种弊端，你对此有何观点？你如何看待美国的政党制度？
2. 华盛顿有句名言“诚实是最好的政策”（Honesty is the best policy），你对这句话如何理解？试举例说明。
3. 华盛顿在告别演讲中论及了如何处理与其他国家尤其是欧洲国家关系的问题。请论述华盛顿在国际关系方面的观点以及其对美国后来的“孤立主义”外交政策的影响。

❑ Translation

乔治·华盛顿：告别演讲

1796年9月17日，刊登于费城的报纸上

各位朋友和同胞：

1. 我们重新选举一位公民来主持美国政府的行政工作，已为期不远。此时此刻，大家必须运用心来考虑这一重任付托给谁。因此，我觉得我现在应当向大家声明，尤其因为这样做有助于使公众意见获得更为明确的表达，那就是我已下定决心，谢绝将我列为候选人。

……

2. 政府的统一，使大家结成一个民族，现在这种统一对你们很珍贵。这是理所当然的，因为你们真正的独立仿佛一座大厦，而政府的统一乃是这座大厦的主要支柱；它支持你们国内的安定、国外的和平；支持你们的安全、你们的繁荣，以及你们如此重视的真正自由。然而不难预见，曾有某些力量试图削弱大家心里对于这种真理的信念，这些力量的起因不一、来源各异，但均将煞费苦心，千方百计地产生作用；其所以如此，乃因统一是你们政治堡垒中一个重点，内外敌人的炮火会最持续不断地、加紧地（虽然常是秘密地与阴险地）进行轰击。因此，最重要的乃是大家应当正确估计这个民族团结对于集体和个人幸福所具有的重大价值；大家应当对它抱着诚挚的、经常的和坚定不移的忠心；你们在思想和言语中要习惯于把它当做大家政治安全和繁荣的保障；

要小心翼翼地守护它。如果有人提到这种信念在某种情况下可以抛弃，即使那只是猜想，也不应当表示支持。如果有人企图使我国的一部分脱离其余部分，或想削弱现在联系各部分的神圣纽带，在其最初出现时，就应当严加指责。

……

3. 研究那些可能扰乱我们联邦的种种原因时，使人想到一件至关重要的事，那就是以地域差别——北方与南方、大西洋与西部——为根据来建立各种党派；因为那些心怀不轨的人可能力图借此造成一种信念，以为地方间真的存在着利益和观点的差异。一个党派想在某些地区赢得影响力而采取的策略之一，是歪曲其他地区的观点和目标。这种歪曲引起的妒忌和不满，是防不胜防的，使那些本应亲如兄弟的人变得互不相容。

……

4. 我已经提醒你们，在美国存在着党派分立的危险，并特别提到按地域差别来分立党派的危险。现在让我从更全面的角度，以最严肃的态度概略地告诫你们警惕党派思想的恶劣影响。

5. 不幸的是，这种思想与我们的本性是不可分割的，并扎根于人类脑海里最强烈的欲望之中。它以各种不同的形式存在于所有政府机构里，尽管多少受到压抑、控制或约束。但那些常见的党派思想的形式，往往是最令人讨厌的，并且确实成为危害政府的最大敌人。

6. 派系斗争因报复情绪而加剧，这在不同国家不同时代曾造成最为恐怖的暴行。两派你胜我败的交替执政本身就是一种可怕的暴政，而且最终还会导致产生一种更为正式的永久性独裁暴政。因为派别纷争带来了动荡和苦难，使人逐渐倾向于建立个人的绝对权力以寻求安全和保障。迟早有某个执政党的首脑，因能力更强或运气比他的竞争对手好，便会利用上述普遍情绪破坏公众自由，以达到个人擢升的目的。

7. 即使事情不至发展至上述极端的地步（不过，我们不该完全忽视这种极端的可能），党派风气经常不断引起祸患，也足以使明智的民族出于责任感和自然利益的考虑而去防范它、抑制它了。

8. 它往往干扰公众会议的进行，并削弱公共管理能力。它在民众中引起无根据的猜忌和莫须有的惊恐；挑拨派别对立；有时还引起骚动和叛乱。它为外国影响和腐蚀打开方便之门。外国影响和腐蚀可以轻易地通过派系倾向的渠道深入到政府机构中来。这样，一个国家的政策和意志就会受到另一个国家政策和意志的影响。

9. 有一种意见，认为自由国家中的政党，是对政府施政的有效牵制，有助于发扬自由精神。在某种限度内，这大概是对的；在君主制的政府下，人民基于爱国心，对于政党精神即使不加袒护，也会颇为宽容。但在民主性质的纯属选任的政府下，这种精神是不应予以鼓励的。从其自然趋势看来，可以肯定，在每一种有益的目标上，总是不乏这种精神的。但这种精神常有趋于过度的危险，因此应当用舆论的力量使之减轻及缓和。它是一团火，我们不要熄灭它，但要一致警惕，以防它火焰大发，变成不是供人取暖，而是贻害于人。

……

10. 我们应当珍视国家的财力，因为这是力量和安全的极为重要的源泉。保存财力的办法之一是尽量少动用它，并维护和平以避免意外开支；但也要记住，为了防患于未然而及时拨款，往往可以避免支付更大的款项来消弭灾祸。同样，我们要避免债台高筑，为此，不仅要节约开支，而且在和平时期还要尽力去偿还不可避免的战争所带来的债务，不要将我们自己应该承受的负担无情地留给后代。

……

11. 一个自由民族应当经常警觉，提防外国势力的阴谋诡计（同胞们，我恳求你们相信我），因为历史和经验证明，外国势力乃是共和政府最致命的敌人之一。不过这种提防，要想做到有效，必须不偏不倚，否则会成为我们所要摆脱的势力的工具，而不是抵御那种势力的工事。对某国过度偏爱，对另外一个过度偏恶，会使受到这种影响的国家只看到一方面的危险，却掩盖甚至纵容另一方所施的诡计。在我们所喜欢的那个国家的爪牙和受他们蒙蔽的人，利用人民的赞赏和信任，诱骗人民放弃本身的利益的同时，那些可能抵制该国诡计的真正爱国志士，反而极易成为怀疑与憎恶的对象。

12. 我们处理外国事务的最重要原则，就是在与它们发展商务关系时，尽量避免涉及政治。我们已订的条约，必须忠实履行。但以此为限，不再增加。欧洲有一套基本利益，它对于我们毫无或甚少关系。欧洲经常发生争执，其原因基本上与我们毫不相干。所以，如果我们卷进欧洲事务，与他们的政治兴衰人为地联系在一起，或与他们友好而结成同盟，或与他们敌对而发生冲突，都是不明智的。

13. 我国独处一方，远离他国，这种地理位置允许并促使我们奉行一条不同的政策路线。如果我们在一个称职的政府领导下保持团结，在不久的将来，我们就可以不怕外来干扰造成的物质破坏；我们就可以采取一种姿态，使我们在任何时候决心保持中立时，都可得到它国严正的尊重；好战国家不能从我们这里获得好处时，也不敢轻易冒险向我们挑战；我们可以在正义的指引下依照自己的利益，在是和是战问题上作出抉择。

14. 我们为什么要摒弃这种特殊环境带来的优越条件呢？为什么要放弃我们自己的立场而站到外国的立场上去呢？为什么要把我们的命运同欧洲任何一部分的命运交织一起，以致把我们的和平与繁荣，陷入欧洲的野心、竞争、利益关系、古怪念头，或反复无常的罗网之中呢？

15. 我们真正的政策，乃是避免同任何外国订立永久的同盟，我的意思是我们现在可自由处理这种问题；但请不要误会，以为我赞成不履行现有的条约。我认为，诚实是最好的政策，这句格言不仅适用于私事，也通用于公务。所以我再重复说一句，那些条约应按其原意加以履行。但我觉得延长那些条约是不必要，也是不明智的。

……

16. 虽然在检讨本人任期内施政时，我未发觉有故意的错误，但是我很明白我的缺点，并不以为我没有犯过很多错误。不管这些错误是什么，我恳切地祈求上帝免除或减轻这些错误所可能产生的恶果。而且我也将怀着一种希望，希望我的国家永远宽恕这些错误；我秉持正直的热忱，献身为国家服务，已经四十五年，希望我因为能力薄弱而犯的过失，会随着我不久以后长眠地下而湮没无闻。
17. 我在这方面和在其他方面一样，均须仰赖祖国的仁慈，我热爱祖国，并受到爱国之情的激励。这种感情，对于一个视祖国为自己及历代祖先的故土的人来说，是很自然的。因此，我以欢欣的期待心情，希望在我殷切期盼的退休之后，我将与我的同胞们愉快地分享自由政府治下完善的法律的温暖——这是我一直衷心向往的目标。并且我相信，这也是我们相互关怀、共同努力和赴汤蹈火的优厚报酬。

Thomas Jefferson

(1743—1826)

托马斯·杰斐逊

3

Thomas Jefferson's First Inaugural Address

Delivered March 4, 1801, in Washington, D.C.

❑ About the Author

托马斯·杰斐逊（Thomas Jefferson, 1743—1826），美利坚合众国第三任总统（1801 年—1809 年），同时也是美国《独立宣言》主要起草人，美国开国元勋中最具影响力者之一。杰斐逊是首位于白宫就职并离任的总统，也是民主共和党党员首次当选总统。截至目前，杰斐逊为唯一担任过美国副总统后又选上总统、而且任满两个任期者。

身为政治学家，杰斐逊秉持古典自由主义与共和主义（republicanism），制定了弗吉尼亚宗教自由法（Virginia Statute for Religious Freedom）。该法日后成为美国宪法第一修正案创设条文之基础，杰斐逊式民主（Jeffersonian democracy）因他而得名。他创立并领导民主共和党，成为今日民主党之前身，统治美国政治达 1/4 世纪。杰斐逊曾任第二任弗吉尼亚州州长（1779 年—1781 年）、第一任美国国务卿（1789 年—1793 年）和第二任美国副总统（1797 年—1801 年）。除政治事业外，杰斐逊也是农业学、建筑学、词源学、考古学与古生物学等学科的专家；又身兼作家、律师与小提琴手；也是弗吉尼亚大学的创办者。许多人认为他是历任美国总统中智慧最高者。杰斐逊任内因崇尚重农主义、个人自由、有限政府及以共和主义激励美国身份认同而知名。尽管杰斐逊以建立有限政府为目的，他在第一任总统任期中执行路易斯安那购地案，并委派进行路易斯与克拉克探勘。在第二任期中他主要处理外交问题，例如在陷入英法之战时保持中立。

杰斐逊受多名欧洲启蒙思想家的见解影响极深，其政治原则尤其受到约翰·洛克不可转让之权利（inalienable rights）与人民主权（popular sovereignty）思想的影响。杰斐逊相信，人皆拥有某种“不可转让之权利”。也就是说，无论政府是否存在，人所拥有的不可创造、夺取或转让的基本权利永存。他对于自由的解释最受后人重视。

杰斐逊极为拥护州权，其于1798年之弗吉尼亚和肯塔基决议（Virginia and Kentucky Resolutions）中，定下敌视联邦扩权之基调，尤其值得注意。然而，他的若干外交政策实际上反而扩充了联邦权力。其中最重要的是，他在1803年的路易斯安那购地案中，以不成文的联邦权力兼并一大块外国土地，连同居住其间的法籍与意大利籍居民。他行使禁运法案，却因与外交政策抵触而失效，显示联邦政府在有战争之虞时，可以强大武力作为后盾，介入地方层级事务以控制贸易往来。

杰斐逊逝世于1826年7月4日，当日为《独立宣言》通过50周年纪念日。他身后葬于其蒙蒂塞洛的产业上。他坚决要求，墓碑除铭刻自己所撰写的句子外，“一个字也不要多”。其墓志铭内容为：弗吉尼亚大学之父，以及《弗吉尼亚宗教自由法》、美国《独立宣言》作者托马斯·杰斐逊长眠于此。

❑ About the Speech

1792年，杰斐逊与詹姆斯·麦迪逊创立民主共和党，并成为党内领袖。1793年，英法两国爆发战争，杰斐逊强烈支持法国，而亚历山大·汉密尔顿与华盛顿方面在缔结《杰伊条约》（*Jay Treaty*）后则支持英国，杰斐逊于是辞职隐退蒙地沙罗，后又获选为美国副总统（1797—1801）。

因与法国进行准战争（两国海军不宣而战），约翰·亚当斯所领导的联邦党加强并增募海陆两军，同时开征新税，为战争作准备，并在1798年制定了《客籍法和惩治叛乱法》(Alien and Sedition Acts)。杰斐逊将此法解读为对他所属的政党的攻击，危险甚于对付外敌。他与麦迪逊为重新集结支持者，匿名著作《肯塔基与弗吉尼亚提案》（Kentucky and Virginia Resolutions），主张宪法仅为各州与联邦政府之间的协定，联邦政府无权行使宪法无明文规定之事项，而各州对联邦政府各项僭越之举可视为无效。此提案为美国史上首次对州权论之陈述，该论述开日后拒行联邦法规与介入论之先河。

杰斐逊重新集结其政党，特别为对付新税开征投入1800年美国总统大选。1800年的选举是美国第四次总统选举，也是第一次两党积极竞选总统职位。托马斯·杰斐逊和艾伦·伯尔在总统大选中获得了相同的选票，须由时为联邦党所控制的美国众议院决断选举结果。经冗长辩论后，汉密尔顿在众议院中说服了同党议员。他认为，选举过程中的流言将腐蚀新生的美国政府；而就政治面而言，杰斐逊较不具伤害性。众议院因于1801年2月17日决议，推举杰斐逊为总统，伯尔为副总统。杰斐逊的当选标志着美国两党轮流执政的开端，史称“1800年革命”。正如汉密尔顿所言，杰斐逊当选后即表现出他是顺应时势的。他毅然从法国手中买下路易斯安那州那块土地，从而使美国的面积扩大了一倍。

杰斐逊于1801年3月宣誓就职，这是美国历史上第一次政府从一个政党（联邦党）

的统治下转到另一个政党（共和党）的手中。当时，党派冲突非常激烈，那些正统的联邦党人悲观地预言在 12 年前精心建立起来的政治和经济制度会因杰斐逊的当政而毁掉。有些人认为杰斐逊会在其就职演说中攻击、批判联邦党的政策，因为杰斐逊曾一直对那些政策持批评态度。然而，事实恰恰相反。为了平息政治斗争，共谋国家大业，杰斐逊发表了这篇充满调和色彩，但又闪烁着资产阶级民主思想的就职演说，宣告实行温和、宽容的政策。由此，杰斐逊在美国历史上创下了又一个先例，那就是，不管在竞选中两党之间的斗争多么激烈，他们都应当接受选举结果，并为国家的利益而精诚合作。

❑ The Speech in Full

Friends and Fellow-Citizens:

1. **Called upon to undertake the duties of the first executive office of our country, I avail[1] myself of the presence of that portion of my fellow-citizens which is here assembled to express my grateful thanks for the favor with which they have been pleased to look toward me, to declare a sincere consciousness that the task is above my talents, and that I approach it with those anxious and awful presentiments[2] which the greatness of the charge and the weakness of my powers so justly inspire.** A rising nation, spread over a wide and fruitful land, traversing[3] all the seas with the rich productions of their industry, engaged in commerce with nations who feel power and forget right, advancing rapidly to destinies beyond the reach of mortal eye—when I contemplate these transcendent[4] objects, and see the honor, the happiness, and the hopes of this beloved country committed to the issue, and the auspices[5] of this day, I shrink from the contemplation, and humble myself before the magnitude[6] of the undertaking. Utterly, indeed, should I despair did not the presence of many whom I here see remind me that in the other high authorities provided by our Constitution I shall find resources of wisdom, of virtue, and of zeal on which to rely under all difficulties. **To you, then, gentlemen, who are charged with the sovereign[7] functions of legislation, and to those associated with you, I look with encouragement for that guidance and support which may enable us to steer with safety the vessel in which we are all embarked[8] amidst[9] the conflicting elements of a troubled world.**

2. During the contest of opinion through which we have passed the animation[10] of discussions and of exertions has sometimes worn an aspect which might impose on strangers unused to think freely and to speak and to write what they think; but this being now decided by the voice of the nation, announced according to the rules

of the Constitution, all will, of course, arrange themselves under the will of the law, and unite in common efforts for the common good. **All, too, will bear in mind this sacred principle, that though the will of the majority is in all cases to prevail[11], that will to be rightful must be reasonable; that the minority possess their equal rights, which equal law must protect, and to violate would be oppression. Let us, then, fellow-citizens, unite with one heart and one mind. Let us restore to social intercourse[12] that harmony and affection without which liberty and even life itself are but dreary[13] things. And let us reflect that, having banished[14] from our land that religious intolerance under which mankind so long bled and suffered, we have yet gained little if we countenance[15] a political intolerance as despotic[16], as wicked, and capable of as bitter and bloody persecutions[17]. During the throes and convulsions of the ancient world[18], during the agonizing spasms of infuriated man[19], seeking through blood and slaughter[20] his long-lost liberty, it was not wonderful that the agitation of the billows[21] should reach even this distant and peaceful shore; that this should be more felt and feared by some and less by others, and should divide opinions as to measures of safety. But every difference of opinion is not a difference of principle. We have called by different names brethren[22] of the same principle. We are all Republicans, we are all Federalists. If there be any among us who would wish to dissolve this Union or to change its republican form, let them stand undisturbed as monuments of the safety with which error of opinion may be tolerated where reason is left free to combat it.** I know, indeed, that some honest men fear that a republican government can not be strong, that this Government is not strong enough; but would the honest patriot, in the full tide of successful experiment, abandon a government which has so far kept us free and firm on the theoretic and visionary fear that this Government, the world's best hope, may by possibility want energy to preserve itself? I trust not. I believe this, on the contrary, the strongest Government on earth. I believe it the only one where every man, at the call of the law, would fly to the standard of the law, and would meet invasions of the public order as his own personal concern. Sometimes it is said that man can not be trusted with the government of himself. Can he, then, be trusted with the government of others? Or have we found angels in the forms of kings to govern him? Let history answer this question.

3. **Let us, then, with courage and confidence pursue our own Federal and Republican principles, our attachment to union and representative government.**

Kindly separated by nature and a wide ocean from the exterminating[23] havoc[24] of one quarter of the globe; too high-minded to endure the degradations of the others; possessing a chosen country, with room enough for our descendants to the thousandth and thousandth generation; entertaining a due sense of our equal right to the use of our own faculties, to the acquisitions of our own industry, to honor and confidence from our fellow-citizens, resulting not from birth, but from our actions and their sense of them; enlightened by a benign religion, professed, indeed, and practiced in various forms, yet all of them inculcating[25] honesty, truth, temperance[26], gratitude, and the love of man; acknowledging and adoring an overruling Providence[27], which by all its dispensations[28] proves that it delights in the happiness of man here and his greater happiness hereafter[29]—with all these blessings, what more is necessary to make us a happy and a prosperous people? Still one thing more, fellow-citizens—a wise and frugal Government, which shall restrain[30] men from injuring one another, shall leave them otherwise free to regulate their own pursuits of industry and improvement, and shall not take from the mouth of labor the bread it has earned. This is the sum of good government, and this is necessary to close the circle of our felicities[31].

4. About to enter, fellow-citizens, on the exercise of duties which comprehend everything dear and valuable to you, it is proper you should understand what I deem[32] the essential principles of our Government, and consequently those which ought to shape its Administration. I will compress[33] them within the narrowest compass they will bear, stating the general principle, but not all its limitations. Equal and exact justice to all men, of whatever state or persuasion, religious or political; peace, commerce, and honest friendship with all nations, entangling[34] alliances with none; the support of the State governments in all their rights, as the most competent administrations for our domestic concerns and the surest bulwarks[35] against anti-republican tendencies; the preservation of the General Government in its whole constitutional vigor, as the sheet anchor of our peace at home and safety abroad; a jealous care of the right of election by the people—a mild and safe corrective of abuses[36] which are lopped[37] by the sword of revolution where peaceable remedies are unprovided; absolute acquiescence[38] in the decisions of the majority, the vital principle of republics, from which is no appeal but to force, the vital principle and immediate parent of despotism; a well disciplined militia, our best reliance in peace and for the first moments of war, till regulars may relieve them; the supremacy[39] of the civil over the military authority; economy in the public

expense, that labor may be lightly burthened[40]; the honest payment of our debts and sacred preservation of the public faith; encouragement of agriculture, and of commerce as its handmaid[41]; the diffusion[42] of information and arraignment[43] of all abuses at the bar of the public reason; freedom of religion; freedom of the press, and freedom of person under the protection of the habeas corpus[44], and trial by juries impartially selected. **These principles form the bright constellation[45] which has gone before us and guided our steps through an age of revolution and reformation. The wisdom of our sages[46] and blood of our heroes have been devoted to their attainment. They should be the creed[47] of our political faith, the text of civic instruction, the touchstone[48] by which to try the services of those we trust; and should we wander from them in moments of error or of alarm, let us hasten to retrace our steps[49] and to regain the road which alone leads to peace, liberty, and safety.**

5. I repair, then, fellow-citizens, to the post you have assigned me. With experience enough in subordinate[50] offices to have seen the difficulties of this the greatest of all, I have learnt to expect that it will rarely fall to the lot of imperfect man to retire from this station with the reputation and the favor which bring him into it. Without pretensions[51] to that high confidence you reposed in our first and greatest revolutionary character, whose preeminent services had entitled him to the first place in his country's love and destined for him the fairest page in the volume of faithful history, I ask so much confidence only as may give firmness and effect to the legal administration of your affairs. I shall often go wrong through defect of judgment. When right, I shall often be thought wrong by those whose positions will not command a view of the whole ground. I ask your indulgence for my own errors, which will never be intentional, and your support against the errors of others, who may condemn what they would not if seen in all its parts. The approbation[52] implied by your suffrage[53] is a great consolation[54] to me for the past, and my future solicitude[55] will be to retain the good opinion of those who have bestowed[56] it in advance, to conciliate[57] that of others by doing them all the good in my power, and to be instrumental to the happiness and freedom of all.

6. Relying, then, on the patronage[58] of your good will, I advance with obedience to the work, ready to retire from it whenever you become sensible how much better choice it is in your power to make. And may that Infinite Power which rules the destinies of

the universe lead our councils to what is best, and give them a favorable issue for your peace and prosperity. (1,727 words)

❑ Notes to the Speech

1. avail [ə'veil] *v.* be of use or advantage 有用于；有助于
   avail oneself of：to make good or profitable use of 利用
2. presentiment [pri'zentimənt] *n.* <formal> an unexplained uncomfortable feeling that something, esp. something bad, is going to happen（尤指对不祥事物的）预感
3. traverse ['trævə(:)s] *v.* <formal> pass across, over, or through 横越，穿过，横过
4. transcendent [træn'sendənt] *adj.* going far beyond ordinary limits 超常的，卓越的，出类拔萃的
5. auspices ['ɔ:spisiz] *n.* <formal> help, support, and favor 资助，赞助，支持
6. magnitude ['mægnitju:d] *n.* <formal> greatness of size or importance 巨大，重要（性）
7. sovereign ['sɔvrin] *adj.* in control of a country; ruling 治国的；权利至高无上的；independent and self-governing 独立自主的，具有独立主权的
8. embark [im'bɑ:k] *v.* go, put, or take on a ship 上船；装船
9. amidst [ə'midst] *prep.* (also amid) in the middle of; among 在……当中，在……中间
10. animation [ˌæni'meiʃən] *n.* excitement; spirit; liveliness 兴奋；生气；活跃
11. prevail [pri'veil] *v.* (continue to) exist or be widespread（继续）盛行；流行；to gain control or victory; win a fight 胜（过）；对……占上风
12. intercourse ['intə(:)kɔ:s] *n.* an exchange of feelings, actions, etc. which make people know each other more closely 交往，沟通，交流
13. dreary ['driəri] *adj.* sad or cheerless; gloomy 令人沮丧的，阴郁的，沉闷的；dull, uninteresting 单调的，乏味的
14. banish ['bæniʃ] *v.* send away by official order, usu. from one's own country, esp. as a punishment 把……驱逐出境；to force to leave; drive away 驱逐，赶走；排除
15. countenance ['kauntinəns] *v.* consent to, give permission 支持，赞同
16. despotic [des'pɔtik] *adj.* 专制的，残暴的，暴虐的
17. persecution [ˌpə:si'kju:ʃən] *n.* cruel and unfair treatment of a person or group, especially because of their religious or political beliefs, or their race 迫害
18. the throes and convulsions of the ancient world：古代社会的剧痛和骚动
    throe [θrəu] *n.* violent sudden pain, esp. caused by dying 突然发作的剧痛
    convulsion [kən'vʌlʃən] *n.* a number of sudden violent uncontrollable shaking movements caused esp. by illness 惊厥，抽搐

19. the agonizing spasms of infuriated man：愤怒之人的痛苦痉挛
    agonize ['ægənaiz] *v.* make a long and anxious effort when considering sth. or trying to make a decision 焦虑，忧愁，苦恼
    spasm ['spæzəm] *n.* a sudden uncontrolled tightening of muscles; a sudden violent effort, feeling, or act 痉挛，抽搐，抽筋；一阵发作
    infuriate [in'fjuərieit] *v.* to make sb. extremely angry 使极为愤怒
20. slaughter ['slɔːtə] *n.* the killing of many people or animals, esp. cruelly, wrongly, or in a battle 屠杀，杀戮
21. the agitation of the billows：巨浪的翻滚
    agitation [ædʒi'teiʃən] *n.* painful excitement of the mind or feelings, anxiety; public argument, action, unrest, etc. for or against political or social change 焦虑，极度不安；鼓动宣传，骚动
    billow ['biləu] *n.* a wave, esp. a very large one 波涛，巨浪
22. brethren ['breðrən] *n.* (plural) the lay members of a male religious order 教友；同胞
23. exterminate [iks'təːmineit] *v.* kill en masse; kill on a large scale; destroy completely, as if down to the roots 消灭；根除
24. havoc ['hævək] *n.* widespread damage or serious disorder 浩劫，大破坏
25. inculcate [in'kʌlkeit] *v.* <formal> fix (ideas, principles, etc.) in the mind of 反复灌输，谆谆教诲
26. temperance ['tempərəns] *n.* total avoidance of alcoholic drinks; self-control in speech, behavior, or esp. the drinking of alcohol 戒酒，禁酒；自我克制，节制
27. an overruling Providence：万能的上帝
    overrule [ˌəuvə'ruːl] *v.* to decide against (sth. already decided) by official power 推翻，否决，驳回
    Providence ['prɔvidəns] *n.* God's care or the kindness of fate 天意，天命，天佑，天道
28. dispensation [ˌdispen'seiʃən] *n.* 特许，豁免；分配，施行；教规，制度
29. hereafter [hiər'ɑːftə] *adv.* <formal> after this time; in the future 此后，今后；将来
30. restrain [ris'trein] *v.* control or prevent from doing sth. esp. by use of force 克制，抑制
31. felicity [fi'lisiti] *n.* <formal> happiness 幸福
32. deem [diːm] *v.* consider; have the opinion; judge 认为；视为；断定为
33. compress [kəm'pres] *v.* force (a substance) into less space; press together; put into fewer words 压缩；压紧；使简练
34. entangle [in'tæŋgl] *v.* cause to become twisted or mixed with sth. else 使纠缠；使陷入

35. bulwark ['bulwə(:)k] *n.* a strong wall built for defence, often made of earth 壁垒，堡垒
36. a mild and safe corrective of abuses：一种矫正种种弊端的温和而安全的手段
37. lop [lɔp] *v.* cut off from a whole 砍伐
38. acquiescence [ˌækwi'esns] *n.* agreement to do what someone wants, or acceptance of what they do 默认，默许
39. supremacy [sju'preməsi] *n.* power to dominate or defeat 最高权力，最高地位
40. burthen ['bəːðən] *v.* weight down with a load; burden 使负重担
41. handmaid ['hændmeid] *n.* a personal maid or female attendant 侍女，女佣人
42. diffusion [di'fjuːʒən] *n.* the spread of social institutions (and myths and skills) from one society to another; the act of dispersing or diffusing sth. 扩散；传播
43. arraignment [ə'reinmənt] *n.* a legal document calling someone to court to answer an indictment 提问，传讯
44. the habeas corpus：人身保护权
    corpus ['kɔːpəs] *n.* a large collection of written or spoken texts that is used for language research 全集，语料库
45. constellation [kɔnstə'leiʃən] *n.* a group of stars which form a pattern and have a name 星座
46. sage [seidʒ] *n.* a person who is regarded as being very wise 哲人，智者；圣人
47. creed [kriːd] *n.* a set of beliefs, principles, or opinions that strongly influence the way people live or work 信条；原则；纲领
48. touchstone ['tʌtʃstəun] *n.* sth. used as a test or standard; criterion 试金石；基准
49. hasten to retrace our steps：匆忙回头
    retrace [ri'treis] *v.* return to the place you started from by going back along the same route 折返；追溯
50. subordinate [sə'bɔːdinit] *adj.* of a lower rank or position; less important 下级的，从属的；不太重要的
51. pretension [priː'tenʃən] *n.* a claim to possess skill, qualities, etc. 自命不凡
52. approbation [ˌæprə'beiʃən] *n.* approval or agreement 认可；批准
53. suffrage ['sʌfridʒ] *n.* the right of people to vote for a government or national leader 选举权，投票权
54. consolation [ˌkɔnsə'leiʃən] *n.* (a person or thing that gives) comfort during a time of sadness or disappointment 慰藉；给人带来安慰的人或事
55. solicitude [sə'lisitjuːd] *n.* anxious concern 关怀；挂念
56. bestow [bi'stəu] *v.* give or present 给予；赠予
57. conciliate [kən'silieit] *v.* try to end a disagreement with sb. 和解，调解；安抚

58. patronage ['pætrənidʒ] *n.* the support and money given by someone to a person or a group such as a charity 资助，赞助

❑ Appreciating the Speech

托马斯·杰斐逊的首次就职演讲是阐述民主哲学的经典之作 (classic work to elaborate on democratic philosophy)，哲理与文采相得益彰 (bring out the best in each other)，堪称不朽之作 (immortal masterpiece)。在演说中，他表现出和解的姿态 (reconciliatory posture)，宣布实行温和宽容的政策 (moderate and tolerant policy)。

从内容上看，他首先强调 (highlight) 国家的团结 (the unity of the nation) 是使美国内求和平繁荣 (peace and prosperity) 和外获安全稳固 (security and stability) 的重要保证 (important guarantee)。他大力赞美民主自由 (praise democratic freedom vigorously)，赞美一个允许各种不同意见共存 (various ideas can coexist) 的"自由的社会"。他主张政府的一切政策都要保护个人生活、自由和追求幸福的权利 (the individual right of life and freedom and the rights to pursue happiness)。他要求国民拥护联邦政府 (support the federal government)，服从共和政体的原则 (comply with the republican principles)，并竭力主张只有允许人民有充分的自由，民主社会方可以繁荣昌盛。最后，他表达了对前任总统的赞誉 (his compliments for the former President)，说了一些自谦之辞并表示了尽忠职守的决心 (his resolution to devote himself to the duty) 和希望国家和平兴旺的美好愿望 (good wishes for the country to remain peaceful and prosperous)。

从语言上看，这篇演说也具有一些比较突出的特点 (outstanding features)。第一，演说中有很多以状语 (adverbial) 开头的句子。比如演讲第一段的第一句，再如第一段的最后一句，等等。另外，长句及复合从句的运用。这增加了句子结构的复杂程度，使表达严肃正式 (serious and formal)。例如第一段中的第一句和第二句，第二段中的第一句，第四段中的第三句，等等。第三，文中运用了很多大词长词，使语言正式稳重，比如 presentiment，convulsions，exterminate，acquiescence，arraignment，approbation，等等。

❑ Culture Links

(1) 杰斐逊的新闻自由思想

在美国独立战争时期，新闻自由的思想进一步深化发展。特别是在《独立宣言》的起草人之一、著名的资产阶级政治家托马斯·杰斐逊的思想中，新闻自由的思想占有极其重要的地位，杰斐逊一生始终坚持新闻自由至上论。他坚定地说："如果让我来决定，到底应该有政府而没有报纸，还是应该有报纸而没有政府，我将毫不犹豫地选择后

者。”临终前，杰斐逊在给法国友人的信中说道：自由报业是开化人类的心灵，促进人类成为理性、道德与社会动物的最佳工具。可以看出，他视新闻自由高于一切，并认为新闻自由是人类一切自由的基石，没有新闻自由，其他自由便成为无本之木。他坚信“人民主权”，提倡出版自由，率先提出并积极努力为新闻自由立法。他认为“出版自由是通往真理的唯一途径”。

简而言之，杰斐逊的新闻自由思想主要包括以下几个方面：第一，新闻自由高于一切。它是作为扼制政府权力、政治专制与思想垄断的对立物而出现的。如果没有它，专制与权力腐败就会因得不到有效的揭露而泛滥，人民的自由表达就会受到阻碍。从这个角度上说，新闻自由是权力的防腐剂与人民的减压阀。第二，奉行新闻自由高于一切的理念，不仅是对人民权利的信任和尊重，而且在政治层面上极大地扩大了美国政治的民主性。因为奉行这一理念就意味着最大多数的民众能够通过新闻媒介来自由参与、自由评论社会中所发生的公共事件和政治事件，从而强有力地保证了民主政治运行需要的民众参与性。因此新闻自由极大地推动了美国民主政治的发展。第三，奉行新闻自由能够启发民智、增长智慧。因为实行新闻自由就必须保证人民的自由表达意见与思想的权利，进而使得民众的意见与政府的决策在思想的市场上自由竞争，其结果便是既启发了民智和智慧，又增强了民众辨别是非、真伪与真理的能力。第四，新闻自由是政府的唯一监督者和民主政治的平衡器。新闻自由通过新闻业的舆论监督功能对一切政府丑闻和政治事件进行着一览无余的涤荡，使政府之恶行无处藏身；在此基础上，使民主政治得到平稳而又有序的发展。杰斐逊的新闻自由思想具有系统、独特以及开放的特点：所谓系统即指从形式到实质、从表面到心灵，他都提出了自己独到的思想；所谓独特是指他不是一个不切实际的空谈家，他的思想大都为了解决政府权限的制约问题和人民大众的舆论监督问题；所谓开放是指他的新闻自由思想其实就是他博大的民主理论当中的一个亮点，他的民主实践的成功在很大程度上归结于他的新闻自由思想焕发出的勃勃生机。

新闻出版自由最终以修正案的方式融入权利法案并成为宪法的重要组成部分，论其贡献，杰斐逊无疑应列首功。在1789年7月制定的《宪法修正案》中的第一条即为：“国会不得制定关于下列事项的法律：确立国教或禁止信教自由；剥夺言论自由或出版自由；或剥夺人民和平集会和向政府请愿伸冤的权利。”这条宪法修正案对美国的民众见解、社会风气以及美国政治都产生了极其深远的影响。

杰斐逊是他那个时代最为真诚的新闻自由主义者，其新闻自由思想实际上与民主理论和哲学理念一脉相承。他不仅是美国新闻自由思想的奠基人，也是美国建国以来最为卓越的新闻自由理论家。

（2）杰斐逊与《独立宣言》

17世纪60年代与70年代间，英属北美13个殖民地与大不列颠王国之间关系持续紧张，终于在1775年爆发莱克星顿与康科德之役（莱克星顿的枪声），成为美国独立战争之先声。彻底独立一开始只是少数人的想法，直到强力压制殖民地自治的“不可容忍法令”（Intolerable Acts）通过后，视不列颠母国为压迫者的观点才传播开来。

1775 年 5 月，杰斐逊出席了在费城召开的第二届大陆会议，奉命参加起草《独立宣言》的委员会。委员会的其他成员——约翰·亚当斯、本杰明·富兰克林、罗伯特·利文斯顿、罗杰·谢尔曼—— 一致认为杰斐逊是起草这个文献的最佳人选，因为他享有文笔犀利的名声，而且他代表了南部殖民地中最有影响的弗吉尼亚。杰斐逊作为一个“沉默的”、但以其“文笔著称的”议员，33 岁时就参与起草了《独立宣言》。《独立宣言》为北美洲 13 个英属殖民地宣告自大不列颠王国独立，并宣明此举正当性之文告。1776 年 7 月 4 日，本宣言由第二次大陆会议于费城批准，之后该日成为美国之独立纪念日。宣言之原件由大陆会议出席代表共同签署，并永久展示于位于首都华盛顿之国家档案与文件署。此宣言为美国最重要的立国文书之一。如同杰斐逊的其他作品一样，《独立宣言》是一篇杰作，其杰出之处不在于创新，而在于它的措辞适当，不仅陈述了革命者的不满情绪，而且维护了他们应有的权益。尽管后来这个宣言经过讨论修改，但宣言中仍明显具有杰斐逊的深刻影响。

《独立宣言》由 4 部分组成。第一部分为前言，简要说明发表宣言的目的。第二部分将“天赋人权”、“社会契约”作为殖民地争取独立的理论根据，鲜明地表达了北美人民向往和追求的理想与信念。第三部分历数了英王迫害掠夺殖民地的 27 条罪状，进一步强调推翻英国殖民统治的必要性和正义性。第四部分庄严宣告独立。《独立宣言》继承并发展了洛克的自然权利学说，其第二段开头的字句：**“We hold these truths to be self-evident, that all men are created equal, that they are endowed by their Creator with certain unalienable Rights, that among these are Life, Liberty and the pursuit of Happiness. That to secure these rights, Governments are instituted among Men, deriving their just powers from the consent of the governed.”**（我们认为这些真理是不言而喻的：人人生而平等，他们都被造物主赋予了某些不可转让的权利，其中包括生命权、自由权和追求幸福的权利。为了保障这些权利，人们才在他们中间建立政府，而政府的正当权利，则是经被统治者同意授予的。”）被称为“改变人类历史的 55 个字”而广为人知。宣言包含多名开国元勋之基本理念，其中若干理念日后被编入美国宪法中。

《独立宣言》表达了北美殖民地追求独立自由的愿望，在动员革命力量、鼓舞人民斗志、赢得战争胜利等方面发挥了巨大作用。它不仅宣告了美利坚合众国这一崭新国家的诞生，而且深深地影响到她的未来。作为美国立国精神最重要的文献之一，《独立宣言》体现的民主思想不仅通过宪法得到了切实的实践，而且至今仍然是吸引一代又一代美国人不断为之奋斗的理想和目标。从世界范围看，《独立宣言》在人类历史上第一次以政治纲领的形式宣告了民主共和国的原则，彻底摧毁了封建专制主义的理论根基，将“人民主权”这些以往只写在学者著作中的思想第一次贯彻到了新兴资产阶级的建国实践中。它不仅直接推动了法国大革命等欧洲资产阶级革命，对亚洲和拉美的民族独立运动也有着深远影响。

❑ Questions Concerning the Speech

1. How does Jefferson feel when he is called upon to undertake the duties of the first executive office of America?
2. What transcendent objects about the country does Jefferson contemplate?
3. How does Jefferson appeal to his fellow-citizens when they have different opinions?
4. According to Jefferson, what can make American people happy and prosperous?
5. What are the essential principles of Jefferson's government?
6. What's the significance of the essential principles of Jefferson's government?
7. What does Jefferson ask his fellow-citizens to do at the end of his speech?

❑ Paraphrase the Following Sentences

1. I shrink from the contemplation, and humble myself before the magnitude of the undertaking.
2. ... but this being now decided by the voice of the nation, announced according to the rules of the Constitution, all will, of course, arrange themselves under the will of the law, and unite in common efforts for the common good.
3. If there be any among us who would wish to dissolve this Union or to change its republican form, let them stand undisturbed as monuments of the safety with which error of opinion may be tolerated where reason is left free to combat it.
4. Without pretensions to that high confidence you reposed in our first and greatest revolutionary character, whose preeminent services had entitled him to the first place in his country's love and destined for him the fairest page in the volume of faithful history, I ask so much confidence only as may give firmness and effect to the legal administration of your affairs.
5. The approbation implied by your suffrage is a great consolation to me for the past, and my future solicitude will be to retain the good opinion of those who have bestowed it in advance, to conciliate that of others by doing them all the good in my power, and to be instrumental to the happiness and freedom of all.

❑ Questions for Discussion

1. 杰斐逊 1800 年当选总统，美国历史上第一次政府从一个政党的统治下转到另一个政党的手中。在这样的历史背景下，杰斐逊是如何调和党派矛盾、平息政治斗争、推动国家发展的?

2. 在杰斐逊的思想中，新闻自由思想占有极其重要的地位。你是如何理解和看待杰斐逊的新闻自由思想的？
3. 1801 年总统大选过后，波士顿一家报纸报道称杰斐逊“骑在奴隶背上进入自由之殿堂”。对此你如何理解，并试论杰斐逊对奴隶制度的影响。

❑ Translation

托马斯·杰斐逊：首任就职演讲

1801 年 3 月 4 日，华盛顿特区

朋友们、同胞们：

1. 我应召担任国家的最高行政长官。值此诸位同胞集会之时，我衷心感谢大家寄予我的厚爱。坦诚来讲，我意识到这项任务非我能力所及，其责任之重大，本人能力之浅薄，自然使我就任时忧惧交加。一个幅员辽阔、物产丰富的新兴国家，带着丰富的工业产品跨海渡洋，同那些自恃强权、不顾公理的国家进行贸易，向着世人无法预见的天命疾进——当我思考这些重大的目标，当我想到这个可爱的国家，其荣誉、幸福和希望都系于这个问题和今天的盛典，我就不敢往下想，在面对这宏图大业时自感德薄能鲜。确实，若不是在这里见到许多先生在场，使我意识到无论遇到什么困难，都可以向宪法规定的另一高级机构寻找智慧、美德和热忱的源泉，我一定会完全失去信心。因此，负有神圣的立法职责的先生们和各位有关人士，我鼓起勇气期望你们给予指引和支持，使我们能够在纷争的乱世中同舟共济，安然前行。
2. 在我们过去的意见交锋中，大家热烈讨论，各展所长，这种紧张气氛，有时会使不习惯于自由思想、不习惯于说出或写下自己想法的人感到不安；但如今，这场争论既已由全国的民意作出决定，而且根据宪法的规定予以公布，大家当然会服从法律的意志，调整自己，为共同的利益齐心协力，大家也会铭记这条神圣的原则；尽管在任何情况下，多数人的意志是起决定作用的，但这种意志必须合理才属公正；少数人享有同等权利，这种权利必须同样受到法律保护，如果侵犯，便是压迫。因此，公民们，让我们同心同德地团结起来。让我们在社会交往中和睦如初、恢复友爱。如果没有这些，自由、甚至生活本身都会枯燥无味，让我们再想一想，我们已经将长期以来造成人类流血、受苦的宗教信仰上的不宽容现象逐出国土，如果我们纵容专横、邪恶并会造成残酷、血腥迫害的政治上的不宽容现象，那么我们必将无所收获。当旧世界经历阵痛和骚动，当愤怒的人挣扎着想通过流血、杀戮来寻求失去已久的自由，那激情甚至也会波涛般冲击这片遥远而宁静的海岸。人们对此的感触和忧患不尽相同，因而对安全措施的意见就出现了分歧，这些都不足为奇。但是，各种意见分歧并不都是原则分歧。

我们虽姓名不同，但都信奉同一原则。我们都是共和党人，我们都是联邦党人，如果我们当中有人想解散这个联邦，或者想改变它的共和体制，那就让他们不受干扰而作为对平安的纪念碑吧，因为有了平安，错误的意见就可得到宽容，理性就得以自由地与之抗争。诚然，我知道有些正直人士担心共和制政府无法成为强有力的政府，担心我们这个政府不够坚强；但是，在成功试验的高潮中，一个诚实的爱国者，难道会因为一种假设的和幻想的疑惧，就以为这个被世界寄予最大希望的政府可能需要力量才得以自存，因而就放弃这个迄今为止带给我们自由和坚定的政府吗？我相信不会。相反，我相信这是世界上最坚强的政府。我相信唯有在这种政府的治理下，每个人才会响应法律的号召，遵从法律准则，像对待切身利益那样去迎击侵犯公共秩序的举动。有时我们听到一种言论，认为不能让人们自己管理自己。那么，能让他去管理别人吗？难道我们在统治人民的君王名单中发现了天使吗？这个问题让历史来回答吧。

3. 因此，让我们鼓足勇气和信心，追求我们自己的联邦与共和原则，拥戴联邦与代议制政府。我们受惠于大自然和大洋的阻隔，幸免于地球上四分之一地区发生的那场毁灭性浩劫；我们品格高尚，不能容忍他人的堕落；我们天赐良邦，其幅员足以容纳子孙万代；我们充分地主张权利平等，包括发挥个人才干，争取劳动所得，受到同胞的尊敬与信赖，而这种尊敬与信赖是出自我们同胞对自身行为的评判而非出自门第。我们尽管教派不同，形式各异，但它们都教人以正直、忠诚、节制、恩义和仁爱；我们承认和崇拜全能的上帝，而天意表明，他乐于使这里的人们得到幸福，今后还将得到更多的幸福——我们有了这些福祉，还需要什么才能够使我们成为快乐而兴旺的民族呢？公民们，我们还需要贤明而节俭的政府，它会制止人们相互伤害，使他们自由地管理自己的实业和进步活动，它不会侵夺人们的劳动果实。这就是良好政府的所有好处，这也是我们达到幸福圆满所必需的。

4. 公民们，我即将履行职责，这些职责包括你们所珍爱的一切。因此，你们应当了解我所认为的政府基本原则是什么，确定其行政依据的原则又是什么。我将尽量扼要地加以叙述，只讲一般原则，不讲其种种限制。实行人人平等和真正的公平，而不论其宗教或政治上的地位或派别；同所有国家和平相处、商务往来、真诚友好，而不与任何国家结盟，维护各州政府的一切权利，将它们作为我国最有权能的内政机构，和抵御反共和趋势的最可靠屏障；维持全国政府在宪制上的全部活力，将其作为国内安定和国际安全的最后依靠；忠实地维护人民的选举权——将它作为一种温和而稳妥的矫正手段，对革命留下的、尚无和平补救办法的种种弊端予以矫正；绝对同意多数人的决定，因为这是共和制的主要原则，反之，不诉诸舆论而诉诸武力乃是专制的主要原则和直接根源；建立一支训练有素的民兵，作为平时和战争初期的最好依靠，直到正规军来接替；实行文职权高于军职权；节约政府开支，减轻劳工负担；诚实地偿还债务，庄严地维护政府信誉；鼓励农业，辅之以商业；传播信息，以公众理论为准绳补偏救弊；实行宗教自由；实行出版自由和人身自由，根据人身保护法和公正选出的陪审团进行审判来保证人身自由。这些原则构成了明亮的星座，照耀在我们的前方，指引我们经历了革命和改革时期。为了实现这些原则，先辈和英雄们都付出过智慧和鲜血。这些原则应当是我们的政治信条，公民教育的课本，检验我们寄予希望者的工作的试金石。如果我们因一时错误或惊恐而背离这些原则，那就让我们悬崖勒马，重返这唯一通向和平、自由和安全的大道。

5. 各位公民，我即将担当起你们委派给我的职务。根据我担任许多较低职务的经验，我已经意识到这是最艰巨的职务，因此，我能够预期，当一个并非尽善尽美的人从这个职位卸任时，很少能像就任时那样深孚众望。我不敢奢望大家如同信任我们第一位最伟大的革命元勋那样对我高度信任，因为他的卓著功勋使他最有资格受到全国的爱戴，使他在忠实的史书中占有最辉煌的一页，我只要求大家给我相当的信任，使人足以坚定地、有效地依法管理大家的事务。由于判断有误，我会常常犯错误。即使我是正确的，那些不是站在统筹全局的立场上看问题的人，也会常常认为我是错误的，我请求你们宽容我自己犯的错误，而这些错误决不是故意犯的，我请求你们支持我反对别人的错误，而这些人如果通盘考虑，也是绝不会犯的。从投票结果来看，大家对我的过去甚为嘉许，这是我莫大的安慰；今后我所渴望的是，力求赐予我好评的各位能保持这种好评，在我职权范围内为其他各位效劳以博得他们的好评，并为所有同胞们的幸福和自由而尽力。

6. 现在，我仰承各位的好意，恭顺地就任此职，一旦你们觉得需要做出你们有权做出的更好的选择，我便准备辞去此职。愿全能的上帝引导我们的机构日臻完善，并为大家的和平与昌盛，赐给它一个值得赞许的结果。

Abraham Lincoln

(1809—1865)

亚伯拉罕·林肯

4

Abraham Lincoln's First Inaugural Address

Delivered 4 March, 1861, in Washington, D.C.

❑ About the Author

亚伯拉罕·林肯 (Abraham Lincoln, 1809—1865)，出生于贫困的肯塔基州边境地区一个农民家庭，父母都是文盲。他一生总共接受了仅仅一年半的学校教育，但他自小聪颖好学，依靠自学成才。青年时代当过雇农、店员、乡邮员、工人、勘测员，日后成为杰出的律师、演说家和政治家。他是美国第16任总统（任期：1861—1865），并在1864年连任，也是首位共和党籍总统。在其总统任内，美国爆发内战，史称南北战争。林肯废除了南方各州的奴隶制度，提出了“民有，民治，民享”的政府理念。虽然林肯一直反对奴隶制度，但在他任职期间，由于各种反动势力的影响，也是为了避免内战，他在政策上曾有过踌躇和动摇。然而，在广大美国人民的支持和推动下，他能够顺应历史潮流，最终签署了著名的《解放宣言》，解决了当时美国社会经济政治生活中存在的主要矛盾。在4年国内战争中，他亲自指挥作战，领导联邦政府同南部农场奴隶主进行了坚决斗争，维护了国家的统一，有力地推动了美国社会的发展。

没有林肯果断、英明的领导，恐怕也就没有今天的美国。联邦的胜利解决了1776年大革命和1789年宪法都没能解决的两个难题：联邦是“永世长存”，还是“从地球上消失”；是否让“大逆不道的”奴隶制继续嘲弄一个“以自由为立国之本”的国家。联邦保住了，奴隶制灭亡了，这便是林肯的不朽功绩。

内战结束后不久，林肯于1865年4月15日遇刺身亡。他是第一个遭到刺杀的美国总统。由于林肯在美国历史上所起的进步作用，他被公认为美国历史上最伟大的总统之一。在美国在线于 2005 年举办的票选活动“最伟大的美国人”中，林肯被选为美国最伟大的人物第二位。

❑ About the Speech

林肯当选美国总统不久，南部 7 个州因担心林肯废除奴隶制而脱离联邦，并组成南部邦联，其他 4 个南方州则宣布它们将反对联邦政府压迫各州的任何企图。1861 年 3 月 4 日林肯在华盛顿特区国会大厦前的台阶上宣誓就职，并发表第一次就职演讲时，美国已处于分裂和内战的边缘。

林肯的就职演讲的主要目的之一就是打消南部各州对取消奴隶制的担忧。在演说中他说，他无意直接或间接地干涉南方蓄奴州业已存在的奴隶制度，因为他相信他“没有这样做的合法权利，也没有这样做的意愿”。他诚恳地呼吁理智和冷静。与此同时，他在演讲中表达了他毫不动摇的信念，即任何一个州都无权退出联邦。他发誓要维持和保护联邦政府的一切财产，包括南部反叛各州已经夺取的要塞。在当时，林肯的这一略带威胁的表态是十分必要的，因为那时南部反叛州已夺取了多个位于其境内的联邦要塞、军火库和海关。但在表达了这一坚定信念之后，他又以平和的语气对南部说，“各位心怀不满的同胞们，内战这个重大问题的关键掌握在你们手中，而不掌握在我手中，政府不会对你们发动攻击。你们不当挑衅者，就不会面临冲突。你们没有对天发誓要毁灭政府，而我却要立下最庄严的誓言：‘坚守、维护和捍卫它。’”他的演说是为维护联邦和避免内战所作出的最后一次努力。

但可悲的是，林肯的恳求没有人听。南方邦联的军队于 1861 年 4 月 12 日炮击南卡罗莱纳州查尔斯顿的萨姆特堡，持续 4 年的美国内战由此爆发。

❑ The Speech *(abridged)*

Fellow-Citizens of the United States:

1. In compliance with[1] a custom as old as the Government itself, I appear before you to address you briefly and to take in your presence the oath prescribed by the Constitution of the United States to be taken by the President "before he enters on the execution of this office."

2. I do not consider it necessary at present for me to discuss those matters of administration about which there is no special anxiety or excitement.

3. Apprehension seems to exist among the people of the Southern States that by the

accession[2] of a Republican Administration their property and their peace and personal security are to be endangered. There has never been any reasonable cause for such apprehension. Indeed, the most ample evidence to the contrary has all the while existed and been open to their inspection. It is found in nearly all the published speeches of him who now addresses you. I do but quote from one of those speeches when I declare that—

I have no purpose, directly or indirectly, to interfere with the institution of slavery in the States where it exists. I believe I have no lawful right to do so, and I have no inclination to do so.

...

4. It is seventy-two years since the first inauguration of a President under our National Constitution. During that period fifteen different and greatly distinguished citizens have in succession[3] administered the executive branch of the Government. They have conducted it through many perils, and generally with great success. Yet, with all this scope of precedent, I now enter upon the same task for the brief constitutional term of four years under great and peculiar difficulty. A disruption[4] of the Federal Union, heretofore only menaced, is now formidably attempted.

5. I hold that in contemplation of [5] universal law and of the Constitution the Union of these States is perpetual. Perpetuity is implied, if not expressed, in the fundamental law of all national governments. **It is safe to assert that no government proper ever had a provision in its organic law[6] for its own termination.** Continue to execute all the express[7] provisions of our National Constitutions, and the Union will endure forever, it being impossible to destroy it except by some action not provided for in the instrument itself.

6. Again: If the United States be not a government proper, but an association of States in the nature of contract merely, can it, as a contract, be peaceably unmade[8] by less than all the parties who made it? **One party to a contract may violate it—break it, so to speak—but does it not require all to lawfully rescind[9] it?**

...

7. It follows from these views that no State upon its own mere motion can lawfully get out of the Union; that resolves and ordinances[10] to that effect are legally void, and that acts of violence within any State or States against the authority of the United States are insurrectionary[11] or revolutionary, according to circumstances.

8. I therefore consider that in view of the Constitution and the laws the Union is unbroken, and to the extent of my ability, I shall take care, as the Constitution itself expressly enjoins[12] upon me, that the laws of the Union be faithfully executed in all the States. Doing this I deem to be only a simple duty on my part, and I shall perform it so far as practicable unless my rightful masters, the American people, shall withhold the requisite[13] means or in some authoritative manner direct the contrary. I trust this will not be regarded as a menace, but only as the declared purpose of the Union that it *will* constitutionally defend and maintain itself.

9. In doing this there needs to be no bloodshed or violence, and there shall be none unless it be forced upon the national authority. The power confided to me will be used to hold, occupy, and possess the property and places belonging to the Government and to collect the duties and imposts; but beyond what may be necessary for these objects, there will be no invasion, no using of force against or among the people anywhere.

...

10. That there are persons in one section or another who seek to destroy the Union at all events and are glad of any pretext to do it I will neither affirm nor deny; but if there be such, I need address no word to them. To those, however, who really love the Union may I not speak?

11. Before entering upon so grave a matter as the destruction of our national fabric, with all its benefits, its memories, and its hopes, would it not be wise to ascertain[14] precisely why we do it? **Will you hazard so desperate a step while there is any possibility that any portion of the ills you fly from have no real existence? Will you, while the certain ills you fly to are greater than all the real ones you fly from, will you risk the commission of so fearful a mistake?**

12. All profess[15] to be content in the Union if all constitutional rights can be maintained. Is it true, then, that any right plainly written in the Constitution has been denied? I think not. Happily, the human mind is so constituted that no party can reach to the audacity[16] of doing this. Think, if you can, of a single instance in which a plainly written provision of the Constitution has ever been denied. If by the mere force of numbers a majority should deprive a minority of any clearly written constitutional right, it might in a moral point of view justify revolution; certainly would if such right were a vital one. But such is not our case. All the vital rights of minorities and of individuals are

so plainly assured to them by affirmations and negations, guaranties and prohibitions, in the Constitution that controversies never arise concerning them. But no organic law can ever be framed with a provision specifically applicable to every question which may occur in practical administration. No foresight can anticipate nor any document of reasonable length contain express provisions for all possible questions. Shall fugitives from labor be surrendered by national or by State authority? The Constitution does not expressly say. *May* Congress prohibit slavery in the Territories[17]? The Constitution does not expressly say. *Must* Congress protect slavery in the Territories? The Constitution does not expressly say.

...

13. One section of our country believes slavery is right and ought to be extended, while the other believes it is wrong and ought not to be extended. This is the only substantial dispute. The fugitive-slave clause of the Constitution and the law for the suppression of the foreign slave trade are each as well enforced, perhaps, as any law can ever be in a community where the moral sense of the people imperfectly supports the law itself. The great body of the people abide by the dry legal obligation[18] in both cases, and a few break over in each. This, I think, can not be perfectly cured, and it would be worse in both cases after the separation of the sections than before. The foreign slave trade, now imperfectly suppressed, would be ultimately revived without restriction in one section, while fugitive slaves, now only partially surrendered, would not be surrendered at all by the other.

14. **Physically speaking, we can not separate. We can not remove our respective sections from each other nor build an impassable wall between them. A husband and wife may be divorced and go out of the presence[19] and beyond the reach of each other, but the different parts of our country can not do this. They can not but remain face to face, and intercourse, either amicable or hostile, must continue between them.** Is it possible, then, to make that intercourse more advantageous or more satisfactory after separation than before? Can aliens[20] make treaties easier than friends can make laws? Can treaties be more faithfully enforced between aliens than laws can among friends? Suppose you go to war, you can not fight always; and when, after much loss on both sides and no gain on either, you cease fighting, the identical old questions, as to terms of intercourse, are again upon you.

15. **This country, with its institutions, belongs to the people who inhabit**

it. Whenever they shall grow weary of the existing Government, they can exercise their constitutional right of amending it or their revolutionary right to dismember or overthrow it. I can not be ignorant of the fact that many worthy and patriotic citizens are desirous of having the National Constitution amended. While I make no recommendation of amendments, I fully recognize the rightful authority of the people over the whole subject, to be exercised in either of the modes prescribed in the instrument itself; and I should, under existing circumstances, favor rather than oppose a fair opportunity being afforded the people to act upon it. I will venture to add that to me the convention mode seems preferable, in that it allows amendments to originate with the people themselves, instead of only permitting them to take or reject propositions originated by others, not especially chosen for the purpose, and which might not be precisely such as they would wish to either accept or refuse. I understand a proposed amendment to the Constitution—which amendment, however, I have not seen—has passed Congress, to the effect that[21] the Federal Government shall never interfere with the domestic institutions of the States, including that of persons held to service. To avoid misconstruction of what I have said, I depart from my purpose not to speak of particular amendments so far as to say that, holding such a provision to now be implied constitutional law, I have no objection to its being made express and irrevocable[22].

16. The Chief Magistrate derives all his authority from the people, and they have referred none upon him to fix terms for the separation of the States. The people themselves can do this if also they choose, but the Executive as such has nothing to do with it. His duty is to administer the present Government as it came to his hands and to transmit it unimpaired by him to his successor.

17. **Why should there not be a patient confidence in the ultimate justice of the people? Is there any better or equal hope in the world?** In our present differences, is either party without faith of being in the right? If the Almighty Ruler of Nations, with His eternal truth and justice, be on your side of the North, or on yours of the South, that truth and that justice will surely prevail by the judgment of this great tribunal of the American people.

18. By the frame of the Government under which we live this same people have wisely given their public servants but little power for mischief[23], and have with equal wisdom provided for the return of that little to their own hands at very short intervals.

While the people retain their virtue and vigilance no Administration by any extreme of wickedness or folly can very seriously injure the Government in the short space of four years.

19. My countrymen, one and all[24], think calmly and well upon this whole subject. **Nothing valuable can be lost by taking time**[25]. If there be an object to hurry any of you in hot haste to a step which you would never take deliberately, that object will be frustrated by taking time; but no good object can be frustrated by it. Such of you as are now dissatisfied still have the old Constitution unimpaired[26], and, on the sensitive point, the laws of your own framing under it; while the new Administration will have no immediate power, if it would, to change either. If it were admitted that you who are dissatisfied hold the right side in the dispute, there still is no single good reason for precipitate[27] action. Intelligence, patriotism, Christianity, and a firm reliance on Him who has never yet forsaken this favored land are still competent to adjust in the best way all our present difficulty.

20. **In your hands, my dissatisfied fellow-countrymen, and not in mine, is the momentous issue of civil war. The Government will not assail**[28] **you. You can have no conflict without being yourselves the aggressors.** You have no oath registered in heaven to destroy the Government, while I shall have the most solemn one to "preserve, protect, and defend it." [29]

21. I am loath to close. **We are not enemies, but friends. We must not be enemies. Though passion may have strained**[30] **it must not break our bonds of affection.** The mystic chords of memory, stretching from every battlefield and patriot grave to every living heart and hearthstone all over this broad land, will yet swell[31] the chorus of the Union, when again touched, as surely they will be, by the better angels of our nature. (2,175 words)

❑ Notes to the Speech

1. in compliance with：按照，依照
2. accession [ək'seʃ(ə)n,æk'seʃən] *n.* 就任，就职
3. in succession：连续（的）；一个接一个（的）
4. disruption [dis'rʌpʃən] *n.* 分裂，瓦解，破坏

5. in contemplation of：对……进行深思
6. organic law：组织法（also called "fundamental law"，即"基本法"）
7. express [iks'pres] *adj.* stated very clearly 明确的，表达清楚的
8. unmake [ʌn'meik] *vt.* cause to disappear, abolish, destroy 撤销，废除，破坏
9. rescind [ri'sind] *vt.* cancel or repeal a law, order, etc. 废除，撤销（法律、命令等）
10. resolves and ordinances：决议和法令
11. insurrectionary [ˌinsə'rekʃənəri] *adj.* 起义的，叛乱的
12. enjoin [in'dʒɔin] *v.* (enjoin sth. on / upon sb.) impose (an action or prohibition) on sb.; order 将（一行动或禁令）强施于某人；命令
13. requisite ['rekwizit] *adj.* necessary because of circumstances or regulations 必要的；需要的
14. ascertain [ˌæsə'tein] *vt.* get to know for certain 查明，弄清，确定
15. profess [prə'fes] *vt.* <formal> claim that something is true 声称；表示，表明
16. audacity [ɔ:'dæsiti] *n.* 大胆，厚颜
17. the Territories：此处指"准州"（即将加入联邦的西部各州）
18. dry legal obligation：枯燥的法律义务
19. go out of the presence：不再见面
比较 in the presence of：在……面前；在（某人）眼前 (= in sb.'s presence)
20. alien ['eiljən] *n.* a foreigner; a being from another world 外国人；外星人
21. to the effect that：with the meaning, or giving the information, that 大意是……
22. irrevocable [i'revəkəbl] *adj.* not able to be changed or revoked 不能改变的；不能取消的
23. mischief ['mistʃif] *n.* harm caused by someone or something 伤害，危害
24. one and all：人人，大家
25. take time：不匆忙，从容行动
26. unimpaired [ˌʌnim'pɛəd] *adj.* not damaged or weakened 未受损害的，未被削弱的
27. precipitate [pri'sipitət] *adj.* done or happening suddenly or without careful thought 仓促的；轻率的
28. assail [ə'seil] *vt.* attack someone violently 攻击，袭击
29. "preserve, protect, and defend it."：引自《美国宪法》第二条第一款
30. strain [strein] *v.* damage or weaken (a part of the body) 因用力过度而损伤（身体的某一部位），此处指（情绪）紧张
31. swell [swel] *v.* (cause to) grow bigger, louder, or more intense（使）膨胀；（使）肿胀；（使声音）变响亮

❑ Appreciating the Speech

1861 年 3 月 4 日林肯发表就职演讲时，南部 7 州已组成南部邦联（the Confederate States of America, also known as the Confederacy），推举杰弗逊·戴维斯为总统，并着手组建军队。由于内战迫在眉睫，林肯的就职仪式是在军队的保护下进行的。但林肯临危不乱，镇定自若地发表了这篇不同凡响的就职演说，充分表现了一位伟大总统和天才演说家的风采。演说的主题 (theme) 是维护联邦 (safeguard the Union)，反对分裂 (oppose disruption)。他首先重申了竞选时许下的诺言 (reiterated his promise made during the election campaigns)，保证尊重各州的现行制度，并执行联邦的有关法令 (pledged to respect the existing institutions and implement the related laws of the Union)。他说："南方各州人民似乎担心，共和党一旦执政，将会危及他们的财产、和平与个人安全。这种担心从来就没有什么合理的根据。实际上，足以说明相反事实的充分证据却一直存在着，并且随时可以进行检查。这种证据在现在同你们讲话的这个人的几乎所有发表过的演说中都可以找到。"从而封住了分离主义者的口舌。接着，他申明大义，分别从宪法、历史和自然条件等多种角度，精辟地论述了维护联邦的正义性和反对分裂的必要性，从而彻底剥夺了分离主义者的行动依据。最后，他仁至义尽地对"各位心怀不满的同胞们"（my dissatisfied fellow-countrymen）进行了规劝，并表达了自己要"坚守、维护和捍卫合众国宪法 (preserve, protect, and defend the Constitution)"的决心。他满怀深情地针对南部各州说："我们不是敌人，而是朋友。我们一定不要成为敌人。尽管情绪紧张，也绝不应割断我们之间的感情纽带。记忆的神秘琴弦，从每一个战场和爱国志士的坟墓伸向这片广阔土地上的每一颗跳动的心和家庭，必将再度被我们善良的天性所拨响，那时就会高奏起联邦大团结的乐章。"其爱国之感至深，同胞之情至浓，令人潸然泪下。林肯的这篇演说逻辑严密、说理深刻、情真意切、一气呵成，堪称就职演说中的精品。

从语言上看，这篇演说的特点主要有两个，一是反问句的使用 (the use of rhetorical questions)，如"If the United States be not a government proper, but an association of States in the nature of contract merely, can it, as a contract, be peaceably unmade by less than all the parties who made it? One party to a contract may violate it—break it, so to speak—but does it not require all to lawfully rescind it?"，严正地表明了任何一方无权单独终止联邦的立场。又如第 17 段林肯又连续用了 3 个反问句，唤起听众的思考，表达了真理和正义必胜，联邦必然永久屹立的信心。本篇的另一个特点是暗喻的使用 (the use of metaphor)，如演讲的最后"The mystic chords of memory, stretching from every battlefield and patriot grave to every living heart and hearthstone all over this broad land, will yet swell the chorus of the Union, when again touched, as surely they will be, by the better angels of our nature."一句中，林肯把"memory"（记忆）比做"mystic chords"（奇妙的琴弦），把"union"（联邦）比做"chorus"（大团结的乐章；本意是

“齐声合唱”)，他用这些生动 (vivid)、贴切的 (appropriate) 比喻，动情地规劝南部各州放弃分裂行为，共同捍卫美利坚这一美国人民用智慧和鲜血换来的自由、民主的国度。

❑ Culture Links

(1) 美国的奴隶制及其废除

美国奴隶制度起源于英国殖民者在北美建立的第一个殖民地——弗吉尼亚。在北美殖民地时期，对非洲黑人奴隶的贩卖和奴役构成了资本原始积累的重要内容。黑人奴隶制在北美殖民地发展的直接原因是殖民地急需大批劳动力。从 1686—1786 年的 100 年间，约有 25 万非洲黑人被贩卖到英属北美殖民地。黑人奴隶成了南方种植园中的主要劳动力，他们以及他们的子女像土地、工具等生产资料一样，是种植园主的私有财产，没有人身自由。美利坚合众国成立后，制定了联邦宪法。但宪法保留了奴隶制，维护了奴隶贸易。到 1860 年，美国黑人奴隶已达到 400 万。

然而，随着资本主义的发展，北方所需要的自由劳动力、商品市场和工业原料越来越受到南方黑人奴隶制的制约，因此北方资本主义经济主张废除奴隶制；而南方种植园经济因需要大量的奴隶，所以南方奴隶主主张维护奴隶制。双方围绕着奴隶制存废问题的矛盾愈演愈烈。双方矛盾到 19 世纪 50 年代在局部地区已酿成武装冲突。在奴隶主的进逼面前，北方人民发起了声势浩大的“废奴运动”，南方黑奴也不断进行反抗。在人民斗争的推动下，北方资产阶级开始主张废除奴隶制度。

1852 年，斯托夫人的小说《汤姆叔叔的小屋》出版，书中对黑人奴隶的悲惨生活作了动人的描述和揭露，在社会上引起强烈反响，有力地推动了废奴运动的发展。1859 年，废奴主义者约翰·布朗率领 21 名白人和黑人起义，把废奴运动推向高潮。

在 1860 年的总统选举中，反对奴隶制的共和党人林肯当选为总统，这预示了奴隶制末日的到来。于是，蓄谋已久的南部奴隶主集团决定脱离联邦，组成南部邦联，从而导致美国南北战争于 1861 年爆发。1862 年 9 月 22 日，林肯审时度势，毅然发表了《解放宣言》，宣布从次年 1 月 1 日起美国 400 万黑人奴隶获得解放。《解放宣言》对美国人的“震撼力是无可估量的”，许多信仰“人人生而平等，平等与自由是造物主所赋予人类不可转让的基本权利”的黑人和白人在阅读了这一法令后，成了“无疑的、坚定的”只有一个美国的拥护者。这一宣言也敲响了南方奴隶制的丧钟。与此同时，林肯还实行了一系列的经济和军事改革，这些措施都极大地调动了北方广大人民的积极性，近百万人踊跃参军，其中包括 23 万黑人士兵，从而从根本上瓦解了南方叛乱各州的战斗力，扭转了战局。1865 年 1 月，美国国会通过了《宪法第 13 修正案》，规定奴隶制或强迫奴役制，不得在合众国境内和管辖范围内存在。1865 年 12 月 18 日，《宪法第 13 修正案》正式生效，从此，奴隶制在美国被废除了。

当然，虽然奴隶制就此废除了，但种族歧视依然存在，种族歧视在美国的消除还有一段很长的路要走。好在在美国宪法和修正案的保障下，在黑人和白人的共同努力下，种族歧视政策最终得到了完全废除，并且因种族歧视而使美国黑人受到的损害也由美国政府通过各种优惠政策给予了尽可能合理的补偿。

（2）两种意义上的美国梦

300多年前，当英格兰移民乘坐着“五月花”号横穿大西洋来到马里兰，寻找一块清教徒能居住的“净土”时，美国梦 (American Dream) 已开始悄然萌芽——美国给了每一个人均等的机会，只要努力奋斗，都可以实现自己的梦想。300年后，这个国家已成富饶之邦，然而美国梦并没有消逝，只是随着历史的变迁，它拥有了更多的“内涵”。而且美国梦早已成为美国文化的重要组成部分。

什么是美国梦？众多历史学家和社会学家观点不一，不同的美国人也有不同的解读。不过，一般而言，人们普遍认为美国梦包含几个要素：美国提供了人人都能成功的机会；成功取决于自己的才能和努力，而不是家世和背景；人人都拥有平等的权利；人人都有信仰的自由。这些要素是与历史密不可分的，也必须和时代背景结合起来看。

从意义上讲，美国梦有广义和狭义之分：广义上讲，它指对美国人崇尚的平等、自由、民主等价值观的追求；狭义上说，它是一种相信在美国只要经过努力不懈的奋斗便能获得更好生活的理想，亦即人们只要通过自己的勤奋工作、勇气、创意和决心就可迈向成功和繁荣，而不必依赖于特定的社会阶级和他人的帮助。

美国梦成为如此强大的力量还因为它是建立在一定现实基础之上，它不仅反映了美国人的理想，而且也反映了美国一定的现实情况。没有一定的现实基础，美国梦会如此深入人心是令人难以想象的。虽然从成功的人数来说可能是少数（实际上，一些研究显示，相比于同一时期的欧洲和亚洲国家，美国人的成功机会确实要多出不少），但一部分人（特别是底层人士）的成功足以形成一种强大的榜样力量。我们或许应该这样理解美国梦：它不仅仅是发财致富、光宗耀祖之梦，它更是实现自身价值，获得公平、公正、自由、平等，权利和尊严得到保障之梦。从这个意义上来讲，美国梦对每一个美国人来说都不是遥不可及的“白日梦”，而是现实之梦，是几乎每个美国人都可以实现的梦。

自1776年美国建国以来，世世代代的美国人都对美国梦深信不疑，从出生于乡间小木屋的林肯到肯尼亚黑人的儿子奥巴马，一个个榜样的力量在激励着美国人民不懈地奋斗。同时美国梦也一直激励着世界各地的青年人来到这片土地创造自己的价值，实现自己的梦想，美国也因此成为全球成功人士的摇篮。

❑ Questions Concerning the Speech

1. What is and what does Lincoln say about the apprehension that seems to exist among the people of the Southern States?

2. What does Lincoln think about a disruption of the Federal Union or the perpetuity of the Union?
3. In what a manner does Lincoln hope to defend and maintain the Union?
4. What is Lincoln's attitude toward the destruction of the national fabric of the United States, with all its benefits, its memories, and its hopes?
5. What is the only substantial dispute in the United States and how shall it be resolved?
6. Why does Lincoln entertain such a patient confidence in the ultimate justice of the people and what does he entreat his countrymen to do?

❑ Paraphrase the Following Sentences

1. Apprehension seems to exist among the people of the Southern States that by the accession of a Republican Administration their property and their peace and personal security are to be endangered.
2. A disruption of the Federal Union, heretofore only menaced, is now formidably attempted.
3. Doing this I deem to be only a simple duty on my part, and I shall perform it so far as practicable unless my rightful masters, the American people, shall withhold the requisite means or in some authoritative manner direct the contrary.
4. Will you, while the certain ills you fly to are greater than all the real ones you fly from, will you risk the commission of so fearful a mistake?
5. No foresight can anticipate nor any document of reasonable length contain express provisions for all possible questions.
6. They can not but remain face to face, and intercourse, either amicable or hostile, must continue between them.
7. Whenever they shall grow weary of the existing Government, they can exercise their constitutional right of amending it or their revolutionary right to dismember or overthrow it.
8. By the frame of the Government under which we live this same people have wisely given their public servants but little power for mischief, and have with equal wisdom provided for the return of that little to their own hands at very short intervals.

❑ Questions for Discussion

1. 林肯被公认为是美国最伟大的总统之一。试举例说明林肯对美国所做出的伟大贡献。
2. 出身卑微的林肯能成为美国历史上最伟大的总统之一。这一点给予我们什么启示?
3. 试分析美国奴隶制与传统奴隶制的异同。

❑ Translation

亚伯拉罕·林肯：首任就职演讲

1861 年 3 月 4 日，华盛顿特区

合众国公民们：

1. 按照一个与政府本身同样悠久的惯例，我来到你们面前发表简短的讲话，并遵照合众国宪法对总统在“就职前”必须宣誓的规定，当着你们的面宣誓。
2. 我想，我现在不必讨论那些并不特别令人忧虑或激动的行政问题。
3. 南方各州人民似乎担心，共和党一旦执政，将会危及他们的财产、和平与个人安全。这种担心从来就没有什么合理的根据。实际上，足以说明相反事实的充分证据却一直存在着，并且随时可以进行检查。这种证据在现在同你们讲话的这个人的几乎所有发表过的演说中都可以找到。我只引述其中的一篇，我曾经宣布——

   “我无意直接或间接地干涉各蓄奴州的奴隶制度。我认为我没有那样做的合法权利，而且也没有那样做的意向。”

   ……
4. 自从第一任总统根据我国宪法就职以来已经 72 年了。在此期间，有 15 位十分杰出的公民相继主持政府的行政部门的工作。他们在许多艰难险阻中履行职责，大致说来都很成功。然而，虽有这样的先例，我现在开始担任这个按宪法规定任期只有短暂 4 年的同一职务时，却处在巨大而特殊的困难之下。联邦的分裂，在此以前只是一种威胁，现在却已成为可怕的行动。
5. 从一般法律和宪法角度来考虑，我认为由各州组成的联邦是永久性的。在各国政府的根本法中，永久性即使没有明确规定，也是不言而喻的。我们有把握说，从来没有哪个正规政府在自己的组织法中列入一项要结束自己执政的条款。继续执行我国宪法明文规定的条款，联邦就将永远存在，毁灭联邦是办不到的，除非采取宪法本身未予规定的某种行动。
6. 再者：假如合众国不是名副其实的政府，而只是具有契约性质的各州的联盟，那么，作为一种契约，这个联盟能够毫无争议地由缔约各方中的少数加以取消吗？缔约的一方可以违约——也可以说毁约——但是，合法地废止契约难道不需要缔约各方全都同意吗？

   ……
7. 根据这些观点可以看出，任何一州都不能单凭自己的动议即可合法地脱离联邦，凡以此为目的制定的任何“决议”和“法令”，在法律上均属无效，而且任何一州或数州以暴力行径反对美国政府，都应视其具体情形定为叛乱或革命。

8. 因此，我认为，根据宪法和法律，联邦是不容分裂的；我将按宪法本身明确授予我的权限，就自己能力所及，使联邦法律得以在各州忠实执行。我认为这仅仅是我分内的职责，我将以可行的方法去完成，除非我的合法主人——美国人民，不给予我必要的手段，或以权威的方式作出相反的指示，我相信大家不会把这看作是一种威胁，而只看作是联邦已宣布过的目标：它将按照宪法保卫和维护它自身。

9. 进行这项工作不需要流血或诉诸暴力，除非强加于国家当局，流血和暴力绝不会发生。委托给我的权力将被用来保持、占有和掌握属于政府的财产和土地，征收普通税和关税；但是，除了为达到这些目的所必须进行的工作外，将不会对人民有任何侵犯，不会对任何地方的人民或在他们之间使用武力。

……

10. 某些地区有人企图破坏联邦，并且爱用各种借口去实现这一点，对此我既不肯定也不否认；但若真有这样的人，对他们我什么话都不必讲。然而，对于真心热爱联邦的那些人，我能不说点什么吗？

11. 把我们的国家大厦连同它所能带来的裨益，它的历史以及它的希望一起毁灭，这是一桩后果极其严重的事情。在着手处理之前，明确我们何以要这样做难道不是明智之举吗？如果你避之不及的那些祸患其实根本就不存在，难道你还会不顾一切地孤注一掷吗？如果确实摆脱了某些祸患，可同时又陷入了更大的灾难，难道你还会冒险犯下如此可怕的错误吗？

12. 大家都声称，如果宪法所规定的各项权利都能得到保证，就愿意留在联邦内。那么，宪法明文规定的权利是否真有哪一项被否定了呢？我认为没有。幸运得很，人的理性使得任何一方都不敢那样做。你们能找出一个例子来说明宪法中明文规定的条款有哪一条曾被否定掉吗？如果多数人只靠数目上的力量就去剥夺少数人应该享受的任何一项明文规定的宪法权利，就道德观点而言，这就可以证明进行革命是有理的；如果那是一项重要的权利，当然应该进行革命。但是我们的情况并非如此。少数人和个人的一切重要权利都得到宪法中所列的各种肯定和否定、保证和禁止的明确保障，在这方面从未引起过任何争议。但是，任何组织法都不能在制定时就针对实际行政工作中可能出现的每一个问题提出专门适用的条款。对于一切可能发生的问题，没有那样的先见之明，也没有任何篇幅适当的文献容得下那么多明文规定。逃避劳役的人应由联邦政府抑或由州政府遣还？宪法未作明确规定。国会可以禁止各个准州的奴隶制吗？宪法未作明确规定。国会应该保护各个准州的奴隶制吗？宪法未作明确规定。

……

13. 我国一部分地区认为奴隶制是正确的，应该得到扩展，而另一部分地区认为它是错误的，不应得到扩展。这就是唯一的实质性争论。在人民的道德观念并不完全支持法律的社会里，宪法中有关逃亡奴隶的条款和禁止贩卖外籍奴隶的法律都得和其他任何法律一样严格执行。人民中的大多数能够遵行这两项枯燥的法律义务，但每一项都被少数人触犯。我认为这是无法完全纠正的。这两种情况在上述两种地区分离之后还会更糟。如外籍奴隶贩卖，现在没有完全遭到禁止，最终会在一个地区不受限制地恢复起来；而逃亡奴隶，另一地区现在只是部分地遣还，那时就根本不会遣还。

14. 以自然条件而言，我们是不能分开的。我们无法把各个地区彼此挪开，也无法在彼此之间筑起一堵无法逾越的墙垣。夫妻可以离婚，不再见面、互不接触，但是我们国家的各个地区却不可能那样做。它们仍得面对面地相处，它们之间还得有或者友好或者敌对的交往。那么，分开之后的交往是否可能比分开之前更有好处，更令人满意呢？外人之间订立条约难道还比朋友之间制定法律容易吗？外人之间执行条约难道还比朋友之间执行法律忠实吗？假定你们进行战争，你们不可能永远打下去；在双方损失惨重，任何一方都得不到好处之后，你们就会停止战斗，那时你们还会遇到诸如交往条件之类的老问题。

15. 这个国家及其机构，属于居住在这个国家里的人民。一旦他们对现存政府感到不能容忍，就可以行使他们的宪法权利去改组政府，或者行使革命权利去解散或推翻政府。我当然知道：许多可敬的、爱国的公民渴望宪法能得到修改。尽管我未提出修改宪法的建议，但我完全承认人民对整个这一问题所具有的合法权利，他们可以施行宪法本身所规定的两种方式中的任何一种；在目前情况下，我应该赞同而不是反对公平地为人民提供对此采取行动的机会。我愿大胆补充说明：在我看来，采取会议的形式是可行的，因为它可以让人民自己提出修正案，而不是只让人民去采纳或反对别人所提出的某些方案，那些人不是专为这一目的而被推选出来的，那些方案也并非恰恰就是人民想要接受或拒绝的。我知道，国会已经通过一项宪法修正案——但我尚未看到那项修正案，其大意是：联邦政府永远不得干涉各州的内部制度，包括对应服劳役者规定的制度。为了避免对我所说的话产生误解，我放弃不谈某些特定修正案的打算，而只是提出：鉴于这样一项条款现在已意味着属于宪法中的条款，我不反对使它成为明确的、不可改变的规定。

16. 总统的一切权力来自人民，但人民没有授权给他为各州的分离规定条件。如果人民有此意愿，那他们可以这样做；而作为总统来说，则不可能这样做。他的责任是管理交给他的这一届政府，并将它完整地移交给他的继任者。

17. 为什么我们不能对人民所具有的最高的公正抱有坚韧的信念呢？世界上还有比这更好或一样好的希望吗？在我们目前的分歧中，难道双方都缺乏相信自己正确的信心吗？如果万国全能的主宰以其永恒的真理和正义支持你北方这一边，或者支持你南方这一边，那么，那种真理和那种正义必将通过美国人民这个伟大法庭的裁决而取得胜利。

18. 就是这些美国人民，通过我们现有的政府结构，明智地只给他们的公仆很小的权力，使他们不能为害作恶，并且同样明智地每隔很短的时间就把那小小的权力收回到自己手中。只要人民保持美德和警惕，无论怎样作恶和愚蠢的执政人员都不能在短短 4 年的任期内十分严重地损害政府。

19. 我的同胞们，大家平静而认真地思考整个这一问题吧。任何宝贵的东西都不会因为从容对待而丧失。假使有一个目标火急地催促你们中随便哪一位采取一个措施，而你绝不能不慌不忙，那么那个目标会因从容对待而落空；但是，任何好的目标是不会因为从容对待而落空的。你们现在感到不满意的人仍然有着原来的、完好无损的宪法，而且，在敏感问题上，你们有着自己根据这部宪法制定的各项法律；而新的一届政府即使想改变这两种情况，也没有直接的权力那样做。那些不满意的人在这场争论中即使被承认是站在正确的一边，也没有一点正当理由采取鲁莽的行动。理智、爱国精神、基督教义以及对从不抛弃这片幸福土地的上帝的信仰，这些仍然能以最好的方式来解决我们目前的一切困难。

20. 各位心怀不满的同胞们，内战这个重大问题的关键掌握在你们手中，而不掌握在我手中。政府不会对你们发动攻击。你们不当挑衅者，就不会面临冲突。你们没有对天发誓要毁灭政府，而我却要立下最庄严的誓言："坚守、维护和捍卫合众国宪法。"

21. 我不愿意就此结束演说。我们不是敌人，而是朋友。我们一定不要成为敌人。尽管情绪紧张，也决不应割断我们之间的感情纽带。记忆的神秘琴弦，从每一个战场和爱国志士的坟墓伸向这片广阔土地上的每一颗跳动的心和家庭，必将再度被我们善良的天性所拨响，那时就会高奏起联邦大团结的乐章。

5

Gettysburg Address by Abraham Lincoln

Delivered 19 November, 1863, in Gettysburg, Pennsylvania

□ About the Speech

《**葛底斯堡演说**》是林肯总统最著名的演说，也是美国历史上被人引用最多的政治性演说。至今，人们还常在许多重要场合提起或朗诵它。

1863 年 7 月 3 日，联邦军队在宾夕法尼亚州葛底斯堡的胜利是南北战争的转折点，这也是南北战争中最为残酷的战役，联邦军队伤亡 23 000 人，而南方邦联军队伤亡失踪的士兵达 28 000 人。北方对葛底斯堡的胜利欢欣鼓舞。1863 年 11 月 19 日，也就是葛底斯堡战役结束的四个半月后，林肯在葛底斯堡国家公墓（Gettysburg National Cemetery）揭幕式上发表这一演说，哀悼在长达五个半月的葛底斯堡之役中阵亡的将士。这篇演说思想深刻、语言精练、修辞细腻、感人至深，自发表以来，一直被认为是英语演讲中的最高典范。

以不到 300 字的字数，在不足 3 分钟的时间里，林肯诉诸独立宣言所支持的“凡人生而平等”之原则，并重新定义这场内战：不只是为联邦存续而奋斗，亦是“自由之新生”，将真平等带给全体公民。我们从演说中可以了解林肯的思想和信念，可以体会到林肯伟大的人格和强大的精神力量。让我们记住世界上这样一个伟大的人物，记住这一流芳千古的佳作，并以他为人生的榜样！

□ The Speech in Full

1. **Fourscore and seven years[1] ago our fathers brought forth on this continent,**

a new nation, conceived[2] in Liberty, and dedicated to the proposition that all men are created equal.

2. Now we are engaged in a great civil war, testing whether that nation or any nation so conceived and so dedicated, can long endure. We are met on a great battle-field of that war. We have come to dedicate a portion of that field as a final resting place for those who here gave their lives that that nation might live. It is altogether fitting and proper that we should do this.

3. But, in a larger sense, we cannot dedicate—we cannot consecrate[3]—we cannot hallow[4]—this ground. The brave men, living and dead, who struggled here, have consecrated it, far above our poor power to add or detract[5]. The world will little note, nor long remember what we say here, but it can never forget what they did here. It is for us the living, rather, to be dedicated here to the unfinished work which they who fought here have thus far so nobly advanced. **It is rather for us to be here dedicated to the great task remaining before us—that from these honored dead we take increased devotion to that cause for which they gave the last full measure of devotion—that we here highly resolve that these dead shall not have died in vain—that this nation, under God, shall have a new birth of freedom—and that government of the people, by the people, for the people[6], shall not perish[7] from the earth.** (270 words)

❑ Notes to the Speech

1. Fourscore and seven years："score"意为"二十"，这个短语意为"八十七年"。用这样的说法是为了创造庄重的气氛。
2. conceive [kən'siːv] *vt.* become pregnant with a child 怀胎，怀孕；孕育
3. consecrate ['kɔnsikreit] *vt.* make or declare sth. holy 使神圣，圣化
4. hallow ['hæləu] *vt.* make holy 使神圣，视为神圣
5. detract [di'trækt] *vt.* make sth. seem less valuable or impressive 减损；贬低
6. of the people, by the people, for the people：直译是"为人民所有，由人民管理，为了人民的利益"，通常译为"民有、民治、民享"，这样既简洁明了，又朗朗上口。
7. perish ['periʃ] *vi.* die 死亡；be completely ruined or destroyed 毁灭；被摧毁

❑ Appreciating the Speech

林肯的《葛底斯堡演说》是美国文学中最感人、最富有诗意的篇章之一。虽然这是一篇庆祝军事胜利的演说，但它没有好战之气 (bellicose)；相反地，这是一篇感人肺腑的颂辞 (moving eulogy)，是一篇表明心志的华章 (magnificent writing)。演说开头，他深情地回顾了先辈们建立崭新的自由、平等国家的功勋 (recalled the contributions of the forefathers in establishing this new and equal country)。接下来，他由衷地赞美了那些为保卫合众国免于分裂而英勇捐躯的人们 (praised those who lost their lives protecting the Union from being split)，以及他们为之献身的那些理想 (and the ideals they devoted to)。最后他以"我们在此下定最大的决心，以不让死者白白牺牲；让这个国家在上帝的保佑下获得自由的新生；让这个民有、民治、民享的政府与世长存。"这样的铿锵话语结束演说，表达了他誓死捍卫合众国、捍卫美国的价值观的坚定决心和信心 (expressed his firm determination and confidence to safeguard the Union and the American values)。其中"民有、民治、民享的政府" (government of the people, by the people, for the people) 这一名言一直在被全世界的人们广为传颂。

从语言上讲，这篇演讲有两个突出特点。一是长句的使用 (the use of long sentences)，如第 1 段即是由一个长句构成，第 2 段的第 3 句也是一个长句。长句的使用增加了本篇演讲的正式性和严肃性。本篇演讲的第二个特点是排比的运用 (the use of parallelism)。如第 3 段第 1 句连用 3 个"We cannot"开头的句子，最后一句连用 4 个"that"从句，而最后一个"that"从句中又包含了一个排比用法"government of the people, by the people, for the people"，这一连串排比的使用使演讲音韵铿锵、气势磅礴，增加了演讲的感召力和鼓动性。

❑ Culture Links

(1) 南北战争及其特点

南北战争是美国历史上唯一的一场内战。交战双方为北方的美利坚合众国（简称联邦）和南方的美利坚联盟国（简称邦联）。战争的主题是奴隶制。这场战争的起因为美国南部 11 州以亚伯拉罕·林肯于 1861 年就任总统为由而陆续退出联邦，另成立以杰斐逊·戴维斯为"总统"的政府，并驱逐驻扎南方的联邦军，而林肯为了维护国家统一下令攻打"叛乱"州。1865 年，南方叛军统帅罗伯特·李向联邦统帅尤里西斯·辛普森·格兰特投降，南北战争结束。此战不但改变了当时美国的政治、经济形势，导致奴隶制度在美国南方最终被废除，也对日后美国的民间社会产生了巨大的影响。

战争的起因：19 世纪 50 年代前后，美国废除奴隶制度的势力加强，林肯旗帜鲜明地反对奴隶制，认为蓄奴不人道，反对扩大蓄奴，因此南方仇视他。1860 年，他当选总统，对南方而言，无异联邦向蓄奴制宣战，南卡罗来纳州在 1861 年首先宣布退出联邦，并用武力驱赶驻守在那里的美国军队，打响了内战的第一枪。随后，其他的一些南方州也退出联邦，建立美国南方邦联，以杰斐逊·戴维斯为总统，一场大规模的战争开始。

战争的经过：战争开始后，由于南方准备充足，致使北方遭遇大失败，许多地方沦陷后都被挂上南方邦联旗帜。林肯为了避免忠于联邦的南方州加入邦联而暂时没有废除奴隶制，但在战事屡战屡败的情况下，共和党激进派要求林肯解放奴隶，林肯于 1862 年签署《解放宣言》，宣布解放叛乱州的奴隶，并接受黑人参与军队。北方的实力因此大大增强，很多沦陷的土地被收复，南方节节溃败。

战争的结果：1865 年，北方收复了南方大部分地区，南方军队由于补给不足，许多士兵饿死。最后罗伯特·李向尤里西斯·辛普森·格兰特请降，南方邦联瓦解，战争以国家重新恢复统一而结束。

战争的影响：南北战争对美国的影响是很深远的，它为美国资本主义的发展扫清了道路，并让美国人吸取教训。从双方伤亡惨重的南北战争中，美国人明白了不论是在一个家庭还是在一个国家，兄弟相残没有赢家。因而，他们更加团结了，此后美国一直没有发生内战。

战争的特点：首先，南北战争不是一场为争得并独霸国家政权为目的的战争（因此有些历史学家认为把南北战争称为内战并不恰当），而是一场以捍卫国家统一为目的的战争。南方打响了南北战争的第一枪，但其目的不是获取国家政权，而是退出联邦，以保存其奴隶制度。北方进行战争是为了联邦的统一，并不是为了使北方永远把持政权。南北战争结束后，联邦依然是全体美国人民（北方人民和南方人民）的联邦，政府依然是按照宪政原则由全体美国人民通过普选产生。

其次，战争的胜利者对待失败者的态度值得褒扬。林肯在得知罗伯特·李将军代表南方投降的消息后，说“南方人又是我们的兄弟了”，他站在维护国家统一和人道的高度，宽容地对待南方叛乱者；被誉为“战神”的南军统帅罗伯特·李将军，在 1865 年放下武器成为败军之将，却也虽败犹荣，与林肯一样被美国人民视为英雄，因为他的行动使国家和人民摆脱了战火的进一步蹂躏。美国人民没有“成王败寇”的观念，胜者宽容，败者镇定，在“维护国家统一”的根本原则下双方尽释前嫌，所以他们都是人民眼中的英雄。

另外，这场导致 60 多万士兵死亡的战争结束后，竟然没有一个战俘。这一“零战俘”现象值得我们深思。战争结束了，北方取得了彻底的胜利，如果此时追究发动战争的责任，大肆逮捕与北方为敌的南方将士，那么国家的统一就只是一个形式，南北双方人民心中的裂痕只会因战争的结束而进一步加大。只有宽容地对待南方的每一个将士，才有可能从形式上和精神上完成国家的真正统一。“零战俘”现象体现了胜利者博大的宽容精神，也为美国日后崛起为大国奠定了精神基础。

（2）“民有、民治、民享”的政府理念

林肯在本篇演讲中简洁而清晰地阐明了他的政府理念，表达了他对政府和人民之间关系的真正理解与准确定位。这实际上也是历届美国政府所遵循的政府理念，即政府要成为“民有、民治、民享”的政府（government of the people, by the people, for the people）。这一理念简明扼要却含义深刻、意义深远。在此，林肯用3个介词生动地体现了政府的性质：

of: 表归属，说明政府属于人民所有，而不是人民属于政府所有；

by: 表执行者，说明政府一切行政权力从根本上讲，是由人民（或其公选的代表）来执行，政府官员只不过是由人民选出，代表人民来行使行政权力；

for: 表目的，指政府以人民的目的为目的，而不是人民以政府的目的为目的。并且，人民愿意“享”这个政府就“享”；不愿意“享”，政府无权要求人民去“享”，否则就违反了“以人民的目的为目的”的原则。

在“民有、民治、民享”中，“民治”（by the people）最为重要，没有它，前面的 of the people 和后边的 for the people 就成了无本之木。检验政府权力的“民”之真伪，不在于它喊没喊出 of the people 和 for the people，而唯一的标准就在于它是否真正做到了 by the people，即政府权力是不是真正是由人民选出的代表来执行。如果政府权力不是经由（by）国民的选举程序，那么它就做不到 for the people，更谈不上 of the people 了。

由此可见，小小的几个常用介词，却表达了丰富、深刻的含义。所以，不要说只有中文才是博大精深，英文同样可以表达深刻、准确的概念。

150 多年前，美国总统林肯以“民有、民治、民享”定义了美国政府的本质。随后，这一政府理念在全世界产生了广泛而深远的影响，以这样的理念为原则的政府在世界各地如雨后春笋般建立起来。

❑ Questions Concerning the Speech

1. What kind of nation did our fathers create on this continent?
2. Why are we met on a great battlefield of that great civil war?
3. Why can't we dedicate, consecrate or hallow this ground?
4. What do we here highly resolve to do?

❑ Paraphrase the Following Sentences

1. Now we are engaged in a great civil war, testing whether that nation or any nation so conceived and so dedicated, can long endure.

2. It is for us the living, rather, to be dedicated here to the unfinished work which they who fought here have thus far so nobly advanced.
3. that we here highly resolve that these dead shall not have died in vain—that this nation, under God, shall have a new birth of freedom—and that government of the people, by the people, for the people, shall not perish from the earth.

❑ Questions for Discussion

1. 试比较美国南北战争与中国解放战争的异同。
2. 试分析林肯“民有、民治、民享”的政府理念与孙中山“三民主义”的承继关系。

❑ Translation

亚伯拉罕·林肯：葛底斯堡演讲

1863 年 11 月 19 日，宾夕法尼亚州，葛底斯堡

1. 八十七年前，我们的先辈在这个大陆上创建了一个新的国家。她孕育于自由之中，奉行人人生而平等的信条。
2. 现在我们正进行一场伟大的内战，以考验这个国家，或者任何一个孕育于自由和奉行人人生来平等信条的国家是否能够长久坚持下去。我们相聚在这场战争的一个伟大战场上，我们来到这里把这战场的一部分奉献给那些为国家生存而捐躯的人们，作为他们最后的安息之所。我们这样做完全是适合的、恰当的。
3. 但是，从更高的意义上说，我们是不能奉献、不能圣化也不能神化这片土地的，因为那些曾经在这里战斗过的人们，活着的和死去的人们，已经圣化了这片土地，他们所做的远非我们的微薄之力所能扬抑。这个世界不大会注意也不会长久记得我们今天在这里所说的话，但是，它永远不会忘记勇士们在这里所做的事。毋宁说，我们活着的人，应该献身于留在我们面前的伟大任务：从这些光荣的死者身上汲取更多的献身精神，以完成他们精诚所至的事业；我们在此下定最大的决心，以不让死者白白牺牲；让这个国家在上帝的保佑下获得自由的新生；让这个民有、民治、民享的政府与世长存。

Woodrow Wilson

(1856—1924)

伍德罗·威尔逊

6

Woodrow Wilson: Ask Congress to Declare War Against Germany

Delivered 2 April 1917, in Washington, D.C.

❑ About the Author

伍德罗·威尔逊（Woodrow Wilson, 1856—1924），出生于弗吉尼亚州斯汤顿，美国第28任总统、第32~33届总统（1913—1921）。威尔逊毕业于霍普金斯大学，获哲学博士学位，曾任普林斯顿大学校长8年，是美国“学术地位最高”的一位总统。

威尔逊1912年获民主党总统候选人提名，战胜西奥多·罗斯福当选总统。上任后，他主张节制“私人企业的垄断”，推行了一系列卓有成效的“新自由”改革：制定联邦储备法，重新组织了美国全国的银行和金融体系；制定了南北战争以来美国最低关税率；采取了联邦累进所得税法；发展了职业教育；实施了铁路部门8小时工作制等。1916年威尔逊连任。当时正值第一次世界大战。开始，威尔逊政府力避参战，但美国的中立政策却未能持久。威尔逊领导美国参战后，动员美国人力、物力，为战争的胜利做出了很大努力。

在战争的最后阶段，威尔逊亲自主导了对德交涉和协定停火。他发表了十四点和平原则，从中阐述了他所认为的能够避免世界再遭战火的新世界秩序。德国战败后，1919年威尔逊作为三巨头之一，带着他提出的被称为“世界和平纲领”的“十四点原则”参加了巴黎和会，缔结了《凡尔赛和约》。威尔逊极力倡导国联方案，为此他东奔西走、竭尽全力，但由于国内孤立主义思潮等种种原因，最终未被美国国会通过。不过，尽管没有美国的加入，国联还是于1920年成立。威尔逊所秉持的理想国际主义，也被后人称为“威尔逊主义”，主张美国登上世界舞台来为民主而战斗。威尔逊始终都对他的祖国充满自豪，他曾深情地说：“我们的伟大建立于我们的自由基础之上——这是个道德的范畴，而不是物质的范畴。”主要由于他对创建国联的特殊贡献，威尔逊于1919年被授予诺贝尔和平奖。他也是继西奥多·罗斯福之后第二位获此殊荣的美国总统。

❑ About the Speech

1917年之前，美国一直恪守1914年的中立宣言。其间，威尔逊为确保一个更宽泛的外交政策，警告美国公民不要在交战阵营中选择他们的所属方。但后来由于德国发起无限制潜艇战，威胁到美国的商业海运，这种中立性开始倾斜。

在认定德国人发起的战争已变成了一个对人类的真正威胁后，为“使世界安全以确保民主”，威尔逊决心将美国带入第一次世界大战。1917年4月2日，他在请求国会对德宣战演讲中说道，美国如不参战，整个西方文明都将被摧毁。威尔逊在讲话中宣告将进行一场“结束一切战争的战争”，说明他希望建立一个和平的基础以防将来战祸再临而招致不必要的死亡与摧毁。这也为他未来将发表的14点原则——一个关于解决领土争端、确保自由贸易和建立维和组织的一揽子建议——铺垫了一个基础。

❑ The Speech *(abridged)*

Gentlemen of the Congress:

1. I have called the Congress into extraordinary session because there are serious, very serious, choices of policy to be made, and made immediately, which it was neither right nor constitutionally permissible that I should assume the responsibility of making.

2. …Vessels of every kind, whatever their flag, their character, their cargo, their destination, their errand, have been ruthlessly sent to the bottom without warning and without thought of help or mercy for those on board, the vessels of friendly neutrals[1] along with those of belligerents[2]. Even hospital ships and ships carrying relief to the sorely bereaved[3] and stricken people of Belgium, though the latter were provided with safe conduct through the proscribed[4] areas by the German Government itself and were distinguished by unmistakable marks of identity, have been sunk with the same reckless lack of compassion or of principle.

…

3. I am not now thinking of the loss of property involved, immense and serious as that is, but only of the wanton[5] and wholesale destruction of the lives

of non-combatants[6], men, women, and children, engaged in pursuits which have always, even in the darkest periods of modern history, been deemed innocent and legitimate. Property can be paid for; the lives of peaceful and innocent people cannot be. The present German submarine warfare against commerce is a warfare against mankind.

4. **It is war against all nations. American ships have been sunk, American lives taken, in ways which it has stirred us very deeply to learn of, but the ships and people of other neutral and friendly nations have been sunk and overwhelmed in the waters in the same way. There has been no discrimination. The challenge is to all mankind.** Each nation must decide for itself how it will meet it. The choice we make for ourselves must be made with a moderation[7] of counsel[8] and temperateness[9] of judgment befitting[10] our character and our motives as a nation. We must put excited feeling away. Our motive will not be revenge or the victorious assertion[11] of the physical might of the nation, but only the vindication[12] of right, of human right, of which we are only a single champion.

5. When I addressed the Congress on the twenty-sixth of February last I thought that it would suffice to assert our neutral rights with arms, our right to use the seas against unlawful interference, our right to keep our people safe against unlawful violence. But armed neutrality, it now appears, is impracticable. ... The German Government denies the right of neutrals to use arms at all within the areas of the sea which it has proscribed, even in the defense of rights which no modern publicist[13] has ever before questioned their right to defend. The intimation is conveyed that the armed guards which we have placed on our merchant ships will be treated as beyond the pale[14] of law and subject to be dealt with as pirates would be. Armed neutrality is ineffectual enough at best; in such circumstances and in the face of such pretensions it is worse than ineffectual[15]; it is likely only to produce what it was meant to prevent; it is practically certain to draw us into the war without either the rights or the effectiveness of belligerents. There is one choice we cannot make, we are incapable of making: we will not choose the path of submission and suffer the most sacred rights of our nation and our people to be ignored or violated. The wrongs[16] against which we now array[17] ourselves are no common wrongs: they cut to the very roots of human life.

6. **With a profound sense of the solemn and even tragical character of the step**

I am taking and of the grave responsibilities which it involves, but in unhesitating obedience to what I deem my constitutional duty, I advise that the Congress declare the recent course of the Imperial German Government to be in fact nothing less than war against the government and people of the United States; that it formally accept the status of belligerent which has thus been thrust upon it; and that it take immediate steps not only to put the country in a more thorough state of defense but also to exert all its power and employ all its resources to bring the Government of the German Empire to terms[18] and end the war.

7. What this will involve is clear.

8. It will involve the utmost practicable cooperation in counsel and action with the governments now at war with Germany, and, as incident to[19] that, the extension to those governments of the most liberal financial credits, in order that our resources may so far as possible be added to theirs.

9. It will involve the organization and mobilization of all the material resources of the country to supply the materials of war and serve the incidental[20] needs of the nation in the most abundant and yet the most economical and efficient way possible.

10. It will involve the immediate full equipment of the navy in all respects but particularly in supplying it with the best means of dealing with the enemy's submarines.

11. It will involve the immediate addition to the armed forces of the United States already provided for by law in case of war at least five hundred thousand men, who should, in my opinion, be chosen upon the principle of universal liability[21] to service, and also the authorization of subsequent[22] additional increments[23] of equal force so soon as they may be needed and can be handled in training.

12. It will involve also, of course, the granting of adequate credits to the Government, sustained, I hope, so far as they can equitably be sustained by the present generation, by well conceived taxation.

13. While we do these things, these deeply momentous things, let us be very clear, and make very clear to the world what our motives and our objects are. ... **our object**

now, as then, is to vindicate[24] the principles of peace and justice in the life of the world as against selfish and autocratic power and to set up amongst the really free and self-governed peoples of the world such a concert[25] of purpose and of action as will henceforth ensure the observance of those principles.

…

14. We have no quarrel with the German people. We have no feeling towards them but one of sympathy and friendship. It was not upon their impulse that their government acted in entering this war. It was not with their previous knowledge or approval. It was a war determined upon as wars used to be determined upon in the old, unhappy days when peoples were nowhere consulted by their rulers and wars were provoked and waged in the interest of dynasties or of little groups of ambitious men who were accustomed to use their fellow men as pawns[26] and tools.

…

15. We are accepting this challenge of hostile purpose because we know that in such a government, following such methods, we can never have a friend; and that in the presence of its organized power, always lying in wait to accomplish we know not what purpose, there can be no assured security of the democratic governments of the world. We are now about to accept a gauge[27] of battle with this natural foe to liberty and shall, if necessary, spend the whole force of the nation to check and nullify[28] its pretensions and its power.

16. We are glad, now that we see the facts with no veil of false pretense about them, to fight thus for the ultimate peace of the world and for the liberation of its peoples, the German peoples included: for the rights of nations great and small and the privilege of men everywhere to choose their way of life and of obedience. The world must be made safe for democracy. Its peace must be planted upon the tested foundations of political liberty. We have no selfish ends to serve.

17. We desire no conquest, no dominion[29]. We seek no indemnities[30] for ourselves, no material compensation for the sacrifices we shall cheerfully make. We are but one of the champions of the rights of mankind. We shall be satisfied when those rights have been made as secure as the faith and the freedom of nations can make them.

…

18. It is a distressing and oppressive duty, Gentlemen of the Congress, which

I have performed in thus addressing you. There are, it may be, many months of fiery trial and sacrifice ahead of us. It is a fearful thing to lead this great peaceful people into war, into the most terrible and disastrous of all wars, civilization itself seeming to be in the balance[31].

19. **But the right is more precious than peace, and we shall fight for the things which we have always carried nearest our hearts, for democracy, for the right of those who submit to[32] authority to have a voice in their own governments, for the rights and liberties of small nations, for a universal dominion of right by such a concert of free peoples as shall bring peace and safety to all nations and make the world at last free.**

20. **To such a task we can dedicate our lives and our fortunes, everything that we are and everything that we have, with the pride of those who know that the day has come when America is privileged[33] to spend her blood and her might for the principles that gave her birth and happiness and the peace which she has treasured. God helping her, she can do no other.** (1,610 words)

❑ Notes to the Speech

1. neutral ['nju:trəl] *n./adj.* (a country) not supporting either side in a dispute or war 中立国；中立的
2. belligerent [bi'lidʒərənt] *adj.* taking part in a war or conflict 交战中的；在斗殴的 *n.* country, group or person engaged in war 交战的国家、群体或个人
3. bereaved [bi'ri:vd] *adj.* deprived of a close relation or friend through their death（因死亡）丧失亲人（或朋友）的
4. proscribe [prə'skraib] *vt.* <formal> forbid 禁止
5. wanton ['wɔntən] *adj.* (of a cruel or violent action) deliberate and unprovoked（残忍或暴力行为）肆意的，恣意的
6. non-combatant [nɔn'kɔmbətənt] *n.* 非作战人员
7. moderation [ˌmɔdə'reiʃən] *n.* the avoidance of extremes in your actions or opinions（行为或观点的）适度，温和
8. counsel ['kaunsəl] *n.* advice 忠告；劝告
9. temperateness ['tempəritnis] *n.* 节制，适度
10. befit [bi'fit] *vt.* <formal> be appropriate for 适合；对……相称
11. assertion [ə'sə:ʃən] *n.* a confident and forceful statement 明确肯定；断言

12. vindication [ˌvindi'keiʃən] *n.* 辩护，辩明，拥护
13. publicist ['pʌblisist] *n.* 国际法专家；宣传员；广告员
14. pale [peil] *n.* a boundary 边界；界限
15. ineffectual [ˌini'fektjuəl] *adj.* ineffective 无效的
16. wrong [rɔŋ] *n.* an unjust, dishonest, or immoral action 不公正行为；欺诈行为；不道德行为
17. array [ə'rei] *vt.* <formal or literary> set in order for battle, show, etc. 使排成阵势
18. bring…to terms：使……屈服
19. as incident to: 相应地，伴随地
20. incidental [ˌinsi'dentl] *adj.* ① happening or appearing irregularly or as a less important part of something important 偶然的，附带的 ② occurring in connection with something else 伴随……发生的；由……引起的
21. liability [ˌlaiə'biliti] *n.* something for which one is responsible, esp. by law（尤指法律规定的）责任，义务
22. subsequent ['sʌbsikwənt] *adj.* coming after something 随后的，后来的
23. increment ['inkrimənt] *n.* an increase in a number or amount 增加量；增加额
24. vindicate ['vindikeit] *vt.* prove to be true or right; free from blame 为……辩护，维护；证明……正确
25. concert ['kɔnsət] *n.* agreement 一致，协调
26. pawn [pɔːn] *n.* a person used by more powerful people for their own purposes 走卒；爪牙
27. gauge [gedʒ] *n.* a standard measure of weight, size, etc. to which objects can be compared（重量、尺寸等的）标准规格
28. nullify ['nʌlifai] *vt.* make something legally invalid 使无效；废除
29. dominion [də'minjən] *n.* supreme power or control 统治；支配
30. indemnity [in'demniti] *n.* a sum of money paid to compensate for damage or loss 赔款；补偿金
31. in the balance：（命运）未定，在危急中；不确定
32. submit [səb'mit] *vt.* (~ to) yield oneself; agree to obey 遵从；顺从；服从
33. privileged ['prividʒid] *adj.* 有特权的；荣幸的

□ Appreciating the Speech

1917 年 4 月 2 日，伍德罗·威尔逊在国会发表了他历史性的请求参战的演讲，即战争咨文（War Message）。

在这篇咨文中，威尔逊着重向国会阐述了美国为什么要参战 (elaborated to the Congress why the US should join the War)。他首先指出各种船只（无论是友好的中立国的，还是交战国的；无论运载了何种货物；无论驶往何地……）在公海上被德国潜艇不加区别地残忍击沉的严酷事实。而令他尤为担忧的，并不是因此造成的船只或财产损失，而是被这些无差别攻击所夺去的无辜生命。威尔逊认为，这是对全人类的战争 (warfare against mankind)，是对世界上所有国家的战争 (war against all nations)。他对国会议员们说，尽管他之前的想法是保持武装中立国地位，但这显然已变得不合时宜。他建议国会作出声明，宣布德意志帝国政府最近所采取的行动已经无异于对美国政府和人民的战争 (advised that the Congress declare the recent course of the Imperial German Government to be in fact nothing less than war against the government and people of the United States)。

威尔逊说，向国会提出参战这一建议对他来说是异常痛苦的。但是为了"捍卫人类世界的和平与公正原则，对抗自私和独裁的强权" (to vindicate the principles of peace and justice in the life of the world as against selfish and autocratic power) 这一目标，这又是必须的，因为"正义比和平更珍贵" (the right is more precious than peace)。为了实现这一目标，他意志坚定地说："为完成这样一个任务，我们可以献出我们的生命、财产，献出我们自己以及我们所有的一切" (To such a task we can dedicate our lives and our fortunes, everything that we are and everything that we have)。演讲结束时，全体听众再次向威尔逊报以热烈的掌声。他的演讲并不只是针对国会，而是也包括美国公众。

就语言来说，本篇演讲的突出特点是排比的运用 (the use of parallelism)。如本篇中间 5 小段，威尔逊连续用 5 个"It will involve ..."开头，语言铿锵、条理清晰地阐明了他对如何进行这场战争、如何赢得这场战争的主张。又如，在倒数第 2 段中，他连续用 5 个"for ..."结构（"for the things ..."、"for the right ..."、"for the dominion ..."），起到节奏鲜明、语势强烈的效果，增强了听众捍卫自由、正义，战胜强权的信心。

❑ Culture Links

（1）美国的孤立主义

美国的孤立主义是指美国外交史上长期存在的一种外交原则。这一由国父华盛顿所确立的原则形成于建国初期，后来很长一段时间内成为美国力主奉行的外交政策的基础。这一原则旨在避免美国陷入欧洲事务，使当时处于弱势地位的美国在强国林立的国际环境中求得了生存和发展。孤立主义并不是闭关自守的防御性政策，美国试图通过这一政策稳定国内环境，集中精力进行本国经济建设，进而发展对外贸易、扩大领土、增强国家实力。

事实上，美国的孤立主义外交政策从来都不是与外界的完全隔离。1796 年 9 月 7 日，美国总统华盛顿在宣布退出政坛时发表的告别演讲中阐述了孤立主义原则："我们对待国外重大行为的准则是在扩大我们的商务关系的同时，应尽可能少与他们发生政治上的牵连。”美国的孤立主义外交在经济和政治上实行着完全不同的政策。

孤立主义是建国初期的美国在处于弱势地位的形势下一种成功与明智的选择，它为新生的美国赢得了发展时间、扩展了空间，为19世纪中后期美国的稳步、快速发展奠定了重要基础。

第一次世界大战爆发后，由于世界形势的巨大变化，民主党总统伍德罗·威尔逊试图努力改变美国的孤立主义外交原则，积极推行通过结盟和建立国际制度实现多边国际合作，调整国际关系和维护美国国家利益的外交政策。然而，美国公众和政治精英们对威尔逊改变美国孤立主义外交传统的做法并不认同。虽然美国最终加入了协约国军事联盟，参加并与盟国一起打赢了第一次世界大战，威尔逊总统也在战后带着他的“十四点计划”远渡重洋参加巴黎和会，并且说服战胜国建立起崭新的多边主义国际合作机制——国际联盟，但是，他却没有能说服他自己的国家改变孤立主义的外交传统，批准《凡尔赛条约》和加入国际联盟。

在20世纪的两次世界大战之间，美国继续维持传统的孤立主义外交原则，在一系列的外交活动中坚持单边主义，拒绝多边的国际合作。在此时期内，美国参议院两度否决美国参加国际法庭，美国国会还在1935年8月通过一项全面反映孤立主义原则的中立法，禁止美国武器运往交战国，并禁止用美国船只运送武器。直至第二次世界大战全面爆发之后，美国的孤立主义外交原则才在富兰克林·罗斯福总统的努力之下逐渐发生变化，以致最终转向加强国际合作、建立反法西斯联盟、彻底打败法西斯、确立维持战后世界和平国际机制的多边“国际主义”外交政策。第二次世界大战后，在美国政府的推动下，旨在维护世界和平、推进国际多边合作的联合国等国际组织也应运而生。

（2）威尔逊理想主义

伍德罗·威尔逊，人称“书生总统”，曾担任威斯莱扬大学的历史学和政治学教授、普林斯顿大学校长及法理学和政治学教授，著有《国会政府》、《美国政治研究》、《美国人民史》和《论国家》等。他于1913年就任美国第28届总统，后获得连任。在第一次世界大战期间，威尔逊系统地提出了理想主义的基本主张，并尽全力去付诸实践，这一主张被称为威尔逊主义或威尔逊理想主义。

威尔逊理想主义以人性本善的假设作为出发点，认为：人性本质上是爱好和平的，世界基本上是和谐的，个人利益与社会利益是协调的，只是由于一些人的良知误入歧途才导致国家间的战争和冲突。所以，只要用道德和正义唤醒他们的良知，消除人与人之间、国家与国家之间的误解，世界就会回到和谐、友善的状态中去。

概括地说，威尔逊关于国际关系和对外政策的理念就是：“和平与正义、国际法律和国际组织，应当也可能是国际社会大家庭共同追求的一种目标和架构。”1918年1月

8日，他对国会发表演说，即著名的“十四点计划”。“十四点计划”是理想主义的政治纲领，其中威尔逊认为务必达成的强制目标包括：公开外交、海洋自由、全面裁军、消除贸易障碍、公正处理殖民地争议和民族自决、恢复比利时、撤出俄罗斯领土以及建立国际联盟。此后，威尔逊又对“十四点计划”进行了补充，提出了四项原则、四个目标、五点具体要求等，完善了他关于最终和平的设想。在威尔逊的不懈努力下，1920年1月国际联盟成立。威尔逊的理想主义计划及其活动受到当时国际社会的普遍欢迎，他本人为此而荣获诺贝尔和平奖。

虽然，从理论上看，理想主义并没有形成一个逻辑严密的理论体系，它更多的是愿望、信念和标准，以及由此重建国际秩序的计划。从实践上看，理想主义根本没能阻止世界大战的再次爆发。它的美好设计被规模更大、更残酷的战争砸得粉碎。然而，理想主义仍被公认为现代国际关系理论发展的起点。威尔逊等理想主义者对国际道德、国际组织和国际法等问题的广泛研究，直接促成了国际联盟和后来联合国的建立。第二次世界大战后，虽然现实主义成为美国对外政策的主要理论基础，但是威尔逊的理想主义并没有失去影响力。在美国的外交政策中，现实主义和理想主义就像一枚硬币的两面，虽然有所侧重，但缺一不可。正如外交史学家沃尔特·罗素·米德所说的：“凡尔赛体系衰落了，但威尔逊的原则却还活着，并且仍在指导着今天的欧洲政治…… 没有一个20世纪的欧洲政治家能发挥如此持久、有益和广泛的影响。”

❑ Questions Concerning the Speech

1. What worries Wilson the most about the German submarine warfare?
2. What does Wilson say about the actual function of the armed neutrality at that time?
3. Why does Wilson say "We have no quarrel with the German people"?
4. In Wilson's opinion, what is the purpose of fighting against Germany?
5. Does Wilson feel proud of leading America into such a terrible war? Why?

Paraphrase the Following Sentences

1. I am not now thinking of the loss of property involved, immense and serious as that is, but only of the wanton and wholesale destruction of the lives of non-combatants,
2. Our motive will not be revenge or the victorious assertion of the physical might of the nation, but only the vindication of right, of human right, of which we are only a single champion.
3. The intimation is conveyed that the armed guards which we have placed on our merchant ships will be treated as beyond the pale of law and subject to be dealt with as pirates would be.

4. With a profound sense of the solemn and even tragical character of the step I am taking and of the grave responsibilities which it involves, but in unhesitating obedience to what I deem my constitutional duty, I advise that the Congress declare the recent course of the Imperial German Government to be in fact nothing less than war against the government and people of the United States...
5. It will involve the utmost practicable cooperation in counsel and action with the governments now at war with Germany...
6. We are now about to accept a gauge of battle with this natural foe to liberty and shall, if necessary, spend the whole force of the nation to check and nullify its pretensions and its power.
7. It is a fearful thing to lead this great peaceful people into war, into the most terrible and disastrous of all wars, civilization itself seeming to be in the balance.
8. To such a task we can dedicate our lives and our fortunes, everything that we are and everything that we have, with the pride of those who know that the day has come when America is privileged to spend her blood and her might for the principles that gave her birth and happiness and the peace which she has treasured.

❑ Questions for Discussion

1. 为什么当时众多的美国人反对美国加入第一次世界大战？如果你是当时的一个美国人，你也会这样做吗？
2. 试论国联对维护当时的世界和平的作用。
3. 试从威尔逊总统主张加入国联的提案未获国会通过这一事实，来讨论一下美国总统与国会的制衡关系。
4. 试析美国的孤立主义与清政府闭关锁国政策的区别。

❑ Translation

伍德罗·威尔逊：要求国会对德宣战

1917 年 4 月 2 日，华盛顿特区

1. 本人提请国会召开临时会议，因为国家必须立即做出严肃、且非常之严肃的决策，而由我来行使此职权既是错误的，也是宪法所不允许的。
2. …… 任何种类的船只，不论它挂什么旗、具有什么性质、载什么货、驶向何处、完成什么使命，全都被击沉，不给预先警告，也全然不顾船上人员的死活；友好中立国的

船只与敌国的船只同样对待。甚至连医护船以及向比利时死伤惨重的人民运送救济物资的船只——后者被德国政府允许安全通过禁海而且带有明确无误的标记——同样也被丧失同情心和原则性的德军击沉。

3. …… 我现在想到的不是德国在海上造成的财产损失，尽管损失惨重，而是对大批平民生命肆无忌惮的屠杀，而这些男人、妇女和儿童所追求的目标向来——甚至在现代历史最黑暗的时期——被认为是无辜和合法的。财产可以赔偿，而和平无辜的人民的生命则无法赔偿。目前德国对付海上贸易的潜艇战其实是以人类为敌。

4. 这是针对所有国家的战争。美国船只被击沉，美国公民葬身海底，消息传来令人震惊。但其他中立或友好国家的船只和人员在海上遭到相同的厄运，没有什么差别。这是对整个人类的挑战。每个国家必须独自决定它应如何对付这一挑战。我们必须适应我国的特点和宗旨审时度势，谨慎考虑，以作出我们自己的决定。我们绝对不应感情用事。我们的动机既非为复仇也不是为了耀武扬威，而仅仅是要做一名维护正义和人权的战士。……

5. 去年 2 月 26 日，我在国会发表讲话时曾想，用武力维护我们中立国的权利——保卫我们在海上的权利，防止非法挑衅，保卫我们人员的安全，防止非法暴力——就足够了。可现在看来，武装中立是不现实的 …… 在失去法律保护的海域内，中立国使用武器的权力还未曾被现代国际法专家质疑过，而德国政府根本就否认这种自卫的权力。德国政府发出通告说，我们在商船上配有武装自卫人员是非法的，将作为海盗对待。其实，武装中立本来就是徒劳无益的。在这种情况下，在这样的要求面前，又岂止是徒劳呢？很可能本来打算阻止战争却引起了战争；但这实际上必然把我们拖入战争而又享受不到参战国的权利和实效。有一条我们不能选择的道路，我们根本也不会选择：那就是屈服的道路，也就是使我们的国家和民族最神圣的权利遭到无视和侵犯的道路。我们现在一致反对的侵权行为不是一般的侵权行为，而是一个将断送人类生活源泉的侵权行为。

6. 我深刻认识到我正采取的步骤的严重乃至悲剧的性质，以及它所包含的重大责任，但是我对履行自己由宪法规定的义务毫不迟疑。正是以这样的态度，我建议国会宣布：德意志帝国最近的行动事实上已是对美国政府和人民发动了战争；美国正式接受已强加于它的交战国地位；美国将立即行动，不仅使国家处于完全的防御状态，而且将竭尽全力、使用一切手段迫使德国政府屈服、结束战争。

7. 这一切意味着什么是明确无误的。

8. 这意味着我们要尽一切可能地与和德国交战的国家进行协商、协调行动，相应地给予他们最慷慨的财政贷款，以便尽可能地让我们的资源能助他们一臂之力；

9. 这意味着我们要组织和调动全国一切资源，以最充足、最经济有效的方式提供战争所需物资，同时满足国家的相关需求；

10. 这意味着即刻开始全方位装备美国海军，尤其是为其提供最精良的武器以对付敌军潜艇；
11. 这意味着即刻招募新兵，依据美国法律战时可增兵至少 50 万。依我之见，人员的选取可依据普遍兵役制原则以及国会授权，即在战争需要和保证训练的情况下，可增加相同规模的军事力量。
12. 这同样也意味着给政府足够的款项，这些开销将由精心策划的税收来支付。

……

13. 当我们行动起来，做这些这些事关至大之事的时候，我们自己应当清楚，也应让全世界明白我们的动机和目的是什么 …… 不论今昔，我们的目的都是维护世界的和平与正义的原则，反对自私和专制的力量，我们要在世界上真正自由和自治的各国人民之中建立起目标与行动上的一致，以确保这些原则得到遵循。当问题涉及世界和平，涉及世界各国人民的自由时，当有组织的势力支持某些专制政府按自己的意志而非人民的意志独断专行，从而对世界人民的和平与自由构成威胁时，中立便不再是可行或可取的了。我们看到，在这种情况下中立已成为历史。我们处在一个新时代的开端，在这个时代中人们坚决要求，凡是文明国家每个公民遵循的关于行为和承担罪责的规范，各个国家和它们的政府也必须同样遵循。
14. 我们与德国人民之间不存龃龉。对他们，我们除了同情和友谊外没有别的情感。他们的政府投入战争并不是因为人民的推动，他们事先一无所知、并未表示赞同。决定进行这场战争与过去不幸的岁月中决定打一场仗的方式相同。旧时统治者从不征求人民的意见，战争的挑起和发动全都是为着王朝的利益或是为野心勃勃的人组成的小集团的利益，这些人惯于利用同胞作为走卒和工具。

……

15. 我们接受这一敌意的挑战，因为我们知道与这样一个采用这种手段的政府是绝对不能做朋友的；只要它组织起来的力量埋伏着准备实现不可告人的目的，世界上一切民主的政府便无法得到安全保障。我们接受的将是一场与这个自由的天敌展开的宏大战役，如有必要，将动用我国的全部力量去制止和粉碎敌人的意图和势力。
16. 我们感到欣慰，因为敌人撕去伪善的面纱，使我们看清了真相，这样我们将为世界最终和平，为世界各国人民包括德国人民的解放而战；为大大小小各国的权利而战；为世界各地人们选择自己的生活方式与被统治方式的权利而战。世界应该让民主享有安全。世界和平应建立在历经考验的政治自由的基础上。我们没有什么私利可图。
17. 我们不想要征服，不想要统治。我们不为自己索取赔偿，对我们将慷慨作出的牺牲不求物质补偿。我们只不过是为人类权利而战的斗士之一。当各国的信念和自由能确保人类权利不可侵犯之时，我们将心满意足。

……

18. 国会议员先生们，这是一种令人痛苦、压力巨大的职责，我此刻向你们讲话就是在履行它。在我们面前很可能有旷日持久的战火考验和惨重牺牲。把我们伟大的、爱好和平的人民卷入战争是件可怕的事。因为这场战争是有史以来最血腥、最残酷的，甚至文明自身似已岌岌可危。

19. 然而正义比和平更宝贵。我们将为自己一向最珍惜的东西而战——为民主而战，为人民能够在自己服从的政府中享有发言权而战，为弱小国家的权利和自由而战，为了自由的民族所主持的正义能一统天下而战。这些民族紧密团结，终会将和平与安全带给各国，使世界最终获得自由。

20. 为完成这样一个任务，我们可以献出我们的生命财产，献出我们自己以及我们所有的一切；我们满怀自豪，因为我们知道，这样的一天已经到来：美国有幸得以用她的鲜血和力量捍卫那些原则，正是它们给予她生命和快乐，给予她一向珍视的和平。上帝保佑她，她别无选择。

Franklin D. Roosevelt

(1882—1945)

富兰克林·D·罗斯福

7

Franklin D. Roosevelt's First Inaugural Address

Delivered 4 March, 1933, in Washington, D.C.

❑ About the Author

富兰克林·D·罗斯福(Franklin D. Roosevelt, 1882—1945)，美国人通常以其姓名缩写 FDR 称之。出生于纽约州一个富裕家庭，先后就读于哈佛大学和哥伦比亚大学，美国第 32 任总统，是 20 世纪美国二三十年代经济危机和第二次世界大战的中心人物之一。从 1933 年至 1945 年间，连续出任 4 届美国总统，且是唯一连任超过两届的美国总统。由于其远房堂叔西奥多·罗斯福是第 26 任美国总统，故常称富兰克林·罗斯福为“小罗斯福”总统，而称西奥多·罗斯福为“老罗斯福”总统。

罗斯福 1907 年从哥伦比亚大学法学院毕业，通过律师资格考试后进入律师事务所任律师。1910 年当选为纽约州参议员，1912 年获连任。1913 年任威尔逊政府海军部副部长。1928 年任纽约州长。由于对农民实行减税，深得人心，1930 年获连任。1932 年竞选总统，提出“新政”计划，以压倒多数选票获胜。在 1930 年代经济大萧条期间，罗斯福推行“新政”以提供失业救济来复苏经济，并成立如公共事业振兴署（WPA）、国家复兴管理局（NRA）和农业调整管理局（AAA）等机构来改革经济和银行体系。虽然直到第二次世界大战爆发为止，美国的经济仍未能完全复苏，但是他所发起的一些计划仍继续在国家的商贸中扮演重要角色。除此之外，在其任内设立的一些制度，包括社会安全系统和全国劳资关系委员会（NLRB）等，仍然保留至今。

早在 1941 年 12 月以前，英国正与纳粹德国作战，而美军还未参与第二次世界大战之际，罗斯福已经利用租借法案向丘吉尔及英国军方提供援助。1941 年 12 月 7 日，日本突然偷袭珍珠港。美国国会应罗斯福之请求，于 12 月 8 日开会，4 小时内通过对日宣战的决议。12月11日，德、意对美宣战。参战后，罗斯福动员了全部工业积极从事军事生产，将美国转变为"民主国家的兵工厂"。他与他的助手哈里·霍普金斯紧密合作，在使美国成为同盟国主要的军火供应商的同时，也使得美国国内产业大幅扩张，实现充分就业，并为非裔和妇女制造了新的机会。进入第二次世界大战后期，同盟国逐渐扭转形势后，罗斯福对塑造战后世界秩序发挥了关键作用，其影响力在雅尔塔会议及联合国的成立中尤其明显。

由于罗斯福在应对20世纪30年代的经济大萧条和第二次世界大战胜利中所做出的重大贡献，他被公认为是美国历史上最伟大的3位总统之一（另外两位是华盛顿和林肯）。他受到美国人民的如此爱戴是因为，虽然他出身富豪家庭，但他相信平凡人的价值，并且为维护百姓的权利而战；他有着慑人的人格魅力，愉快地工作，对未来充满信心；他带领美国走出经济困境，改变了美国人的生活方式；他以捍卫民主、自由的政治体制为己任，使世界变得更安全。

❑ About the Speech

当罗斯福于1933年3月就职时，美国正遭受经济危机的严重打击。有1/4的劳动人口失业。农民随着农产品价格下降了60%而正处于极度贫困之中。工业生产自1929年以来下降了一半以上，导致200万人无家可归。时至3月4日晚间为止，48州中的32州以及哥伦比亚特区当地银行都已关闭。纽约联邦储备银行无法在5日开门，因为巨额国库存款已被几天前恐慌的客户挤兑一空。整个国家前景惨淡，人们对未来缺乏信心。

在1933年3月4日下午，罗斯福发表了这篇富有激情的就职演讲，在演讲中罗斯福表现出一种压倒一切的自信，他告诉人们：我们唯一害怕的就是害怕本身。同时，他指责经济危机祸首在于银行家和金融家对利润的追求、建立在自身利益基础上的资本主义。新总统轻松愉快的乐观态度和决心，"点燃了举国同心同德的新精神之火"，在很大程度上恢复了美国人民的信心，消除了美国人民的恐惧。

历史学家把罗斯福的计划定位为"救济、复兴和改革"。"救济"是为了解决数以千万失业人口的迫切需要。"复兴"指的是刺激经济以恢复常态。"改革"则意味着制定长期方案以修正出错的体系，特别是金融和银行制度。在当时美国内政和外交遇到严重困难的情况下，罗斯福提出了睦邻政策，缓和了美国与其他美洲国家之间的矛盾。

众所周知，罗斯福对于美国及整个资本主义体系做出了巨大的贡献，而这篇首次就职演说，为他成功地翻开了他光辉政治生涯的第一页。

❑ The Speech in Full

1. I am certain that my fellow Americans expect that on my induction[1] into

the Presidency I will address them with a candor[2] and a decision which the present situation of our Nation impels. This is preeminently[3] the time to speak the truth, the whole truth, frankly and boldly. Nor need we shrink from honestly facing conditions in our country today. This great Nation will endure as it has endured, will revive[4] and will prosper. So, first of all, let me assert my firm belief that the only thing we have to fear is fear itself—nameless, unreasoning, unjustified terror which paralyzes needed efforts to convert retreat into advance. In every dark hour of our national life a leadership of frankness and vigor has met with that understanding and support of the people themselves which is essential to victory. I am convinced that you will again give that support to leadership in these critical days.

2. In such a spirit on my part and on yours we face our common difficulties. They concern, thank God, only material things. Values have shrunken to fantastic levels; taxes have risen; our ability to pay has fallen; government of all kinds is faced by serious curtailment[5] of income; the means of exchange are frozen in the currents of trade; the withered leaves of industrial enterprise[6] lie on every side; farmers find no markets for their produce; the savings of many years in thousands of families are gone.

3. More important, a host of[7] unemployed citizens face the grim problem of existence, and an equally great number toil[8] with little return. Only a foolish optimist can deny the dark realities of the moment.

4. **Yet our distress comes from no failure of substance. We are stricken by no plague of locusts. Compared with the perils[9] which our forefathers conquered because they believed and were not afraid, we have still much to be thankful for. Nature still offers her bounty[10] and human efforts have multiplied it. Plenty is at our doorstep, but a generous use of it languishes[11] in the very sight of the supply.** Primarily this is because the rulers of the exchange of mankind's goods have failed, through their own stubbornness and their own incompetence, have admitted their failure, and abdicated[12]. Practices of the unscrupulous[13] money changers stand indicted[14] in the court of public opinion, rejected by the hearts and minds of men.

5. **True they have tried, but their efforts have been cast in the pattern of an outworn tradition. Faced by failure of credit they have proposed only the lending of more money. Stripped[15] of the lure of profit by which to induce our people**

to follow their false leadership, they have resorted to exhortations[16], pleading tearfully for restored confidence. They know only the rules of a generation of self-seekers. They have no vision, and when there is no vision the people perish[17].

6. The money changers have fled from their high seats in the temple of our civilization. We may now restore that temple to the ancient truths. The measure of the restoration lies in the extent to which we apply social values more noble than mere monetary profit.

7. **Happiness lies not in the mere possession of money; it lies in the joy of achievement, in the thrill of creative effort. The joy and moral stimulation of work no longer must be forgotten in the mad chase of evanescent[18] profits. These dark days will be worth all they cost us if they teach us that our true destiny is not to be ministered[19] unto but to minister to ourselves and to our fellow men.**

8. Recognition of the falsity of material wealth as the standard of success goes hand in hand with the abandonment of the false belief that public office and high political position are to be valued only by the standards of pride of place and personal profit; and there must be an end to a conduct in banking and in business which too often has given to a sacred trust the likeness of callous[20] and selfish wrongdoing. **Small wonder[21] that confidence languishes, for it thrives only on honesty, on honor, on the sacredness of obligations, on faithful protection, on unselfish performance; without them it cannot live.**

9. Restoration calls, however, not for changes in ethics alone. This Nation asks for action, and action now.

10. **Our greatest primary task is to put people to work. This is no unsolvable problem if we face it wisely and courageously. It can be accomplished in part by direct recruiting by the Government itself, treating the task as we would treat the emergency of a war, but at the same time, through this employment, accomplishing greatly needed projects to stimulate and reorganize the use of our natural resources.**

11. Hand in hand with this we must frankly recognize the overbalance of population

in our industrial centers and, by engaging on a national scale in a redistribution, endeavor to provide a better use of the land for those best fitted for the land. The task can be helped by definite efforts to raise the values of agricultural products and with this the power to purchase the output of our cities. It can be helped by preventing realistically the tragedy of the growing loss through foreclosure[22] of our small homes and our farms. It can be helped by insistence that the Federal, State, and local governments act forthwith[23] on the demand that their cost be drastically reduced. It can be helped by the unifying of relief activities which today are often scattered, uneconomical, and unequal. It can be helped by national planning for and supervision of all forms of transportation and of communications and other utilities which have a definitely public character. There are many ways in which it can be helped, but it can never be helped merely by talking about it. We must act and act quickly.

12. Finally, in our progress toward a resumption[24] of work we require two safeguards against a return of the evils of the old order; there must be a strict supervision of all banking and credits and investments; there must be an end to speculation[25] with other people's money, and there must be provision for an adequate but sound currency.

13. There are the lines of attack. I shall presently urge upon a new Congress in special session detailed measures for their fulfillment, and I shall seek the immediate assistance of the several States.

14. Through this program of action we address ourselves to[26] putting our own national house in order and making income balance outgo[27]. Our international trade relations, though vastly important, are in point of time and necessity secondary to the establishment of a sound national economy. I favor as a practical policy the putting of first things first. I shall spare no effort to restore world trade by international economic readjustment, but the emergency at home cannot wait on that accomplishment.

15. The basic thought that guides these specific means of national recovery is not narrowly nationalistic. It is the insistence, as a first consideration, upon the interdependence of the various elements in all parts of the United States—a recognition of the old and permanently important manifestation[28] of the American spirit of the pioneer. It is the way to recovery. It is the immediate way. It is the strongest assurance that the recovery will endure.

16. In the field of world policy I would dedicate this Nation to the policy of the good neighbor—the neighbor who resolutely respects himself and, because he does so, respects the rights of others—the neighbor who respects his obligations and respects the sanctity[29] of his agreements in and with a world of neighbors.

17. **If I read the temper of our people correctly, we now realize as we have never realized before our interdependence on each other; that we can not merely take but we must give as well; that if we are to go forward, we must move as a trained and loyal army willing to sacrifice for the good of a common discipline, because without such discipline no progress is made, no leadership becomes effective.** We are, I know, ready and willing to submit our lives and property to such discipline, because it makes possible a leadership which aims at a larger good. This I propose to offer, pledging that the larger purposes will bind upon us all as a sacred obligation with a unity of duty hitherto[30] evoked only in time of armed strife.

18. With this pledge taken, I assume unhesitatingly the leadership of this great army of our people dedicated to a disciplined attack upon our common problems.

19. Action in this image and to this end is feasible under the form of government which we have inherited from our ancestors. Our Constitution is so simple and practical that it is possible always to meet extraordinary needs by changes in emphasis and arrangement without loss of essential form. That is why our constitutional system has proved itself the most superbly enduring political mechanism the modern world has produced. It has met every stress of vast expansion of territory, of foreign wars, of bitter internal strife[31], of world relations.

20. It is to be hoped that the normal balance of executive and legislative authority may be wholly adequate to meet the unprecedented task before us. But it may be that an unprecedented demand and need for undelayed action may call for temporary departure from that normal balance of public procedure.

21. I am prepared under my constitutional duty to recommend the measures that a stricken nation in the midst of[32] a stricken world may require. These measures, or such other measures as the Congress may build out of its experience and wisdom, I shall seek, within my constitutional authority, to bring to speedy adoption.

22. **But in the event that[33] the Congress shall fail to take one of these two courses, and in the event that the national emergency is still critical, I shall not evade the clear course of duty that will then confront me.** I shall ask the Congress for the one remaining instrument to meet the crisis—broad Executive power to wage a war against the emergency[34], as great as the power that would be given to me if we were in fact invaded by a foreign foe.

23. For the trust reposed[35]in me I will return the courage and the devotion that befit the time. I can do no less.

24.We face the arduous[36] days that lie before us in the warm courage of the national unity; with the clear consciousness of seeking old and precious moral values; with the clean satisfaction that comes from the stern performance of duty by old and young alike. We aim at the assurance of a rounded and permanent national life.

25.We do not distrust the future of essential democracy. The people of the United States have not failed. In their need they have registered a mandate[37] that they want direct, vigorous action. They have asked for discipline and direction under leadership. They have made me the present instrument of their wishes. In the spirit of the gift I take it.

26. In this dedication of a Nation we humbly ask the blessing of God. May He[38] protect each and every one of us. May He guide me in the days to come. (1,902 words)

Notes to the Speech

1. induction [in'dʌkʃən] *n.* a procedure or ceremony for introducing someone to a new job, organization, or way of life 入门；就职仪式
2. candor ['kændə] *n.* the quality of speaking honestly and openly about things 直率；直言不讳
3. preeminently [priː'eminəntli] *adv.* 卓越地，超群地
4. revive [ri'vaiv] *v.* become active, popular, or successful again; become conscious again 恢复；复兴；使苏醒
5. curtailment [kəː'teilmənt] *n.* the act of reducing or limiting 缩减，缩短
6. the withered leaves of industrial enterprise：工业企业枯萎的落叶

wither ['wiðə] *v.* dry up and die; become weak 枯萎，凋谢；衰弱，凋敝

7. a host of：许多，一大群
8. toil [tɔil] *v.* work very hard doing unpleasant or tiring tasks 苦干，辛苦劳动
9. peril ['peril] *n.* great danger 危险
10. bounty ['baunti] *n.* something that is provided in large amounts 慷慨，丰富
11. languish ['læŋgwiʃ] *v.* be forced to remain and suffer in an unpleasant situation（被迫）受苦，受折磨
12. abdicate ['æbdikeit] *v.* give up the position of being king or queen; refuse to be responsible for something 退位；放弃（责任），失职
13. unscrupulous [ʌn'skru:pjuləs] *adj.* behaving in an unfair or dishonest way 不诚实的，不道德的
14. indict [in'dait] *v.* <law, especially American English> officially charge someone with a criminal offence 控告，起诉，告发
15. strip [strip] *v.* remove something that is covering the surface of something else; take away something important from someone as a punishment 剥去；剥夺
16. exhortation [ˌegzɔ:'teiʃən, ˌeksɔ:-] *n.* the act of trying very hard to persuade someone to do something 劝诫；劝告
17. perish ['periʃ] *v.* <formal or literary> die, especially in a terrible or sudden way 死亡；毁灭
18. evanescent [ˌi:və'nesnt] *adj.* quickly fading; soon disappearing from memory 迅速消失的；不久便淡忘的
19. minister ['ministə] *v.* give help to someone who needs it, especially someone who is sick or old 辅助；帮助
20. callous ['kæləs] *adj.* not caring that other people are suffering 铁石心肠的，无情的
21. small wonder：难怪，不足为奇
22. foreclosure [fɔ:'kləuʒə(r)] *n.* 丧失抵押品赎回权；排斥
23. forthwith [ˌfɔ:θ'wiθ] *adv.* <formal> immediately 立刻，立即
24. resumption [ri'zʌmpʃən] *n.* <formal> the act of starting an activity again after stopping or being interrupted 恢复，重新开始
25. speculation [ˌspekju'leiʃən] *n.* an investment that is very risky but could yield great profits; the act of making guesses about its nature or identity or about what might happen 投机；猜测
26. address oneself to：<formal> direct one's attention or efforts to 致力于；着手
27. outgo [aut'gəu] *n.* money paid out 支出；消耗

28. manifestation [ˌmænifes'teiʃən] *n.* <formal> the act of showing or making clear and plain 表明，显示
29. sanctity ['sæŋktiti] *n.* holiness; sacredness 神圣；庄严；不可侵犯
30. hitherto [ˌhiðə'tuː] *adv.* <formal> until this/that time; up until now 迄今，至今，到目前为止
31. bitter internal strife：激烈的内战
    strife [straif] *n.* strong disagreement or fighting 严重不和；争斗
32. in the midst of：在……之中
33. in the event that：如果，万一；在……情况下
34. wage a war against the emergency：向非常情况开战
    wage [weidʒ] *v.* be involved in a war against someone, or a fight against something 进行，发动
35. repose [ri'pəuz] *v.* lie or be placed on; place on 休息；安放
36. arduous ['ɑːdjuəs] *adj.* involving a lot of strength and effort 努力的，费力的
37. mandate ['mændeit] *n.* the right and power given to a government, or any body of people chosen to represent others, to act according to the wishes of those who voted for it 授权，委任
38. He [hiː; hi] *n.* God 上帝

❑ Appreciating the Speech

富兰克林·德拉诺·罗斯福的这篇就职演说通篇洋溢着乐观 (optimistic)、进取 (enterprising)、坚定 (firm)、执著 (persistent)、务实 (pragmatic) 的精神，富有强烈的感染力和号召力 (strong appeal and charisma)，堪称演说中的典范 (example or paradigm)。在就职演说中，罗斯福首先鼓励美国人民勇敢面对眼前的困难 (face the present difficulties courageously)，强调 (emphasize or highlight) 精神的力量。他以“我们唯一害怕的就是害怕本身” (the only thing we have to fear is fear itself) 这样的铿锵话语，掷地有声地给美国人民打气，呼吁大家摆脱恐惧心理 (get rid of fear)，恢复自信心 (restore the confidence)，果断行动以应付危机 (take decisive actions to cope with crisis)。他宣布推行“新政” (the new deal)，其核心内容 (core content) 是复兴 (recovery)、救济 (relief)、改革 (reform)，主要包括整顿金融秩序 (rectify financial order)，增加公共开支 (increase public expenditure)，加强竞争力 (strengthen the competitiveness) 等政策，帮助美国摆脱经济危机 (get rid of the economic crisis)。其次，在外交 (diplomatic) 方面，他提出“睦邻政策” (the policy of good neighbor)，决心尊重自己与邻国的权

利与义务 (respect the rights and obligations of his own country and the neighboring country)，力图缓和美国与拉丁美洲各国之间的紧张关系 (attempt to ease the tension between America and the countries in Latin America)。最后他号召全国民众协同努力 (concerted effort) 以实现政治抱负和国家富强 (to realize the political aspiration and national prosperity)。

从语言上来讲，这篇演讲最突出的特点是排比 (parallelism) 的大量运用。这种修辞手法既能起到突出演说主题 (highlight the theme of the speech) 的作用，又能令句子流畅，读起来朗朗上口，使演讲极具感染力。例如在第 8 段最后一句号召国民增强信心 (call on the citizens to boost their confidence) 时连用了 5 个 "on..." 结构；第 11 段中提及完成对人口重新分配，为最善于利用土地的人提供更好地利用土地的条件时，用了 5 个 "It can be helped by..." 结构；第 12 段中谈及防止旧秩序的弊病卷土重来时，连用了 3 个 "there must be" 结构；第 25 段中谈到美国人民并没有失败时，连用了 3 个 "they have..." 结构。这些排比结构的使用突出强调作用，颇具感召力和鼓动性。另外演说中还有很多富于真理 (truth) 和人生哲理 (life philosophy) 的句子，比如 "When there is no vision the people perish."（如果没有远见，一个民族就要灭亡）。还有 "Happiness lies not in the mere possession of money; it lies in the joy of achievement, in the thrill of creative effort"（幸福不仅仅在于对金钱的拥有，它源于取得成就时的喜悦及创造性努力带来的激动）。这样的句子有很多，发人深省 (thought-provoking)，可成为读者工作、学习、生活中的座右铭 (motto)。

❑ Culture Links

（1）大萧条与"罗斯福新政"

大萧条 (Great Depression) 是指 1929 年至 1933 年之间的全球性经济大衰退，它发端于美国，影响比历史上任何一次经济衰退都要深远。这次经济萧条是以农产品价格下跌为起点，农业衰退由于金融的大崩溃而进一步恶化，尤其在美国，一股投机热导致大量资金从欧洲抽回，随后在 1929 年 10 月发生了令人恐慌的华尔街股市暴跌。随着股票市场的崩溃，美国经济随即全面陷入毁灭性的灾难之中，可怕的连锁反应很快发生：疯狂挤兑、银行倒闭、工厂关门、工人失业、贫困来临、有组织的抵抗。农业资本家和大农场主大量销毁"过剩"的产品，用小麦和玉米替代煤炭做燃料，把牛奶倒进密西西比河，使这条河变成"银河" (Milky Way)。资本的短缺，在所有的工业化国家中都带来了出口和国内消费的锐减：没有市场必然使工厂关闭；货物越少，货物运输也就越少，这必然会危害船运业和造船业。

在所有国家中，经济衰退的后果是大规模人口失业：美国 1 370 万，德国 560 万，英国 280 万（1932 年的最大数据）。这次经济危机很快从美国蔓延到其他工业国家。大萧条也造成了严重的社会问题：大萧条期间约有 200 万 ~400 万中学生辍学，许多人忍受不了生理和心理的痛苦而自杀，社会治安日益恶化。

由于大萧条的普遍影响，各国为维护本国利益，加强贸易保护的措施和手段，提高政府对经济的政策参与性，其中很富成效的如罗斯福新政时期实行的一些经济政策及建立的一些监管机构。“罗斯福新政”（The New Deal）是指 1933 年富兰克林·罗斯福就任美国总统后所实行的一系列经济政策，其核心是 3 个 R：救济（Relief）、改革（Reform）和复兴（Recovery），因此有时也被称为“3R 新政”。

“罗斯福新政”的主要内容包括：（1）举办救济和公共工程（例如公共事业振兴署、田纳西河谷管理局兴办的一些基建项目）。（2）整顿银行业，克服金融危机。新政从整顿银行开始，罗斯福在就职的第三天下令所有银行停业整顿。3 月 9 日，国会通过《紧急银行法》。该法的实施使银行与金融秩序恢复了正常，人们恢复了对银行的信心。（3）恢复工业与农业的生产。1933 年 5 月，国会通过《农业调整法》和《国家产业复兴法》，政府用行政手段调节农业生产，减少农产品过剩、保证农民利益；并将生产的各个环节置于国家监督之下，以减少盲目生产；并由国家干预，调节企业关系和劳资关系，对农业复苏起到积极作用，为企业复兴创造良好条件。（4）保护劳工权利，制定最低工资和最高工时规定。出台《联邦紧急救济法》并成立联邦紧急救济署，此后又将救济改成“以工代赈”，解决失业问题。（5）建立社会保障体系。通过一系列社保法规，同时推动工会建设。

“罗斯福新政”恢复了公众对美国政治制度的信心，强化了联邦政府机构。“新政”中采取的一系列经济政策以增加政府对经济直接或间接干预的方式大大缓解了大萧条所带来的经济危机与社会矛盾，缓解了美国在内政和外交上的严重困难，并由此使美国的工业、农业逐渐全面恢复。在罗斯福第一个任期结束的 1936 年，美国国民收入增幅达到 50%。因此，罗斯福在 1936 年再次当选总统，也就不足为怪了。

（2）罗斯福与美国社会保障制度

1932 年在经济危机的背景之下，罗斯福以“新政”为口号赢得了大选，美国进入了罗斯福时代。罗斯福政府颁布《社会保障法》作为美国第一个全国性的由联邦政府承担义务的社会保障立法。《社会保障法》可以说在“新政”社会保障政策中最具有深远影响和奠基作用。它于 1935 年 8 月 14 日出台，为美国的社会保障政策提供了法律依据，其内容主要以失业保险、养老保险和社会救济为主。

因为社会保障维系到社会稳定和经济安全，“弱势群体”面对生存的考验，急需政府进行强有力的社会保障。另一方面，社会保障制度的建立也与罗斯福的个人因素有着密切的关系。罗斯福正值壮年时得了骨髓炎，再加上医疗不当导致他腰部以下瘫痪，以至于他后半生在行走中一直需要人扶持，两腿还得装上笨重的钢撑架。由于他是一个身体残疾的人，因此罗斯福对“弱势群体”有着强烈的个人情感，对“弱势群体”也比较关注。在经济大危机中，他采取“抑富济贫”的方式，使得穷人的生存环境得到改善。罗斯福认为联邦政府应该承担起保障人们生活的责任，他的主张为《社会保障法》的制订提供了理论依据。1941年在《四大自由论》中，罗斯福强调“与我们社会经济有关的许多问题和要求需要立即得到改善”，例如：应该使更多的人享受养老金和失业保险；应该扩大医疗保健制度；应该建立更好的制度，使能够并且需要从事有酬工作的人得到工作。

罗斯福政府开创了国家干预经济、社会生活的新模式，成功地为美国社会保障制度的发展和完善奠定了基础，使美国福利在远远落后于一些西欧发达国家的情况下形成了具有自己特色的保障制度，对于维护社会稳定和促进社会的发展具有重大影响。

当然，在美国有很多人，尤其是作为社会中坚的中产阶级群体，并不赞同政府扩大社会福利的趋向。他们的逻辑很简单：美国的体制给个人奋斗提供了平等的机会，政府应该尽量不干预、少干预；过度发达的社会福利和救济体系，一方面会扩大政府的公权力，另一方面会增加吃大锅饭的懒汉，从而加重了辛苦地工作着的纳税人的负担。美国人爱强调的是，美国保障的是“追求幸福的权利”和“机会的平等”，而非“幸福的权利”和“平等的幸福”。

❑ Questions Concerning the Speech

1. What's the firm belief President Roosevelt asserted at the beginning of the speech ?
2. What do the common difficulties in the second paragraph refer to?
3. Does the distress of American people come from the failure of substance? Why?
4. What's the greatest primary task of Roosevelt government to restore the nation?
5. What are the two safeguards that are required against a return of the evils of the old order?
6. What are some of the specific means of national recovery Roosevelt proposes?
7. How do you understand Roosevelt's foreign policy?
8. Under what situation will not President Roosevelt evade the clear course of duty that will confront him?

❑ Paraphrase the Following Sentences

1. I am certain that my fellow Americans expect that on my induction into the Presidency I will address them with a candor and a decision which the present situation of our Nation impels.
2. Nature still offers her bounty and human efforts have multiplied it. Plenty is at our doorstep, but a generous use of it languishes in the very sight of the supply.

3. Stripped of the lure of profit by which to induce our people to follow their false leadership, they have resorted to exhortations, pleading tearfully for restored confidence.
4. These dark days will be worth all they cost us if they teach us that our true destiny is not to be ministered unto but to minister to ourselves and to our fellow men.
5. Through this program of action we address ourselves to putting our own national house in order and making income balance outgo.
6. But it may be that an unprecedented demand and need for undelayed action may call for temporary departure from that normal balance of public procedure.
7. But in the event that the Congress shall fail to take one of these two courses, and in the event that the national emergency is still critical, I shall not evade the clear course of duty that will then confront me.

❑ Questions for Discussion

1. 幸福是由物质财富决定吗？请说明幸福与物质财富的关系并给出理由。
2. 罗斯福在演讲中有句名言“我们唯一不得不害怕的就是害怕本身”。你是如何理解的？你赞同这种说法吗？为什么？
3. 30 年代爆发的经济危机产生了巨大的破坏性影响。试论导致 30 年代经济危机的根本原因是什么，它对我们当今社会有什么启示？

❑ Translation

富兰克林·罗斯福：首任就职演讲

1933 年 3 月 4 日，华盛顿特区

1. 今天，对我们的国家来说，是一个神圣的日子。我肯定，同胞们都期待我在就任总统时，会像我国目前形势所要求的那样，坦率而果断地向他们讲话。现在正是坦白、勇敢地说出实话，说出全部实话的最好时刻。我们不必畏首畏尾，不老老实实面对我国今天的情况。这个伟大的国家会一如既往地坚持下去，它会复兴和繁荣起来。因此，让我首先表明我的坚定信念：我们唯一不得不害怕的就是害怕本身——一种莫名其妙、丧失理智的、毫无根据的恐惧，它把人转退为进所需的种种努力化为泡影。凡在我国生活阴云密布的时刻，坦率而有活力的领导都得到过人民的理解和支持，从而为胜利准备了必不可少的条件。我相信，在目前的危急时刻，大家会再次给予同样的支持。
2. 我和你们都要以这种精神，来面对我们共同的困难。感谢上帝，这些困难只是物质方

面的。价值难以想象地萎缩了；课税增加了；我们的支付能力下降了；各级政府面临着严重的收入短缺；交换手段在贸易过程中遭到了冻结；工业企业枯萎的落叶到处可见；农场主的产品找不到销路；千家万户多年的积蓄付之东流。

3. 更重要的是，大批失业公民正面临严峻的生存问题，还有大批公民正以艰辛的劳动换取微薄的报酬。只有愚蠢的乐天派会否认当前这些阴暗的现实。

4. 但是，我们的苦恼绝不是因为缺乏物资。我们没有遭到什么蝗虫的灾害。我们的先辈曾以信念和无畏一次次转危为安，比起他们经历过的险阻，我们仍大可感到欣慰。大自然仍在给予我们恩惠，人类的努力已使之倍增。富足的情景近在咫尺，但就在我们见到这种情景的时候，宽裕的生活却悄然离去。这主要是因为主宰人类物资交换的统治者们失败了，他们固执己见而又无能为力，因而已经认定失败了，并撒手不管了。贪得无厌的货币兑换商的种种行径将受到舆论法庭的起诉，将受到人类心灵理智的唾弃。

5. 是的，他们是努力过，然而他们用的是一种完全过时的方法。面对信贷的失败，他们只是提议借出更多的钱。当利润失去了吸引力，不能再引诱人民追随他们的错误引导时，他们只得求助于规劝，泪流满面地恳求人们恢复信心。他们只知自我追求者们的处世规则。他们没有远见，而没有远见的民族是要灭亡的。

6. 如今，货币兑换商已从我们文明庙堂的高处落荒而逃。我们要以千古不变的真理来重建这座庙宇。至于能恢复到什么程度，则取决于我们如何运用比金钱利益更高尚的社会价值观。

7. 幸福并不在于单纯地占有金钱；幸福还在于取得成就后的喜悦，在于创造性努力时的激情。务必不能再忘记劳动带来的喜悦和激励，而去疯狂地追逐那转瞬即逝的利润。如果这些暗淡的时日能使我们认识到，我们真正的天命不是要别人侍奉，而是为自己和同胞们服务，那么我们付出的代价就完全是值得的。

8. 认识到把物质财富当做成功的标准是错误的，我们就会抛弃以地位尊严和个人收益为唯一标准，来衡量公职和高级政治地位的错误信念；我们必须制止银行界和企业界的一种行为，它常常使神圣的委托混同于无情和自私的不正当行为。难怪信心在减弱，信心只有靠诚实、信誉、忠心维护和无私履行职责。而没有这些，就不可能有信心。

9. 然而，复兴不仅仅只要改变伦理观念。这个国家要求行动起来，现在就行动起来。

10. 我们最大、最基本的任务是让人民投入工作。只要我们英明、勇敢地去面对，这个问题就可以解决。这可以部分由政府直接招募完成，就像对待临战的紧要关头一样。但同时，通过这种招募，我们能通过促进和重组我们对自然资源的使用，来组成一些非常需要的工程。

11. 我们齐心协力，但必须坦白地承认工业中心的人口失衡，我们必须在全国范围内重新分配，使土地在最适合的人手中发挥更大的作用。明确地为提高农产品价值并以此购买城市产品所做的努力，会有助于任务的完成。避免许多小家庭业、农场业被取消赎取抵押品的权利的悲剧也有助于任务的完成。坚决主张联邦、州及地方政府立即对大幅度地削减开支的要求采取行动，有助于任务的完成。将现在常常是分散不经济、不平等的救济活动统一起来有助于任务的完成。对所有公共交通运输、通信及其他涉及公众生活的设施作全国性的计划及监督有助于任务的完成。许多事情都有助于任务完成，但这些决不包括空谈。我们必须行动，而且立即行动。

12. 最后，为了重新开始工作，我们需要两手防御，来抗御旧秩序恶魔卷土重来；一定要有严格监督银行业、信贷及投资的机制；一定要杜绝投机；一定要有充足而健康的货币供应。

13. 以上这些，朋友们，就是施政方针。我要在特别会议上敦促新国会给予详细实施方案，并且，我会立即向各州寻求支援。

14. 通过行动，我们将予以我们自己一个有秩序的国家大厦，使收入大于支出。我们的国际贸易，虽然很重要，但现在在时间和必要性上，次于对本国健康经济的建立。我建议，作为可行的策略、首要事务先行。虽然我将不遗余力地通过国际经济重新协调所来恢复国际贸易，但我认为国内的紧急情况无法等待这重新协调的完成。

15. 指导这一特别的全国性复苏的基本思想并非狭隘的国家主义。我首先考虑的是坚持美国这一整体中各部分的相互依赖性——这是对美国式的开拓精神的古老而永恒的证明的体现。这才是复苏之路，是即时之路，是保证复苏功效持久之路。

16. 在国际政策领域，我将使美国采取睦邻政策。做一个决心自重，因此而尊重邻国的国家。做一个履行义务，尊重与他国协约的国家。

17. 如果我对本国人民的情绪了解正确的话，我想我们已认识到了我们从未认识的问题，我们是互相依存的，我们不可以只索取，我们还必须奉献。我们前进时，必须像一支训练有素的忠诚的军队，愿意为共同的原则而献身。因为，没有这些原则，就无法取得进步，领导就不可能得力。我知道，我们都准备好了并愿意为此原则献出生命和财产，因为这将使政府能够领导人民朝着更大的幸福目标迈进。我将提供这样的领导，保证这些伟大的目标如同一项神圣的义务把我们所有人团结起来，迄今为止，这种责任感仅仅在战争时期才能被唤起。

18. 有了这样的誓言，我将毫不犹豫地承担领导伟大人民大军的任务，致力于对我们普遍问题的强攻。

19. 这样的行动，这样的目标，在我们从祖先那里继承的政府形式中是可行的。我们的宪法如此简单，实在。它随时可以应付特殊情况，只需对重点和安排加以修改而不丧失中心思想，正因为如此，我们的宪法体制已自证为是最有适应性的政治体制。它已应付过巨大的国土扩张、外战、内乱及国际关系所带来的压力。

20. 我们希望行政部门与司法部门的正常平衡会足以应对我们所面临的史无前例的重任。然而史无前例的要求和立刻行动的必要也可能要求我们暂时背离公共程序上的正常平衡（指三权分立）。

21. 根据宪法赋予我的职责，我准备提出一些措施，在一个危难世界中的一个危难民族，也许需要这些措施。对于这些措施，以及国会根据本身的经验和智能可能制订的这类其他措施，我将在宪法赋予我的权限内，设法予以迅速的采纳。
22. 但是，如果国会拒不采纳这两条路线中的一条，如果国家紧急情况依然如故，我将不回避我所面临的明确的尽职方向。我将要求国会准许我使用唯一剩下的手段来应付危机——向非常情况开战的广泛的行政权，就像我们真的遭到外敌入侵时授予我那样的广泛权力。
23. 对大家给予我的信任，我将以时代所要求的勇气和献身精神予以回报。我会竭尽全力。
24. 让我们正视面前的严峻岁月，怀着举国一致给我们带来的热情和勇气，怀着寻求传统的、珍贵的道德观念的明确意识，怀着老老少少都能通过恪尽职守而得到的问心无愧的满足。我们的目标是要保证国民生活的圆满和长治久安。
25. 我们并不怀疑基本民主制度的未来。合众国人民并没有失败。他们在困难中表达了自己的委托，即要求采取直接而有力的行动。他们要求有领导的纪律和方向。他们现在选择我作为实现他们的愿望的工具。我接受这一重托。
26. 在此举国奉献之际，我们谦卑地请求上帝赐福。愿上帝保佑我们大家和每一个人，愿上帝在未来的日子里指引我。

8

Franklin D. Roosevelt: The Four Freedoms

Delivered 6 January, 1941, in Washington, D.C.

❑ About the Speech

1941年1月6日，罗斯福在他致国会的年度咨文中表达了美国对不断扩大的国际冲突的反应，要求国会提供必要的武器装备给那些其防御对美国利益至关重要的国家。

就在发表这篇演讲的几个月前，随着德国纳粹的入侵，法国落入了希特勒之手。在罗斯福发表这篇演讲的同时，英国正积极抵抗纳粹的空袭。在那几个月里，英国军事很有可能崩溃。在这篇演说中，罗斯福为积极援助美国的盟国做了舆论准备。他也努力通过中立立法使美国不参与到欧洲战争，同时使那些受战争威胁和攻击的国家变强大。他的目标是使美国成为能给盟国提供军事装备的“民主国家的兵工厂”。1941年3月，国会通过了《租借法案》给那些反抗德国纳粹的国家提供援助。

在这篇演说中，罗斯福提出了著名的“四大自由论”——言论与表达意见的自由；每个人以自己的方式崇拜上帝的自由；免于匮乏的自由；免于恐惧的自由。“四大自由”是罗斯福在法西斯势力步步紧逼、威胁到美国生存的情况下提出的，它从言论、信仰、经济和安全方面阐释了人的基本权利，旨在调动美国及世界各国人民参与反法西斯战争的积极性。作为一种信仰和理念，“四大自由”丰富并创造性地发展了美国传统中的自由民主思想，有助于确立美国在世界反法西斯战争中的领导地位。罗斯福强调指出，这些自由应在全球范围内得到保障：它们将成为一个安定的国际秩序的基础。

总之，罗斯福的此次演讲在美国历史上具有极其重要的意义，尤其是“四大自由论”，被认为是美国人民准备为之奋斗的原则的最简要声明。

❑ The Speech in Full

Mr. President, Mr. Speaker, members of the 77th Congress:

1. I address you, the members of this new Congress, at a moment unprecedented[1] in the history of the union. I use the word "unprecedented" because at no previous time has American security been as seriously threatened from without as it is today.

2. Since the permanent formation of our government under the Constitution in 1789, most of the periods of crisis in our history have related to our domestic affairs. And, fortunately, only one of these—the four-year war between the States—ever threatened our national unity. Today, thank God, 130,000,000 Americans in 48 States have forgotten points of the compass[2] in our national unity.

3. It is true that prior to 1914 the United States often has been disturbed by events in other continents. We have even engaged in two wars with European nations and in a number of undeclared wars in the West Indies, in the Mediterranean and in the Pacific, for the maintenance of American rights and for the principles of peaceful commerce. But in no case had a serious threat been raised against our national safety or our continued independence.

4. What I seek to convey is the historic truth that the United States as a nation has at all times maintained opposition—clear, definite opposition—to any attempt to lock us in behind an ancient Chinese wall while the procession[3] of civilization went past. Today, thinking of our children and of their children, we oppose enforced isolation for ourselves or for any other part of the Americas.

5. That determination of ours, extending over all these years, was proved, for example, in the early days during the quarter century of wars following the French Revolution.

6. While the Napoleonic struggles did threaten interests of the United States because

of the French foothold[4] in the West Indies and in Louisiana, and while we engaged in the War of 1812 to vindicate[5] our right to peaceful trade, it is nevertheless clear that neither France nor Great Britain nor any other nation was aiming at domination of the whole world.

7. And in like fashion, from 1815 to 1914—ninety-nine years—no single war in Europe or in Asia constituted a real threat against our future or against the future of any other American nation.

8. Except in the Maximilian interlude[6] in Mexico, no foreign power sought to establish itself in this hemisphere[7]. And the strength of the British fleet in the Atlantic has been a friendly strength; it is still a friendly strength.

9. Even when the World War broke out in 1914, it seemed to contain only small threat of danger to our own American future. But as time went on, as we remember, the American people began to visualize[8] what the downfall of democratic nations might mean to our own democracy.

10. We need not overemphasize imperfections in the peace of Versailles. We need not harp[9] on failure of the democracies to deal with problems of world reconstruction. We should remember that the peace of 1919 was far less unjust than the kind of pacification[10] which began even before Munich, and which is being carried on under the new order of tyranny[11] that seeks to spread over every continent today. The American people have unalterably[12] set their faces against that tyranny.

11. I suppose that every realist knows that the democratic way of life is at this moment being directly assailed[13] in every part of the world—assailed either by arms or by secret spreading of poisonous propaganda[14] by those who seek to destroy unity and promote discord[15] in nations that are still at peace.

12. During 16 long months this assault has blotted out the whole pattern of democratic life[16] in an appalling[17] number of independent nations, great and small. And the assailants are still on the march, threatening other nations, great and small.

13. Therefore, as your President, performing my constitutional duty to "give to the

Congress information of the state of the union," I find it unhappily necessary to report that the future and the safety of our country and of our democracy are overwhelmingly involved in events far beyond our borders.

14. Armed defense of democratic existence is now being gallantly[18] waged in four continents. If that defense fails, all the population and all the resources of Europe and Asia, and Africa and Austral-Asia will be dominated by conquerors. And let us remember that the total of those populations in those four continents, the total of those populations and their resources greatly exceed the sum total of the population and the resources of the whole of the Western Hemisphere—yes, many times over.

15. In times like these it is immature—and, incidentally, untrue—for anybody to brag that an unprepared America, single-handed and with one hand tied behind its back, can hold off the whole world.

16. No realistic American can expect from a dictator's peace international generosity, or return of true independence, or world disarmament[19], or freedom of expression, or freedom of religion—or even good business. Such a peace would bring no security for us or for our neighbors. Those who would give up essential liberty to purchase a little temporary safety deserve neither liberty nor safety.

17. **As a nation we may take pride in the fact that we are soft-hearted; but we cannot afford to be soft-headed. We must always be wary of those who with sounding brass[20] and a tinkling cymbal[21] preach[22] the "ism" of appeasement[23]. We must especially beware of that small group of selfish men who would clip the wings of the American eagle[24] in order to feather their own nests.**

18. I have recently pointed out how quickly the tempo of modern warfare could bring into our very midst the physical attack which we must eventually expect if the dictator nations win this war.

19. There is much loose talk[25] of our immunity from immediate and direct invasion from across the seas. Obviously, as long as the British Navy retains its power, no such danger exists. Even if there were no British Navy, it is not probable that any enemy

would be stupid enough to attack us by landing troops in the United States from across thousands of miles of ocean, until it had acquired strategic bases from which to operate.

20. But we learn much from the lessons of the past years in Europe—particularly the lesson of Norway, whose essential seaports were captured by treachery[26] and surprise built up over a series of years. The first phase of the invasion of this hemisphere would not be the landing of regular troops. The necessary strategic points would be occupied by secret agents and by their dupes[27]—and great numbers of them are already here and in Latin America. As long as the aggressor nations maintain the offensive they, not we, will choose the time and the place and the method of their attack.

21. **And that is why the future of all the American Republics is today in serious danger. That is why this annual message to the Congress is unique in our history. That is why every member of the executive branch of the government and every member of the Congress face great responsibility, great accountability[28]. The need of the moment is that our actions and our policy should be devoted primarily—almost exclusively—to meeting this foreign peril. For all our domestic problems are now a part of the great emergency.**

22. **Just as our national policy in internal affairs has been based upon a decent respect for the rights and the dignity of all our fellow men within our gates, so our national policy in foreign affairs has been based on a decent respect for the rights and the dignity of all nations, large and small. And the justice of morality must and will win in the end.**

23. Our national policy is this: First, by an impressive expression of the public will and without regard to partisanship[29], we are committed to all-inclusive[30] national defense. Secondly, by an impressive expression of the public will and without regard to partisanship, we are committed to full support of all those resolute[31] people everywhere who are resisting aggression and are thereby keeping war away from our hemisphere. By this support we express our determination that the democratic cause shall prevail, and we strengthen the defense and the security of our own nation. Third, by an impressive expression of the public will and without regard to partisanship, we are committed to the proposition[32]that principles of morality and considerations for our own security

will never permit us to acquiesce[33] in a peace dictated by aggressors and sponsored by appeasers. We know that enduring peace cannot be bought at the cost of other people's freedom.

24. In the recent national election there was no substantial difference between the two great parties in respect to that national policy. No issue was fought out on this line before the American electorate[34]. And today it is abundantly evident that American citizens everywhere are demanding and supporting speedy and complete action in recognition of obvious danger.Therefore, the immediate need is a swift and driving increase in our armament production.

25. Leaders of industry and labor have responded to our summons[35]. Goals of speed have been set. In some cases these goals are being reached ahead of time. In some cases we are on schedule; in other cases there are slight but not serious delays. And in some cases—and, I am sorry to say, very important cases—we are all concerned by the slowness of the accomplishment of our plans.

26. The Army and Navy[36], however, have made substantial progress during the past year. Actual experience is improving and speeding up our methods of production with every passing day. And today's best is not good enough for tomorrow.

27. I am not satisfied with the progress thus far made. The men in charge of the program represent the best in training, in ability, and in patriotism. They are not satisfied with the progress thus far made. None of us will be satisfied until the job is done. No matter whether the original goal was set too high or too low, our objective is quicker and better results.

28. To give you two illustrations: We are behind schedule in turning out finished airplanes. We are working day and night to solve the innumerable[37] problems and to catch up. We are ahead of schedule in building warships, but we are working to get even further ahead of that schedule.

29. To change a whole nation from a basis of peacetime production of implements of peace to a basis of wartime production of implements of war is no small task. And the

greatest difficulty comes at the beginning of the program, when new tools, new plant facilities, new assembly lines, new shipways must first be constructed before the actual material begins to flow steadily and speedily from them.

30. The Congress of course, must rightly keep itself informed at all times of the progress of the program. However, there is certain information, as the Congress itself will readily recognize, which, in the interests of our own security and those of the nations that we are supporting, must of needs[38] be kept in confidence.

31. New circumstances are constantly begetting[39] new needs for our safety. I shall ask this Congress for greatly increased new appropriations[40] and authorizations to carry on what we have begun.

32. I also ask this Congress for authority and for funds sufficient to manufacture additional munitions[41] and war supplies of many kinds, to be turned over to those nations which are now in actual war with aggressor nations. Our most useful and immediate role is to act as an arsenal[42] for them as well as for ourselves. They do not need manpower, but they do need billions of dollars' worth of the weapons of defense.

33. The time is near when they will not be able to pay for them all in ready cash. We cannot, and we will not, tell them that they must surrender merely because of present inability to pay for the weapons which we know they must have.

34. I do not recommend that we make them a loan of dollars with which to pay for these weapons—a loan to be repaid in dollars. I recommend that we make it possible for those nations to continue to obtain war materials in the United States, fitting their orders into our own program. And nearly all of their material would, if the time ever came, be useful in our own defense.

35. Taking counsel of expert military and naval authorities, considering what is best for our own security, we are free to decide how much should be kept here and how much should be sent abroad to our friends who, by their determined and heroic resistance, are giving us time in which to make ready our own defense.

36. For what we send abroad we shall be repaid, repaid within a reasonable time

following the close of hostilities, repaid in similar materials, or at our option in other goods of many kinds which they can produce and which we need.

37. **Let us say to the democracies: "We Americans are vitally concerned in your defense of freedom. We are putting forth our energies, our resources, and our organizing powers to give you the strength to regain and maintain a free world. We shall send you in ever-increasing numbers, ships, planes, tanks, guns. That is our purpose and our pledge."**

38. In fulfillment of this purpose we will not be intimidated by the threats of dictators that they will regard as a breach of international law or as an act of war our aid to the democracies which dare to resist their aggression. Such aid—Such aid is not an act of war, even if a dictator should unilaterally[43] proclaim[44] it so to be.

39. And when the dictators—if the dictators—are ready to make war upon us, they will not wait for an act of war on our part.

40. They did not wait for Norway or Belgium or the Netherlands to commit an act of war. Their only interest is in a new one-way international law, which lacks mutuality in its observance and therefore becomes an instrument of oppression. The happiness of future generations of Americans may well depend on how effective and how immediate we can make our aid felt. No one can tell the exact character of the emergency situations that we may be called upon to meet. The nation's hands must not be tied when the nation's life is in danger.

41. Yes, and we must prepare, all of us prepare, to make the sacrifices that the emergency—almost as serious as war itself—demands. Whatever stands in the way of speed and efficiency in defense, in defense preparations of any kind, must give way to the national need.

42. **A free nation has the right to expect full cooperation from all groups. A free nation has the right to look to the leaders of business, of labor, and of agriculture to take the lead in stimulating effort, not among other groups but within their own group.**

43. The best way of dealing with the few slackers[45] or trouble-makers in our midst is, first, to shame them by patriotic example, and if that fails, to use the sovereignty[46] of government to save government.

44. **As men do not live by bread alone, they do not fight by armaments alone. Those who man our defenses and those behind them who build our defenses must have the stamina[47] and the courage which come from unshakable belief in the manner of life which they are defending. The mighty action that we are calling for cannot be based on a disregard of all the things worth fighting for.**

45. The nation takes great satisfaction and much strength from the things which have been done to make its people conscious of their individual stake[48] in the preservation of democratic life in America. Those things have toughened the fiber[49] of our people, have renewed their faith and strengthened their devotion to the institutions we make ready to protect.

46. Certainly this is no time for any of us to stop thinking about the social and economic problems which are the root cause of the social revolution which is today a supreme factor in the world. For there is nothing mysterious about the foundations of a healthy and strong democracy. The basic things expected by our people of their political and economic systems are simple. They are: Equality of opportunity for youth and for others; jobs for those who can work; security for those who need it; the ending of special privilege for the few; the preservation of civil liberties for all; the enjoyment of the fruits of scientific progress in a wider and constantly rising standard of living. These are the simple, the basic things that must never be lost sight of in the turmoil[50] and unbelievable complexity of our modern world. The inner and abiding strength of our economic and political systems is dependent upon the degree to which they fulfill these expectations.

47. **Many subjects connected with our social economy call for immediate improvement. As examples:**

We should bring more citizens under the coverage of old-age pensions and unemployment insurance.

We should widen the opportunities for adequate medical care.

We should plan a better system by which persons deserving or needing gainful employment may obtain it.

48. I have called for personal sacrifice, and I am assured of the willingness of almost all Americans to respond to that call. A part of the sacrifice means the payment of more money in taxes. In my budget message I will recommend that a greater portion of this great defense program be paid for from taxation than we are paying for today. No person should try, or be allowed to get rich out of the program, and the principle of tax payments in accordance with ability to pay should be constantly before our eyes to guide our legislation.

49. If the Congress maintains these principles, the voters, putting patriotism ahead pocketbooks[51], will give you their applause. In the future days, which we seek to make secure, we look forward to a world founded upon four essential human freedoms.

The first is freedom of speech and expression—everywhere in the world.

The second is freedom of every person to worship God in his own way—everywhere in the world.

The third is freedom from want[52], which, translated into world terms, means economic understandings which will secure to every nation a healthy peacetime life for its inhabitants—everywhere in the world.

The fourth is freedom from fear, which, translated into world terms, means a world-wide reduction of armaments to such a point and in such a thorough fashion that no nation will be in a position to commit an act of physical aggression against any neighbor—anywhere in the world.

50. That is no vision of a distant millennium[53]. It is a definite basis for a kind of world attainable in our own time and generation. That kind of world is the very antithesis[54] of the so-called "new order" of tyranny which the dictators seek to create with the crash of a bomb.

51. To that new order we oppose the greater conception—the moral order. A good society is able to face schemes of world domination and foreign revolutions alike without fear.

52. Since the beginning of our American history we have been engaged in change, in a perpetual, peaceful revolution, a revolution which goes on steadily, quietly, adjusting itself to changing conditions without the concentration camp or the quicklime[55] in the ditch. The world order which we seek is the cooperation of free countries, working together in a friendly, civilized society.

53. **This nation has placed its destiny in the hands and heads and hearts of its millions of free men and women, and its faith in freedom under the guidance of God. Freedom means the supremacy[56] of human rights everywhere. Our support goes to those who struggle to gain those rights and keep them. Our strength is our unity of purpose. To that high concept there can be no end save[57] victory.** (3,428 words)

❑ Notes to the Speech

1. unprecedented [ʌn'presidəntid] *adj.* having no precedent; novel 空前的，无前例的
2. points of the compass：指南针上的罗盘点，意指不同的地域和方向
3. procession [prə'seʃən, prəu-] *n.* the group action of a collection of people or animals or vehicles moving ahead in more or less regular formation 队伍，行列
4. foothold ['futhəuld] *n.* a strong or favorable position from which further advances or progress may be made; a place such as a small hole or area of rock where you can safely put your foot when climbing 立足点；立足处
5. vindicate ['vindikeit] *v.* prove that someone who was blamed for something is in fact not guilty; prove that someone or something is right or true 证明……无辜；证明……正确
6. interlude ['intə(:)ˌlu:d, -lju:d] *n.* a short period of time when an activity or situation stops and something else happens 插曲，穿插
7. hemisphere ['hemisfiə] *n.* one half of the earth; one half of the brain（地球的）半球；（大脑的）半球
8. visualize ['vizjuəlaiz, 'viʒ-] *v.* form a picture of someone or something in the mind 使形象化；想象，设想
9. harp [hɑ:p] *n.* a large musical instrument consisting of a row of strings stretched from the top to the bottom of a frame 竖琴 *v.* (~on) keep talking about something in a boring way 唠叨；喋喋不休
10. pacification [ˌpæsifi'keiʃ(ə)n] *n.* 平定；绥靖；和解；讲和

11. tyranny ['tirəni] *n.* a cruel, harsh, and unfair government in which a person or small group of people have power over everyone else 暴政，苛政
12. unalterably [ʌn'ɔːltərəbli] *adv.* not possible to change 不可改变地，坚定不移地
13. assail [ə'seil] *v.* criticize strongly or attack violently 猛烈抨击；猛烈袭击
14. propaganda [ˌprɔpə'gændə] *n.* information which is false or which emphasizes just one part of a situation, used by a government or political group to make people agree with them（政治组织的）宣传
15. discord ['diskɔːd] *n.* disagreement and argument between people 不一致，不合，纷争
16. blot out the whole pattern of democratic life：毁掉了整个民主生活的方式
    blot out：抹去，清除；遮盖，遮蔽
17. appalling [ə'pɔːliŋ] *adj.* very unpleasant and shocking; emphasizing that something is very great or severe 令人惊骇的，极为恶劣的；非常的，极其严重的
18. gallantly ['gæləntli] *adv.* bravely and honourably 勇敢地
19. disarmament [dis'ɑːməmənt] *n.* the act of reducing the number of weapons, especially nuclear weapons, that a country has 裁军
20. sounding brass：浮夸的言辞，空话
    brass [brɑːs] *n.* 黄铜，铜管乐器
21. tinkling cymbal：发出叮叮响的铙钹
22. preach [priːtʃ] *v.* talk about a religious subject in a public place, especially in a church during a service; talk about how good or important something is and try to persuade other people about this; give someone advice, especially about their behavior, in a way that they think is boring or annoying 说教；讲道；鼓吹；宣扬
23. appeasement [ə'piːzmənt] *n.* the act of making someone less angry or stop them from attacking you by giving them what they want 缓和，平息
24. American eagle：a large eagle of North America that has a white head and dark wings and body 北美秃鹰，美国国徽上的中心图案，是美国的国鸟，也是美国的象征。
25. loose talk：随意言谈；信口胡说
26. treachery ['tretʃəri] *n.* behavior or an action in which someone betrays their country or betrays a person who trusts them 背叛；变节
27. dupe [djuːp] *n.* someone who is tricked, especially into becoming involved in something illegal 上当者，易受骗的人 *v.* trick or deceive someone 欺骗，愚弄
28. accountability [əˌkauntə'biliti] *n.* being responsible for the effects of the actions and willing to explain or be criticized for them 有义务，有责任，可说明性
29. partisanship ['pɑːtizænʃip,'pɑːtizən-] *n.* support for a person or group without fair consideration of the facts and circumstances 盲目支持；偏袒

30. all-inclusive [ɔ:l in'klu:siv] *adj.* including the cost of everything in the price charged 包括一切的
31. resolute ['rezəlju:t] *adj.* doing something in a very determined way because you have very strong beliefs, aims, etc. 坚决的，果断的
32. proposition [ˌprɔpə'ziʃən] *n.* a statement that consists of a carefully considered opinion or judgment; an offer or suggestion, especially in business or politics; a suggested change or addition to the law of a state of the US, which citizens vote on 见解，观点；提议，提案
33. acquiesce [ˌækwi'es] *v.* <formal> do what someone else wants, or allow something to happen, even though you do not really agree with it 默许；勉强同意
34. electorate [i'lektərət] *n.* all the people who have the right to vote in an election 全体选民
35. summon ['sʌmən] *n.* an official order to appear in a court of law 传唤 *v.* order someone to come to a place; order someone to come to a court of law; try very hard to have enough of something such as courage, energy, or strength 召唤，召集；鼓起
36. the Army and Navy：陆军和海军
37. innumerable [i'nju:mərəbl] *adj.* very many, or too many to be counted 无数的，数不清的
38. must of needs：一定；必须
39. beget [bi'get] *v.* <old use> become the father of a child; cause sth. or make it happen 成为……的父亲；招致，引起
40. appropriation [əˌprəupri'eiʃən] *n.* the process of saving money for a special purpose, or the money that is saved, especially by a business or government; the act of taking control of something without asking permission 拨款；挪用
41. munitions [mju'niʃənz] *n.* (plural) military supplies such as bombs and guns 军火；军需品
42. arsenal ['ɑ:sinl] *n.* a large collection of weapons and military equipment held by a country, group, or person; a building where weapons and military equipment are stored 储藏的武器，军备；军火库
43. unilaterally [ˌju:ni'lætərəli] *adv.* done by or having an effect on only one side, esp. one of the political groups in an agreement 单方面地，单边地
44. proclaim [prə'kleim] *v.* say publicly or officially that something important is true or exists 宣告，声明
45. slacker ['slækə(r)] *n.* someone who is lazy and does less work than he should 懒鬼，怠工者

46. sovereignty ['sɔvrinti] *n.* complete freedom and power to govern; the power that an independent country has to govern itself 主权；主权国家
47. stamina ['stæminə] *n.* the physical or mental energy needed to do a tiring activity for a long time 持久力，毅力
48. stake [steik] *n.* 桩；(比赛或行动的) 赌注，风险；利害关系；重大利益；(企业等中的) 股份
49. fiber ['faibə] *n.* a slender and greatly elongated solid substance; strength of character 纤维；性格，气质，骨气
50. turmoil ['tə:mɔil] *n.* a violent disturbance; violent agitation 混乱，骚动
51. pocketbook ['pɔkitˌbuk] *n.* personal financial means; a pocket-size case for holding papers and paper money 经济来源；钱包
52. want [wɔnt] *n.* the state of extreme poverty; the state of needing something that is absent or unavailable 穷困；匮乏
53. millennium [mi'leniəm] *n.* a period of one thousand years 一千年
54. antithesis [æn'tiθisis] *n.* <formal> the complete opposite of something 对立面，对照
55. quicklime ['kwiklaim] *n.* a white powder that is made by heating 生石灰
56. supremacy [sju'preməsi] *n.* the position in which a person is more powerful or advanced than anyone else 霸权；至高无上
57. save [seiv] *prep.* <formal> except 除……之外

❑ Appreciating the Speech

富兰克林·德拉诺·罗斯福在 1941 年不断扩大的国际冲突 (expanding international conflict) 背景下致以国会的咨文在美国历史上具有相当大的影响力和意义 (be of considerable influence and significance)。在文中，他威严 (grave and dignified)、自信 (self-confident)、坚决 (steadfast)、果断 (decisive)，号召美国人民坚定信心，反对暴政 (fight against tyranny)；要求国民致力于应付外来危险 (to devote to meeting the foreign peril)，提出国家政策 (national policy)；要求国会把必要的武器装备 (necessary munitions and war supplies) 提供给那些总统认为其防御对美国利益至关重要 (of crucial importance to the American interests) 的国家；号召人民作出牺牲 (to call on everyone to make sacrifices)，建立四项基本自由基础之上的世界 (a world founded upon four essential human freedoms)，并宣布了他所认为的四项人类基本自由。

从语言上来讲，演讲中不乏排比 (parallelism)、反复 (repetition) 等修辞手法的灵活运用，使语言更富感染力和鼓动性。例如第 21 段中指出美国当务之急的行动和政策的时候用了 3 个 "that is why" 结构；第 42 段中提及自由国家有权利做的事情时用了两个 "a free nation has the right to”结构；第 47 段中在为需要立即改善的与我们社会经济有关的事项举例时用了 3 个“we should”结构，起到强调作用，增强了感召力。另外，文中第 23 段中申明国家政策时，“by an impressive expression of the public will and without regard to partisanship”重复了 3 遍；第 49 段宣布“四大自由”时“freedom”强调了 4 遍，加深了听众印象 (deepen the impression of the audience)，增强了语势。

❑ Culture Links

(1)《租借法案》

租借法案 (Lend-Lease Program) 是美国国会 1941 年通过的向反法西斯国家提供援助的重要法案，目的是使美国不卷入战争的同时，为盟国提供战争物资。

第二次世界大战的爆发使美国日益受到纳粹德国侵略扩张的威胁。德国入侵西欧后，罗斯福政府为了美国自身的安全和防御，并扩大势力范围，确立战后世界中美国的领导地位，决定加强对处境困难、财政拮据的英国给予援助。1940 年 12 月 17 日，罗斯福总统发表讲话，提出美国可以借出军火，并用生动的比喻加以说明：假设邻居失火，我只能把浇园的水龙带借给他去灭火，而不应让他事先付钱买这条水龙带，待火灭后邻居原物送还即可。他还说：“美国必须成为民主国家的兵工厂。”1941 年 3 月 11 日，《租借法案》正式生效。法案授权总统可以以出售、交换、转让和租借的形式向被认为其防御对美国安全具有重大意义的国家提供武器、军用物资、粮食等任何军需品。据此，美国共向英、苏、法、中等几十个反法西斯国家提供 500 多亿美元的物资，首先获得援助和获得援助最多的是英国。1941 年 5 月 6 日，罗斯福正式宣布，《租借法案》适用于中国，到 1945 年 9 月 3 日止，美国给予中国 8.45 亿美元的援助。第二次世界大战结束后《租借法案》停止执行。

《租借法案》的通过埋葬了中立法，是美国由孤立主义走向参战的决定性重要步骤。它改变了原来军事物资需要现金交易的惯例，对反法西斯战争的胜利起到了积极的作用。

(2) 珍珠港事件

珍珠港事件是日本政府策划的于 1941 年 12 月 7 日突然袭击美国太平洋珍珠港海军基地的事件。攻击珍珠港的计划来自日本与美国的外交冲突。日本自 1937 年发动对中国的战争后，长期无法脱身，经济也每况愈下。为了继续对中国的战争，日本国家政策逐渐走向夺取他国资源的计划。美国则对日本实行禁运，并逐渐升级，并于 1941 年连同荷兰和英国停止对日本的一切石油进口。另外，日本军队统帅们认为只有美国海军有力量阻止日本的扩张。为此，日本拟定了攻击珍珠港的计划。日本海军派出了 6 艘航空母舰和 300 多架飞机的兵力，分两波进行攻击。由于美军受到突袭，日军取得重大成果，击沉与重创 8 艘战列舰、3 艘巡洋舰和 3 艘驱逐舰、188 架飞机被摧毁，并造成 2 402 人阵亡和 1 282 人受伤。

这场军事攻击对第二次世界大战的发展有着重大的影响。美国公众舆论由于日本这次未宣而战的行动愤怒不已。美国、加拿大和英国于 1941 年 12 月 8 日向日本宣战。德国和意大利于 12 月 11 日向美国宣战。第二次世界大战因此演变成一场全球冲突。珍珠港事件发生后，罗斯福发表了著名的《国耻演说》，声称 12 月 7 日将成为"一个遗臭万年的日子"(a date which will live in infamy)，这一天后来成为了美国的纪念日。

❑ Questions Concerning the Speech

1. What does the United States as a nation oppose to in the history and today according to Roosevelt?
2. What happened to the democratic way of life when the speech was delivered?
3. What's the situation of the democratic existence like in the four continents at that time?
4. Since the future of all the American Republics was in serious danger, what needed to be done at that moment?
5. What is the basis of the American national policy?
6. What's the President's requirement towards the Congress?
7. What was the American purpose and American pledge with regard to democracies?
8. What kind of world order are American people seeking for?

❑ Paraphrase the Following Sentences

1. What I seek to convey is the historic truth that the United States as a nation has at all times maintained opposition—clear, definite opposition—to any attempt to lock us in behind an ancient Chinese wall while the procession of civilization went past.
2. And in like fashion, from 1815 to 1914—ninety-nine years—no single war in Europe or in Asia constituted a real threat against our future or against the future of any other American nation.
3. In times like these it is immature—and, incidentally, untrue—for anybody to brag that an unprepared America, single-handed and with one hand tied behind its back, can hold off the whole world.
4. As a nation we may take pride in the fact that we are soft-hearted; but we cannot afford to be soft-headed. We must always be wary of those who with sounding brass and a tinkling cymbal preach the "ism" of appeasement. We must especially beware of that small group of selfish men who would clip the wings of the American eagle in order to feather their own nests.

5. However, there is certain information, as the Congress itself will readily recognize, which, in the interests of our own security and those of the nations that we are supporting, must of needs be kept in confidence.
6. For what we send abroad we shall be repaid, repaid within a reasonable time following the close of hostilities, repaid in similar materials, or at our option in other goods of many kinds which they can produce and which we need.
7. If the Congress maintains these principles, the voters, putting patriotism ahead pocketbooks, will give you their applause.

❑ Questions for Discussion

1. 文中罗斯福提到“我们作为一个国家感到骄傲的是，我们心地善良，但我们绝不能头脑过于简单（As a nation we may take pride in the fact that we are soft-hearted; but we cannot afford to be soft-headed.）”对此你作何理解，并试举例说明。
2. 请对比罗斯福提出的“四大自由”与中国背景下的自由。请问你对自由是如何定义的，在什么情况下我们才能得到更大程度的自由?
3. 第二次世界大战初期，美国通过租借法案，以出售、交换、转让和租借的形式向被认为其防御对美国安全具有重大意义的国家提供武器、军用物资、粮食等任何军需品。试论此法案对中国抗日战争的意义和影响。

❑ Translation

富兰克林·罗斯福：论四大自由

1941 年 1 月 6 日，华盛顿特区

总统先生，议长先生，第 77 届议会的议员们：

1. 我是在美国历史上一个史无前例的时刻向你们——新议员先生们——发表讲话。我说史无前例，是因为美国的安全过去从未像今天这样受到外来的威胁。
2. 自从 1789 年根据宪法成立政府以来，历史上的多数危机时期都与国内事务有关。幸运的是，只有一次各州之间的为期 4 年的战争威胁到我国的统一。感谢上帝，今天美国的 48 个州、1.3 亿人口打破地域而团结一致。
3. 1914 年之前，美国经常受到其他大洲事件的扰乱。为了保卫美国的利益和和平贸易原则，我们甚至参加了两次欧洲国家的战争和西印度群岛、地中海和太平洋的不宣而战。但任何情况均未对我国的安全和独立造成威胁。

4. 我要说的是这样一条历史真理，即美国一贯反对——明确而不含糊地——反对任何将我们关在中国古城墙后面的企图，那样会使我们错过文明发展的机会。今天，考虑到我们的孩子及他们的后代，我们反对将我们或美洲任何部分强行孤立起来。
5. 我们这些年来一直保持的决心，在例如法国大革命后四分之一世纪的战争中得到证实。
6. 虽然拿破仑战争的确威胁到美国的利益，因为法国在西印度群岛和路易斯安那建立了立脚点，虽然我们 1812 年发动了战争以获得和平贸易的权利，但无论法国还是英国或任何其他国家都没有要控制整个世界。
7. 同样，从 1815 年到 1914 年这 99 年的时间里，欧洲或亚洲的任何异常战争都没有对我国的未来或其他美洲国家的未来构成真正的威胁。
8. 除了墨西哥的马西米连插曲，没有任何外国势力试图在本半球插足。当时大西洋英国舰队友好的兵力，现在仍然如此。
9. 甚至 1914 年世界大战的骤然爆发似乎对我们美国本身的前途也仅有轻微的威胁。但是，随着时间的推移，美国人民开始体会到各民主国家的沦陷对我们美国的民主制度会意味着什么。
10. 我们无须过分强调《凡尔赛和约》的不完善，我们也无须反复谈论各民主国家未能进行世界重建。我们应该记住，1919 年的和约与早在慕尼黑会议以前就开始的绥靖政策相比，其不公正的程度要小得多；而在那力图向世界各大洲扩展的暴政新秩序下，这种绥靖政策仍在延续着。美国人民已坚定地表示反对那种暴政。
11. 我想每一个现实主义者都知道，民主的生活方式目前正在世界各地遭到直接攻击——或者是武力的进攻，或者是秘密散布的恶毒宣传的进攻。散布这种宣传的是那些企图在仍然维持着和平的国家中破坏团结、制造混乱的人。
12. 16 个月来，这种攻击已在数目惊人的一批大小独立国家中毁掉了整个民主生活的方式。进攻者仍在步步进逼，威胁着大大小小的其他国家。
13. 因此，作为你们的总统，执行宪法加诸于我的向国会报导联邦情况的责任，我认为必须向你们报告，我们国家和我们民主政治的前途与安全已经和远离我们国境的许多事件不可抗拒地牵连在一起了。
14. 以武力保卫民主生存的战争，现正在四大洲英勇地进行。如果这场保卫战失败，所有在欧洲、亚洲、非洲和澳洲的人口和一切资源，均将为征服者所控制。不要忘记，这些人口和资源合计起来，远超过整个西半球的全部人口和资源的总数。是的，要超过很多倍。
15. 这种情况下，如果任何人吹嘘说，一个准备不充分的美国，单枪匹马，甚至一只手绑在背后就可以抵挡整个世界，这是幼稚的，也是不符合实际情况的。
16. 任何一个现实的美国人都不会期望从独裁者的和平中得到国与国之间的宽容，或者真正的独立、世界裁军、言论自由或宗教信仰自由，或甚至自由经商的机会。这样的和平不会给我们或我们的邻国带来安全。放弃基本的自由来换取暂时的平安既不会得到自由也不会得到安全。

17. 我们作为一个国家感到骄傲的是，我们心地善良，但我们绝不能头脑过于简单。我们必须警惕那些大肆宣扬绥靖主义的人。我们必须特别警惕那一小撮自私自利的人，他们拔掉我们北美秃鹰翅膀上的羽毛来编造他们自己的窝。

18. 我最近曾指出，现代战争进展迅速，如果独裁国家赢得战争，很快就会把战争推进到我们腹地。

19. 现在有许多漫不经心的谈论，说我国可以免于海外的直接入侵。的确，只要英国海军保持其战斗力，这种危险就不会存在。甚至没有英国海军，敌人也不会愚蠢到在获得战略基地之前，就跨过万里海洋，运送军队登陆美国发动进攻。

20. 但是我们接受了这几年欧洲的教训，特别是挪威的教训，它的重要海港在几年的时间里由于出卖、叛变和突然袭击而被占领。对本半球入侵的第一阶段不会是正规军队的登陆。关键的战略要点将会被他们的特工和受他们欺骗的人占领，他们很多人早已在这里和拉丁美洲潜伏。只要侵略国家维持攻势，那就会由他们，而不是我们，选择进攻的时间、地点和方法。

21. 这就是为什么我们说今天所有美洲国家处于严重危险之中。这就是为什么这次国情咨文在美国历史上具有独特地位。这就是为什么政府和国会的每个成员都肩负着重大责任。当务之急是，我们的行动和我们的政策都应首先，差不多全部致力于应付外来的危险。我们国内的所有问题现在只是这紧急情况的一个部分。

22. 正如在国内事务上，我们的国策是以尊重国门以内所有同胞的权利和尊严为基础，在外交事务上，我们的国策也以尊重所有大小国家的权利与尊严为基础。道德的公正原则最后将会并且也必然会获得胜利。

23. 我们国家的政策是：

第一，根据公众的明确意愿，不分党派，我们决心致力于全面的国防。

第二，根据公众的明确意愿，不分党派，我们决定对于任何地方反抗侵略致使战火远离我们半球的所有英勇民族，予以全力支持。我们用这种支持，来表示我们对民主事业必胜的决心；我们要加强我国本身的防御和安全。

第三，根据公众的明确意愿，不分党派，我们决定声明，道德的原则和国家安全的考虑将不允许我们默许侵略者强制推行的并有绥靖者支持的和平。我们知道，永久的和平不能以其他人民的自由为代价。

24. 在最近的全国选举中，两大政党在这一国家政策方面没有实质性差别。美国选民们在这方面没什么争论的问题。现在很明显各地的美国公民都认识到这一危险，正要求和支持迅速的统一的行动。因此，目前最需要的是迅速大力加强军火生产。

25. 劳资双方的领袖都对我们的号召作出了回应。加快速度的目标也被制订出来。一些目标我们已经提前实现，一些目标正按计划进行，也有些出现了微小的、不严重的延误。

但我非常遗憾地说，有些非常重要的目标，计划完成的缓慢程度令我们大家非常担忧。

26. 但是，陆军和海军在过去的一年里都有了实质性的进展。实际经验正在一天天地改善和加快着我们的生产方法。今天最好的明天就不够好了。

27. 我对目前已取得的进展并不满意。负责计划的人在训练、能力和爱国主义思想方面都是最好的。他们也不满意目前已取得的进展。在工作完成之前我们都不会感到满意。不管最初的目标定得过高或过低，我们的目标是要取得更快更好的结果。

28. 举两个例子：在制造飞机方面我们落后于预定计划。我们日夜工作以解决成堆的难题来赶上进度。我们在制造战舰方面超出计划，但我们仍在努力使计划更提前完成。

29. 将和平时期的生产转变为战时生产是一项艰巨的任务。最大的困难在于，计划开始时，必须首先制造或建造新的工具、新的生产设施、新的装配线和新的船台，然后实际的材料才能从中平稳地迅速地生产出来。

30. 当然，国会必须随时了解计划的进展情况。但国会也明白，为了我国和那些我们支持的国家的安全，必须对某些信息保密。

31. 新情况不断为我们的安全带来新的需要。我将要求国会大量增加新的拨款并授权继续进行我们已开始的工作。

32. 我也要求本届国会给予充分的授权和款项，以生产额外的军需品与战争装备，供给那些正与侵略国实际作战的国家。我们最有效和最直接的任务是充当他们和我们自己的军火库。他们不需人力，他们所需的是价值以十亿美元计的防卫武器。

33. 用不了多久，他们将无力用现款偿付这些防御武器。我们不能也不会只因为他们无力支付我们知道他们必须拥有的武器，便告诉他们必须投降。

34. 我并不建议给他们美金贷款用于支付购买武器的费用，然后用美金还贷款。我建议由我们设法使那些国家继续从美国取得作战物资，并使他们的订单与我们自己的计划配合起来。在适当的时候，他们的几乎全部物资都会有利于我们自己的防卫。

35. 征询陆军和海军权威专家的意见，并且考虑到什么是最有利于我们自身安全，我们可以自由地决定应该在国内保留多少，应该运给我们的外国朋友多少。他们坚定英勇抗敌，使我们赢得时间为我们自己的防卫作准备。

36. 我们送到国外的东西将会得到偿还，在战争结束后一段时间内用类似的物资或我们选择接受的多种其他物资偿还。这些物资他们能够生产，我们又很需要。

37. 让我们对民主国家申明："我们美国人十分关注你们保卫自由的战争。我们正用我们的实力、我们的资源和我们的组织力量，使你们有能力恢复和维系一个自由的世界。我们会给你们送来数量日增的舰艇、飞机、坦克和大炮。这是我们的目标，也是我们的誓言。"

38. 为了实现这个目标，我们不会被独裁者的威胁吓倒，这些人认为我们对那些敢于抵抗他们侵略的民主国家进行支持，是违犯国际公法的或是战争的行为。但即使独裁者单方面宣布，这种援助也绝不是战争行为。

39. 如果独裁者要对我们发动战争，当他们发动战争时，他们不会等我们采取战争行动。
40. 他们没等挪威或比利时或荷兰采取战争行动。他们唯一感兴趣的是一种新的单方面的国际法。它只要求一方遵守，因此就沦为他们侵略的工具。未来一代美国人的幸福取决于我们如何使我们的援助高效并迅速发挥作用。没有人会知道我们将会被迫应付怎样紧急的形势。当国家的命运处于危机之中时，我们的双手一定不能被捆住。
41. 是的，我们必须准备，每个人都必须准备，准备为战争一样的严重紧急情况作出牺牲。任何事情如果妨碍防卫的速度和效率、妨碍任何形式的防卫准备，都应该让位给国家的需要。
42. 一个自由的国家有权要求各行各业的充分合作。一个自由的国家有权期待其商业、劳工和农业的领袖在自己行业之内而不是之外鼓励大家作出努力。
43. 对那些我们当中为数不多的怠工者和捣乱分子，对付他们最好的方法就是首先用爱国者的榜样使他们感到羞愧。如果这不奏效，就用政府的权威来拯救政府。
44. 如同人们并非单靠面包生活一样，他们也并非单靠武器来作战。那些坚守我们防御工事的人以及在他们后面建立防御工事的人必须具有耐力和勇气，而所有这些均来自对他们正在保卫的生活方式所抱的不可动摇的信念。我们所号召的伟大行动，是不可能以忽视所有值得奋斗的东西为基础的。
45. 国家对于为使其人民认识到捍卫美国民主生活与其休戚相关所做的一切感到满意，并且从中汲取了巨大力量。这些事情使人民的气质坚强起来，重建了他们的信心，也加强了他们对我们准备保卫的制度的忠诚。
46. 当然，现在并非停止考虑各种社会和经济问题的时候，这些问题都是社会革命的根本原因，而这种革命则是今天世界的一个主要因素。一个健全巩固的民主体制的基础没有任何神秘的东西。我们人民对政治和经济制度所抱的基本期望十分简单，这包括：给青年和其他人以均等机会；给能工作的人提供工作；给需要保障的人提供保障；终止少数人享有的特权；保护所有人的公民自由权；在生活水平更普遍和不断提高的情况下，享受科学进步的成果。在我们这个混乱和极端复杂的现代世界中，这些是决不应忽视的简单而基本的事项。我们的各种经济和政治体制的内在和持久的力量，取决于它们满足这些期望的程度。
47. 有不少与我们社会经济有关的事项，需要立即改善。例如：我们应当使更多的公民得到老年退休金和失业保险的保障。我们应当扩大那种使人们得到充分医疗照顾的机会。我们应当制订一套更好的制度，使那些应当并需要获得有薪工作的人们能够工作。
48. 我曾经号召大家作个人的牺牲。我已得到保证，几乎每个美国人都心甘情愿响应我这个号召。这种牺牲的一个部分就是缴纳更多的税。我在预算咨文中建议，巨大的防卫计划中更大的部分由税收支付。任何人不应也不允许从这一计划中发财。应不断根据纳税能力缴税的原则制定我们的法律。

49. 如果国会坚持这些原则，视爱国重于个人钱财的选举人就会为你们鼓掌。在我们力求安定的未来的岁月里，我们期待一个建立在四项人类基本自由之上的世界。

第一是在全世界任何地方，人人都有发表言论和表达意见的自由。

第二是在全世界任何地方，人人有以自己的方式来崇拜上帝的自由。

第三是免于匮乏的自由——这种自由，用通俗的话来讲，就是一种经济上的融洽关系，它将保证全世界每一个国家的居民都过上健康和平的生活。

第四是免除恐惧的自由——这种自由，用通俗的话来讲，就是进行世界性的彻底裁军，使世界上没有一个国家有能力向全世界任何地区的任何邻国进行武力侵略。

50. 这不是对遥远未来的黄金时代的幻想。这是我们这个时代和我们这一代人可以实现的一种世界的坚实基础。这种世界，和独裁者想用炸弹爆炸来制造的所谓“新秩序”的暴政，是截然相反的。

51. 对于他们那个新秩序，我们是以一种伟大的观念——道德秩序来与之相对抗的。一个好的社会能够毫无畏惧地面对企图主宰世界以及在国外制造革命的各种阴谋。

52. 自美国有史以来，我们一直在从事改革—— 一种永久性的和平革命—— 一种连续不断而静悄悄地适应环境变化的革命。我们的革命没有集中营，也没有万人冢。我们所追求的世界秩序，是自由国家间的合作，以及在友好、文明的社会里共同努力。

53. 我们的国家已把她的命运交到她千百万自由男女公民的双手里，头脑里和心灵里；把她对于自由的信仰交由上帝指引。自由意味着人权在任何地方都是至高无上的。凡是为了取得或保持这种权利而斗争的人，我们都予以支持。我们的力量来自我们的目标一致。为了实现这一崇高的观念，我们是不获全胜绝不罢休的。

Harry S. Truman

(1884—1972)

哈利·S·杜鲁门

9

Harry S. Truman's Inaugural Address

Delivered January 20, 1949, in Washington, D.C.

❑ About the Author

哈里·S·杜鲁门(Harry S. Truman，1884—1972)，出生于密苏里州拉马尔一个农场主家庭。在第一次世界大战期间，杜鲁门参加了炮兵，并且成为一名上尉，在法国作战。杜鲁门退役后，在民主党地方组织的支持下逐步进入政界，1922年任县法官，1926年后又任县首席法官、县长。1934年当选为密苏里州参议员，并于1940年再次当选。第二次世界大战期间，他担任参议院战争调查委员会主席，负责调查军方有关行政混乱、浪费和诈骗资源等丑闻，为国家节省了大约150亿美元，他对军方实施的“常识节流措施”，更使杜鲁门受到了广泛的支持和敬重，而杜鲁门更因此出现在了《时代周刊》的封面上。

1944年杜鲁门当选为富兰克林·D·罗斯福的副总统。1945年4月罗斯福总统病逝，在美国历史的重大时刻，杜鲁门以副总统身份继任美国第33任总统(1945—1953)。面对一系列棘手问题，杜鲁门做出了许多与美国、世界有关的重大决定，对第二次世界大战以后美国的外交政策和国际关系的发展产生深刻的影响。杜鲁门执政后不久即对制定联合国宪章作出安排；部署接受德国无条件投降事宜；参加波茨坦会议；签署命令在长崎、广岛投放原子弹，使日本迅速投降；提出遏制政策，与苏联进行冷战；提出并推行杜鲁门主义；批准并推行“马歇尔计划”；订立北大西洋公约；建立中央情报局；应对朝鲜战争。

杜鲁门是位素以友善和谦逊闻名的总统，他的不少警句，如“推卸责任止于此”(The buck stops here!)和“怕热就别进厨房”(If you can't stand the heat, get out of the kitchen.)等，成为家喻户晓的名言。相比前任总统，杜鲁门的支持度不算高，但他谨慎果断的性格令他得以在面对险峻的国际情势时，可以克服许多艰巨的挑战。今日的历史学者仍视他为最出色的美国总统之一。

❑ About the Speech

杜鲁门执政时，冷战开始并愈演愈烈。从此美国自觉地承当起"自由世界"领导者的"天命"，也是第一次有了明确的敌人，那就是"共产主义"，具体体现就是苏联和以苏联为首的社会主义阵营。1948年杜鲁门在选举中赢得了惊人的压倒性胜利，在就职前的一两天，演说稿中还只有联合国、马歇尔计划、北大西洋公约等三项，但在杜鲁门的坚持下，最后把对不发达国家进行技术援助的计划写进了演说稿。

1949年1月20日，杜鲁门在国会大厦东门廊宣誓就职，就职典礼在电视和广播上都进行了转播。就职演说持续了20多分钟，几乎全部讲对外事务，重点是"四项主要的行动计划"。当讲到美国计划在拉美搞小规模的技术援助时，他特意提高了嗓门，加重了语气，称之为"一项新的大胆的计划"。这开创了在和平时期政府实施对外援助的先河，使对外援助与美国外交政策紧密地结合在一起。他还宣称美国致力的世界目标是："所有的国家和所有的民族，可以自由地以其自认合宜的方式治理本身。"美国不会追求纯粹的国家利益，"我们不谋求别国领土，也不会将我们的意志强加于人"。美国将以提供"军事顾问和设备给予自由国家，使之与我们合作，维持和平与安全"，"来加强爱好自由的国家之力量以迎战侵略之险"。于是保卫自由、保卫和平和保卫美国安全都联系在一起。世界每一个角落都关系到美国的"战略利益"，"世界任何地方的人民的命运都与美国有关，美国有责任帮助他们"，"只有通过帮助人类大家庭中那些最不幸的成员自助，人类才能过上体面的、令人满意的、人人有权享受的生活。"在这些绚丽的词句后面透露出杜鲁门强烈的民族优越感和全球扩张主义思想。正如基辛格分析的那样，这些都源于"他对美国实力的自豪；以及他深信美国的最大天职是作为全人类自由与进步之源泉"。

❑ The Speech *(abridged)*

1. Mr. Vice-President, Mr. Chief Justice, and fellow citizens, I accept with humility the honor which the American people have conferred upon[1] me. I accept it with a deep resolve to do all that I can for the welfare of this Nation and for the peace of the world.

2. In performing the duties of my office, I need the help and prayers of every one of you. I ask for your encouragement and your support. The tasks we face are difficult, and we can accomplish them only if we work together.

3. **Each period of our national history has had its special challenges. Those that confront us now are as momentous[2] as any in the past. Today marks the beginning not only of a new administration, but of a period that will be eventful, perhaps decisive, for us and for the world.**

4. It may be our lot[3] to experience, and in large measure to bring about, a major turning point in the long history of the human race. The first half of this century has been marked by unprecedented[4] and brutal attacks on the rights of man, and by the two most frightful wars in history. The supreme need of our time is for men to learn to live together in peace and harmony.

5. **The peoples of the earth face the future with grave uncertainty, composed almost equally of great hopes and great fears**. In this time of doubt, they look to the United States as never before for good will, strength, and wise leadership.

6. It is fitting, therefore, that we take this occasion to proclaim[5] to the world the essential principles of the faith by which we live, and to declare our aims to all peoples.

7. The American people stand firm in the faith which has inspired this Nation from the beginning. **We believe that all men have a right to equal justice under law and equal opportunity to share in the common good. We believe that all men have the right to freedom of thought and expression. We believe that all men are created equal because they are created in the image of God.**

8. **From this faith we will not be moved**.

9. The American people desire, and are determined to work for, a world in which all nations and all peoples are free to govern themselves as they see fit, and to achieve a decent and satisfying life. Above all else, our people desire, and are determined to work for, peace on earth—a just and lasting peace—based on genuine agreement freely arrived at by equals.

...

10. Since the end of hostilities, the United States has invested its substance and its energy in a great constructive effort to restore peace, stability, and freedom to the world.

11. We have sought no territory and we have imposed our will on none. We have asked for no privileges we would not extend to others.

12. We have constantly and vigorously supported the United Nations and related agencies as a means of applying democratic principles to international relations. We have consistently advocated and relied upon peaceful settlement of disputes among nations.

13. We have made every effort to secure agreement on effective international control of our most powerful weapon, and we have worked steadily for the limitation and control of all armaments[6].

14. We have encouraged, by precept[7] and example, the expansion of world trade on a sound and fair basis.

15. Almost a year ago, in company with 16 free nations of Europe, we launched the greatest cooperative economic program in history. The purpose of that unprecedented effort is to invigorate[8] and strengthen democracy in Europe, so that the free people of that continent can resume their rightful place in the forefront of civilization and can contribute once more to the security and welfare of the world.

16. Our efforts have brought new hope to all mankind. We have beaten back despair and defeatism. We have saved a number of countries from losing their liberty. Hundreds of millions of people all over the world now agree with us, that we need not have war—that we can have peace.

17. The initiative[9] is ours.

18. We are moving on with other nations to build an even stronger structure of international order and justice. We shall have as our partners countries which, no longer solely concerned with the problem of national survival, are now working to improve the standards of living of all their people. We are ready to undertake new projects to strengthen the free world.

19. In the coming years, our program for peace and freedom will emphasize four major courses of action.

20. First, we will continue to give unfaltering[10] support to the United Nations and related agencies, and we will continue to search for ways to strengthen their authority and increase their effectiveness. We believe that the United Nations will be strengthened by the new nations which are being formed in lands now advancing toward self-government under democratic principles.

21. Second, we will continue our programs for world economic recovery.

22. This means, first of all, that we must keep our full weight behind the European recovery program. We are confident of the success of this major venture in world recovery. We believe that our partners in this effort will achieve the status of self-supporting nations once again.

23. In addition, we must carry out our plans for reducing the barriers to world trade and increasing its volume. Economic recovery and peace itself depend on increased world trade.

24. Third, we will strengthen freedom-loving nations against the dangers of aggression.

25. We are now working out with a number of countries a joint agreement designed to strengthen the security of the North Atlantic area. Such an agreement would take the form of a collective defense arrangement within the terms of the United Nations Charter[11].

26. We have already established such a defense pact for the Western Hemisphere by the treaty of Rio de Janeiro[12].

27. The primary purpose of these agreements is to provide unmistakable proof of the joint determination of the free countries to resist armed attack from any quarter. Each country participating in these arrangements must contribute all it can to the common defense.

28. If we can make it sufficiently clear, in advance, that any armed attack affecting our national security would be met with overwhelming force, the armed attack might never occur.

29. I hope soon to send to the Senate a treaty respecting the North Atlantic security plan.

30. In addition, we will provide military advice and equipment to free nations which will cooperate with us in the maintenance of peace and security.

31. Fourth, we must embark on[13] a bold new program for making the benefits of our scientific advances and industrial progress available for the improvement and growth of underdeveloped areas.

32. More than half the people of the world are living in conditions approaching misery. Their food is inadequate. They are victims of disease. Their economic life is primitive and stagnant[14]. Their poverty is a handicap and a threat both to them and to more prosperous areas.

33. For the first time in history, humanity possesses the knowledge and the skill to relieve the suffering of these people.

34. The United States is pre-eminent[15] among nations in the development of industrial and scientific techniques. **The material resources which we can afford to use for the assistance of other peoples are limited. But our imponderable[16] resources in technical knowledge are constantly growing and are inexhaustible**.

35. I believe that we should make available to peace-loving peoples the benefits of our store of technical knowledge in order to help them realize their aspirations for a better life. And, in cooperation with other nations, we should foster capital investment in areas needing development.

36. Our aim should be to help the free peoples of the world, through their own efforts, to produce more food, more clothing, more materials for housing, and more mechanical power to lighten their burdens.

37. We invite other countries to pool their technological resources in this undertaking. Their contributions will be warmly welcomed. This should be a cooperative enterprise in which all nations work together through the United Nations and its specialized agencies wherever practicable. It must be a worldwide effort for the achievement of peace, plenty, and freedom.

38. With the cooperation of business, private capital, agriculture, and labor in this country, this program can greatly increase the industrial activity in other nations and can raise substantially their standards of living.

39. Such new economic developments must be devised and controlled to benefit the peoples of the areas in which they are established. Guarantees to the investor must be balanced by guarantees in the interest of the people whose resources and whose labor go into these developments.

40. The old imperialism[17]—exploitation for foreign profit—has no place in our plans. What we envisage[18] is a program of development based on the concepts of democratic fair-dealing.

41. All countries, including our own, will greatly benefit from a constructive program for the better use of the world's human and natural resources. Experience shows that our commerce with other countries expands as they progress industrially and economically.

42. **Greater production is the key to prosperity and peace. And the key to greater production is a wider and more vigorous application of modern scientific and technical knowledge.**

43. **Only by helping the least fortunate of its members to help themselves can the human family achieve the decent, satisfying life that is the right of all people.**

44. **Democracy alone can supply the vitalizing force to stir the peoples of the world into triumphant action, not only against their human oppressors, but also against their ancient enemies—hunger, misery, and despair.**

45. On the basis of these four major courses of action we hope to help create the conditions that will lead eventually to personal freedom and happiness for all mankind.

46. If we are to be successful in carrying out these policies, it is clear that we must have continued prosperity in this country and we must keep ourselves strong.

47. Slowly but surely we are weaving a world fabric of international security and growing prosperity.

48. We are aided by all who wish to live in freedom from fear—even by those who live today in fear under their own governments.

49. We are aided by all who want relief from the lies of propaganda—who desire truth and sincerity.

50. We are aided by all who desire self-government and a voice in deciding their own affairs.

51. We are aided by all who long for economic security—for the security and abundance that men in free societies can enjoy.

52. We are aided by all who desire freedom of speech, freedom of religion, and freedom to live their own lives for useful ends.

53. Our allies are the millions who hunger and thirst after righteousness[19].

54. In due time, as our stability becomes manifest, as more and more nations come to know the benefits of democracy and to participate in growing abundance, I believe that those countries which now oppose us will abandon their delusions[20] and join with the free nations of the world in a just settlement of international differences.

55. Events have brought our American democracy to new influence and new responsibilities. They will test our courage, our devotion to duty, and our concept of liberty.

56. But I say to all men, **what we have achieved in liberty, we will surpass in greater liberty**.

57. Steadfast in our faith in the Almighty, we will advance toward a world where man's freedom is secure.

58. To that end we will devote our strength, our resources, and our firmness of resolve. With God's help, the future of mankind will be assured in a world of justice, harmony, and peace. (1,911 words)

❑ Notes to the Speech

1. confer upon: officially give someone a title, etc., especially as a reward for something they have achieved 给予，赋予
2. momentous [məu'mentəs] *adj.* very important, consequential 重大的，重要的
3. lot [lɔt] *n.* fortune 命运
4. unprecedented [ʌn'presidəntid] *adj.* never having happened before 史无前例的，空前的
5. proclaim [prə'kleim] *vt.* <formal> say publicly or officially that something important is true or exists 宣告；公布
6. armament ['ɑːməmənt] *n.* the weapons and military equipment used by an army 军备，装备武器
7. precept ['priːsept] *n.* a rule on which a way of thinking or behaving is based 规则；教训
8. invigorate [in'vigəreit] *vt.* heighten or intensify 鼓舞
9. initiative [i'niʃiətiv] *n.* if you have or take the initiative, you are in a position to control a situation and decide what to do next 主动。文中这句话的意思是"主动权掌握在我们手中。"
10. unfaltering ['ʌn'fɔːltəriŋ] *adj.* marked by firm determination or resolution; not shakable 坚定的，坚决的，专心的
11. the United Nations Charter:《联合国宪章》
12. the treaty of Rio de Janeiro:《里约热内卢公约》，亦称《美洲国家互助条约》，因于1947年9月在巴西的里约热内卢签署，故名。美洲21国在公约上签字，同意一致行动，共同维护美洲安全。
13. embark on: start something, especially something new, difficult, or exciting 开始；从事

14. stagnant ['stægnənt] *adj.* not growing or changing; without force or vitality 停滞的，迟钝的
15. pre-eminent [pri'eminənt] *adj.* greatest in importance or degree or significance or achievement 卓越的；显著的
16. imponderable [im'pɔndərəbl] *adj.* difficult or impossible to evaluate with precision 不可估计的
17. old imperialism：旧式帝国主义，指 15、16 世纪以来英、法、西班牙等国那种侵夺土地、掠取财富和占领殖民地的做法。
18. envisage [in'vizidʒ] *vt.* form a mental image of something that is not present or that is not the case 设想；正视
19. righteousness ['raitʃəsnis] *n.* adhering to moral principles 公正，正直，正当
20. delusion [di'lu:ʒən] *n.* a mistaken or unfounded opinion or idea 错觉；妄想

❑ Appreciating the Speech

杜鲁门在就职演说中，首先表达了自己就任总统的心情和恪尽职守的决心 (determination to fulfill the duties)，并指出当时所面临的严峻挑战 (severe challenges)，在经历了历史上最可怕的两场战争之后，人类面前的迫切任务是"学会和睦相处"(learn to live together in peace and harmony)。接着他向全世界宣告指导美国人生活的信念的基本原则及目标。最后杜鲁门声明了美国和平自由纲领 (program for peace and freedom) 的四项主要行动计划 (four major courses of action)：支持联合国 (support the United Nations)、战后欧洲经济复兴计划 (European Economic Recovery Program) (即马歇尔计划 Marshall Plan)、援助自由世界抵御侵略 (aid freedom-loving nations against aggression) (体现于北大西洋公约组织 North Atlantic Treaty Organization 的建立) 和对不发达地区实行经济技术援助 (economic and technical assistance)，并着重阐述了第四项，称它是"旨在执行一项利用美国先进的科学和发达的工业来改进和发展不发达地区的新的果敢计划" (a bold new program for making the benefits of American scientific advances and industrial progress available for the improvement and growth of underdeveloped areas)。

这篇演讲态度鲜明，条理清晰；句式简洁，铿锵有力；语言通俗易懂，明白畅晓。最大的特色是排比结构 (parallelism) 的运用。例如，在谈到美国人民自美国建国以来就一直坚信的信念时，"We believe that all men have a right to equal justice under law and equal opportunity to share in the common good. We believe that all men have the right to freedom of thought and expression. We believe that all men are created equal because they are created in the image of God."，内容集中，读起来朗朗上口，有一股强大的力量，从而增强了语言的气势和表达效果。再比如，演说结尾部分连续使用 5 个"We are aided by all who”的排比结构作为每一段的开头，增强了语势，体现出一种节奏感，条理分明地论述了美国在构建国际安全和日益繁荣的世界体系时 (weave a world fabric of international security and growing prosperity) 拥有了众多追求正义 (desire justice) 人们帮助的事实，深化了中心。此外，演说中还用了层进 (climax) 的修辞手法 (figures of speech)，如“Greater production is the key to prosperity and peace. And the key to greater production is a wider and more vigorous application of modern scientific and technical knowledge.”，叙事透辟，加强感染力 (appeal)，使听众易于对演讲者论点产生认同感 (sense of identity)。需要一提的是，演说中用了大量的短句独立成段，如“From this faith we will not be moved.”“The initiative is ours.”等等，强调了主题 (theme)，值得读者仔细品味。

❑ Culture Links

（1）马歇尔计划

马歇尔计划（The Marshall Plan），官方名称为欧洲经济复兴计划（European Economic Recovery Program），是第二次世界大战后美国对被战争破坏的西欧各国进行经济援助、协助重建的计划，对欧洲国家的发展和世界政治格局产生了深远的影响。

第二次世界大战欧洲战场胜利后，美国凭借其在第二次世界大战后的雄厚实力，为帮助其欧洲盟国恢复因世界大战而濒临崩溃的经济体系，并同时抗衡苏联和共产主义势力在欧洲的进一步渗透和扩张而提出此计划。1947年6月5日，时任美国国务卿的乔治·马歇尔在哈佛大学的毕业典礼上提出了欧洲恢复计划，这就是著名的马歇尔计划。

该计划于1947年7月正式启动，并整整持续了4个财政年度之久。在这段时期内，西欧各国通过参加经济合作发展组织（OECD）总共接受了美国包括粮食、燃料、原材料、金融、技术和机械设备等各种形式的援助合计达130亿美元。

马歇尔计划实施期间，西欧国家的国民生产总值增长25%，工农业生产提高到战前水平上，大大地促进了国际贸易；该计划也有利于美国，因为它为美国的产品扩大了欧洲的市场。马歇尔计划是战后美国对外经济技术援助最成功的计划，它为北大西洋公约组织和欧洲经济共同体的建立奠定了基础，对西欧的联合和经济的恢复起了促进作用。

（2）麦卡锡主义

麦卡锡主义（McCarthyism）是在20世纪50年代初由美国参议员约瑟夫·麦卡锡（Joseph Raymond McCarthy）煽起的美国全国性反共“十字军运动”。麦卡锡是共和党人，原在威斯康星州担任律师，1946年被选为参议员。他任参议员期间，经常发表攻击共产党的演说，谴责杜鲁门和马歇尔对待共产主义的软弱态度，大肆渲染共产党侵入政府和舆论界的危险性，促使成立“非美调查委员会”（House Committee on Un-American

Activities），在文艺界和政府部门煽动人们互相揭发，恶意诽谤、肆意迫害共产党和民主进步人士，许多著名人士，如演员查理·卓别林和发明原子弹的科学家罗伯特·奥本海默等，都受到迫害和怀疑。

1950 年 2 月，麦卡锡公开指责有 205 名共产党人混入美国国务院，引起全国关注，但未能提供任何具体的人名。参议院对外关系委员会调查了国务院，但并没有发现共产党或共产党的同情者。然而麦卡锡提出更多的指控，并赢得了很多支持者。指控和调查涉及数千人，图书馆管理员、大学教授、演员、记者、神职人员及其他各色人等受到怀疑。一些公司拒绝雇用被控与共产党有牵连的人。许多雇员为了保住饭碗，按要求宣誓忠于政府。1954 年春天，他又指控陆军部窝藏共产党分子，从事颠覆活动。为此参议院常设调查小组委员会举行了长达 36 天的听证会，同时向全国进行电视直播。在听证会上，麦卡锡进行了拙劣的表演。他那种信口雌黄的政治手段遭到陆军特别顾问约瑟夫·韦尔奇的揭露。自此，麦卡锡一蹶不振。美国国内外的舆论开始指责他是"蛊惑民心的煽动家"。11 月美国中期选举，共和党失去参议院的多数，麦卡锡被免去非美调查委员会主席的职务。12 月 2 日参议院以 67 票对 22 票通过决议，正式谴责麦卡锡"违反参议院传统"的行径，从而结束了"麦卡锡主义"时代。然而麦卡锡主义毁了许多清白的美国人的声誉和职业生涯，从 1955 年至 1958 年，美国最高法院做出一系列判决，以保护被控同情共产主义的人的权益。

从 1950 年初麦卡锡主义开始泛滥，到 1954 年底彻底破产的前后 5 年里，它的影响波及美国政治、外交和社会生活的方方面面。麦卡锡主义时期是美国历史上违反传统政治自由和民主的最不光彩的一段时期。此后，麦卡锡主义成为一个专有名词，也成为政治迫害的代名词。

（3）杜鲁门主义与世界霸权

第二次世界大战结束后，杜鲁门政府奉行扩张主义。1947 年 3 月 12 日，杜鲁门在致国会的关于援助希腊和土耳其的咨文中，提出了以遏制共产主义作为国家政治意识形态和对外政策的指导思想。后来这一指导思想被称为"杜鲁门主义"（Truman Doctrine），成为第二次世界大战后美国的对外政策核心。

咨文阐明援助希腊、土耳其的直接原因是美国要接替英国、填补东地中海的真空；进而指出在世界上任何地区发生社会主义革命，都"危害着国际和平的基础和美国的安全"，宣称世界已分为两个敌对的营垒，一边是"极权政体"，一边是"自由国家"，每个国家都面临着两种不同生活方式的抉择；因而宣布"美国的政策必须是支持那些正在抵抗武装的少数人或外来压力的征服企图的自由民族"，即美国要承担"自由世界"守护神的使命，充当世界警察的角色。杜鲁门还认为如果丧失希腊，就会立刻危及土耳其和整个中东，其影响将不仅是东方，还将殃及西方的民主制度。这就是多米诺骨牌理论的早期说法。因此，他要求国会立即采取果断行动，向希腊和土耳其提供 4 亿美元的军事援助。1947 年 5 月 22 日，杜鲁门正式签署《援助希腊、土耳其法案》。根据该法案，1947—1950 年，美国援助希、土两国 6.59 亿美元。由美国出钱出枪，重新武装和改编了的希腊政府军队，在 1949 年扑灭了共产党领导的希腊革命。

杜鲁门主义是美国战后对外政策的重大转折点。当时它与马歇尔计划共同构成美国对外政策的基础，标志着美苏在第二次世界大战中的同盟关系的结束及冷战的正式开始，也标志着美国作为战后第一大国的世界霸主地位的确立。随后，美国对苏联实行全面的"遏制"政策，与苏联在全球范围内展开争霸竞赛。为了在争霸中取胜，杜鲁门政府出台各种外交政策、开展各种外交活动，这些政策和活动也就具体地构成了美国全球战略的实施。在此后长达 30 年的时间内，杜鲁门主义一直作为美国对外政策的基本原则并起着支配性作用。

❑ Questions Concerning the Speech

1. What is the supreme need of the time when the address is delivered?
2. Explain briefly the American people's faith which they stand firm in.
3. Why does America launch with free nations of Europe the cooperative economic program?
4. Who will the United States have as her partners?
5. What role does the increased world trade play?
6. Why will America strengthen the ties with freedom-loving countries?
7. How does Truman describe the living conditions of the people on the edge of misery?
8. What should be made available to help peace-loving peoples realize their aspirations for a better life?
9. How can the human family eventually lead a decent and satisfying life?

❑ Paraphrase the Following Sentences

1. Today marks the beginning not only of a new administration, but of a period that will be eventful, perhaps decisive, for us and for the world.
2. It is fitting, therefore, that we take this occasion to proclaim to the world the essential principles of the faith by which we live, and to declare our aims to all peoples.
3. We shall have as our partners countries which, no longer solely concerned with the problem of national survival, are now working to improve the standards of living of all their people.
4. Guarantees to the investor must be balanced by guarantees in the interest of the people whose resources and whose labor go into these developments.

5. In due time, as our stability becomes manifest, as more and more nations come to know the benefits of democracy and to participate in growing abundance, I believe that those countries which now oppose us will abandon their delusions and join with the free nations of the world in a just settlement of international differences.
6. But I say to all men, what we have achieved in liberty, we will surpass in greater liberty.

❑ Questions for Discussion

1. 杜鲁门在其就职演说中提出了美国全球战略的四点行动计划，其中最后一点“我们必须实行一项新的、大胆的计划，利用先进的科学和发达的工业来改进和发展不发达地区”，这就是后来俗称的“第四点计划”。试论“第四点计划”的出台背景、实施情况与历史影响。
2. 第二次世界大战还没有结束，美国总统杜鲁门就讲了一段耐人寻味的话：“美国在世界上处于领导地位……恺撒、成吉思汗、路易十四、拿破仑或其他任何一个伟大的领袖所担负的责任，都不能同美国总统今天所担负的责任相比拟。”谈谈你对杜鲁门这段话的理解。
3. 朝鲜战争是怎样爆发的？当时中国国内面临怎样的形势？在此形势下我们该不该出兵，为什么？朝鲜战争对中国产生了什么影响？

❑ Translation

哈里·杜鲁门：就职演讲

1949 年 1 月 20 日，华盛顿特区

1. 副总统先生，首席大法官先生，同胞们，我谨以谦恭的心情接受美国人民授予我的荣誉，并以坚定的决心为美国人民的幸福和世界和平竭尽全力。
2. 在履行公职时，我需要诸位的协助和祈祷。我请求你们给予我鼓励和支持。我们面临的任务是艰巨的，因此，我们只有携手并肩才能完成这些任务。
3. 我国历史上的各个时期都曾面临特殊的挑战。我们现在面临的挑战和以往面临的任何挑战一样严重。今天不仅标志着一届新政府的起点，而且标志着一个新时期的开始。这一时期对我们以及对整个世界来说，将是个多事之秋，或许还将是决定性的岁月。
4. 也许命运注定我们要去经历，或者在更大程度上是去促成人类漫长历史中的一个重大转折。本世纪上半叶的特点是，人权遭到史无前例的粗暴践踏，并经历了历史上最可怕的两场战争。当代人们最迫切的需要就是学会和睦相处。

5. 世界各国人民都怀着忐忑不安的心情面对着未来，他们既充满希望又满腹忧虑。在这迷惘的时刻，他们比以往任何时候更期待着合众国的善意、力量和明智的领导。
6. 因此，我们审时度势，利用这一时机向全世界宣告指导我们生活的信念的基本原则，向所有的民族宣布我们的目标。
7. 美国人民坚信自美国建国以来就一直激励着全国上下的信念。我们相信在法律面前人人平等，分享公共利益的机会均等。我们相信所有的人都有思想与言论自由的权利。我们相信人人生而平等，因为他们是按照上帝的形象创造的。
8. 我们坚持这一信念，绝不动摇。
9. 美国人民渴望所有国家、所有民族能自由选择他们认为合适的方式来管理自己，过上体面而满意的生活，并决心致力于建设这样的世界。美国人民尤其渴望在地球上实现和平，一种以平等自愿达成真诚一致为基础的公正和持久的和平，并决心为此而作出努力。

……

10. 战争结束以来，美国为恢复世界和平、稳定、自由作出了巨大的建设性努力，并为此投入了物资和能源。
11. 我们并没有谋求别国的领土，也没有把我们的意志强加于人。我们不要求特权，也不把特权送给任何人。
12. 我们经常积极支持联合国及其有关机构，以便能把民主原则运用到国际关系中。我们一贯主张国家之间的争端应和平解决，并依赖这种解决方法。
13. 我们已尽一切努力以达成国际协议来有效的控制我们最强大的武器。我们不断致力于限制和控制军备。
14. 鉴于教训和先例，我们鼓励在公平合理的基础上扩大世界贸易。
15. 大约在一年前，我们和欧洲的 16 个自由国家共同发起了历史上规模最大的经济合作计划。这项史无前例的计划旨在鼓励并加强欧洲的民主，使欧洲大陆的自由人民在文明前沿恢复其合法地位，并能再次对世界安全和幸福作出贡献。
16. 我们的努力已为全人类带来新的希望。我们已战胜绝望和失败主义。我们拯救了许多正在失去自由的国家。全世界数亿人民现在都同意我们的观点：我们不需要战争，我们能够实现和平。
17. 主动权掌握在我们手中。
18. 我们和其他国家一起，正在建立一个维护国际秩序与公正的更加强大的组织。我们将把那些不再仅仅关心国家生存问题，而正在努力改善人民生活水平的国家作为伙伴。我们准备实施新方案，以巩固自由世界。
19. 在今后几年，我们的和平自由纲领将着重于四项主要的行动计划。
20. 第一，我们将继续坚定不移地支持联合国及其有关机构，继续寻求途径来加强这些机构的权威并提高其效率。今天，不少新的国家正在成立，正在民主原则的指引下向自治方向迈进。我们相信，联合国将随着这些新国家的加入而得到加强。

21. 第二，我们将继续施行我们制订的世界经济复兴计划。
22. 这意味着我们必须首先全力支持欧洲复兴计划。对于世界复兴计划这一重大事业的成功，我们充满了信心。我们相信，通过复兴计划，我们的友邦将再次取得自给自足的国家地位。
23. 此外，我们还必须执行为减少世界贸易壁垒、增加世界贸易额而制订的计划。经济复兴与和平本身都取决于世界贸易的增长。
24. 第三，我们要加强热爱自由的国家的力量，以抵御侵略的威胁。
25. 我们现在正与一些国家起草一项旨在加强北大西洋地区安全的共同协议。该协议将根据联合国宪章的条款，采取集体防御协定的形式。
26. 我们根据《里约热内卢条约》已经为西半球建立了这样一个防御协定。
27. 这些协议的主要目的是明确表明自由国家抵抗来自任何地区的武装进攻的共同决心。参加这些协议的每个国家必须为共同防御贡献全部力量。
28. 如果我们能预先充分地表明，任何影响到我们国家安全的武装进攻都会遭到强大的反击，也许武装进攻就永远不会发生。
29. 我希望不久能向参议院呈送关于北大西洋安全计划的条约。
30. 此外，我们还将向那些同我们合作以维护和平与安全的自由国家提供军事顾问和装备。
31. 第四，我们必须着手拟定一项大胆的新计划，使不发达地区的进步与发展能受益于我们先进的科学和发达的工业。
32. 全世界半数以上的人口正濒临悲惨的境地，他们食物匮乏、疾患加身。他们的经济生活原始落后、停滞不前。他们的贫困无论是对自己还是对较为繁荣的地区都是一种阻碍和威胁。
33. 人类有史以来第一次掌握了能解除这些人苦难的知识和技能。
34. 在众多的国家中，美国的工业和科学技术的发展是卓越的。尽管我们用来援助其他国家人民的物质资源是有限的，但我们在技术知识方面的资源却是无法估量的，是不断增长和用之不竭的。
35. 我认为，我们应该向爱好和平的民族提供我们的技术知识，以便帮助他们实现追求美好生活的愿望。同时，我们还应该和其他国家合作，鼓励对于那些需要开发的地区进行投资。
36. 我们的目标应该是帮助世界上各个自由民族通过他们自己的努力，生产更多的粮食，更多的衣物，更多的建筑材料，以及更多的机器来减轻他们的负担。
37. 我们邀请其他国家向该计划汇集他们的技术资源。他们的贡献将会受到热烈欢迎。这是一项所有国家通过联合国及其专门机构在任何可行方面进行合作的计划。为实现和平、富足和自由，这必须是世界范围内的努力。
38. 在我国的企业、私人资本、农业、劳工等协作下，这一计划能够极大增强其他国家的工业活动，从实质上提高他们的生活水平。

39. 这种新的经济发展必须加以规划和控制，从而使被开发地区的人民有所得益。在保证投资者利益的同时，必须兼顾那些在这项发展计划中提供资源和劳力的人民的利益。
40. 在我们的计划中，剥削他国利润的老牌帝国主义没有立足之地。我们对该发展规划的设想是基于民主的公平交易的观点上的。
41. 所有国家，包括我国在内，将极大地受益于一项建设性计划，该计划是为更合理地使用世界上的人力资源和自然资源而制定的。经验表明，我们同其他国家的贸易将随着这些国家在工业和经济上的发展而扩大。
42. 繁荣与和平的关键是提高生产，而提高生产的关键是更广泛、更积极地运用现代科学技术知识。
43. 人类大家庭只有帮助那些最不幸的成员自食其力，才能过上所有人都有权享受的体面的、令人满意的生活。
44. 只有民主政治才能产生生机勃勃的力量，以激励世界人民不仅为反抗人类的压迫者，而且还为反抗人类古老的敌人——饥饿、痛苦、绝望——而斗争。
45. 根据这四项主要的行动计划，我们希望有助于创造各种条件，最终实现个人自由和全人类的幸福。
46. 显然，如果我们要成功的执行这些政策，就必须继续保持国家的繁荣，保持自身的强大。
47. 我们正在逐步但肯定无疑的编织一张国际安全和日益繁荣的世界网络。
48. 我们得到了所有希望摆脱恐惧而自由生活的人们的帮助，甚至还得到了那些至今在其政府统治下过着恐惧生活的人们的帮助。
49. 我们得到了所有希望摆脱宣传的谎言、渴望真理和真诚的人们的帮助。
50. 我们得到了所有渴望自治，渴望在决定自己事务中能表达其意志的人们的帮助。
51. 我们得到了所有渴望在经济上有保障的人们，渴望在自由社会里能够享有安全和富足的人们的帮助。
52. 我们得到了所有渴望言论自由、宗教自由以及有权选择自己满意的生活方式的人们的帮助。
53. 千百万如饥似渴追求正义的人们都是我们的盟友。
54. 随着我们国家日益稳定，随着越来越多的国家了解到民主政治的益处并分享不断增长的富足，我相信，到适当的时候，那些现在反对我们的国家便会放弃他们的妄想，并和世界上的自由国家一起，公正地解决国际分歧。
55. 许多事件给美国的民主政治带来了新的影响和新的责任。这些事件将考验我们的勇气，考验我们对职责的忠诚以及我们的自由信念。
56. 但我要告诉所有的人，我们已经实现了自由，我们还要向更高的自由目标迈进。
57. 怀着对全能的上帝的坚定信念，我们将朝着一个人类自由有保障的世界迈进。
58. 为了达到这个目标，我们将奉献出我们的力量、才智和坚定的决心。在上帝的福佑下，人类的未来无疑是个公正、和谐与和平的世界。

John F. Kennedy

(1917—1963)

约翰·F·肯尼迪

10

John F. Kennedy's Inaugural Address

Delivered 20 January, 1961, in Washington, D.C.

About the Author

约翰·菲茨杰拉德·肯尼迪(John Fitzgerald Kennedy, 1917—1963)，通常被称作约翰·F·肯尼迪（John F. Kennedy）、JFK或杰克·肯尼迪（Jack Kennedy），生于马萨诸塞州，是美国第35任总统，并被大多数美国人视为历史上最伟大的总统之一。约翰·F·肯尼迪是美国颇具影响力的肯尼迪政治家族的一员，被视为美国自由主义的代表。他也是美国历史上最年轻的当选总统，第一位生于20世纪的总统，还是美国历史上第一位信奉罗马天主教的总统和迄今为止唯一获得普利策奖的总统。

约翰·F·肯尼迪在任总统期间，内政上，致力于摆脱经济衰退，重振经济活力，并在保障黑人和妇女的平等权利等方面作出了不懈的努力。外交上，他处理了古巴导弹危机，并与当时的苏联集团继续对抗。正当肯尼迪踌躇满志要进一步干一番事业的时候，他于1963年11月22日在得克萨斯州达拉斯市遇刺身亡。他的遇刺被视为对美国历史的发展产生重大决定性影响的事件之一，因为这一事件在其后数十年中一直影响着美国政治的发展方向。

About the Speech

肯尼迪于1961年1月20日正式宣誓就任美国第35任总统，那是两大阵营（前苏联和西方）冷战激烈的时代。肯尼迪在演讲中表达了他对自由的执著追求和对和平的向往。他在对国际事务给予了极大关注的同时，呼吁美国民众承担起更多的义务，为世界和平与人类进步作出更大的牺牲。肯尼迪的就职演说与富兰克林·德拉诺·罗斯福的第一次就职演说被并称为 20 世纪最令人难忘的两次美国总统就职演说，共计 1 355 个单词的演说成为激励型语言和呼吁公民义务的典范之作。

肯尼迪从当选之后就开始考虑就职演说，他不想在演说中偏激地指责当前事务，也不喜欢重新阐述有关于冷战的陈词滥调或论述一些有可能加剧美苏紧张关系的有关共产主义威胁的问题。他希望用词可以激起和平的希望，确定一个新时代的乐观基调。

在演说中，他呼吁全人类团结起来，共同反对专制、贫困、疾病和战争，他在演说中提到的：**"不要问你的国家能为你做些什么，而要问一下你能为你的国家做些什么。"** (Ask not what your country can do for you, ask what you can do for your country.) 更是成为了美国总统历次就职演说中最脍炙人口的语句之一。

The Speech in Full

Vice-President Johnson, Mr. Speaker, Mr. Chief Justice, President Eisenhower, Vice-President Nixon, President Truman, reverend clergy, fellow citizens,

1. **We observe today not a victory of party, but a celebration of freedom—symbolizing an end, as well as a beginning—signifying renewal, as well as change.** For I have sworn before you and Almighty God the same solemn oath[1] our forebears prescribed nearly a century and three quarters ago[2].

2. **The world is very different now. For man holds in his mortal hands[3] the power to abolish all forms of human poverty and all forms of human life. And yet the same revolutionary beliefs for which our forebears fought are still at issue[4] around the globe—the belief that the rights of man come not from the generosity of the state, but from the hand of God.**

3. We dare not forget today that we are the heirs of that first revolution. Let the word go forth[5] from this time and place, to friend and foe alike, that **the torch has been passed to a new generation of Americans—born in this century, tempered by war, disciplined by a hard and bitter peace[6], proud of our ancient heritage—and unwilling to witness or permit the slow undoing[7] of those human rights to which this Nation has always been committed[8], and to which we are committed today at home and around the world.**

4. Let every nation know, whether it wishes us well or ill, that **we shall pay any**

price, bear any burden, meet any hardship, support any friend, oppose any foe, in order to assure the survival and the success of liberty.

5. This much we pledge—and more.

6. To those old allies whose cultural and spiritual origins we share, we pledge the loyalty of faithful friends. **United, there is little we cannot do in a host of cooperative ventures. Divided, there is little we can do—for we dare not meet a powerful challenge at odds[9] and split asunder[10].**

7. To those new States whom we welcome to the ranks of the free[11], we pledge our word that one form of colonial control shall not have passed away merely to be replaced by a far more iron tyranny[12]. We shall not always expect to find them supporting our view. But we shall always hope to find them strongly supporting their own freedom—and to remember that, in the past, those who foolishly sought power by riding the back of the tiger ended up inside[13].

8. To those peoples in the huts and villages across the globe struggling to break the bonds of mass misery, we pledge our best efforts to help them help themselves, for whatever period is required—not because the Communists may be doing it, not because we seek their votes, but because it is right. **If a free society cannot help the many who are poor, it cannot save the few who are rich.**

9. To our sister republics south of our border, we offer a special pledge—to convert our good words into good deeds—in a new alliance for progress—to assist free men and free governments in casting off[14] the chains of poverty. But this peaceful revolution of hope cannot become the prey[15] of hostile powers. Let all our neighbors know that we shall join with them to oppose aggression or subversion anywhere in the Americas. And let every other power know that this Hemisphere intends to remain the master of its own house.

10. To that world assembly of sovereign states, the United Nations, our last best hope in an age where the instruments of war[16] have far outpaced the instruments of peace, we renew our pledge of support—to prevent it from becoming merely a forum

for invective[17]—to strengthen its shield of the new and the weak—and to enlarge the area in which its writ[18] may run.

11. Finally, to those nations who would make themselves our adversary, we offer not a pledge but a request: that both sides begin anew the quest for peace, before the dark powers of destruction unleashed by science engulf all humanity in planned or accidental self-destruction.

12. We dare not tempt them with weakness. For only when our arms are sufficient beyond doubt can we be certain beyond doubt that they will never be employed.

13. But neither can two great and powerful groups of nations take comfort from our present course—both sides overburdened by the cost of modern weapons, both rightly[19] alarmed by the steady spread of the deadly atom, yet both racing to alter that uncertain balance of terror that stays the hand of[20] mankind's final war.

14. So let us begin anew—remembering on both sides that civility is not a sign of weakness, and sincerity is always subject to[21] proof. **Let us never negotiate out of fear. But let us never fear to negotiate.**

15. Let both sides explore what problems unite us instead of belaboring those problems which divide us.

16. Let both sides, for the first time, formulate serious and precise proposals for the inspection and control of arms—and bring the absolute power to destroy other nations under the absolute control of all nations.

17. Let both sides seek to invoke[22] the wonders of science instead of its terrors. Together let us explore the stars, conquer the deserts, eradicate disease, tap[23] the ocean depths, and encourage the arts and commerce.

18. Let both sides unite to heed in all corners of the earth the command of Isaiah[24]—to "undo[25] the heavy burdens ... and to let the oppressed go free."

19. And if a beachhead[26] of cooperation may push back the jungle of suspicion, let

both sides join in creating a new endeavor, not a new balance of power, but a new world of law, where the strong are just and the weak secure and the peace preserved.

20. All this will not be finished in the first 100 days. Nor will it be finished in the first 1,000 days, nor in the life of this Administration, nor even perhaps in our lifetime on this planet. But let us begin.

21. **In your hands, my fellow citizens, more than in mine, will rest the final success or failure of our course.** Since this country was founded, each generation of Americans has been summoned to give testimony to[27] its national loyalty. The graves of young Americans who answered the call to service surround the globe.

22. **Now the trumpet summons us again—not as a call to bear arms[28], though arms we need; not as a call to battle, though embattled[29] we are—but a call to bear the burden of a long twilight struggle[30], year in and year out, "rejoicing in hope, patient in tribulation[31]"—a struggle against the common enemies of man: tyranny, poverty, disease, and war itself.**

23. Can we forge[32] against these enemies a grand and global alliance, North and South, East and West, that can assure a more fruitful life for all mankind? Will you join in that historic effort?

24. **In the long history of the world, only a few generations have been granted the role of defending freedom in its hour of maximum danger. I do not shrink from this responsibility—I welcome it. I do not believe that any of us would exchange places with any other people or any other generation. The energy, the faith, the devotion which we bring to this endeavor will light our country and all who serve it—and the glow from that fire can truly light the world.**

25. **And so, my fellow Americans: ask not[33] what your country can do for you—ask what you can do for your country.**

26. **My fellow citizens of the world: ask not what America will do for you, but what together we can do for the freedom of man.**

27. **Finally, whether you are citizens of America or citizens of the world, ask of us the same high standards of strength and sacrifice which we ask of you. With a good conscience our only sure reward, with history the final judge of our deeds, let us go forth to lead the land we love, asking His blessing and His help, but knowing that here on earth God's work must truly be our own.** (1,391 words)

❑ Notes to the Speech

1. solemn oath：庄严的誓言。1787 年美国通过宪法，规定总统就职前应宣誓。
2. nearly a century and three quarters ago：肯尼迪于 1961 年 1 月 20 日发表本就职演说，距离 1787 年将近 175 年。
3. in his mortal hands：在人类的手中
   mortal ['mɔːtl] *adj.* having to die at some time 终将死亡的
4. at issue：under discussion; in dispute 在讨论中；在争议中
5. go forth：发布，发表。此处意为"让……听到"
6. tempered by war, disciplined by a hard and bitter peace：在战争中受过锻炼，在艰难困苦的和平时期受过磨炼。
   temper ['tempə] *vt.* make somebody stronger through exposure to hardship 使锻炼
   discipline ['disiplin] *vt.* train sb. to be obedient or self-controlled 训练，训导
   bitter peace：此处指第二次世界大战后的"冷战"
7. undoing [ʌn'duːiŋ] *n.* the ruin or downfall of sb. or sth. 毁灭；崩溃
8. commit [kə'mit] *vt.* promise (esp. oneself, one's property, etc.) to a certain cause, opinion, or course of action（与 to 连用）（尤指自身或自己的财产等）献身；奉献；致力于
9. at odds：in disagreement 意见不一致，不和
10. asunder [ə'sʌndə(r)] *adv.* <esp. literary> apart or into pieces 分开；离散
11. ranks of the free：自由国家的行列
12. iron tyranny：残酷的暴政
    tyranny ['tirəni] *n.* government by a cruel ruler with complete power 暴政；专制
13. ended up inside：葬身其中（葬身虎腹之中）
    end up: eventually reach or come to a particular state or place 最终到达某处或达到某状态
14. cast off：throw away or abandon 丢弃，抛弃。此处指"挣脱，摆脱"
15. prey [prei] *n.* an animal that is hunted and eaten by another animal 被捕食的动物；牺牲品

16. instruments of war：战争手段
    instrument ['instrumənt] *n.* something or someone that is used to get a particular result 手段；工具
17. invective [in'vektiv] *n.* rude and insulting words that someone says when they are very angry 痛骂，漫骂
18. writ [rit] *n.* a document from a court that orders someone to do or not to do something 公文；命令，票
19. rightly ['raitli] *adv.* correctly, or for a good reason 正确地；恰当地；当然
20. stay the hand of：stop, prevent 制止，阻止
21. (be) subject to：depending on 取决于
22. invoke [in'vəuk] *vt.* request or beg for 恳求，祈求
23. tap [tæp] *vt.* use or draw from 开发，利用；发掘
24. Isaiah [ai'zaiə] 以赛亚，公元前 8 世纪希伯来预言家
25. undo [ˌʌn'duː] *vt.* unfasten (what is tied or wrapped) 解开，打开，松开
26. beachhead ['biːtʃhed] *n.* an area of shore that has been taken from an enemy by force, and from which the army can prepare to attack a country 滩头阵地
27. give testimony (to sth.)：give evidence in support of sth.（对某事的）见证，证明
28. bear arms：拿起武器
    bear [bɛə] *vt.* carry 携带
29. embattled [im'bætld] *adj.* (of an army, etc.) drawn up and prepared for battle（指军队等）严阵以待的，做好战斗准备的
30. a long twilight struggle：为迎接黎明而肩负起的漫长斗争
    twilight ['twailait] *n.* the time when night is about to become day or (more usually) when day is about to become night 黄昏；黎明
31. tribulation [ˌtribju'leiʃən] *n.* great trouble or suffering 忧患，苦难
32. forge [fɔːdʒ] *vt.* form by heating and hammering 锻造；（喻）缔造
33. ask not = do not ask

❑ Appreciating the Speech

肯尼迪总统的就职演说一直被认为是演说中的典范，受到广泛的赞誉。该演说短小精悍、布局合理、逻辑严密、充满激情。

在这篇短短 1 300 多字的演讲开头，他称颂了美国的民主制度 (spoke highly of the democratic system of the United States)，激励美国人民维护和传播这一优越的制度 (motivated the American people to safeguard and spread this superior system)，反对一

切独裁专制 (opposed all forms of dictatorship)，保卫世界和平 (defended world peace)。接下来，他依次论述了与其同盟国、新独立国家、亚非贫困国家、拉美诸国、联合国及苏联集团的关系和政策。最后，他号召美国人民及世界各国的人民肩负起自己的神圣职责 (shoulder their own sacred responsibilities)，为自己国家的进步、为人类的自由而奋斗 (struggle for the advancement of their own countries and for the freedom of mankind)。

从语言上看，这篇演讲突出特点是句式整齐，生动形象。作者运用了多种修辞手段 (figure of speech)，主要包括平行结构 (parallelism)、对照 (antithesis)、暗喻 (metaphor)、引用 (quotation) 等。例如，①在论述与不同国家的关系和政策时，肯尼迪连用 6 个以 "To those ..." 起头的结构相同的介词短语引领的句子（平行结构），层次分明、清晰地表达了对这些国家的不同态度。②在论述与同盟国关系时，他使用了对照的手法，"United, there is little we cannot do in a host of cooperative ventures. Divided, there is little we can do—for we dare not meet a powerful challenge at odds and split asunder."，这里 united（团结）与 divided（分裂），little we can not do（无所不能）与 little we can do（一事无成）的相互对照，形象而生动地显示出团结与分裂将会产生的截然不同的结果，激励同属同盟国阵营的国家携手并肩、精诚团结、与对手抗衡。③在谈及与新独立国家的关系时，他恰当、传神地运用了暗喻的手法，以 "But we shall always hope to find them strongly supporting their own freedom—and to remember that, in the past, those who foolishly sought power by riding the back of the tiger ended up inside. "，警示那些国家要珍惜来之不易的自由，如执迷不悟投向前苏联阵营，定会遭受"落入虎腹"的可悲下场。④在谈到希望世界两大对立阵营联合起来时，他说："Let both sides unite to heed in all corners of the earth the command of Isaiah—to 'undo the heavy burdens ... and to let the oppressed go free.'" 这句话引自《圣经·旧约全书·以赛亚书》第 58 章第 6 节。《圣经》中的原句是 "to undo the thongs of the yoke, to let the oppressed go free."（解下轭上的索，使被压迫者得自由）。作者通过对圣经的引用，增加了演说的庄重感，易于引起信仰上帝的美国人民的共鸣，使演说更具鼓动性 (agitating) 和说服力 (convincing)。

☐ Culture Links

（1）肯尼迪与古巴导弹危机

古巴导弹危机 (Cuban Missile Crisis)，又称加勒比海导弹危机，是 1962 年冷战时期在美国、苏联与古巴之间爆发的一场极其严重的政治、军事危机。事件爆发的直接原因是苏联在古巴部署导弹。这个事件被看做是冷战的顶峰和转折点。在世界史上，人类从未如此近地处于一场核战争的边缘。

该危机始于 1962 年 10 月 14 日，美军 U-2 间谍侦察机拍到了正在古巴建设中的苏联制中程导弹发射井的照片。这张照片在 1962 年 10 月 16 日被提交给肯尼迪。照片预示美国很快就会陷入严峻的核弹威胁中，肯尼迪也因此陷于两难境地：如果美国攻击这个导弹发射井，可能会直接导致与苏联的核战争；但是如果美国不采取任何行动，则要一直忍受近距离的核弹威胁。由于距离太接近，如果对方在毫无警告的情况下发射核弹，美国很可能会在未还击之前就被击垮。另一个方面的考虑则是，美国会在它所在的西半球内成为弱者。

许多军事专家和内阁成员希望对核弹发射井进行空袭，但肯尼迪则派遣海军监视所有抵达古巴的船只并做好封港准备。他开始与苏联谈判并要求苏方撤回一切在古巴的防御武器及器械，并警告说，如果不这么做的话，古巴则要面临封港。

最后（10 月 28 日），秘密外交谈判终于成功，双方达成以下协议：苏联撤回部署在古巴的导弹，美国同意不入侵古巴，并秘密撤回部署在土耳其的导弹。这次把整个世界向核战争拉近的危机是前所未有的，但所幸被两个领导人的人性所阻挡下来。

在这一危机的处理过程中，肯尼迪一直行事果断、毫不妥协。他认识到，无论苏联战略能力陡增两倍或三倍所带来的军事影响是什么，政治影响都可能是毁灭性的。

肯尼迪勇敢的鹰派作风和冷静灵活的应对措施阻挠了这一计谋的实现，为美国人赢得了胜利，还羞辱了苏联人。

（2）“天赋人权”观念

“天赋人权”一语源于拉丁文 jus nafural，应译为“自然权利”；中国早年译成“天赋人权”,后一直沿用。“天赋人权”观（“自然权利”观），源自于古希腊哲学的自然法理论，文艺复兴以来，成为西方法律与政治思想的重要议题。它是近代自然法学派的一个重要概念，意指人具有与生俱来的生存、自由、追求幸福和财产的权利。17、18 世纪，荷兰思想家、法学家**格劳秀斯**（1583—1645）和哲学家**斯宾诺莎**（1632—1677），英国思想家、哲学家**洛克**（1632—1704），法国思想家、法学家**孟德斯鸠**（1689—1755）和思想家、哲学家**卢梭**（1712—1778）等对这一思想进行了重要的发展。

“天赋人权”观念的起源亦与基督教的教义有着密不可分的关系。基督教认为，人是神（造物主、上帝、天）创造的，神按照他自己的样子造人，因此，人是神圣的。神造人的目的，是叫人荣耀神。神造人的同时，也赋予了人管理万物的职责。再者，由于每个人都是神创造的，所以在神的面前人人平等。由此演绎出了人权的基本观念：

人是神圣的，是应当受到尊重的，是不可侮辱的；

人是神创造的，故有生存、自由、追求幸福等基本权利；

为了荣耀神，为了管理万物，人有寻求发展、接受教育、选择管理者（政府）等的权利；

人的权利是神授（天赋）的、生来俱有的，而不是另外某人赋予的，因而亦是不可侵犯的；在神面前，每个人的人权都是平等的。

“天赋人权”的观念第一次被文字清晰地表达出来，是在美国的《独立宣言》中。两百多年前，1776 年 7 月 4 日通过的《独立宣言》铿锵有力地宣告："我们认为这些真理是不言而喻的：人人生而平等，造物主赋予他们若干不可让与的权利，其中包括生命权、自由权和追求幸福的权利。为了保障这些权利，所以才在人们中间成立政府。而政府的正当权力，则系于被统治者的同意。任何形式的政府一旦对这些目标的实现起破坏作用时，人民有权来改变它或废除它，以建立新的政府。"《独立宣言》指导了美国的独立战争，创建了长治久安的民主制度。

肯尼迪在演讲开头所说的"人的权利并非来自国家的慷慨，而是来自上帝的恩赐"，即是指的"天赋人权"。美国的政治家和人民从来就坚定地相信，世界上所有人都享有与生俱来的权利，这些权利使人具有追求自由、幸福和尊严的可能，这些权利不是任何政府的恩赐，而保障这些权利是任何一个政府的义不容辞的责任。

❑ Questions Concerning the Speech

1. Why does Kennedy say that "The world is very different now"?
2. What belief is still at issue around the globe? Do you agree with him?
3. What does Kennedy pledge to the old allies of the United States?
4. What is his stated policy towards Latin America?
5. What does he say to the nations who he considers to be "our adversaries"?
6. What does Kennedy ask his fellow Americans and fellow citizens of the world to do?
7. Do you agree that freedom was in its hour of maximum danger when Kennedy assumed office? Why?

❑ Paraphrase the Following Sentences

1. And yet the same revolutionary beliefs for which our forebears fought are still at issue around the globe.
2. This much we pledge—and more.
3. United, there is little we cannot do in a host of cooperative ventures. Divided, there is little we can do.
4. the United Nations, our last best hope in an age where the instruments of war have far outpaced the instruments of peace.
5. before the dark powers of destruction unleashed by science engulf all humanity in planned or accidental self-destruction.
6. yet both racing to alter that uncertain balance of terror that stays the hand of mankind's final war.

7. So let us begin anew—remembering on both sides that civility is not a sign of weakness, and sincerity is always subject to proof.
8. each generation of Americans has been summoned to give testimony to its national loyalty

❑ Questions for Discussion

1. 肯尼迪总统在演讲中说，“不要问国家能为你们做些什么，而要问你们能为国家做些什么。”请问，我们是否有权利让国家为我们做些什么？为什么？
2. 如果你身处 20 世纪 60 年代初的美苏争霸年代，你会站在谁的一边？请说明具体理由。
3. 请谈一下肯尼迪在保障黑人及妇女的平等权利方面所做出的贡献。

❑ Translation

约翰·肯尼迪：就职演讲

1961 年 1 月 20 日，华盛顿特区

约翰逊副总统、议长先生、首席法官先生、艾森豪威尔总统、尼克松副总统、杜鲁门总统、尊敬的牧师、各位公民：

1. 今天我们庆祝的不是政党的胜利，而是自由的胜利。这象征着一个结束，也象征着一个开端，表示了一种更新，也表示了一种变革。因为我已在你们和全能的上帝面前，宣读了我们的先辈在 170 多年前拟定的庄严誓言。
2. 现在的世界已大不相同了，人类的巨手掌握着既能消灭人间的各种贫困，又能毁灭人间的各种生活的力量。但我们的先辈为之奋斗的那些革命信念，在世界各地仍然有着争论。这个信念就是：人的权利并非来自国家的慷慨，而是来自上帝的恩赐。
3. 今天，我们不敢忘记我们是第一次革命的继承者。让我们的朋友和敌人同样听见我此时此地的讲话：火炬已经传给新一代美国人。这一代人在本世纪诞生，在战争中受过锻炼，在艰难困苦的和平时期受过陶冶，他们为我国悠久的传统感到自豪——他们不愿目睹或听任我国一向保证的、今天仍在国内外作出保证的人权渐趋毁灭。
4. 让每个国家都知道——不论它希望我们繁荣还是希望我们衰落——为确保自由的存在和自由的胜利，我们将付出任何代价、承受任何负担、应付任何艰难、支持任何朋友、反抗任何敌人。
5. 这些就是我们的保证——而且还有更多的保证。
6. 对那些和我们有着共同文化和精神渊源的老盟友，我们保证待以诚实朋友那样的忠诚。

我们如果团结一致，就能在许多合作事业中无往而不胜；我们如果分歧对立，就会一事无成——因为我们不敢在争吵不休、四分五裂时迎接强大的挑战。

7. 对那些我们欢迎其加入到自由行列中来的新国家，我们恪守我们的誓言：绝不让一种更为残酷的暴政来取代一种消失的殖民统治。我们并不总是指望他们会支持我们的观点。但我们始终希望看到他们坚强地维护自己的自由——而且要记住，在历史上，凡愚蠢地骑在虎背上谋求权力的人，都以葬身虎口而告终。

8. 对世界各地身居茅舍和乡村、为摆脱普遍贫困而斗争的人们，我们保证尽最大努力帮助他们自立，不管需要花多长时间——之所以这样做，并不是因为共产党可能正在这样做，也不是因为我们需要他们的选票，而是因为这样做是正确的。自由社会如果不能帮助众多的穷人，也就无法保全少数富人。

9. 对我国南面的姐妹共和国，我们提出一项特殊的保证——在争取进步的新同盟中，把我们善意的话语变为善意的行动，帮助自由的人们和自由的政府摆脱贫困的枷锁。但是，这种充满希望的和平革命决不可以成为敌对国家的牺牲品。我们要让所有邻国都知道，我们将和他们在一起，反对在美洲任何地区进行侵略和颠覆活动。让所有其他国家都知道，本半球的人仍然想做自己家园的主人。

10. 联合国是主权国家的世界性议事机构，是我们在战争手段大大超过和平手段的时代里最后的、最美好的希望所在。因此，我们重申予以支持；防止它仅仅成为谩骂的场所；加强它对新生国家和弱小国家的保护；扩大它行使法令的管束范围。

11. 最后，对那些想与我们作对的国家，我们提出一个要求而不是一项保证：在科学释放出可怕的破坏力量、把全人类卷入到预谋的或意外的自我毁灭的深渊之前，让我们双方重新开始寻求和平。

12. 我们不敢以怯弱来引诱他们。因为只有当我们毫无疑问地拥有足够的军备时，我们才能毫无疑问地确信永远不会使用这些军备。

13. 但是，这两个强大的国家集团都无法从目前所走的道路中得到安慰——发展现代武器所需的费用使双方负担过重，致命的原子武器的不断扩散理所当然使双方忧心忡忡，但是，双方却都在争着打破这种制止人类最后战争的不确定的恐怖均势。

14. 因此，让我们双方重新开始——双方都要牢记，礼貌并不意味着怯弱，诚意永远有待于验证。让我们绝不要由于畏惧而谈判，但我们决不能畏惧谈判。

15. 让双方都来探讨使我们团结起来的问题，而不要操心那些使我们分裂的问题。

16. 让双方首次为军备检查和军备控制制订认真而又明确的提案，把毁灭他国的绝对力量置于所有国家的绝对控制之下。

17. 让双方寻求利用科学的奇迹，而不是科学造成的恐怖。让我们一起探索星球，征服沙漠，根除疾患，开发深海，并鼓励艺术和商业的发展。

18. 让双方团结起来，在全世界各个角落倾听以赛亚的训令——“解下轭上的索，使被欺压的得自由。”
19. 如果合作的滩头阵地会逼退猜忌的丛林，那么就让双方共同作一次新的努力：不是建立一种新的均势，而是创造一个新的法治世界，在这个世界中，强者公正、弱者安全、和平将得到维护。
20. 所有这一切不可能在第一个一百天内完成，也不可能在第一个一千天或者在本届政府任期内完成，甚至在我们的有生之年内也不可能完成。但是，让我们开始吧。
21. 公民们，我们方针的最终成败与其说掌握在我手中，不如说掌握在你们手中。自从合众国建立以来，每一代美国人都曾受到召唤去证明他们对国家的忠诚。响应召唤而献身的美国青年的坟墓遍及全球。
22. 现在，号角已再次吹响——不是召唤我们拿起武器，虽然我们需要武器；不是召唤我们去作战，虽然我们严阵以待。它召唤我们为迎接黎明而肩负起漫长斗争的重任，年复一年，“从希望中得到欢乐，在苦难中保持坚韧”，去反对人类共同的敌人——专制、贫困、疾病和战争本身。
23. 为反对这些敌人，确保人类更为丰裕的生活，我们能够组成一个包括东西南北各方的全球大联盟吗？你们愿意参加这一历史性的努力吗？
24. 在漫长的世界历史中，只有少数几代人在自由处于最危急的时刻被赋予保卫自由的责任。我不会推卸这一责任，我欢迎这一责任。我不相信我们中间有人想同其他人或其他时代的人交换位置。我们为这一努力所奉献的精力、信念和忠诚，将照亮我们的国家和所有为国效劳的人，而这火焰发出的光芒定能照亮全世界。
25. 因此，美国同胞们，不要问国家能为你们做些什么，而要问你们能为国家做些什么。
26. 全世界的公民们，不要问美国将为你们做些什么，而要问我们共同能为人类的自由做些什么。
27. 最后，不论你们是美国公民还是其他国家的公民，你们理应要求我们献出我们同样要求于你们的高度力量和牺牲。问心无愧是我们唯一可靠的奖赏，历史是我们行动的最终裁判，让我们走向前去，引导我们所珍爱的国家。我们祈求上帝的福佑和帮助，但我们知道，确切地说，上帝在尘世的工作必定是我们自己的工作。

Lyndon B. Johnson

(1908—1973)

林登·B·约翰逊

11

Lyndon B. Johnson: We Shall Overcome

Address to a Joint Session of Congress on Voting Legislation

Delivered 15 March, 1965, in Washington, D.C.

❑ About the Author

林登·B·约翰逊 (Lyndon B. Johnson，1908—1973)，出生于得克萨斯州基利斯比县的石墙，约翰逊家族曾参与了约翰逊城的建设。约翰逊是民主党人，年轻时开始从政，1937年国会补缺选举中当选为众议员，是罗斯福总统“新政”的积极支持者。1941年至1942年自愿报名在海军服役，担任少校，多次涉险，因临危不惧、表现勇敢，由麦克阿瑟将军亲自授予银星勋章。1948年约翰逊当选为参议员。1951年，在参议院工作仅3年，他就成为了民主党的领袖。1960年，约翰逊未能获得民主党总统候选人提名，转而接受肯尼迪提名为副总统的建议。1963年11月，肯尼迪总统遇刺身亡，副总统约翰逊旋即在达拉斯机场的空军1号总统专机的机舱里宣誓就职，成为美国第36任总统（1963年11月22日—1965年1月20日，1965年1月20日—1969年1月20日）。在继任总统一职后，1964年约翰逊以空前优势赢得总统选举。

在内政上，约翰逊总统提出与“新政”、“公平施政”、“新边疆”一脉相承的改革计划，即“伟大社会”施政纲领。他在任期间，控制有权势的政客以推动立法，不遗余力地推行各项福利法案、签署民权法案、消灭贫穷法案和减税法，得到了民主党的大力支持。他著名的“向贫穷开战”的口号，引导全国在生活富裕时考虑到饥饿和匮乏的棘手问题，深得人心。在其任期内，数百项涉及民权、税收、教育、医疗、就业、养老、住宅、环保、地方建设的法案陆续获得通过，这在美国历史上前所未有。

但是在外交上，他奉行前任总统约翰·肯尼迪的既订政策，使得越南战争不断升级。随着战争的拖延，约翰逊总统的声望持续下降。尽管其外交政策遭受失败，但是因为他的国内政策成绩斐然，尤其是他提出的“伟大社会计划”确实给予了美国人以巨大的精神动力，并成为美国人的奋斗目标，因此，约翰逊在美国民众心目中的地位还是比较高的，并且在一些史学家对历届总统的评价中依然获得高排名。

❑ About the Speech

正如1868年第十四修正案无法保障被释放奴隶的完整权利，1964年的民权法案也无法确保奴隶的后代在社会中拥有合法权利。民权领袖知道，法律与法庭禁止种族歧视之裁决本身绝对不会让非洲裔美国人完整参与国家政治生活。如果黑人要有更好的经济与政治地位，他们必须有更多能参与投票的机会。

美国阿拉巴马州的塞尔玛市是个典型南方城市，虽然有半数以上的人口是黑人，却只有少数黑人拥有投票权。为了使受到的不公正昭然天下，当地黑人领袖与学生非暴力委员会以及南方基督教领袖会议协调一致，从塞尔玛市到该州首府蒙哥马利市，发起了争取投票权的示威游行。1965年3月7日，大约500名游行者启程出发，他们安全地度过了埃德蒙德·佩图斯大桥(Edmund Pettus Bridge)，但是在桥的另一端，全副武装的州警队制止他们继续前进。游行民众试图和对方开展谈判对话，他们退到了人行道上，但答复他们的只有冷冰冰的警棍、鞭子和催泪瓦斯，结果造成流血冲突，50多名示威者入院就医。白人还攻击了到塞尔玛市准备参加进军的黑人牧师们，并致其中一人死亡。这起被称为“血色星期日”的事件，通过电视的广泛报道引起全国轰动。数小时内，成千上万的自愿者往南加入这场游行，要求白宫进行联邦干预的呼吁也从各地纷至沓来。

塞尔玛事件一爆发，约翰逊就要求联邦法官发布允许进军的司法解释，并告诫阿拉巴马州长不得干涉进军。他还对刚刚正式担任司法部长的尼古拉斯·卡岑巴赫（Nicholas Katzenbach）发布新命令：放弃宪法修正案的缓慢程序；迅速准备选举权提案。3月15日，约翰逊总统在国会两院联席会议上发表电视转播的讲话，要求国会通过选举法案。许多当时学者认为这是约翰逊最棒的一场演说，是使用西奥多·罗斯福所谓的“最佳讲坛”的完美例证，也就是总统职务作为领导美国民主之讲台的道德职权。约翰逊把大众对南方白人暴力的反感与其政治技巧相结合，呼吁美国终结种族歧视。当约翰逊引述圣歌“我们终将攻克难关！”（We Shall Overcome）时，几乎无人不为此感动，而这也成为民权运动的圣歌。在此演说中，他首次以总统身份全力支持民权运动，清楚地表达的不只是黑人成为完整公民的期盼，而且也是民主社会中其他无法补足的体悟。7 000万美国人通过三大电视网看到了19年来美国总统第一次亲自到国会就国内事务直接呼吁立法。约翰逊的这篇演讲受到舆论的一致赞扬，民权评论家称之为“总统在民权方面所作的最激进的讲话”。

❑ The Speech in Full

Mr. Speaker, Mr. President, Members of the Congress:

1. I speak tonight for the dignity of man and the destiny of democracy. I urge every member of both parties, Americans of all religions and of all colors, from every section of this country, to join me in that cause.

2. **At times history and fate meet at a single time in a single place to shape a turning point in man's unending search for freedom. So it was at Lexington and Concord. So it was a century ago at Appomattox. So it was last week in Selma, Alabama.** There, long-suffering men and women peacefully protested the denial of their rights as Americans. Many were brutally assaulted. One good man, a man of God, was killed.

3. **There is no cause for pride in what has happened in Selma. There is no cause for self-satisfaction in the long denial of equal rights of millions of Americans. But there is cause for hope and for faith in our democracy in what is happening here tonight.** For the cries of pain and the hymns and protests of oppressed people have summoned into convocation[1] all the majesty of this great government—the government of the greatest nation on earth. Our mission is at once the oldest and the most basic of this country: to right wrong, to do justice, to serve man.

4. In our time we have come to live with the moments of great crisis. Our lives have been marked with debate about great issues—issues of war and peace, issues of prosperity and depression. **But rarely in any time does an issue lay bare the secret heart of America itself. Rarely are we met with a challenge, not to our growth or abundance, or our welfare or our security, but rather to the values, and the purposes, and the meaning of our beloved nation.**

5. The issue of equal rights for American Negroes is such an issue.

6. **And should we defeat every enemy, and should we double our wealth and conquer the stars, and still be unequal to this issue, then we will have failed as a people and as a nation.** For with a country as with a person, "What is a man profited, if he shall gain the whole world, and lose his own soul?"

7. **There is no Negro problem. There is no Southern problem. There is no Northern problem. There is only an American problem. And we are met here tonight as Americans—not as Democrats or Republicans. We are met here as Americans to solve that problem.**

8. This was the first nation in the history of the world to be founded with a purpose. **The great phrases of that purpose still sound in every American heart, North and South: "All men are created equal," "government by consent[2] of the governed," "give me liberty or give me death".** Well, those are not just clever words, or those are not just empty theories. In their name Americans have fought and died for two centuries, and tonight around the world they stand there as guardians of our liberty, risking their lives.

9. **Those words are a promise to every citizen that he shall share in the dignity of man. This dignity cannot be found in a man's possessions; it cannot be found in his power, or in his position. It really rests on his right to be treated as a man equal in opportunity to all others.** It says that he shall share in freedom, he shall choose his leaders, educate his children, provide for his family according to his ability and his merits as a human being. To apply any other test—to deny a man his hopes because of his color, or race, or his religion, or the place of his birth is not only to do injustice, it is to deny America and to dishonor the dead who gave their lives for American freedom.

10. Our fathers believed that if this noble view of the rights of man was to flourish, it must be rooted in democracy. The most basic right of all was the right to choose your own leaders. The history of this country, in large measure, is the history of the expansion of that right to all of our people. Many of the issues of civil rights are very complex and most difficult. But about this there can and should be no argument.

11. Every American citizen must have an equal right to vote.

12. There is no reason which can excuse the denial of that right. There is no duty which weighs more heavily on us than the duty we have to ensure that right.

13. Yet the harsh fact is that in many places in this country men and women are kept

from voting simply because they are Negroes. Every device of which human ingenuity is capable has been used to deny this right. The Negro citizen may go to register only to be told that the day is wrong, or the hour is late, or the official in charge is absent. And if he persists, and if he manages to present himself to the registrar, he may be disqualified because he did not spell out his middle name or because he abbreviated a word on the application. And if he manages to fill out an application, he is given a test. The registrar is the sole judge of whether he passes this test. He may be asked to recite the entire Constitution, or explain the most complex provisions of State law. And even a college degree cannot be used to prove that he can read and write.

14. For the fact is that the only way to pass these barriers is to show a white skin. Experience has clearly shown that the existing process of law cannot overcome systematic and ingenious[3] discrimination. No law that we now have on the books—and I have helped to put three of them there—can ensure the right to vote when local officials are determined to deny it. In such a case our duty must be clear to all of us. **The Constitution says that no person shall be kept from voting because of his race or his color. We have all sworn an oath before God to support and to defend that Constitution. We must now act in obedience to that oath.**

15. Wednesday, I will send to Congress a law designed to eliminate illegal barriers to the right to vote.

16. The broad principles of that bill will be in the hands of the Democratic and Republican leaders tomorrow. After they have reviewed it, it will come here formally as a bill. I am grateful for this opportunity to come here tonight at the invitation of the leadership to reason with my friends, to give them my views, and to visit with my former colleagues. I've had prepared a more comprehensive analysis of the legislation which I had intended to transmit to the clerk tomorrow, but which I will submit to the clerks tonight. But I want to really discuss with you now, briefly, the main proposals of this legislation.

17. This bill will strike down[4] restrictions to voting in all elections—Federal, State, and local—which have been used to deny Negroes the right to vote. This bill will establish a simple, uniform standard which cannot be used, however ingenious the effort, to flout[5] our Constitution. It will provide for citizens to be registered by

officials of the United States Government, if the State officials refuse to register them. It will eliminate tedious, unnecessary lawsuits which delay the right to vote. Finally, this legislation will ensure that properly registered individuals are not prohibited from voting.

18. I will welcome the suggestions from all of the Members of Congress—I have no doubt that I will get some—on ways and means to strengthen this law and to make it effective. But experience has plainly shown that this is the only path to carry out the command of the Constitution.

19. To those who seek to avoid action by their National Government in their own communities, who want to and who seek to maintain purely local control over elections, the answer is simple: open your polling places to all your people.

20. Allow men and women to register and vote whatever the color of their skin.

21. Extend the rights of citizenship to every citizen of this land.

22. There is no constitutional issue here. The command of the Constitution is plain. **There is no moral issue. It is wrong—deadly wrong—to deny any of your fellow Americans the right to vote in this country. There is no issue of States' rights or national rights. There is only the struggle for human rights. I have not the slightest doubt what will be your answer.**

23. But the last time a President sent a civil rights bill to the Congress, it contained a provision to protect voting rights in Federal elections. That civil rights bill was passed after eight long months of debate. And when that bill came to my desk from the Congress for my signature, the heart of the voting provision had been eliminated. **This time, on this issue, there must be no delay, or no hesitation, or no compromise with our purpose.**

24. We cannot, we must not, refuse to protect the right of every American to vote in every election that he may desire to participate in. And we ought not, and we cannot, and we must not wait another eight months before we get a bill. We have already waited a hundred years and more, and the time for waiting is gone.

25. So I ask you to join me in working long hours—nights and weekends, if necessary—to pass this bill. And I don't make that request lightly. For from the window where I sit with the problems of our country, I recognize that from outside this chamber is the outraged conscience of a nation, the grave concern of many nations, and the harsh judgment of history on our acts.

26. But even if we pass this bill, the battle will not be over. What happened in Selma is part of a far larger movement which reaches into every section and State of America. It is the effort of American Negroes to secure for themselves the full blessings of American life. **Their cause must be our cause too. Because it's not just Negroes, but really it's all of us, who must overcome the crippling[6] legacy of bigotry[7] and injustice.**

27. And we shall overcome[8].

28. As a man whose roots go deeply into Southern soil, I know how agonizing racial feelings are. I know how difficult it is to reshape the attitudes and the structure of our society. But a century has passed, more than a hundred years since the Negro was freed. And he is not fully free tonight.

29. It was more than a hundred years ago that Abraham Lincoln, a great President of another party, signed the Emancipation Proclamation; but emancipation is a proclamation, and not a fact. **A century has passed, more than a hundred years, since equality was promised. And yet the Negro is not equal. A century has passed since the day of promise. And the promise is un-kept.**

30. The time of justice has now come. I tell you that I believe sincerely that no force can hold it back. It is right in the eyes of man and God that it should come. And when it does, I think that day will brighten the lives of every American. For Negroes are not the only victims. How many white children have gone uneducated? How many white families have lived in stark[9] poverty? How many white lives have been scarred by fear, because we've wasted our energy and our substance to maintain the barriers of hatred and terror?

31. And so I say to all of you here, and to all in the nation tonight, that those who appeal to you to hold on to the past do so at the cost of denying you your future.

32. This great, rich, restless country can offer opportunity and education and hope to all, all black and white, all North and South, sharecropper[10] and city dweller. These are the enemies: poverty, ignorance, disease. They're our enemies, not our fellow man, not our neighbor. And these enemies too—poverty, disease, and ignorance: we shall overcome.

33. Now let none of us in any section look with prideful righteousness on the troubles in another section, or the problems of our neighbors. There's really no part of America where the promise of equality has been fully kept. In Buffalo as well as in Birmingham, in Philadelphia as well as Selma, Americans are struggling for the fruits of freedom. This is one nation. What happens in Selma or in Cincinnati is a matter of legitimate concern to every American. **But let each of us look within our own hearts and our own communities, and let each of us put our shoulder to the wheel to root out injustice wherever it exists.**

34. As we meet here in this peaceful, historic chamber tonight, men from the South, some of whom were at Iwo Jima, men from the North who have carried Old Glory to far corners of the world and brought it back without a stain on it, men from the East and from the West, are all fighting together without regard to religion, or color, or region, in Vietnam. Men from every region fought for us across the world twenty years ago.

35. And now in these common dangers and these common sacrifices, the South made its contribution of honor and gallantry[11] no less than any other region in the Great Republic—and in some instances, a great many of them, more.

36. And I have not the slightest doubt that good men from everywhere in this country, from the Great Lakes to the Gulf of Mexico, from the Golden Gate to the harbors along the Atlantic, will rally now together in this cause to vindicate[12] the freedom of all Americans.

37. For all of us owe this duty; and I believe that all of us will respond to it. Your President makes that request of every American.

38. **The real hero of this struggle is the American Negro. His actions and protests, his courage to risk safety and even to risk his life, have awakened**

the conscience of this nation. His demonstrations have been designed to call attention to injustice, designed to provoke change, designed to stir reform. He has called upon us to make good the promise of America. And who among us can say that we would have made the same progress were it not for his persistent bravery, and his faith in American democracy.

39. **For at the real heart of battle for equality is a deep seated belief in the democratic process. Equality depends not on the force of arms or tear gas but depends upon the force of moral right; not on recourse to violence but on respect for law and order.**

40. And there have been many pressures upon your President and there will be others as the days come and go. But I pledge you tonight that we intend to fight this battle where it should be fought—in the courts, and in the Congress, and in the hearts of men.

41. We must preserve the right of free speech and the right of free assembly. But the right of free speech does not carry with it, as has been said, the right to holler[13] fire in a crowded theater. We must preserve the right to free assembly. But free assembly does not carry with it the right to block public thoroughfares[14] to traffic.

42. We do have a right to protest, and a right to march under conditions that do not infringe the constitutional rights of our neighbors. And I intend to protect all those rights as long as I am permitted to serve in this office.

43. We will guard against violence, knowing it strikes from our hands the very weapons which we seek: progress, obedience to law, and belief in American values.

44. **In Selma, as elsewhere, we seek and pray for peace. We seek order. We seek unity. But we will not accept the peace of stifled rights, or the order imposed by fear, or the unity that stifles protest. For peace cannot be purchased at the cost of liberty.**

45. In Selma tonight—and we had a good day there—as in every city, we are working for a just and peaceful settlement. And we must all remember that after this

speech I am making tonight, after the police and the FBI and the Marshals have all gone, and after you have promptly passed this bill, the people of Selma and the other cities of the Nation must still live and work together. And when the attention of the nation has gone elsewhere, they must try to heal the wounds and to build a new community.

46. This cannot be easily done on a battleground of violence, as the history of the South itself shows. It is in recognition of this that men of both races have shown such an outstandingly impressive responsibility in recent days—last Tuesday, again today.

47. The bill that I am presenting to you will be known as a civil rights bill. But, in a larger sense, most of the program I am recommending is a civil rights program. Its object is to open the city of hope to all people of all races.

48. Because all Americans just must have the right to vote. And we are going to give them that right. All Americans must have the privileges of citizenship—regardless of race. And they are going to have those privileges of citizenship—regardless of race.

49. But I would like to caution you and remind you that to exercise these privileges takes much more than just legal right. It requires a trained mind and a healthy body. It requires a decent home, and the chance to find a job, and the opportunity to escape from the clutches[15] of poverty.

50. Of course, people cannot contribute to the nation if they are never taught to read or write, if their bodies are stunted[16] from hunger, if their sickness goes untended, if their life is spent in hopeless poverty just drawing a welfare check. So we want to open the gates to opportunity. But we're also going to give all our people, black and white, the help that they need to walk through those gates.

51. My first job after college was as a teacher in Cotulla, Texas, in a small Mexican-American school. Few of them could speak English, and I couldn't speak much Spanish. My students were poor and they often came to class without breakfast, hungry. And they knew, even in their youth, the pain of prejudice. They never seemed to know why people disliked them. But they knew it was so, because I saw it in their eyes. I often walked home late in the afternoon, after the classes were finished, wishing there was

more that I could do. But all I knew was to teach them the little that I knew, hoping that it might help them against the hardships that lay ahead.

52. And somehow you never forget what poverty and hatred can do when you see its scars on the hopeful face of a young child. I never thought then, in 1928, that I would be standing here in 1965. It never even occurred to me in my fondest dreams that I might have the chance to help the sons and daughters of those students and to help people like them all over this country.

53. But now I do have that chance—and I'll let you in on[17] a secret—I mean to use it.

54. And I hope that you will use it with me.

55. **This is the richest and the most powerful country which ever occupied this globe. The might of past empires is little compared to ours. But I do not want to be the President who built empires, or sought grandeur[18], or extended dominion.**

56. **I want to be the President who educated young children to the wonders of their world.**

57. **I want to be the President who helped to feed the hungry and to prepare them to be tax-payers instead of tax-eaters.**

58. **I want to be the President who helped the poor to find their own way and who protected the right of every citizen to vote in every election.**

59. **I want to be the President who helped to end hatred among his fellow men, and who promoted love among the people of all races and all regions and all parties.**

60. **I want to be the President who helped to end war among the brothers of this earth.**

61. And so, at the request of your beloved Speaker, and the Senator from Montana,

the majority leader, the Senator from Illinois, the minority leader, Mr. McCulloch, and other Members of both parties, I came here tonight—not as President Roosevelt came down one time, in person, to veto a bonus bill, not as President Truman came down one time to urge the passage of a railroad bill—but I came down here to ask you to share this task with me, and to share it with the people that we both work for. I want this to be the Congress, Republicans and Democrats alike, which did all these things for all these people.

62. **Beyond this great chamber, out yonder in fifty States, are the people that we serve. Who can tell what deep and unspoken hopes are in their hearts tonight as they sit there and listen. We all can guess, from our own lives, how difficult they often find their own pursuit of happiness, how many problems each little family has. They look most of all to themselves for their futures. But I think that they also look to each of us.**

63. Above the pyramid on the great seal of the United States[19] it says in Latin: "God has favored our undertaking." God will not favor everything that we do. It is rather our duty to divine[20] His will.

64. But I cannot help believing that He truly understands and that He really favors the undertaking that we begin here tonight. (3, 813 words)

❑ Notes to the Speech

1. convocation [ˌkɔnvəˈkeiʃən] *n.* <formal> the process of arranging for a large meeting to be held 召集
2. consent [kənˈsent] *n.* agreement about something 同意，允许
3. ingenious [inˈdʒiːnjəs] *adj.* marked by originality, resourcefulness, and cleverness in conception or execution（物体、计划、思想等）精巧的；新颖独特的；巧妙的
4. strike down：say that a law, decision etc. is illegal and officially end it 取消，删去
5. flout [flaut] *vt.* treat with contemptuous disregard 公然藐视，无视（法律等）
6. crippling [ˈkripliŋ] *adj.* causing so much damage or harm that something no longer works or is no longer effective 极有害的；有严重后果的
7. bigotry [ˈbigətri] *n.* the intolerance of a person who is stubbornly devoted to his or her own opinions and prejudices 偏执，顽固

8. *We Shall Overcome*：1963 年 8 月在华盛顿举行的近 25 万人参加的民权示威游行中，民谣皇后 Joan Baez 演唱了 *We Shall Overcome*。现在在美国，每年 1 月的第三个星期一是马丁·路德·金日，纪念黑人民权领袖马丁·路德·金。无数群众，包括白人、黑人，扶老携幼，唱起 *We Shall Overcome*，和平地纪念他的逝世。歌曲歌词如下：

We shall overcome,	我们要战胜一切，
we shall overcome,	我们要战胜一切，
we shall overcome someday.	我们总有一天能战胜一切。
Oh, deep in my heart I do believe.	我从心灵深处，坚决相信：
That we shall overcome someday.	我们总有一天能战胜一切。
We shall live in peace,	我们要和平的生活，
we shall live in peace,	我们要和平的生活，
we shall live in peace someday.	我们总有一天会和平的生活。
Oh, deep in my heart I do believe.	我从心灵深处，坚决相信：
That we shall overcome someday.	我们总有一天能战胜一切。
We'll walk hand in hand,	我们要团结向前，
we'll walk hand in hand,	我们要团结向前，
we'll walk hand in hand someday.	我们总有一天会团结前进。
Oh, deep in my heart I do believe.	我从心灵深处，坚决相信：
That we shall overcome someday.	我们总有一天能战胜一切。

9. stark [stɑːk] *adj.* complete or extreme 完全的，十足的
10. sharecropper ['ʃɛəˌkrɔpə] *n.* a poor farmer who uses someone else's land, and gives the owner part of the crop in return 佃农
11. gallantry ['gæləntri] *n.* exceptional or heroic courage when facing danger (especially in battle) 勇敢
12. vindicate ['vindikeit] *vt.* maintain, uphold, or defend 维护
13. holler ['hɔlə] *vt.* <informal> (especially American English) to shout loudly 大声叫喊
14. thoroughfare ['θəːrəˌfɛə] *n.* a public road from one place to another 通路，大道
15. clutch [klʌtʃ] *n.* influence, or control 掌握，控制
16. stunted ['stʌntid] *adj.* not developing properly or to full size（发育、生长等）受妨碍的；发育不良的
17. let sb. in on：allow sb. to share one's secret 告知，透露；让某人参与
18. grandeur ['grændʒə] *n.* impressive beauty, power, or size 壮观；显赫
19. the great seal of the United States：美国国徽
20. divine [di'vain] *vt.* <literary> discover or guess something 猜测，预测

❑ Appreciating the Speech

1965 年，民权运动游行者 (civil rights marchers) 在塞尔玛遭到了无耻的、持续的暴力攻击 (brutal attack) 后，3 月 15 日约翰逊总统在参众两院联席会议 (joint session of Congress) 上发表了声情并茂 (affectionate) 的特别咨文 (State of the Union Address)，并引述圣歌 (hymn)《我们终将攻克难关》(*We Shall Overcome*)，呼吁美国一定要改变种族隔离的现状 (the status quo of racial segregation)，终结种族歧视 (racial discrimination)，从而推动了选举权法 (Voting Rights Act) 的通过。从内容上看，演说发生在特定背景下，针对性强，有的放矢 (targeted); 语言自然朴素，极具感染力; 通过充实的事例，晓之以理，使听众明确努力的方向和行动的目标，富有说服力 (persuasive)。

演说一开始，约翰逊即表明立场，说明此次演讲的目的是为了“人类的尊严和民主的命运”(the dignity of man and the destiny of democracy)。他列举了黑人选民受到登记限制 (registration restriction) 的种种实例，并阐述如何保障其投票权的方案。接下来他宣称：“这不是道德问题，否认任何一位美国同胞在这个国家拥有选举权是错误的——是致命的错误。这不是州权利与国家权利的问题，而仅仅是为人权而抗争。”(“There is no moral issue. It is wrong—deadly wrong—to deny any of your fellow Americans the right to vote in this country. There is no issue of States' rights or national rights. There is only the struggle for human rights.”)，这也是全文的点睛之笔 (best line)；他表示“不拖延、不犹豫、不妥协”(no delay, no hesitation, no compromise) 地进行选举权立法 (voting legislation)。总统还把自己的政治权力 (political power) 与民权运动的道德因素 (moral factor) 融合起来，“他们的事业也必定是我们的事业。因为不仅是黑人，实际上我们所有人都应当克服偏执和不公正的遗毒。”(Their cause must be our cause too. Because it's not just Negroes, but really it's all of us, who must overcome the crippling legacy of bigotry and injustice.)。最后，约翰逊还论述了政府的目标及其愿望，即“要成为一位使幼有所学、饥有所食、贫有所立的总统，要成为一位保护每一次选举中每一个选民的权利的总统”。

从语言上看，排比句的运用是这篇演讲的显著特点 (outstanding feature)。如“So it was at Lexington and Concord. So it was a century ago at Appomattox. So it was last week in Selma, Alabama.”此处排比句有一个明显的特点，就是时间和空间的对比。所提及的地方由远及近，时间亦是从“百年前”到“上周”，条理清晰。统一的“So it was”句式也起到了强调各自主语，明确比较主体的作用。再如“There is no Negro problem. There is no Southern problem. There is no Northern problem. There is only an American problem.”此处约翰逊强调，问题不存在南北之分，存在的只有“美国”这个国家的整体问题。演说将结束时，连续用了 5 个“I want to be the President who”的句型单独成段，排山倒海的气势 (grandeur) 增强了表达效果。同样，第 3 段“There is no cause for… There is no cause for… But there is cause for…”；第 22 段 “There is no constitutional issue… There is no moral issue… There is no issue of…. There is only…”；第 38 段 “His demonstrations have been designed to call attention to injustice, designed to provoke change, designed to stir reform.” 等也运用了排比句。倒装句 (inverted sentence)、强调句型 (emphatic pattern)、虚拟语气 (subjunctive mood) 的多处体现也使演讲者的思想表达得更充分、更鲜明，如第 4 段、25 段、39 段中的倒装结构；第 46 段 “It is in recognition of this that…” 的强调句；第 6 段、38 段的虚拟句等。此外，层进 (climax)、暗喻 (metaphor) 等多种修辞的灵活运用更易引起听众的认同。如 “we *ought not*, and we *cannot*, and we *must not* wait… ” 语气强烈、充满感情，表达了政府支持民权法案的坚定决心 (steadfast determination)。而 50 段 “drawing a welfare check”（领到一张福利支票）则形象地表现出了政府许诺和现实之间的距离，富于感召力。

❑ Culture Links

（1）我有一个梦想

在 20 世纪 60 年代，美国人逐渐认识到，南北战争所致力的解放黑奴运动，并没有产生使美国黑人成为完全平等公民的预期效果。19 世纪后期，美国黑人的公民权利受到州和地方歧视黑人的法规和惯例层层约束和限制。在日常生活中，美国黑人常常被隔离开来，不能与白人同在一个学校上学，乘坐同一公共交通工具，同在一个地方居住。黑人不能充分参与美国社会生活，甚至在 100 年后仍然和奴隶一样被剥夺各种权利，他们生活水准的提高与国家的发展并非完全相称。因此美国黑人的平等问题成为一个严重的社会问题。

1963 年 8 月 28 日，美国著名民权运动黑人领袖马丁·路德·金在华盛顿哥伦比亚特区主持了有 25 万人参加的集会，然后领导群众浩浩荡荡地从华盛顿纪念碑出发，分两路游行到林肯纪念堂。在林肯纪念堂前，马丁·路德·金发表了举世闻名的演说《我有一个梦想》，为反对种族歧视、争取平等发出呼喊。他说：“今天，我高兴地同大家一起，参加这次将成为我国历史上为争取自由而举行的最伟大的示威集会。”“我的梦想深深扎根于美国的梦想之中。我梦想有一天我们这个国家挺身屹立，真正实践其信条的真谛，即我们认为真理是不言而喻的，人人生而平等。”“梦想有一天在佐治亚的红山上，昔日奴隶的儿子与昔日奴隶主的儿子坐在一起，共叙兄弟情谊；梦想有一天在密西西比州自由与正义替代压迫与剥削。”“终有一天，我们会自由。”

有新闻记者指出，马丁·路德·金的演讲 “充满林肯和甘地精神的象征和圣经的韵律”。他既义正言辞又有节制，公开宣扬非暴力的改革途径；并且侃侃陈词，扣人心弦。他用高昂雄辩的言语自觉地将宗教修辞与人们耳熟能详的爱国主义象征熔为一炉，表达了一种对理想世界的预言和振奋人心的观念。这篇演说词作为对民权运动目标的精辟阐述迅速进入了美国语言和全民意识。在 20 世纪 60 年代和 70 年代，美国国会、总统和法院将马丁·路德·金在讲演中提到的各种法律障碍一一解除了。

马丁·路德·金领导的非暴力抵抗运动，不但赢得了蒙哥马利城公共汽车种族隔离制度的废除，而且赢得了全国、全世界对伯明翰市黑人运动的关注和同情；不但胜利地组织了美国历史上影响深远的向首都华盛顿的“自由进军”运动，为全美国的黑人争取人权，而且深深地打动了包括总统在内各阶层白人的心；不但促成了美国国会通过民权法案，从法律上正式结束美国黑人的被歧视地位，而且影响了英国国会通过反种族歧视法和反性别歧视法。1964 年 11 月，马丁·路德·金由于对美国的反对种族歧视、争取黑人自由平等的斗争所做的杰出贡献，而获得了该年度的诺贝尔和平奖。

（2）约翰逊政府与民权法案

1964 年 5 月，林登·约翰逊在密歇根大学演讲说，他要使美国步入“一个伟大的社会”，这就是他对内政策的标志。随后他推行了这项计划，计划的核心是“保障民权，并向贫困宣战”，扩大公共福利的范围和对象。在就业、医疗、教育、生活和住房、城市发展等一系列民生领域，约翰逊都扩大了政府用于公共福利的财政支出。

约翰逊的政治前途与黑人民权法案息息相关，南方的种族歧视传统曾使他在黑人民权问题上犹豫和沉默，但他最终认识到：沉默固然可以使他成为代表某一地域的国会议员，但无法使他成为美国人民的领袖。因此他对法案从公开反对转变为积极支持，他从顽固保守的南方阵营中出来，促成了一系列民权法案的通过，从而动摇了南方种族隔离制的社会根基和白人至上的政治信念。

约翰逊政府先后促使国会通过了 3 个民权法案：① 1964 年民权法，最高法院法官阿瑟·戈德堡称之为“人的尊严的证明”。该法案的目标是消除因种族、肤色、宗教和国籍背景所产生的一切歧视。规定黑人可以同白人一样享用旅馆、饭店、娱乐休息等公共场所，禁止在公共场所实行种族隔离；② 1965 年《选民登记法》(又称《选举权法》)，约翰逊在签字仪式上说，这项法案粉碎了对黑人“古老束缚的最后一个主要枷锁”，禁止在选民登记时采取文化考查和其他歧视性措施；③ 1968 年民权法 (又称《开放住房法》)，是重建以来美国通过的第一个住宅法。它规定：1970 年该法全部生效时，80% 的住宅在出售或出租时禁止歧视。

这一系列民权法案改变了许多美国人的人生，特别是黑人和其他少数民族。1964 年 7 月约翰逊签署具有历史性意义的《民权法案》时，一户黑人家庭从电视上看到了这一历史时刻并对约翰逊心生感激。40 年后，这家的女儿康多莉扎·赖斯成为美国历史上第一位黑人女国务卿。2008 年奥巴马以非洲裔的身份当选美国首位黑人总统，打破了白人垄断美国总统的历史。目前美国从联邦到地方，黑人参政的现象是非常普遍的。约翰逊在一个需要变革的时代，顺应历史潮流、及时地把握了时机、做出正确的变革。有人称其为“民权总统”，对此他当之无愧。

（3）越南战争

越南战争（Vietnam War），简称越战，是南越（越南共和国）及美国对抗共产主义的北越（越南民主共和国）及“越南南方民族解放阵线”（又称越共）的一场战争。最早开始援助南越的美国总统是艾森豪威尔；约翰·肯尼迪开始支持在越南作战；林登·约翰逊将战争扩大。在尼克松执政时期，美国因国内的反战浪潮而逐步将军队撤出越南。北越军和南越共军最终打败了南越政府军队，占领了全越南。

早在杜鲁门和艾森豪威尔政府时期，为避免共产主义在东南亚国家的蔓延，遏制前苏联、制裁中国，维护其在亚太地区的利益，美国就确定了干涉越南的政策。1961 年肯尼迪政府以“顾问团”名义派遣军事人员直接插手越南战争，在那里进行一场“特种战争”。约翰逊上台后，把“特种战争”升级为“局部战争”，扩大战争规模，开始对越南北方进行轰炸袭击。1965 年，约翰逊下令采取“雷声隆隆”行动，在南越不再局限于使用傀儡军，美国直接派军队参战。侵越美军迅速增加，达到 50 万人。

约翰逊政府大规模武装侵略越南非但没有动摇越南人民抗美救国的决心，相反，在中国和其他国家的援助下，越南人民艰苦抗战、不断取得胜利，使美国在越战中泥足深陷，带来一系列严重后果。军事上，美军人员伤亡惨重，厌战情绪高涨，士兵逃亡剧增；经济上，由于越战军费开支大幅度增加，加剧了国内通货膨胀，加速了经济危机的到来；政治上，美国国内进行了一场声势浩大的反战运动。

这场和平反战运动从校园反叛，街头抗议，到非暴力反抗，赢得了广大美国民众的支持与同情，从而影响了公众舆论的导向以及政府政策的制定，使越南战争得以提前结束，昭示了和平和民众的强大力量，增强了人们实现世界和平的信心。

（4）“《纽约时报》诉沙利文案”

在约翰逊总统任上的 1964 年，美国联邦最高法院对“《纽约时报》诉沙利文案”（*New York Times Co. v. Sullivan*）的判决，是美国新闻史上里程碑式的判例，这一案件的影响一直延续至今。联邦最高法院确立的“真实恶意原则”使美国各新闻媒体在批评国家公职人员方面获得了几乎不受限制的特权，进一步保证了舆论对公权力的有效监督。

纽约时报案发生在 20 世纪 60 年代美国民权运动风起云涌的时期。1960 年 3 月 29 日，《纽约时报》刊载了题为“留心他们高涨的呼声”（Heed Their Rising Voices）的政治宣传广告，为民权运动募捐基金，并猛烈地抨击了美国南方各级政府镇压民权示威的行径，其中特别谴责阿拉巴马州蒙哥马利市警方对示威学生施行的“滥用公权的暴力行为”。可是，后来有人发现，广告中有个别细节不够真实。比如，广告中说有几位黑人学生因领导和平示威而被警察驱出大学校园，实际上这几位学生是因进入一家仅供白人就餐的餐厅抗议，使餐厅无法正常营业，违反了当时阿拉巴马州的种族隔离法和社会治安法而被驱，警察的行为基本上属于依法行事。又如，黑人领袖马丁·路德·金只被政府逮捕过 4 次，广告中却说 7 次。广告引发了警方的强烈不满。看过报纸后的蒙哥马利市政官员、警察局局长沙利文，向蒙哥马利巡回法庭提起诉讼。《纽约时报》的员工和律师试图证明报社并没有诽谤警察局长，因为广告上根本没有提到沙利文的名字，但沙利文的律师们用各种方法证明这些内容“指涉而且关系到”沙利文。1960 年 11 月 3 日，沙利文的这一诉讼请求获得了巡回法庭的支持，法官判决《纽约时报》败诉，并向沙利文赔偿 50 万美元，这一判决于 1962 年 8 月 30 日再次获得阿拉巴马州高级法院的支持，州法院遵循普通法的惯例，认为当言论造成他人的声誉、职业、交易、商业活动等损失时，该言论即构成诽谤。

《纽约时报》不服两级法院的判决，上诉到联邦最高法院。1964 年 1 月 6 日，“《纽约时报》诉沙利文案”正式开庭。庭辩结束两个月后，1964 年 3 月 9 日，联邦最高法院 9 位大法官以 9 票对 0 票作出判决，撤销原判，裁定《纽约时报》公司胜诉。联邦最高法院在判决书中指出，对于政府官员的公职行为的诽谤案中，阿拉巴马法院在适用法律时，缺乏对联邦宪法第一修正案和第十四修正案所赋予的言论自由和新闻自由的保障。判决进一步指出，“公民履行批评官员的职责，如同官员恪尽管理社会的职责”，为了保障新闻自由，政府官员不得单纯因新闻报道中的内容有失实的部分而提出诽谤起诉。除非他们能证明媒体的报道存在“真实恶意”（actual malice，即“真实恶意原则”），并且还需证明自己的实际利益因为这一部分失实的内容确实受到了伤害。但是在这个案件中，警察局长沙利文无法证明《纽约时报》公司的这个报道存在真实恶意，因此判其败诉。

该案是保障新闻自由的关键判决。“真实恶意原则”要求，诽谤案件的原告必须证明，所诉的报道出版者明知报道是假的，或者罔顾报道真伪。由于原告承担了极重的举证责任，而且证明一个人内心的活动较为困难，当涉及公众人物时，此类案件极少会胜诉。“真实恶意原则”实际上是为了保障媒体和公民有权批评任何一个政府官员，而给官员诉讼设置障碍，要他们知难而退。

❑ Questions Concerning the Speech

1. How could a man realize his dignity according to Johnson?
2. Why are people in many places in America kept from voting?
3. Please explain the functions of the bill that Johnson plans to submit to the clerks.
4. What is the solution for people who seek to maintain purely local control over elections?
5. Why does Johnson say “what happened in Selma is part of a far larger movement” in Paragraph 26?
6. Who are the enemies that Americans shall overcome?
7. Why is the American Negro the real hero of the struggle for democracy?
8. Does equality depend on the force of arms or violence?
9. What does it take if people want to exercise the privileges of citizenship?

❑ Paraphrase the Following Sentences

1. For with a country as with a person, “What is a man profited, if he shall gain the whole world, and lose his own soul?”

2. Every device of which human ingenuity is capable has been used to deny this right.
3. For from the window where I sit with the problems of our country, I recognize that from outside this chamber is the outraged conscience of a nation, the grave concern of many nations, and the harsh judgment of history on our acts.
4. But let each of us look within our own hearts and our own communities, and let each of us put our shoulder to the wheel to root out injustice wherever it exists.
5. People cannot contribute to the nation if they are never taught to read or write, if their bodies are stunted from hunger, if their sickness goes untended, if their life is spent in hopeless poverty just drawing a welfare check.
6. "God has favored our undertaking." God will not favor everything that we do. It is rather our duty to divine His will.

❑ Questions for Discussion

1. 1965 年 3 月，民权运动支持者自阿拉巴马州的塞尔玛进行了 3 次示威游行后，最终到达首府蒙哥马利，并递交了请愿书。为什么说蒙哥马利是游行的终点、自由的起点?
2. 早在中国春秋战国时代，墨子就提出了“兼爱”思想，希望天下人人平等。他曾经说过：“使天下人兼相爱，爱人若爱其身——爱得万民——爱人者必见爱，而恶人者必见恶也。”试分析墨子思想和美国之平等观的异同点。
3. 邓小平在 1992 年视察南方时指出，我们“必须大胆吸收和借鉴人类社会创造的一切文明成果”。而作为资产阶级自由主义的社会改革并体现那个时代社会精英的行动主义精神，约翰逊的“伟大社会”又对中国推进“和谐社会”建设有何启示?

❑ Translation

林登·约翰逊：我们终将攻克难关

国会两院联席会议上关于投票立法的演说

1965 年 3 月 15 日，华盛顿特区

议长先生、总统、国会成员：

1. 今晚我为人类的尊严和民主的命运而演说。我呼吁两党所有成员、所有宗教与肤色的美国人以及来自这个国家各地的人，一同和我参与这项理念。
2. 有时历史和命运于某个时间在某处相会，而形成人类对自由之无止尽追寻过程的转折

点，这发生于列克星敦和康科德事件中，发生于一个世纪前的阿波马托克斯，也于上周发生在阿拉巴马州的塞尔玛。在那里，长期受苦的男女们和平地抗议身为美国人的权利被拒绝。许多人被残忍地攻击，有一个善良的人，一个上帝的子民，被杀害了。

3. 塞尔玛事件没有什么值得骄傲的理由；长久以来数百万美国人的平等权利遭拒绝，没有自满的理由。但是今晚在这里，我们有理由对民主制度抱以希望与信念。因为被压迫人们所发出的痛苦呼喊、圣歌以及抗议之声已召集了这个世界上最伟大国家的政府的所有威严。我们眼前所需做的是这个国家最古老与最基本的任务：纠正错误、执行正义、服务人民。

4. 现在，我们正经历重大的危急时刻。关于重大议题的争论是我们生活的标志：战争与和平议题、繁荣与萧条议题。但任何时代少有能够揭露美国本身内心秘密的议题。我们甚少面临挑战，并非关于成长或富裕、福利或保障，而是关于我们热爱的祖国的价值、目标及意义。

5. 美国黑人的平等权问题就是这样一个议题。

6. 假如我们战胜每个敌人、增加我们的财富并征服星球，却仍对此议题持不平等态度，那么我们将是个失败的民族与国家。因为一个国家就如同一个人，“如果赢得整个世界却失去自己的灵魂，又有什么益处呢？”

7. 没有黑人的问题，没有南方问题，没有北方问题，只有美国人的问题。而今晚我们在此相遇，我们都是美国人，不是民主党或共和党，我们是以美国人的身份在这里解决问题。

8. 这是世界历史上第一个为某一目标而创建的国家，那些伟大的话语仍回响在每个美国人心中，无论是北方或南方：“所有人生而平等”、“征得被统治者同意的政府”、“不自由毋宁死”。这些不只是漂亮的词语，也不是空洞的理论。两个世纪以来，美国人以自己的名义抗争并牺牲，而今晚，他们在全世界以捍卫者之姿冒着生命危险保卫我们的自由。

9. 这些语句是对每个公民的承诺，应许他们拥有人类的尊严。这种尊严在一个人的财产中是不可能找到的；在他的权力或地位中也是不可能找到的。它真正仰赖的是拥有与他人一样被平等对待的权利。也就是如同人类一样依据自己的能力和优点分享自由、可以选择自己的领袖、教育孩子并供养家庭。运用任何其他的测试——因为肤色或种族、宗教或出生地而拒绝给予一个人希望——不仅仅是不公平之举，也是否认美国并且侮辱为美国人的自由生活而献身的先辈。

10. 我们的祖先认为，人权这一崇高理念若要兴旺发达，必须深植于民主制度中。所有权利中，最基本的便是选择领袖的权利。我们国家的历史在很大意义上也是把此项权利扩大给所有人民的历史。许多公民权利的问题非常复杂，也是最困难的。但是关于此点则不能也不应有争议。

11. 每个美国公民必须有平等的投票权。

12. 没有理由为拒绝此项权利而辩解。没有比确保这项权利还要重要的职责。

13. 然而残忍的事实却是全国很多地方的男女只因为他们是黑人而被禁止投票。人类的所有灵巧智能都使用在拒绝这项权利上。前去登记的黑人公民不是被告知日期错误与时间太晚，就是负责的官员缺席。如果黑人坚持并设法到登记处，他也许会因为没有写中间名或在申请表上省略一个字而被取消资格。如果他设法填写申请表，他则必须接受测试。而登记员是唯一判定他能否通过测试的人。他可能会被要求背诵完整的宪法或解释州法中最复杂的条款。即使是大学学位也不能证明其有读写能力。

14. 而实际上，唯一可以通过这些阻碍的方法就是证明你是白种人。经验清楚表明现行的法律程序不可能消除这种系统的处心积虑的歧视。现在我们在书上拥有的法律——我已在那边放了三本——如果地方官员决意拒绝，则无法保障投票权。在这种情况下，我们必须清楚我们的职责。宪法声明任何人不得因他的种族或肤色而被禁止投票。我们已在上帝面前发誓支持并捍卫宪法。我们现在必须遵守誓言行动。

15. 星期三我将送交国会一条消除非法阻碍投票权的法令。

16. 明天该法案的广泛原则将会在民主党与共和党的领导人手中。他们审阅过后，将会正式成为法案。我很感谢今晚能有机会受邀前来规劝我的朋友，让他们了解我的想法并且拜访我的前同僚们。我已准备了更为全面的立法分析，我本来打算明天交给职员，但是我今晚便会送交。而现在我确实要与你们简短地讨论这项立法的主要提议。

17. 这项法案将会打破所有选举投票的限制——联邦、州以及地方——这些限制曾经拒绝黑人投票。这项法案将会精心设立一个简单的、统一的标准，并且不能被用于藐视宪法。如果州官员拒绝公民投票，法案将会保证他们通过美国政府官员的登记。法案将消除冗长的且不必要的延迟投票权的诉讼。最后，立法将确保正当登记的人们不被禁止投票。

18. 我将欢迎所有国会成员关于加强此法案并使之有效的方法与手段之建议——我毫不怀疑我会获得一些建议。但是经验已清楚表明这是实施宪法命令的唯一途径。

19. 对于那些寻求在他们的社区避开联邦政府行动的人；对于希望并寻求维持纯粹地方控制选举的人，答案很简单：开放你们的投票地点给所有人。

20. 无论肤色，允许所有人登记投票。

21. 给予我们国家所有公民以公民权。

22. 这不是宪法问题，宪法命令非常清楚。这不是道德问题，否认任何一位美国同胞在这个国家拥有选举权是错误的——是致命的错误。这不是州权利与国家权利的问题，而仅仅是为人权而抗争。我丝毫不怀疑你们将作出怎样的回答。

23. 上次总统将公民权法案送交国会，其中包含了一项保护联邦选举权的条款。该法案在经过长达八个月的辩论之后才通过。当国会将该法案送至我的办公桌等我签名时，投票条款的核心已被删除。这次，在此议题上，不能够有拖延、犹豫以及对目标的妥协。

24. 我们不能，我们绝对不能拒绝保护每个美国人欲参与投票之选举权。我们不应、不能也不必再一次等待八个月以通过法案。我们已等待一百多年，等待时间已结束。

25. 因此，我要求你们与我一起长时间努力——数个夜晚与周末，如果必须的话——通过法案。我并非草率地作出此要求，因为我坐在国家问题的窗口边，并认识到在这个房间外，是一个国家愤怒的良心、许多国家的严肃关切以及历史对我们的行为的严厉评判。

26. 但即使我们通过法案，战斗也不会结束，塞尔玛发生的事件只是触及美国各地更大型运动的一部分。这是美国黑人为保障自己美国生活美满幸福而做的努力。他们的事业也必定是我们的事业。因为不仅是黑人，实际上我们所有人都应当克服偏执和不公正的遗毒。

27. 而我们终将攻克难关。

28. 本质深植于南方国土的我知道种族情感是多么令人痛苦。我知道要改造我们社会的态度与结构是多么困难。但是一个世纪已经过去了，一百多年来黑人仍然没有自由，并且到今晚都还没有完全自由。

29. 一百多年前另一党的伟大总统亚伯拉罕·林肯签署了《解放宣言》，但是解放只是一项宣言而非事实。自从承诺平等以来，一个世纪过去了，超过一百年，而黑人却仍遭受不平等的待遇。承诺的日子已经过一个世纪之久，而承诺没有被兑现。

30. 正义的时刻已来到，而我真诚地认为没有任何力量能够阻挡这一时刻。在人类与上帝眼中这一刻应该来，来临时，我想那天将会照亮每个美国人的生活。黑人不是唯一受害者。多少白人小孩未受教育？多少白人家庭生活极其贫困？因为我们浪费了精力与物资去维护仇恨与恐怖这些障碍，多少白人的生活因恐惧留下了创伤？

31. 因此今晚我要告诉在座的所有人以及全国同胞，那些恳求你坚持过去做法的人这么做是以拒绝你的未来为代价。

32. 这个伟大、富有、永不止息的国家能够提供机会、教育和希望给所有人：所有黑人和白人、整个南方和北方、佃农和城市居民。这些是敌人：贫穷、无知、疾病。他们才是我们的敌人而不是我们的同胞与邻居。而这些贫穷、疾病与无知也是我们必须战胜的敌人。

33. 在任何地区，我们都不要以高傲的正义对其他地区的麻烦或我们邻居的问题冷眼旁观。美国没有任何地区能完全维持平等的承诺。在布法罗以及伯明翰，在费城以及塞尔玛，美国人都在争取自由。这是一个国家。在塞尔玛或辛辛那提发生的事件是每个美国人关切的合法事务。但是以我们人人都关注一下我们自己的内心和我们所在的社区，让我们鼎力相助，消除存在于任何地方的不公平。

34. 今晚我们在这和平与历史性的会场碰面时，那些来自南方的人，其中某些人曾在硫磺岛；那些从北方来的人，他们把美国国旗带至世界各地，并且毫无瑕疵地将之带回；

还有从东部、西部来的人，所有这些人不分宗教、肤色或地域，正在越南一起作战。来自每个地区的人二十年前都在为我们在世界各地奋战。

35. 在这些共同的危险与牺牲中，南方贡献的荣誉与英勇不比这个伟大共和国其他地区少——在某些例子中甚至还更多。

36. 我毫不怀疑这个国家各地的所有好人，从北美五大湖到墨西哥湾，从金门到沿大西洋海港的人会为此理念而群起维护所有美国人的自由。

37. 因为这是我们的职责，并且我相信我们所有人都会响应这个号召。你们的总统向每个美国人提出要求。

38. 这场斗争的真正英雄是美国黑人。他们的行动与抗议以及冒险失去安全甚至生命的勇气，已经唤醒了这个国家的良知。他们的示威运动旨在引起对于不公正的关注、激起改变、推动改革。他们号召我们要完成美国的承诺。若不是他们百折不挠的勇敢以及对美国民主的信念，在我们之中，有谁能说我们会取得如此的进展了?

39. 平等之战的真正精神在于深植于民主过程的信念。平等并非仰赖武器或催泪瓦斯的力量，而是依赖道德权利；并非依赖暴力而是对法律和秩序的尊重。

40. 你们的总统有许多压力，未来的日子里还会有其他压力。但是今晚我保证我们将为这场战斗而奋斗到底；在法庭、国会以及人们的心中。

41. 我们必须保护言论自由与集会自由的权利，但是如上所述，言论自由并不代表有在拥挤的剧院大喊失火的权利。我们必须保护集会自由权利，但是自由集会并不代表有权阻碍交通畅通之权利。

42. 在不侵犯邻里宪法权利的情况下，我们有权抗议以及游行。而我打算保护所有那些权利，只要我仍在此职位上。

43. 我们要防止暴力，我们知道暴力从我们手中打击我们寻求的武器——进步、对法律的遵守以及对美国价值的信念。

44. 在塞尔玛如在别处，我们寻求并祈祷和平，我们寻求秩序，我们寻求团结。但是我们不会接受阻止权利的和平、加诸恐惧的秩序或是遏制抗议的团结。因为追求和平不能以付出自由为代价。

45. 今晚在塞尔玛，以及其他我们曾拥有美好日子的各城市，我们为了安定的正义与和平而努力。我们所有人必须记得在我今晚演说之后，在警察、联邦调查局和执行官们离开之后，以及你们快速通过该法案之后，塞尔玛以及国家其他城市的人民仍必须一起生活与工作。当国家的注意力转移到其他地方，他们必须要设法治愈创伤并建立一个新的社会。

46. 在这暴力的战场上无法轻易达成目标，南方历史已历历在目。值得褒扬的是，最近两个种族人民已证明了这项明显深刻的责任——上个星期二以及今天。

47. 我现在所提出的法案即是民权法案，但更广义地说，我所提议的大部分方案都是民权方案，其目标在于将希望之城开放给所有种族的人民。
48. 因为所有美国人都必须拥有投票权，因此我们将给予他们投票权。不分种族，所有美国人都必须拥有公民特权，而无论什么种族，他们都将得到公民特权。
49. 但是我想告诫并提醒你们：要行使这些特权不只需要正当的合法权利，还需要训练有素的心智与健康的身体，需要像样的家、找工作的机会以及脱离穷困潦倒的机会。
50. 当然，如果人们从来没有被教导读与写，如果他们的身体因饥饿而营养不良，如果他们的疾病得不到照料，如果他们生活在无望的贫困中而仅能领到一张福利支票，人民就不可能为国家做贡献。因此我们希望打开机会大门，但是我们将协助所有的黑人与白人走过这些大门。
51. 大学毕业后，我的第一份工作是在德州科土拉一所小型墨西哥裔美国人的学校教书，他们当中几乎没有人能说英语，而我也不会说西班牙文。我的学生非常贫穷，他们通常没有早餐吃，饥饿地来到学校。他们在年轻时就知道受歧视的痛苦，他们不知道为什么人们不喜欢他们，但他们知道情况就是这样，因为我从他们的眼神中可以得知。上完课之后，我经常下午很晚才回家，希望我能做得更多。但我只知道教授他们我的知识，希望能有助于他们对抗未来的艰辛。
52. 当你看到贫穷与仇恨在年轻孩童充满希望的脸上留下伤疤时，绝对忘不了这带来的伤害。在 1928 年，我绝对想不到我会于 1965 年站在这里，我甚至从来没有梦想过能有机会帮助那些学生的子女们以及全国像他们一样的人。
53. 但我现在的确有机会——我会告诉你们一个秘密——我一定会利用它。
54. 而我希望你们会与我一起利用这个机会。
55. 这是全球有史以来最富有最强大的国家。过去所有帝国的力量几乎无法与我们比拟。但我不希望成为建立帝国、寻求显赫或扩张领土的总统。
56. 我希望成为教育孩子们了解世界奇观的总统。
57. 我希望成为帮助贫穷者不再饥饿并让他们成为纳税人而非纳税者之负担的总统。
58. 我希望成为帮助穷人解决贫困以及保护所有公民选举投票权的总统。
59. 我希望成为帮助结束同胞之间仇恨以及促进所有种族、区域以及党派人民之间的爱之总统。
60. 我希望成为帮助结束地球上兄弟之间战争的总统。
61. 因此在敬爱的议长与蒙大拿州参议员、多数党领袖，伊利诺伊州参议员、少数党领袖麦克卡罗其先生以及两党其他成员的请求下，今晚我来到这里——并非是罗斯福总统亲自来此否决一项红利法案的那一次，也不是杜鲁门总统到此敦促通过铁路法案的那一次——而是我到此要求你们与我一同承担此项任务，并与我们为之效力的人们一起分享。我希望国会、共和党人与民主党人一起为所有人民做这些事情。

62. 此会议室外，远处的那五十个州，有我们服务的人民。谁能说出今晚倾听演说的人民心中有多么深厚与不可言喻的希望。我们都可从自身生活中猜到他们追求幸福的困难以及每个家庭遭遇了多少难题。他们的未来大部分都得仰赖自己，但是我认为他们也仰赖我们每个人。
63. 美国国徽金字塔图案的上方，用拉丁文写着："上帝赞同我们的基业。"上帝不会赞成我们所做的每件事，预测上帝的意愿才是我们的职责。
64. 但是我禁不住相信上帝真的了解同时也赞成我们今晚在这里开始的基业。

Ronald W. Reagan

(1911—2004)

罗纳德·W·里根

12

Ronald W. Reagan's First Inaugural Address

Delivered January 20, 1981, in Washington, D.C.

❑ About the Author

罗纳德·W·里根(Ronald W. Reagan, 1911—2004)，生于伊利诺伊州坦皮科城。美国第40任总统（1981—1989）。他也是一名伟大的演讲家。在踏入政坛前，里根担任过体育节目广播员、电影演员、电视节目主持人等，第二次世界大战期间应征入伍，在空军服役。他还先后两次担任美国影视演员协会（Screen Actors Guild）主席。他的演说风格高明而极具说服力，被媒体誉为“伟大的沟通者”(The Great Communicator)。“大器晚成”的里根是创下最多纪录的美国总统：他是当选时年龄最大且最长寿的总统；他是历任总统中唯一一位演员出身的总统；他是中美两国建交后首位在任时访华的总统；他没有学过经济专业，却创立了“里根经济学”；他是最受共和党人推崇的20世纪美国总统；民主党人最喜欢的20世纪共和党总统。

里根早年参加民主党。1962年改入共和党后活跃于政坛。1966年至1974年连任两届加利福尼亚州州长。1968年和1976年两次争取共和党总统候选人的提名，但均未成功。1969年被选为共和党州长协会主席。

1980年11月4日里根再度竞选总统获胜，当选为美国第49届总统，1981年1月20日宣誓就职。1984年11月竞选连任成功，当选为美国第50届总统，1989年1月去职。在任期间，里根推行经济复兴计划，主张缩减政府规模和权力，减少税收，降低通货膨胀率和削减社会福利。在对外政策上，他对苏联采取强硬政策，谴责它是一个“邪恶的帝国”，认为苏联最恶劣的是“与人类历史的潮流相背，抹灭其人民的自由和尊严”，并提出了主动战略防御计划，被称为“星球大战”计划。1987年12月8日里根和苏联总统戈尔巴乔夫签署了旨在彻底销毁和禁止两国核武器的《中程核力量条约》(**Intermediate Nuclear Forces Treaty**)。

1993 年里根获总统自由勋章。1994 年 11 月 5 日，里根向公众宣布，他患了老年痴呆症。2004 年 6 月 5 日，他于家中辞世，享年 93 岁。

❑ About the Speech

里根总统于 1981 年 1 月 20 日发表首任就职演说。他的首任就职典礼安排在国会大厦西侧，这在美国历史上是第一次。

面对日益严重的失业和通货膨胀，里根在演讲中明确表示，“在当前这场危机中，政府不是问题的解决办法，政府就是问题所在。”他说：“我们是一个拥有政府的国家——而不是一个拥有国家的政府”，并坚定地阐明了他的目标：减少政府在国家经济中所扮演的角色，缩小联邦政府的规模。因为，依里根哲学的观点，联邦政府的管制抑制了就业机会的增加，阻碍了工业领域的创新精神。

他承诺要减轻美国人的惩罚性税收负担，实施刺激经济增长的政策。他深情地寄语美国人民，以先辈为榜样，以无愧于自己的行动，使美国继续成为“自由的楷模和希望的灯塔”。他坚信，美国人民“只要齐心协力，在上帝的帮助下，就能够而且必将解决面临的各种问题”。因为，他激励大家，“我们毕竟都是美国人”。

罗纳德·里根，这位民主价值观的坚定支持者和传播者，使美国人民对他们的国家机制重新树立起信心，这是他作为总统的一项重要成就。

❑ The Speech in Full

Senator Hatfield, Mr. Chief Justice, Mr. President, Vice-President Bush, Vice-President Mondale, Senator Baker, Speaker O'Neill, Reverend Moomaw, and my fellow citizens:

1. **To a few of us here today this is a solemn and most momentous occasion. And, yet, in the history of our nation it is a commonplace occurrence. The orderly transfer of authority as called for in the Constitution routinely takes place as it has for almost two centuries and few of us stop to think how unique we really are. In the eyes of many in the world, this every-four-year ceremony we accept as normal is nothing less than a miracle.**

2. Mr. President, I want our fellow citizens to know how much you did to carry on

this tradition. By your gracious cooperation in the transition process you have shown a watching world that we are a united people pledged to maintaining a political system which guarantees individual liberty to a greater degree than any other. And I thank you and your people for all your help in maintaining the continuity which is the bulwark[1] of our republic.

3. The business of our nation goes forward.

4. These United States are confronted with an economic affliction[2] of great proportions. We suffer from the longest and one of the worst sustained inflations in our national history. It distorts our economic decisions, penalizes[3] thrift, and crushes the struggling young and the fixed-income elderly alike. It threatens to shatter the lives of millions of our people. Idle industries have cast workers into unemployment, human misery and personal indignity.

5. Those who do work are denied a fair return for their labor by a tax system which penalizes successful achievement and keeps us from maintaining full productivity. But great as our tax burden is, it has not kept pace with public spending. For decades we have piled deficit upon deficit[4], mortgaging[5] our future and our children's future for the temporary convenience of the present. To continue this long trend is to guarantee tremendous social, cultural, political, and economic upheavals[6].

6. You and I, as individuals, can, by borrowing, live beyond our means, but for only a limited period of time. Why then should we think that collectively, as a nation, we are not bound by that same limitation?

7. **We must act today in order to preserve tomorrow. And let there be no misunderstanding—we're going to begin to act beginning today. The economic ills we suffer have come upon us over several decades. They will not go away in days, weeks, or months, but they will go away. They will go away because we as Americans have the capacity now, as we have had in the past, to do whatever needs to be done to preserve this last and greatest bastion[7] of freedom.**

8. **In this present crisis, government is not the solution to our problem; government is the problem.**

9. From time to time we've been tempted to believe that society has become too complex to be managed by self-rule, that government by an elite group is superior to government for, by, and of the people. But if no one among us is capable of governing himself, then who among us has the capacity to govern someone else?

10. All of us together—in and out of government—must bear the burden. The solutions we seek must be equitable[8] with no one group singled out to pay a higher price.

11. We hear much of special interest groups. Well our concern must be for a special interest group that has been too long neglected. It knows no sectional boundaries, or ethnic and racial divisions, and it crosses political party lines. It is made up of men and women who raise our food, patrol our streets, man[9] our mines and factories, teach our children, keep our homes, and heal us when we're sick—professionals, industrialists, shopkeepers, clerks, cabbies[10], and truck drivers. They are, in short, "We the People." This breed called Americans.

12. Well, this Administration's objective will be a healthy, vigorous, growing economy that provides equal opportunities for all Americans with no barriers born of bigotry[11] or discrimination. Putting America back to work means putting all Americans back to work. Ending inflation means freeing all Americans from the terror of runaway[12] living costs.

13. All must share in the productive work of this "new beginning," and all must share in the bounty[13] of a revived economy.

14. With the idealism and fair play which are the core of our system and our strength, we can have a strong and prosperous America at peace with itself and the world. So as we begin, let us take inventory[14].

15. We are a nation that has a government—not the other way around. And this makes us special among the nations of the earth. Our Government has no power except that granted it by the people. It is time to check and reverse the growth of government which shows signs of having grown beyond the consent of the governed.

16. It is my intention to curb the size and influence of the Federal establishment and to demand recognition of the distinction between the powers granted to the Federal Government and those reserved to the states or to the people.

17. **All of us—all of us need to be reminded that the Federal Government did not create the states; the states created the Federal Government.**

18. **Now, so there will be no misunderstanding, it's not my intention to do away with government. It is rather to make it work—work with us, not over us; to stand by our side, not ride on our back. Government can and must provide opportunity, not smother[15] it; foster productivity, not stifle[16] it.**

19. **If we look to the answer as to why for so many years we achieved so much, prospered as no other people on earth, it was because here in this land we unleashed the energy and individual genius of man to a greater extent than has ever been done before. Freedom and the dignity of the individual have been more available and assured here than in any other place on earth. The price for this freedom at times has been high, but we have never been unwilling to pay that price.**

20. It is no coincidence that our present troubles parallel and are proportionate to the intervention and intrusion in our lives that result from unnecessary and excessive growth of Government. It is time for us to realize that we are too great a nation to limit ourselves to small dreams. We're not, as some would have us believe, doomed to an inevitable decline. **I do not believe in a fate that will fall on us no matter what we do. I do believe in a fate that will fall on us if we do nothing.**

21. So with all the creative energy at our command, let us begin an era of national renewal. Let us renew our determination, our courage, and our strength. And let us renew our faith and our hope. We have every right to dream heroic dreams.

22. Those who say that we're in a time when there are no heroes—they just don't know where to look. You can see heroes every day going in and out of factory gates. Others, a handful in number, produce enough food to feed all of us and then the world beyond. You meet heroes across a counter—and they're on both sides of that counter. There are entrepreneurs[17] with faith in themselves and faith in an idea who create

new jobs, new wealth and opportunity. There are individuals and families whose taxes support the Government and whose voluntary gifts support church, charity, culture, art, and education. Their patriotism is quiet but deep. Their values sustain our national life.

23. Now I have used the words "they" and "their" in speaking of these heroes. I could say "you" and "your" because I'm addressing[18] the heroes of whom I speak—you, the citizens of this blessed land. Your dreams, your hopes, your goals are going to be the dreams, the hopes, and the goals of this Administration, so help me God.

24. We shall reflect the compassion that is so much a part of your make-up[19]. How can we love our country and not love our countrymen—and loving them reach out a hand when they fall, heal them when they're sick, and provide opportunity to make them self-sufficient so they will be equal in fact and not just in theory?

25. Can we solve the problems confronting us? Well the answer is an unequivocal[20] and emphatic "Yes." To paraphrase[21] Winston Churchill, I did not take the oath I've just taken with the intention of presiding over the dissolution[22] of the world's strongest economy.

26. In the days ahead, I will propose removing the roadblocks that have slowed our economy and reduced productivity. Steps will be taken aimed at restoring the balance between the various levels of government. Progress may be slow—measured in inches and feet, not miles—but we will progress. It is time to reawaken this industrial giant, to get government back within its means, and to lighten our punitive[23] tax burden. And these will be our first priorities, and on these principles there will be no compromise.

27. On the eve or our struggle for independence a man who might've been one of the greatest among the Founding Fathers, Dr. Joseph Warren, President of the Massachusetts Congress, said to his fellow Americans, **"Our country is in danger, but not to be despaired of. On you depend the fortunes of America. You are to decide the important question upon which rest the happiness and the liberty of millions yet unborn. Act worthy of yourselves[24]."**

28. **Well I believe we, the Americans of today, are ready to act worthy of ourselves, ready to do what must be done to insure happiness and liberty for**

ourselves, our children, and our children's children. And as we renew ourselves here in our own land, we will be seen as having greater strength throughout the world. We will again be the exemplar[25] of freedom and a beacon of hope for those who do not now have freedom.

29. To those neighbors and allies who share our freedom, we will strengthen our historic ties and assure them of our support and firm commitment. We will match loyalty with loyalty. We will strive for mutually beneficial relations. We will not use our friendship to impose on their sovereignty, for our own sovereignty is not for sale.

30. As for the enemies of freedom, those who are potential adversaries, they will be reminded that peace is the highest aspiration of the American people. We will negotiate for it, sacrifice for it; we will not surrender for it—now or ever. Our forbearance[26] should never be misunderstood. Our reluctance for conflict should not be misjudged as a failure of will. When action is required to preserve our national security, we will act. We will maintain sufficient strength to prevail[27] if need be, knowing that if we do so, we have the best chance of never having to use that strength.

31. **Above all we must realize that no arsenal or no weapon in the arsenals of the world is so formidable as the will and moral courage of free men and women. It is a weapon our adversaries in today's world do not have. It is a weapon that we as Americans do have. Let that be understood by those who practice terrorism and prey upon[28] their neighbors.**

32. I am—I'm told that tens of thousands of prayer meetings are being held on this day; and for that I am deeply grateful. We are a nation under God, and I believe God intended for us to be free. It would be fitting and good, I think, if on each inaugural day in future years it should be declared a day of prayer.

33. This is the first time in our history that this ceremony has been held, as you've been told, on this West Front of the Capitol.

34. Standing here, one faces a magnificent vista[29], opening up on this city's special beauty and history. At the end of this open mall are those shrines[30] to the giants on whose shoulders we stand. Directly in front of me, the monument to a

monumental man. George Washington, father of our country. A man of humility who came to greatness reluctantly. He led America out of revolutionary victory into infant nationhood. Off to one side[31], the stately memorial to Thomas Jefferson. The Declaration of Independence flames with his eloquence. And then beyond the Reflecting Pool, the dignified columns of the Lincoln Memorial. Whoever would understand in his heart the meaning of America will find it in the life of Abraham Lincoln.

35. Beyond those monuments—those monuments to heroism is the Potomac River, and on the far shore the sloping hills of Arlington National Cemetery[32], with its row upon row of simple white markers bearing crosses or Stars of David. They add up to only a tiny fraction of the price that has been paid for our freedom.

36. Each one of those markers is a monument to the kind of hero I spoke of earlier. Their lives ended in places called Belleau Wood, the Argonne, Omaha Beach, Salerno, and halfway around the world on Guadalcanal, Tarawa, Pork Chop Hill, the Chosin Reservoir, and in a hundred rice paddies and jungles of a place called Vietnam[33].

37. Under one such a marker lies a young man, Martin Treptow, who left his job in a small town barber shop in 1917 to go to France with the famed Rainbow Division[34]. There, on the Western front, he was killed trying to carry a message between battalions[35] under heavy fire. We're told that on his body was found a diary. On the flyleaf under the heading, "My Pledge," he had written these words: "America must win this war. Therefore, I will work; I will save; I will sacrifice; I will endure; I will fight cheerfully and do my utmost, as if the issue of the whole struggle depended on me alone."

38. **The crisis we are facing today does not require of us the kind of sacrifice that Martin Treptow and so many thousands of others were called upon to make. It does require, however, our best effort, and our willingness to believe in ourselves and to believe in our capacity to perform great deeds; to believe that together with God's help we can and will resolve the problems which now confront us.**

39. And after all, why shouldn't we believe that? We are Americans.

40. God bless you and thank you. Thank you very much. (2,493 words)

❑ Notes to the Speech

1. bulwark ['bulwə(:)k] *n.* a strong wall built for defense or protection 堡垒，壁垒
2. affliction [ə'flikʃən] *n.* <formal>something causing suffering or grief 痛苦，苦难；苦恼
3. penalize ['pi:nəlaiz] *vt.* punish, sometimes unfairly（有时指不公正地）处罚
4. we have piled deficit upon deficit: 我们的赤字不断增加
5. mortgage ['mɔ:gidʒ] *vt.* give the right or the claim to the ownership of (a house, land, etc.) in return for money lent for a certain period 抵押；把……作抵押品
6. upheaval [ʌp'hi:vəl] *n.* a big change that causes a lot of upset or disruption 剧变；动乱
7. bastion ['bæstiən] *n.* something that protects or preserves particular principles or activities 堡垒
8. equitable ['ekwitəbl] *adj.* fair and impartial 公平的，公正的
9. man [mæn] *vt.* provide a place or machine with people to operate or defend it 给（场所或机器）配置人员（或兵力）
10. cabby ['kæbi] *n.* <informal> taxi driver [口] 出租车司机
11. bigotry ['bigətri] *n.* intolerance toward people who hold different views, especially on matters of politics, religion, or ethnicity 褊狭，顽固
12. runaway ['rʌnəwei] *adj.* (of an animal or vehicle, etc.) running out of control（动物、车辆等）失控的
13. bounty ['baunti] *n.* generosity 慷慨，恩惠
14. take inventory：盘点存货（inventory *n.* 存货清单）
15. smother ['smʌðə] *v.* die or kill from lack of air（使）窒息；闷死
16. stifle ['staifl] *vt.* prevent from breathing freely 使窒息；闷死
17. entrepreneur [ˌɔntrəprə'nə:] *n.* a person who is successful in setting up businesses 企业家
18. address [ə'dres] *vt.* make a speech or remark to 对……发表演说；对……讲话
19. make-up ['meikʌp] *n.* the combination of qualities (in a person's character) 性格
20. unequivocal [ʌni'kwivəkəl] *adj.* totally clear in meaning 不含糊的
21. paraphrase ['pærəfreiz] *vt.* restate something using other words, especially in order to make it simpler or shorter（用易懂的语言或文字）重新表达
22. dissolution [disə'lu:ʃən] *n.* the breaking up or destruction of an organization or institution 分解；解体；解散
23. punitive ['pju:nitiv] *adj.* intended as punishment 惩罚性的
24. Act worthy of yourselves：做出无愧于你们自己的行动

25. exemplar [ig'zemplə] *n.* a person or thing that is a good or typical example of something 典型；模范；榜样
26. forbearance [fɔː'bɛərəns] *n.* patient self-control（耐心的）克制，自制
27. prevail [pri'veil] *vi.* be more powerful than 占优势，占上风
28. prey [prei] *vi.* (~ upon) hunt and kill another animal for food 猎捕，捕食；take advantage of or cause distress to someone 劫掠；折磨
29. vista ['vistə] *n.* a distant view, to which the eye is directed between narrow limits 狭长的景色，远景
30. shrine [ʃrain] *n.* a place connected with a holy person or event 神殿；圣坛
31. off to one side：（华盛顿纪念碑的）旁边
32. Arlington National Cemetery：阿灵顿国家公墓（美国最大和最著名的国家军人公墓，坐落于美国弗吉尼亚州阿灵顿郡）
33. 里根在这里提到的一些地名都是美国历史上一些著名战役的地点。
34. Rainbow Division：彩虹师，即美国陆军新编第 42 师。1917 年 10 月该师被派往法国参加第一次世界大战。
35. battalion [bə'tæljən] *n.* an army unit forming part of a brigade [军事] 营

❑ Appreciating the Speech

里根的这篇就职演说以其对政府作用的清醒认识 (clear-headed understanding of the function of government)、对国内外政策、原则和立场的精当阐述 (appropriate expounding of foreign and domestic policies, principles, and standpoint) 以及对美国必将战胜困难的坚定信念 (strong confidence in America's triumph over difficulties)，给听众留下了难以忘怀的印象。

演说中，他首先指出了美国正面临的种种困难与问题 (the various kinds of difficulties and problems the United States was faced with)，表示“政府不是问题的解决办法，政府本身才是问题所在 (government is not the solution to our problem; government is the problem)”，号召全体美国人民“共同肩负起(振兴美国的)责任”。他告诉大家，美国人民的梦想、希望和目标将成为本届政府的梦想、希望和目标 (the dreams, hopes and aims of the American people will be the dreams, hopes and aims of his administration)。他号召美国人民“采取无愧于自己的行动，去做确保自己和子孙后代的幸福和自由所必需的事情”。他告诫潜在的对手，“和平是美国人民最崇高的愿望……但我们永远不会为了和平而投降。”在演说的最后，面对着华盛顿纪念碑、杰斐逊纪念馆、林肯纪念堂和庄严肃穆的阿灵顿国家公墓，他深情地回顾了先人们的丰功伟绩和付出的巨大牺牲，表达了由衷的敬仰之情，然后很自然的转回到现实中来，激励美国人民，“只要齐心协力，在上帝的帮助下，

就能够而且必将解决面临的各种问题 (together with God's help we can and will resolve the problems which now confront us)”。

从语言上讲，这篇演讲的显著特点是对照和反问的使用 (the use of antithesis and rhetorical questions)。首先，本篇多次使用了对照的修辞手法。如，在演讲的开头，里根用“To a few of us here today, this is a solemn and most momentous occasion; and yet, in the history of our Nation, it is a commonplace occurrence.”，使用 yet 一词，使前后两句形成了鲜明的对比，表现了对美国的平稳的权力交接的自豪之情。在演讲中间，他用“I do not believe in a fate that will fall on us no matter what we do. I do believe in a fate that will fall on us if we do nothing.”一句，又一次以鲜明的对比表达了他鲜明的观点，即：美国人民的命运掌握在美国人民手中，如果他们无所作为，厄运必将降临。其次，本篇演讲中还几次运用了反问的修辞手法，如，在演讲的前半部分，里根用“Why, then, should we think that collectively, as a nation, we are not bound by that same limitation?”一句反问，引起听众的深思，表明作为一个国家，应该像个人一样，放弃“靠借贷过一种入不敷出的生活”；又如，在演讲的结尾处，他又以一句反问“And, after all, why shouldn't we believe that? We are Americans.”，掷地有声地激发美国人民的信心和斗志，号召大家同心协力、战胜困难。

❑ Culture Links

（1）里根总统遇刺案与美国法律

1981 年 3 月 30 日，美国总统里根与美国劳工代表，在首府华盛顿的希尔顿饭店共进午餐并发表演说。走出饭店时，围观人群中的一个青年突然用小手枪开枪，保镖迅即将里根推入等候的加长轿车内。那青年 3 秒连发 6 枪。白宫新闻秘书、一名警察和一名保镖中弹。最后一颗子弹打到车子后跳飞“射进”里根肺部。在回白宫路上，里根咳嗽吐血，才知道中弹了，马上转道急送附近乔治·华盛顿大学医疗中心急救。里根命大，子弹在心脏附近穿过。进手术室，里根还能跟医生幽默一下：“我希望你们都是共和党人。”医生回答：“总统先生，我们今天都会支持共和党的。”

凶手 26 岁，名叫约翰·欣克利，他刺杀总统的目的只是为了赢得女演员朱迪·福斯特的芳心。福斯特因在电影《出租汽车司机》中扮演一个妓女而名声大振。影片描写了一个孤独的出租汽车司机，为了表达对那个妓女的爱情，而去刺杀一位总统候选人。欣克利十分崇拜福斯特，给她写信、打电话，百般纠缠。但福斯特一次也没见他，因此，他决定用刺杀总统这一具有历史意义的行动来博得福斯特的尊敬和爱情。

欣克利当场被捕。美国人做事相当古板，必须按法律程序一步步来，不能因为刺杀总统而“从速从严”枪毙了事。审讯过程中，发现他的刺杀动机，如他事先给福斯特的信中所说，就是为了给她一个印象（to impress her）、表示他对她的爱（to express his love for her）。

这种动机和行为，在我们看来，和一个精神病患者根本挨不上边。可是，在欣克利被捕的第五天，其父母声明他患有精神病。依据美国法律，法庭请精神病专家进行了诊断，结果确定欣克利患有精神病（insanity）。一年多经过多次听证和庭审，1982年6月21日，法庭根据陪审团的裁决，判定欣克利无罪（Not guilty）。但因他具有暴力伤害危害性，所以被送进精神病医院治疗，直到确能证明他对本人与社会都不再构成威胁时才能释放。2005年12月，联邦法官判定他不再有暴力危害性，开始可以定期回家"看望"（visits）。

对于给予欣克利的无罪判决即使在美国也引起了不少争议。根据美国法律，必须由原告方证明被告的精神健全，被告才负法律责任。而要证明一个人精神健全比证明一个人精神错乱困难得多，因为被告方只要提出若干用常理无法解释的证据，就可以证明被告精神错乱。因此，两个多月后，里根向国会提出刑事审判改革法案，其中专有一部分对以精神失常为理由作辩护的法律提出修改。尽管该案反映了美国法律中的不尽如人意之处，同时，在美国个别人滥用美国宪法中规定的个人可以拥有枪支的权利，致使在美国不时发生枪击事件，引起民众担忧和恐慌，但美国的司法独立、法律程序至上等特点仍然得到了普遍的肯定。

（2）"政府本身才是问题所在"

里根上任之际正赶上美国经济急剧衰退之时，当时通货膨胀将近10%，失业率达到两位数，如何振兴经济成为里根的当务之急。当今世界各国遇到经济危机的做法普遍是加大政府干预力度，以期在最短的时间内摆脱危机，恢复增长。耐人寻味的是，里根的做法恰恰相反，正如他在首任就职演说中所说的，"政府并不是解决问题的方法，政府本身才是问题所在。"他对政府在处理经济问题上的能力持怀疑态度，因而，他的解决方法是"不为"，即撤回政府的干预，让自由市场机制自动修正所面临的问题。为此，他采取降低所得税、降低利率、对商业行为撤销管制、削减联邦开支、减少预算赤字等措施，这些措施产生了积极的效果。从1982年12月起，美国经济逐渐走出衰退，经济复苏势头比战后历次经济复苏都强劲有力。至1988年5月，美国经济持续增长65个月，成为战后和平时期经济增长持续时间最长的一次。美国国民生产总值占世界的比重也由1980年的23%上升到1986年的25.2%，由此开创出一个"里根时代"（1981—1989），这使得里根离开华盛顿时比他到这里时更受欢迎。

客观地讲，政府作为一种必要的存在，是能发挥一定作用的，但如果它变成"无所不为"的全能政府，那就会走向反面，成为"制造问题"的根源。里根虽然不是经济学家，却深知"有所为，有所不为"的道理。当然，他并不是真正意义上的"不为"，只是收回了政府不必要、不应该伸出的"手"，让"市场的回归市场"、"社会的回归社会"。他深知，资源由市场自由支配是最符合经济发展规律的逻辑，社会自组织功能的有效整合是民众权利得到切实维护的最好途径。这种理念也反映在他上海复旦大学演讲中，他当时这样说道："我认为我们的价值之根本就在于个人自由，而个人自由的核心是经济上的自由；如果人民群众在经济上得到了自由，就不再需要任何人向他们发号施令了。"而在大洋彼岸，我们还可看到另一位国家领导人的相同的理念和举措，那就是德国总理默克尔。在 2011—2012 年欧洲经济大衰退中，德国作为欧洲最大的经济体在这一惊涛骇浪中表现相当不俗，经济增长稳中有升，失业率小幅下降。默克尔和她的政府的做法也是"不为"，默克尔说："结构健康的市场经济都有很强的自我调节能力，不应该过分依靠政府行为。"

的确，在一个正常社会里，政府只需发挥有限的作用即可。一个包揽一切的全能政府对百姓而言绝对是祸不是福。

❑ Questions Concerning the Speech

1. How difficult a situation was America facing at the time of Regan's first inaugural address?
2. What role does Reagan think government should play in resolving the present crisis?
3. What does Reagan mean by "a special interest group"?
4. What is Reagan's understanding of the nature of "Government"?
5. Whom would Reagan call heroes?
6. How can the Reagan Administration solve the problems confronting the American people?
7. What characterizes Reagan's foreign policy?
8. Why does Reagan tell the story of Martin Treptow?

❑ Paraphrase the Following Sentences

1. The orderly transfer of authority as called for in the Constitution routinely takes place as it has for almost two centuries and few of us stop to think how unique we really are.
2. But great as our tax burden is, it has not kept pace with public spending.
3. It is time to check and reverse the growth of government which shows signs of having grown beyond the consent of the governed.
4. If we look to the answer as to why for so many years we achieved so much, prospered as no other people on earth, it was because here in this land we unleashed the energy and individual genius of man to a greater extent than has ever been done before.
5. It is no coincidence that our present troubles parallel and are proportionate to the intervention and intrusion in our lives that result from unnecessary and excessive growth of Government.
6. Well I believe we, the Americans of today, are ready to act worthy of ourselves, ready to

do what must be done to insure happiness and liberty for ourselves, our children, and our children's children.

7. George Washington, father of our country. A man of humility who came to greatness reluctantly. He led America out of revolutionary victory into infant nationhood.
8. I will fight cheerfully and do my utmost, as if the issue of the whole struggle depended on me alone.

❑ Questions for Discussion

1. 试论政府的性质及其合理运作。
2. 在美国，枪击案时有发生。有的枪击案甚至造成重大伤亡，震惊世界。但美国政府却无法做到禁止美国人购买和持有枪支。请分析其中原因并提出你的合理化建议。
3. 1994 年 11 月，83 岁的里根向公众宣布他患了老年痴呆症。他的这一作法对我们有什么启示?

❑ Translation

罗纳德·里根：首任就职演讲

1981 年 1 月 20 日，华盛顿特区

海特菲尔德参议员、首席法官先生、总统先生、布什副总统、蒙代尔副总统、贝克参议员、奥尼尔议长、尊敬的摩麦牧师，我的美国同胞们：

1. 今天对于我们中间的一些人来说，是一个非常庄严隆重的时刻。然而，对于这个国家的历史来说，却是一件普通的事情。按照宪法要求，政府权力正在有序地移交，我们已经如此“例行公事”了两个世纪，很少有人觉得这有什么特别的。但在世界上更多人看来，这个我们已经习以为常的四年一次的仪式，却实在是一个奇迹。
2. 总统先生，我希望我们的同胞们都能知道你为了这个传承而付出的努力。通过移交程序中的通力合作，你向正在注视着我们的世界表明：我们是发誓要团结起来维护这样一个政治体制的团体，这样的体制保证了我们能够得到比其他政体更为广泛的个人自由。同时我也要感谢你和你的伙伴们的帮助，因为你们坚持了这样的传承，而这恰恰是我们共和国的根基。
3. 我们国家的事业在继续前进。
4. 合众国正面临巨大的经济困难。我们遭遇到我国历史上历时最长、最严重之一的通货膨胀。它扰乱着我们的经济决策，打击着节俭的风气，压迫着正在挣扎谋生的青年人和收入固定的中年人，威胁着要摧毁我国千百万人民的生计。停滞的工业使工人失业、蒙受痛苦并失去了个人尊严。

5. 即使那些有工作的人，也因税收制度的缘故而得不到公正的劳动报酬，因为这种税收制度使我们无法在事业上取得成就，使我们无法保持充分的生产力。尽管我们的纳税负担相当沉重，但还是跟不上公共开支的增长。数十年来，我们的赤字额屡屡上升，我们为图目前暂时的方便，把自己的前途和子孙的前途抵押出去了。这一趋势如果长此以往，必然引起社会、文化、政治和经济等方面的大动荡。
6. 作为个人，你们和我可以靠借贷过一种入不敷出的生活，然而只能维持一段有限的时期。我们怎么可以认为，作为一个国家整体，我们就不应受到同样的约束呢？
7. 为了保住明天，我们今天就必须行动起来。大家都要明白无误地懂得——我们从今天起就要采取行动。我们深受其害的经济弊病，几十年来一直袭击着我们。这些弊病不会在几天、几星期或几个月内消失，但它们终将消失。它们之所以终将消失，是因为我们作为现在的美国人，一如既往地有能力去完成需要完成的事情，以保存这个最后而又最伟大的自由堡垒。
8. 在当前这场危机中，政府不是问题的解决办法，政府本身才是问题所在。
9. 我们时常误以为，社会已经越来越复杂，已经不可能凭借自治方式加以管理，而一个由杰出人物组成的政府要比民享、民治、民有的政府高明。可是，假如我们之中没有人能够管理自己，那么谁又能够去管理他人呢。
10. 我们大家——不论政府官员还是平民百姓——必须共同肩负起这个责任。我们谋求的解决办法必须是公平的，不要使任何一个群体付出较高的代价。
11. 我们听到许多关于特殊利益集团的谈论，然而，我们必须关心一个被忽视了太久的特殊利益集团。这个集团没有区域之分、没有人种之分、没有民族之分、没有政党之分，这个集团由许许多多的男人与女人组成，他们生产粮食、巡逻街头、管理厂矿、教育儿童、照料家务和治疗疾病。他们是专业人员、实业家、店主、职员、出租汽车司机和货车驾驶员。总而言之，他们就是“我们人民”——这个称之为美国人的民族。
12. 本届政府的目标是必须建立一种健全的、生气勃勃的和不断发展的经济，为全体美国人民提供一种不因偏执或歧视而造成障碍的均等机会，让美国重新工作起来，意味着让全体美国人重新工作起来。制止通货膨胀，意味着让全体美国人从失控的生活费用所造成的恐惧中解脱出来。
13. 人人都应分担“新开端”的富有成效的工作，人人都应分享经济复苏的硕果。
14. 我国制度和力量的核心是理想主义和公正态度。有了这些，我们就能建立起强大、繁荣、国内稳定并同全世界和平相处的美国。因此，在我们开始之际，让我们看看实际情况。
15. 我们是一个拥有政府的国家——而不是一个拥有国家的政府。这一点使我们在世界各国中独树一帜，我们的政府除了人民授予的权力，没有任何别的权力。目前，政府权力的膨胀已显示出超出了人民意愿的迹象，制止并扭转这种状况的时候到了。

16. 我打算压缩联邦机构的规模和权力，并要求大家承认联邦政府被授予的权力同各州或人民保留的权利这两者之间的区别。

17. 我们大家都需要提醒：不是联邦政府创立了各州，而是各州创立了联邦政府。

18. 因此，大家不要产生误解，我的意思不是要取消政府，而是要它发挥作用——同我们一起合作，而不是凌驾于我们之上；同我们并肩而立，而不是骑在我们的背上。政府能够而且必须提供机会，而不是扼杀机会，它能够而且必须促进生产力，而不是抑制生产力。

19. 如果我们要探究这么多年来我们为什么能取得这么大成就，并获得了世界上任何一个民族未曾获得的繁荣昌盛。其原因是在这片土地上，我们使人类的能力和个人的才智得到了前所未有的发挥。在这里，个人所享有并得以确保的自由和尊严超过了世界上任何其他地方。为这种自由所付出的代价有时相当高昂，但我们从来没有不愿意付出这代价。

20. 我们目前的困难，与政府机构因为不必要的过度膨胀而干预、侵扰我们的生活同步增加，这绝不是偶然的巧合。我们是一个泱泱大国，不能自囿于小小的梦想。现在正是认识到这一点的时候。我们并非注定走向衰落，尽管有些人想让我们相信这一点。我不相信，无论我们做些什么，我们都将命该如此；但我相信，如果我们什么也不做，我们将的确命该如此。

21. 为此，让我们以掌握的一切创造力来开创一个国家复兴的时代吧。让我们重新拿出决心、勇气和力量，让我们重新建立起我们的信念和希望吧。我们完全有权去做英雄梦。

22. 有人说我们处于一个没有英雄的时代——其实他们是不知道到哪去找英雄。你每天都可以看见英雄们进出工厂的大门。还有一部分，人数不多，但生产的粮食不仅养活我们全体美国人，还有世界上的其他人。你在柜台前就能遇见英雄们，他们在柜台的两侧。有很多企业家带着自信和对理想的信仰创造新工作、新财富和新机会。有很多个人和家庭的税收支持着政府，他们的志愿捐赠支持着宗教、慈善、文化、艺术和教育。他们的爱国主义含蓄而深沉。他们的价值维系国民生计。

23. 现在，谈及这些英雄时，我用了“他们”和“他们的”。我可以用“你们”和“你们的”，因为我正在我谈及的英雄们面前演讲，你们是这片福地上的公民。你们的梦想、你们的希望和你们的目标将是本届政府的梦想、希望和目标。上帝保佑！

24. 我们将体现出你们天性中最光辉的一面——同情心。我们如何能热爱国家却不爱国人——热爱他们那就在他们跌倒时伸手扶他们一把，他们病了就给他们治病，给他们提供机会使他们能经济上独立，这样他们才能享受事实上的平等而不是理论上的平等？

25. 我们能解决面对的问题吗？回答是掷地有声和斩钉截铁的“能”。我这样诠释丘吉尔的一句名言：“我发誓不做让这个世界上最强大的经济体土崩瓦解的总统。”

26. 在以后的日子里，我将提议铲除延缓经济发展和降低生产力的路障。旨在回复各级政府之间的平衡的措施会陆续出台。进步会很缓慢——只能用英寸英尺而不是英里来度量——但是我们将不断进步。现在到了唤醒这个工业巨人、让政府回归本位和减少惩罚性税收负担的时候了。这些将是我们的第一要务。在这些原则上，没有任何妥协的余地。

27. 在我们的独立战争开始的前夕，一个本可以成为我们伟大的国父之一的人，约瑟夫·华伦博士对他的同胞们说：“我们的国家处于危难之中，但还有希望。美国的未来在你们手上。你们将决定成千上万尚未出生的美国人的自由和幸福的问题。做无愧于自己的事吧。”

28. 我相信我们今天的美国人已经做好了准备做无愧于自己的事，做好了准备做保证我们的自由和幸福及我们的子孙万代的自由和幸福所必须做的一切。我们在国内更新自己，而在全世界看来我们更加强大了。我们将在此成为现在还没有自由的人们的自由榜样和希望灯塔。

29. 对分享我们自由的我们的邻国和盟友，我们将加强历史悠久的纽带并且坚定我们的支持和承诺。我们将以忠诚回报忠诚。我们将倾力打造一个互利的关系。我们不会把我们的友谊强加于他们的主权之上，因为我们自己的主权是不能出卖的。

30. 对自由的敌人，他们是我们的潜在敌人，他们要知道和平是美国人民的最高热望。我们可以用谈判换和平，用牺牲换和平，但我们不会用投降换和平——现在不会，永远不会。我们的容忍不容误解。我们不愿打仗不是意志崩溃。如果为了国家安全我们必须行动，我们将会行动。我们将维持取胜所必需的武力。因为只有这样，我们才有可能永远不使用武力。

31. 最重要的是我们要认识到世界上没有任何武器比自由人的意志和正义勇气更具威力。这种武器当今世界上我们的对手没有。这种武器我们美国人却有。这一点那些大搞恐怖主义和觊觎邻国的国家须知。

32. 我听说今天有无数的祝福聚会；我对此深表感谢。我们是上帝光辉普照的国家，我坚信上帝希望我们自由。我想，如果今后每个总统就职日都被作为祝福日，那倒是非常合适和令人欣喜的。

33. 正如你们所知，这个仪式在国会大厦西门举行历史上还是第一次。

34. 站在这里，一幅极其美丽的历史画卷在眼前展开。在开敞林荫道的尽头是巨人们的纪念碑、纪念堂，他们的肩上站着我们。在我的正前方是最值得纪念的国父华盛顿的纪念碑。他为人谦虚，不愿被当做伟人。他领导美国取得革命的胜利并建立了年轻的合众国。纪念碑的一侧，是杰斐逊纪念堂，独立宣言闪烁着他雄辩的火焰。倒映池的那边，是林肯纪念堂庄严的大理石柱。无论谁如果真心想理解美国的含义，他可以从林肯的一生读懂。

35. 在这些纪念碑的远处便是波多马克河，河的彼岸是阿灵顿国家公墓的斜坡，坡上有一排排的带有十字和大卫星的白色墓碑，纪念英雄们。这些简朴的墓碑仅仅是我们为自由付出的代价的一小部分。

36. 每一块碑纪念一个我前面所说的英雄。他们牺牲在贝卢伍德、阿尔贡、奥马哈海滩、萨莱诺港，以及相隔半个地球之遥的瓜达尔纳尔岛、塔拉瓦岛、猪排山、长津水库和到处是稻田和丛林的地方——越南。

37. 在其中一个墓碑下，安息着一个年轻人，马丁·特里普托，他在 1917 年辞去一个小镇理发店的工作加入著名的彩虹师来到法国。在那里的西线，他在炮火下为阵地间传递消息，不幸牺牲。我们知道在他身上找到一个日记本。扉页上有一个标题“我的誓言”，下面写道：“美国必须赢得战争。因此，我将愉快地尽全力工作、拯救、牺牲、坚守战斗，如同这个胜利靠我一个人一样。”

38. 我们今天面对的危机不要求我们付出马丁·特里普托和千百万其他人付出的牺牲。然而它需要我们最大的努力和相信我们自己及相信我们干大事的能力的愿望；相信在上帝的保佑下，我们一起能够也将要解决我们当前面对的问题。

39. 我们为什么不应该相信这一点呢？毕竟我们都是美国人！

40. 上帝保佑你们。非常感谢各位！

George Bush

(1924—　)

乔治·布什

13

George Bush's Inaugural Address

Delivered January 20, 1989, in Washington, D.C.

❑ About the Author

乔治·布什 (George Bush，1924—　)，出生于马萨诸塞州密尔顿。父亲是华尔街银行家、康涅狄格州前参议员。布什家教很严，年轻时受到良好教育。第二次世界大战期间，参加海军当飞行员，因战功卓著被授予飞行十字勋章。退伍后在耶鲁大学攻读经济学，毕业后到得克萨斯州经营石油业。

20 世纪 60 年代初，布什开始从事政治活动。1966 年至 1970 年任国会众议员，曾任众议院筹款委员会委员。1971 年至 1973 年任常驻联合国代表。1973 年至 1974 年任共和党全国委员会主席。1974 年至 1975 年任美国驻中国联络处主任。1976 年至 1977 年任中央情报局局长。后任赖斯大学副教授，并在得克萨斯州经商。1980 年布什当选为美国副总统，并于 1984 年连任。1988 年大选中布什战胜民主党对手迈克尔·杜卡基斯入主白宫，任美国第 41 任总统（1989 年 1 月—1993 年 1 月）。

布什执政后，内政平平，但外交十分活跃。1989 年 5 月，宣布对苏联实行“超越遏制”战略。1990 年，与苏联就削减战略性核武器等有关军备控制等问题达成协议。在布什任期内，东欧剧变、苏联解体，世界格局发生了根本变化。布什提出“新大西洋主义”，调整与盟国关系。还提出了建立“世界新秩序”的战略构想。1990 年 8 月，伊拉克军队入侵科威特，推翻科威特政府并宣布吞并科威特。布什坚决主张由联合国出兵干涉，亲自参与并指挥了代号为“沙漠风暴”的军事行动，对科威特和伊拉克境内的伊拉克军队发动进攻，打赢了海湾战争。但其好战的作风使他对国内经济有所轻视，因而于 1992 年大选中败给比尔·克林顿，谋求连任失败。

20 世纪 70 年代，布什任美国驻中国联络处主任期间，他和夫人经常骑着自行车走街串巷，深入中国普通百姓的生活。这位来自“汽车王国”的外交官的行为一时被传为佳话，有人把布什称为“骑自行车的大使”。他们给路人照“立拍得”，到友谊商店买邮票，去全聚德吃烤鸭，在使馆区遛狗，努力传达一个友善的美国形象。这段时光为他的后半生留下了深刻的中国情结。2009 年 9 月，美国休斯敦地区华侨华人把“2009 年杰出中国之友奖”授予老布什夫妇，表彰他们 30 多年来为促进中美关系发展所做出的杰出贡献。

❑ About the Speech

自乔治·华盛顿 1789 年在纽约的市政厅宣誓就任美国第 1 任总统，到 1989 年 1 月 20 日乔治·布什在华盛顿国会大厦西边的台阶上宣誓成为第 41 任总统，刚好 200 年。布什的就职仪式也因此尤为盛大，名字就叫做“从乔治到乔治——200 周年”典礼。这次庆典包括总统就职舞会、“海滩小子”乐队演奏的音乐会、从航空母舰上起飞的 21 架飞机的列队表演、“空中骑士团”的跳伞表演以及长达近 4 小时的就职游行等。扎成花瓣状的红白蓝 3 色彩带和历届总统的巨幅画像悬挂在沿街的建筑物上，30 万观众从四面八方涌到宾夕法尼亚大道，两旁的观礼台上挤满了欢呼者，到处是一派热闹的景象。

新总统在首席大法官伦奎斯特的主持下宣读了 35 个字的誓词，这意味着里根时代的结束。接着布什发表了 20 分钟的就职演说。他仿效艾森豪威尔总统在 1953 年的做法，先念了一小段祈祷词。他还感谢里根总统“为美国做出的伟大贡献”。因为 1981 年初里根入主白宫时，美国经济停滞、通货膨胀达两位数，营救被伊朗扣押的美国人质失败。此后的 8 年中，美国经历了长达六年多的战后和平时期最长的经济发展时期。目前工业开工率和就业人数达到多年来的最高水平，通货膨胀连续两年保持在 4.4% 的低水平。对外事务方面，和苏联改善了关系、推动一些地区冲突的平息式“降温”，国际形势有了明显缓和。

布什就职演说主要集中在国内问题上。在外交方面，新政府将保持里根外交政策的延续性。还应指出的是：演说的着重点并不在于阐释解决内政外交问题的具体政策或行动计划，而是要向全国表明其施政意向和施政原则。他强调白宫和国会要以“妥协”与“和谐”的精神共同迎接挑战。美国各界对新总统的就职演说基本持欢迎态度。一些舆论界人士认为，布什指出了当前美国人最为关心的问题。他将是一位务实的、温和的、谦虚的总统。

❑ The Speech in Full

Mr. Chief Justice, Mr. President[1], Vice-President Quayle[2], Senator Mitchell, Speaker Wright, Senator Dole, Congressman Michel, and fellow citizens, neighbors, and friends:

1. There is a man here who has earned a lasting place in our hearts and in our history. President Reagan, on behalf of our Nation, I thank you for the wonderful things that you have done for America.

2. I have just repeated word for word the oath taken by George Washington 200 years ago, and the Bible on which I placed my hand is the Bible on which he placed his. It is right that the memory of Washington be with us today, not only because this is our Bicentennial Inauguration[3], but because Washington remains the Father of our Country. And he would, I think, be gladdened by this day; for today is the concrete expression of a stunning fact: our continuity these 200 years since our government began.

3. We meet on democracy's[4] front porch, a good place to talk as neighbors and as friends. For this is a day when our nation is made whole, when our differences, for a moment, are suspended.

4. And my first act as President is a prayer. I ask you to bow your heads:

5. Heavenly Father[5], we bow our heads and thank You for Your love. Accept our thanks for the peace that yields this day and the shared faith that makes its continuance likely. Make us strong to do Your work, willing to heed[6] and hear Your will, and write on our hearts these words: **"Use power to help people." For we are given power not to advance our own purposes, nor to make a great show in the world, nor a name. There is but one just use of power, and it is to serve people.** Help us to remember it, Lord. Amen.

6. I come before you and assume the Presidency at a moment rich with promise. We live in a peaceful, prosperous time, but we can make it better. **For a new breeze is blowing, and a world refreshed by freedom seems reborn; for in man's heart, if not in fact, the day of the dictator is over. The totalitarian[7] era is passing, its old ideas blown away like leaves from an ancient, lifeless tree. A new breeze is blowing, and a nation refreshed by freedom stands ready to push on. There is new ground to be broken, and new action to be taken. There are times when the future seems thick as a fog; you sit and wait, hoping the mists will lift and reveal the right path. But this is a time when the future seems a door you can walk right through into a room called tomorrow.**

7. **Great nations of the world are moving toward democracy through the door to freedom. Men and women of the world move toward free markets through the door to prosperity. The people of the world agitate for[8] free expression and free thought through the door to the moral and intellectual satisfactions that only liberty allows.**

8. **We know what works: Freedom works. We know what's right: Freedom is right. We know how to secure a more just and prosperous life for man on Earth: through free markets, free speech, free elections, and the exercise of free will unhampered by the state.**

9. For the first time in this century, for the first time in perhaps all history, man does not have to invent a system by which to live. We don't have to talk late into the night about which form of government is better. We don't have to wrest[9] justice from the kings. We only have to summon it from within ourselves. We must act on what we know. I take as my guide the hope of a saint: **In crucial things, unity; in important things, diversity; in all things, generosity.**

10. America today is a proud, free nation, decent and civil, a place we cannot help but love. We know in our hearts, not loudly and proudly, but as a simple fact, that this country has meaning beyond what we see, and that our strength is a force for good. But have we changed as a nation even in our time? Are we enthralled[10] with material things, less appreciative of the nobility of work and sacrifice?

11. **My friends, we are not the sum of our possessions. They are not the measure of our lives. In our hearts we know what matters. We cannot hope only to leave our children a bigger car, a bigger bank account. We must hope to give them a sense of what it means to be a loyal friend, a loving parent, a citizen who leaves his home, his neighborhood and town better than he found it.** What do we want the men and women who work with us to say when we are no longer there? That we were more driven to succeed than anyone around us? Or that we stopped to ask if a sick child had gotten better, and stayed a moment there to trade a word of friendship?

12. No President, no government, can teach us to remember what is best in what we are. But if the man you have chosen to lead this government can help make a difference;

if he can celebrate the quieter, deeper successes that are made not of gold and silk, but of better hearts and finer souls; if he can do these things, then he must.

13. America is never wholly herself unless she is engaged in high moral principle. We as a people have such a purpose today. It is to make kinder the face of the Nation and gentler the face of the world. My friends, we have work to do. There are the homeless, lost and roaming. There are the children who have nothing, no love, no normalcy[11]. There are those who cannot free themselves of enslavement to whatever addiction — drugs, welfare, the demoralization[12] that rules the slums. There is crime to be conquered, the rough crime of the streets. There are young women[13] to be helped who are about to become mothers of children they can't care for and might not love. They need our care, our guidance, and our education, though we bless them for choosing life.

14. The old solution, the old way, was to think that public money alone could end these problems. But we have learned that is not so. And in any case, our funds are low. We have a deficit to bring down. We have more will than wallet; but will is what we need. We will make the hard choices, looking at what we have and perhaps allocating it differently, making our decisions based on honest need and prudent safety. And then we will do the wisest thing of all. We will turn to the only resource we have that in times of need always grows: the goodness and the courage of the American people.

15. I am speaking of a new engagement in the lives of others, a new activism, hands-on and involved, that gets the job done. We must bring in the generations, harnessing[14] the unused talent of the elderly and the unfocused energy of the young. For not only leadership is passed from generation to generation, but so is stewardship. And the generation born after the Second World War has come of age.

16. I have spoken of a thousand points of light, of all the community organizations that are spread like stars throughout the Nation, doing good. We will work hand in hand, encouraging, sometimes leading, sometimes being led, rewarding. We will work on this in the White House, in the Cabinet agencies. I will go to the people and the programs that are the brighter points of light, and I will ask every member of my government to become involved. **The old ideas are new again because they are not old, they are timeless: duty, sacrifice, commitment, and a patriotism that finds its expression in taking part and pitching in[15].**

17. We need a new engagement, too, between the Executive and the Congress. The challenges before us will be thrashed out[16] with the House and the Senate. We must bring the Federal budget into balance. And we must ensure that America stands before the world united, strong, at peace, and fiscally sound. But, of course, things may be difficult. **We need compromise; we have had dissension[17]. We need harmony; we have had a chorus of discordant[18] voices.**

18. For Congress, too, has changed in our time. There has grown a certain divisiveness. We have seen the hard looks and heard the statements in which not each other's ideas are challenged, but each other's motives[19]. And our great parties have too often been far apart and untrusting of each other. It has been this way since Vietnam. That war cleaves[20] us still. But, friends, that war began in earnest a quarter of a century ago, and surely the statute of limitations[21] has been reached. This is a fact: The final lesson of Vietnam is that no great nation can long afford to be sundered[22] by a memory. A new breeze is blowing, and the old bipartisanship[23] must be made new again.

19. To my friends—and yes, I do mean friends—in the loyal opposition—and yes, I mean loyal: I put out my hand. I am putting out my hand to you, Mr. Speaker. I am putting out my hand to you, Mr. Majority Leader. For this is the thing: **This is the age of the offered hand.** We can't turn back clocks, and I don't want to. But when our fathers were young, Mr. Speaker, our differences ended at the water's edge[24]. And we don't wish to turn back time, but when our mothers were young, Mr. Majority Leader, the Congress and the Executive were capable of working together to produce a budget on which this nation could live. Let us negotiate soon and hard. But in the end, let us produce[25]. The American people await action. They didn't send us here to bicker[26]. They ask us to rise above the merely partisan. "In crucial things, unity" —and this, my friends, is crucial.

20. To the world, too, we offer new engagement and a renewed vow: We will stay strong to protect the peace. The "offered hand" is a reluctant fist; but once made, strong, and can be used with great effect. There are today Americans who are held against their will in foreign lands, and Americans who are unaccounted for. Assistance can be shown here, and will be long remembered. **Good will begets[27] good will. Good faith can be a spiral that endlessly moves on.**

21. Great nations like great men must keep their word. When America says

something, America means it, whether a treaty or an agreement or a vow made on marble steps. We will always try to speak clearly, for candor is a compliment, but subtlety, too, is good and has its place. While keeping our alliances and friendships around the world strong, ever strong, we will continue the new closeness with the Soviet Union[28], consistent both with our security and with progress. One might say that our new relationship in part reflects the triumph of hope and strength over experience. But hope is good, and so are strength and vigilance.

22. Here today are tens of thousands of our citizens who feel the understandable satisfaction of those who have taken part in democracy and seen their hopes fulfilled. But my thoughts have been turning the past few days to those who would be watching at home, to an older fellow who will throw a salute by himself when the flag goes by, and the woman who will tell her sons the words of the battle hymns. **I don't mean this to be sentimental. I mean that on days like this, we remember that we are all part of a continuum, inescapably connected by the ties that bind.**

23. Our children are watching in schools throughout our great land. And to them I say, thank you for watching democracy's big day. **For democracy belongs to us all, and freedom is like a beautiful kite that can go higher and higher with the breeze.** And to all I say: No matter what your circumstances or where you are, you are part of this day, you are part of the life of our great nation.

24. A President is neither prince nor pope, and I don't seek a window on men's souls. In fact, I yearn for a greater tolerance, an easy-goingness about each other's attitudes and way of life.

25. There are few clear areas in which we as a society must rise up united and express our intolerance. The most obvious now is drugs. And when that first cocaine was smuggled in on a ship, it may as well have been a deadly bacteria, so much has it hurt the body, the soul of our country. And there is much to be done and to be said, but take my word for it: This scourge[29] will stop.

26. And so, there is much to do; and tomorrow the work begins. **I do not mistrust the future; I do not fear what is ahead. For our problems are large, but our heart**

is larger. Our challenges are great, but our will is greater. And if our flaws are endless, God's love is truly boundless.

27. Some see leadership as high drama, and the sound of trumpets calling, and sometimes it is that. **But I see history as a book with many pages, and each day we fill a page with acts of hopefulness and meaning. The new breeze blows, a page turns, the story unfolds. And so today a chapter begins, a small and stately story of unity, diversity, and generosity—shared, and written, together.**

28. Thank you. God bless you and God bless the United States of America. (2,344 words)

❑ Notes to the Speech

1. Mr. President：指第40任总统罗纳德·威尔逊·里根
2. Vice-President Quayle：詹姆斯·丹福思·奎尔，曾任国会众议员、参议员，1988年作为布什的竞选伙伴当选副总统。
3. Bicentennial Inauguration：（美）首任总统就职200周年纪念日
   bicentennial ['baisen'tenjəl] *adj.* of or relating to or completing a period of 200 years 200年的，每200年的
4. democracy's：指国会大厦
5. Heavenly Father：天父，指上帝
6. heed [hi:d] *vt.* <formal> pay attention to someone's advice or warning 注意，留心
7. totalitarian [ˌtəutæli'teəriən] *adj.* characterized by a government in which the political authority exercises absolute and centralized control 极权主义的
8. agitate ['ædʒiteit] *v.* (for) argue strongly in public for something you want, especially a political or social change（尤指为法律、社会状况的改变而）激烈争论，鼓动
9. wrest [rest] *vt.* obtain by seizing forcibly or violently, also metaphorically 夺取，费力取得
10. enthrall [en'θrɔ:l] *vt.* make someone very interested and excited, so that they listen or watch something very carefully 迷惑，迷醉，奴役
11. normalcy ['nɔ:məlsi] *n.* expectedness as a consequence of being usual or regular or common 常态
12. demoralization [diˌmɔrəlai'zeiʃn] *n.* destroying the moral basis for a doctrine or policy 道德颓废，堕落
13. young women：此处指未婚怀孕的妇女

14. harness ['hɑːnis] *vt.* control and use the natural force or power of something 治理；利用
15. pitch in：start working energetically 大干起来，加油干
16. thrash out：discuss vehemently in order to reach a solution or an agreement 研究解决
17. dissension [di'senʃən] *n.* disagreement among a group of people 意见不同；纠纷，争执
18. discordant [dis'kɔːdənt] *adj.* not in agreement or harmony 不调和的，不和的；[乐] 不悦耳的，不和谐的；此句的意思是："我们需要和谐，因为我们中间出现过不和谐的声音。"
19. in which not each other's ideas are challenged, but each other's motives：此处指在第 40 任总统里根当政时期，行政部门与国会经常为一些意识形态方面的问题发生争执。
20. cleave [kliːv] *vt.* <formal> divide something into completely separate parts 劈开，把……分成几个小部分（或小派别等）
21. statute of limitations：a statute prescribing the time period during which legal action can be taken 限定法律行动有效时限的法令

    statute ['stætjuːt] *n.* a law passed by a parliament, council, etc., and formally written down 法令，条例
22. sunder ['sʌndə] *vt.* <literary> break something into parts, especially violently [= split] 分裂；分离
23. bipartisanship [bai'pɑːtizənʃip] *n.* [美] 两党合作
24. our differences ended at the water's edge：我们的分歧只局限于国内问题上。
25. Let us negotiate soon and hard. But in the end, let us produce：该句指，布什上任时，民主党乃是国会的多数党，所以他极力谋求两党合作，以改变里根时期的冲突与不和。
26. bicker ['bikə] *vi.* argue over petty things 斗嘴
27. beget [bi'get] *vt.* cause something or make it happen < 书 > 招致，产生，引起；此句的意思是"善有善报"。
28. we will continue the new closeness with the Soviet Union：自 1985 年米哈依·戈尔巴乔夫出任苏联共产党总书记后，苏联对外政策发生重大变化，美苏关系也由强硬对抗逐渐转向缓和与合作，并举行了多次最高级会晤。
29. scourge [skəːdʒ] *n.* something that causes misery or death 祸害；祸根；灾害

❑ Appreciating the Speech

从演说内容上看，布什首先感谢前任 (predecessor) 总统里根对美国做出的杰出贡献，

然后缅怀华盛顿总统，表明政府“服务于人民”(to serve people) 的宗旨。接下来布什论述了当时的国内外形势 (current situation at home and abroad)，表达了人们追求自由的理想 (the pursuit of the ideal of freedom)。他明确了自己的行动指南 (guideline)，“在关键问题上，要团结一致；在重大问题上，允许多样性；在所有问题上，则须宽宏大量”(In crucial things, unity; in important things, diversity; in all things, generosity.)。布什还强调了道德准则 (moral principle) 的重要性，诠释了成功的真谛 (true essence)，指出美国的目标旨在“使国家的面貌变得更加仁厚善良，使这个世界的面貌变得更加温文尔雅”(make kinder the face of the Nation and gentler the face of the world)。紧接着布什列举了政府面临的任务，并重申美国人民的“善良品质和无畏勇气”(the goodness and the courage of the American people) 是解决问题的根本。他号召白宫和参众两院协同努力 (concerted effort)，两大党派摒弃纷争 (abandon partisanship)、团结一致 (solidarity)，共同应对挑战，因为这是一个“握手言和”的时代 (This is the age of the offered hand)。谈到外交事务，布什宣称要“加强与盟国的关系，发展友谊，使之永远牢不可破；同时还将继续密切与苏联的联系”(While keeping our alliances and friendships around the world strong, ever strong, we will continue the new closeness with the Soviet Union.)。在处理社会明显存在的诸如毒品问题时，布什明确表示决不宽容 (intolerance)。最后，他表达了自己对未来充满信心，并号召人民共同撰写美国历史的新篇章 (new chapter)。

从语言上看，象征 (symbolization) 和明喻 (simile) 的使用是该篇演说的最大特色。①象征手法（It refers to the act of expressing indirectly by an image, form, or model. 指借用某种具体形象的事物暗示特定的人物或事理，以表达真挚的感情和深刻的寓意，丰富人们的联想，耐人寻味。)：如，文中多次出现的“a new breeze is blowing”（一阵清新的和风正在吹拂），象征着一个充满希望的时刻。给人以简练、形象的实感，意境无穷。②明喻：例如，“…its old ideas blown away *like* leaves from an ancient, lifeless tree.” 布什把陈旧的观念比作“衰老枯萎的树上随风凋落的叶子”。又如，“There are times when the future *seems* thick *as* a fog.”（有时候浓雾沉沉，前途迷茫）。再如，“But this is a time when the future *seems* a door you can walk right through into a room called tomorrow.” 此处，他把未来比作一扇门。谈到专行善事的社区组织之多，布什说：“…of all the community organizations that are spread *like* stars throughout the Nation.”(这些组织像繁星一样遍布全国)。提及美国人在国际事务中向来说话算数，他说：“Great nations *like* great men must keep their word.”（伟大的民族也像伟人一样必须信守诺言)。谈到自由，“…freedom is *like* a beautiful kite that can go higher and higher with the breeze”，他把自由比作“一只美丽的风筝”。布什在演讲的最后用了诗情画意 (poetic) 的描述：“Some see leadership *as* high drama,… But I see history *as* a book with many pages, and each day we fill a page with acts of hopefulness and meaning.”（有人把领导看做一出高亢激越的戏剧……但我把历史看做是一本鸿篇巨制，每天我们都在用充满希

望和富有意义的行动书写一页历史)。演讲者借用比喻使语言精练、形象、生动，增强了语言的具体性、实感性、鲜明性，从而使听众加深对事物的理解，体会真切、感受深刻。③辅韵 (consonance)：According to Merriam-Webster's Collegiate Dictionary, consonance refers to the recurrence or repetition of consonant sounds especially at the end of stressed syllables without the similar correspondence of vowels. 辅韵是指辅音重复（尤指位于词尾的），但前面无相同或相似的元音。如，"And if our flaws are *endless*, God's love is truly *boundless*."（如果说我们的缺点无穷无尽，上帝的爱则更是无边无垠。），就赋予了语言韵律与节奏美 (rhyme and rhythm beauty)，且声响和谐。

❑ Culture Links

（1）美国人的成功观

美国人的成功观是在他们的祖先成功地建立自己的民族和国家的过程中确立起来的。崇尚成功是推动美国人及美国社会的基本动力。

今天美国人的成功观虽然经过了一个世纪以来各种变化的影响，一定的时期可能侧重于某一个方面，但基本的信念并没有本质的差异。美国人成功观的基本信念包括五个方面：第一，他们相信美国的自然环境和美国民主使美国人超越任何限制，使每个人的潜力得以充分发挥，为个人成功提供物质和社会保证；第二，成功的基本信念是通过勤劳致富；第三个信念是现代企业精神。在现代社会，科技与企业管理对个人成功起着决定性作用这一事实早已被大众所接受；第四个信念是成功所需要的个人素质。理想的美国式成功是不仅仅为自己而奋斗，更重要的是为自我完善而奋斗，即不仅要自己努力工作，还要努力提高自己；第五个信念是运气，这大概是美国文化中的一个独特现象。

上述成功的第四个信念也体现在该篇演讲的字里行间，"My friends, we are not the sum of our possessions. They are not the measure of our lives. In our hearts we know what matters.We cannot hope only to leave our children a bigger car, a bigger bank account. We must hope to give them a sense of what it means to be a loyal friend, a loving parent, a citizen who leaves his home, his neighborhood and town better than he found it." , "But if the man you have chosen to lead this government can help make a difference; if he can celebrate the quieter, deeper successes that are made not of gold and silk, but of better hearts and finer souls; if he can do these things, then he must." 即美国人认为成功不单意味着只为自己奋斗，为自己堆积财富。成功不一定是物质上的积累，而是得到某种认可；更重要的是在道德上、在观念上不断提高和自我完善，并贡献自己的才智于社会、于大众，从而推动社会的进步。所以在美国，人们很少看重金钱本身，它更多的是一种标志、一种工具。成功的果实被看做具有全民共享的价值。当一个人的地位提高时，人们对他的要求也相应提高。去看看《名人录》，随便找几个知名商人的条目，

就会发现他们参加的公益性委员会和协会有多么多，他们的捐赠金额有多么惊人。福特、卡耐基、洛克菲勒，都为自己创造了极大的财富，与此同时他们也以各种方式主动地回报社会，给成千上万的美国人创造了更多的工作岗位和更好的受教育机会。无论怎样，这就是成功的内涵。

（2）美国人的宽容性

美国是个移民之国，他们的祖先来自于全球各地。人们移居美国时，不仅仅在地理位置上挪动一下，而且还把他们所在国的传统和风俗习惯带到了新的居住地。因为杂，人们各自的差异十分突出；因为差异十分普遍，人们就不特别注重统一性。久而久之，美国人的文化习俗中形成了较高程度的宽容性（tolerance），对异质文化和不同传统持容忍、接受的态度。

从政治上讲，这种宽容性表现在对自由的追求和对自由权利的维护，尤其是对思想和言论的宽容。美国社会和政府包容一切异端邪说、批评指责。即使用最激烈、刻薄的语言抨击时政、挖苦总统，也不用担心受到迫害，更无须担心牢狱之忧。这种包容不是来自社会和政府的恩赐，而是来自美国宪法的制度保障。美国宪法中对言论自由、出版自由等基本人权的保障，不仅仅写在了纸面上，而真正是一条条庄严的承诺，被一丝不苟地付诸实践。芝加哥大学政治学教授邹谠先生曾说："如果我讲了一百句话，其中有九十九句错，美国会吸收我说对的那一句，而不计较说错的九十九句……"，这是对美国的包容的最好诠释。

从宗教上说，它体现在不同信仰的和谐共存。从生活范围上看，它显现在不同种族、不同族裔社区的平安相处。一言以蔽之，在美国，每个人基本上可以任意选择不同的观念、信仰、生活方式和传统习惯；人们也可以在相当程度上保持自己的习俗。譬如，美国华人可以在唐人街用华语生活和工作；同样的道理，越南移民能够在他们的"小西贡"按越南的方式经营业务，从事各种活动。

美国人的宽容性，除了上面的美国是个移民国这个因素外，还与美国人的频繁迁徙有关。众所周知，美国历史发展中的一个重要部分是她的西部开发史。那时，美国拓荒者或徒步跋涉、或骑马坐车，从东到西、从南到北，哪里有机遇，就往那里移居。频繁的迁移和不断地更换居处使人们始终处于"流动"状态，对其面临的各种现象更易于宽容和接受。此外，经常迁移还能够帮助人们扩大眼界、见多识广，对不同的习俗持同情、理解的态度，并逐渐形成多样性胜于单一性的开放性观念。

由于美国人的宽容性较强，所以美国人很少把自己的意志强加在其他人身上，这与中国孔夫子"己所不欲，勿施于人"的古训十分相似。譬如说，丈夫是个共和党人，但他决不能逼迫拥护民主党的妻子改变政治立场。同理，母亲也许是个天主教徒，但她决不能强迫已皈依穆斯林教的儿子改变宗教信仰。在日常生活和平时事务处理中，这种宽容精神更是屡见不鲜。也许正是这种“宽容”的情怀成就了今日美国的民族理性，成就了美国包容开放的社会，成就了美国今天的辉煌。

（3）美国人的宗教信仰

在美国这个世界上科技最发达、经济最繁荣、物质生活最丰富的国家，按理说其国民的宗教意识应该非常薄弱。但事实恰恰相反，宗教信仰的烙印在美国随处可见，宗教的巨大影响渗透到了美国人生活的方方面面。美国人的宗教信仰特点可归纳为以下几点：

① 宗教信仰的普遍性：今天的美国，每 10 个人中就有 9 个人自称相信上帝，有 6 个人每天祈祷，有一半以上的人认为上帝是美国民主的道德引导力量；美国的钞票上赫然印着“我们信仰上帝”；美国的国歌里有“上帝保佑美国”的歌词；美国总统就职，要手按《圣经》，在最高法院大法官的主持下进行宣誓，牧师站在一旁作证。他们的就职演讲总是以“上帝保佑美国”做结语。在美国，《圣经》从来都是最畅销的书，宗教音乐的音像制品销售量远远超过爵士乐、古典音乐及其他各种流行音乐。可以说，美国人生活的各个方面都和宗教有着密切的关系，正如德国著名社会学家马克斯·韦伯所说：“美国是世界上最世俗的国家，又是最信奉宗教的国家。”

② 宗教多元化：美国是世界上最大的移民国家，这就使宗教多元化成为必然。更重要的是宪法第一修正案为宗教多元化提供了法律保障。各种宗教派别和平相处，新兴宗教层出不穷。不过，尽管美国有形形色色的宗教派别，起主流作用的仍然是基督教，这不仅表现在教徒数量上的优势，关键是其代表的价值观念和行为方式体现着美国社会的主流方向。

③ 宗教世俗化：美国的宗教重社会实用功能，轻神学功能。宗教不再是通往天国的必经之路，而是为满足人们现实精神生活的需要。美国人去教堂是一种信念，但更多的是出于社会和个人的要求。在美国，教堂被看做是人们生活中的一个重要场所。它不仅是举行宗教仪式的地方，还是教育、文化和社交中心。在这里他们可以从牧师的讲道中得到心灵的慰藉，可以提高自己的道德修养，可以交到志同道合的知心朋友。

④ 宗教对政治的影响：众所周知，美国是一个政教分离的国家。然而，这种政教分离的制度并不意味着政治与宗教不相干。这种分离只是机构的分离，并不是文化的分离。“教”指的是“教会”组织，而不是“宗教”；“政”指的是“国家”机构，而非“社会”。在美国，宗教与政治从来都是相互信赖、相互配合，共同为美国的事业服务。当然，宗教对美国政治的影响不表现在对政治的直接干预上，而主要表现在两个方面：一是对美国政治文化传统的深远影响（如美国人向外推行美国价值观的做法就是受基督教徒的“使命观”的影响）；二是对某些具体政策施加影响（如对社会福利政策、堕胎问题等）。

在美国，宗教对美国人的价值观念、生活态度以及道德标准产生了巨大影响，促进了美国多元文化的形成，铸造了美国人乐观向上、勤奋节俭、乐善好施、仗义执言的性格。至今，宗教在美国人生活的各个方面仍然起着不可替代的作用。

❑ Questions Concerning the Speech

1. According to the address, how to secure a more just and prosperous life for man on Earth?
2. What is the guideline for Bush to follow when he is faced with various problems?
3. Does Bush favor the idea of madly pursuing material things?
4. What should Americans leave their future generations based on the address?
5. How could America be wholly herself?
6. What does the "old solution" refer to in Paragraph 14?
7. Why does Bush mention an older fellow and a woman in Paragraph 22?
8. How will Bush deal with people's different attitudes and way of life?
9. Why are drugs described as "deadly bacteria"?

❑ Paraphrase the Following Sentences

1. The people of the world agitate for free expression and free thought through the door to the moral and intellectual satisfactions that only liberty allows.
2. Are we enthralled with material things, less appreciative of the nobility of work and sacrifice?
3. We will turn to the only resource we have that in times of need always grows: the goodness and the courage of the American people.
4. The final lesson of Vietnam is that no great nation can long afford to be sundered by a memory.
5. This is the age of the offered hand.
6. There are today Americans who are held against their will in foreign lands, and Americans who are unaccounted for.

❑ Questions for Discussion

1. 如果说“贫穷是一切罪恶的根源”，在创业摆脱贫穷创造价值的同时，财富是人生的唯一价值吗?
2. 荷兰哲学家斯宾诺沙 (Spinoza) 说：“The heart is not conquered by force, but by love and tolerance. (人心不是靠武力征服的，而是靠爱和宽容大度征服的。)”你同意这种观点吗? 试举例论证。
3. 布什在演说中明确了其行动指南，即“一致性、多样性、宽容性” (unity, diversity,

generosity)，在某种程度上它和中国的“求同存异，百家争鸣”有异曲同工之妙。请具体说明在当今社会如何才能体现出一致性、多样性和宽容性。

☐ Translation

乔治·布什：就职演讲

1989 年 1 月 20 日，华盛顿特区

首席法官先生、总统先生、副总统奎尔先生、米切尔参议员、赖特议长、多尔参议员、米歇尔众议员、同胞们、邻友们、朋友们：

1. 今天我们当中有这样一个人，他在我们心中，在我国历史上，赢得了一个永恒的地位。他就是里根总统。在此，我代表全国人民向您表示感谢，感谢您为美国做出的伟大贡献。
2. 我刚才逐字逐句复述了乔治·华盛顿在二百年前宣读过的誓言，我的手所按的也正是他当年按过的那部《圣经》。今天，我们应当铭记华盛顿，这不仅因为今天是首任总统就职二百周年的纪念日，而且因为华盛顿始终是我们的国父。我想，他的在天之灵一定会为今天而感到高兴。因为今天具体体现了一个值得称颂的事实，那就是，我们的政府自创建二百年以来始终保持一贯。
3. 我们相聚在民主大厦的前门廊，这是我们以邻居和朋友身份进行交谈的好地方，因为今天是我们暂时撇开彼此的分歧，全国人民团结一致的日子。
4. 我作为总统的第一个行动是请求各位同我一起低头祈祷：
5. “天国的圣父，我们俯首感谢您的垂爱。为了和平，也为了我们共同的信念，请接受我们的感谢。因为和平创造了今天，而我们的共同信念则使今天得以延续。请赐予我们力量，使我们得以完成您赋予的任务。我们愿聆听和遵从您的旨意，把‘运用权力帮助人民’这一箴言铭刻在心头。因为我们获得权力不是为了促进实现我们自己的目的，不是为了炫耀于世，更不是为了追逐浮名。权力只有一个正当用途，那就是服务于人民。主啊，请帮助我们牢记这一点。阿门！”
6. 在这个充满希望的时刻，我来到你们面前就任总统之职。我们生活在和平、繁荣的时代，我们能够使它更加美好。因为现在吹拂着一阵清新的和风，一个沐浴在自由之中使人感到清新的世界似乎已经重新降生；因为即使不是实际上，至少也在人们心中，独裁者的时代已经过去。极权主义时代正在消逝，它那陈旧的观念就像一株衰老枯萎的树上的叶子随风凋落。一阵清新的和风正在吹拂，一个经历过自由洗礼的国家准备继续奋进。新的天地有待开辟，新的行动有待采取。有时候浓雾沉沉，前途迷茫。大

家坐下来等待，盼望云开雾散，显露出正确的道路。但此时此刻，未来就像你可以立即跨过的大门，走进一个叫做明天的殿堂。

7. 世界上的伟大国家正在经过通向自由的大门走向民主。全世界的男男女女则经过通向繁荣的大门进入自由市场。全世界人民正在经过通向只有自由才能赋予的道德与智力满足的大门，奋力争取言论自由和思想自由。

8. 我们知道什么能起作用：自由能起作用。我们知道什么是正确的：自由是正确的。我们知道如何为地球上的人类争得更公正、更富裕的生活：通过自由市场、自由言论、自由选举，和不受国家阻挠地行使自由意志。

9. 本世纪第一次，也许是有史以来第一次，人类不必发明一种赖以生存的制度了。我们不必为哪种形式的政府更好而讨论到深夜了。我们也不必从君主手里夺取正义了。我们只需从自身内部唤起正义。我们必须按照我们知道的事实采取行动。我把一位圣徒的期望作为行动的指南：在关键的问题上，做到团结一致；在重大的问题上，允许多样性；在所有问题上，则须宽宏大量。

10. 今天的美国是骄傲、自由的礼仪之邦，是我们由衷热爱的国度。在我们心中，我们固然不必大声张扬和自负自傲，但我们却从内心懂得一个简单的事实，即这个国家的意义决不仅限于我们所看到的一切，我们拥有的实力乃是一种向善的力量。但即使在我们这个时代，作为一个国家，我们是否已经发生了变化？我们是否迷恋于物质的东西而不那么崇尚勤奋与奉献这一高贵的品质呢？

11. 朋友们，我们并不是我们财产的总和。财产不是衡量我们生活的尺度。我们心中懂得什么最重要。我们不能只希望给我们的后代留下一辆更豪华的轿车和更丰厚的存款。我们应当希望给他们留下这样一种意识，让他们懂得一个忠诚的朋友，一个慈爱的父母，一个能使自己的家庭、街区和城镇变得更加美好的公民意味着什么。当我们不在某一个地方时，我们希望那些曾经同我们一道共事的人说些什么呢？是希望他们说我们比周围任何人都更不顾一切地追求成功？还是说我们能抽空去询问一个孩子的病情是否好转，或者稍停片刻与他友好地交谈？

12. 任何总统，任何政府都不能教会我们记住我们当中什么是最好的。但是，如果你们选出的政府领导人能有所作为；如果他能取得那种不是由黄金和丝绸、而是由更美好的心灵所带来的虽不显眼但意义深远的成就；如果他能做到这一切，他就必须这样去做。

13. 美国只有追求崇高的道德准则才能称为一个完全的美国。今天，作为一个民族，我们应当具有这样的目标，那就是使这个国家变得更为仁慈，使这个世界变得更加美好。朋友们，我们还有许多事情要做。世界上还有许多人无家可归、迷惘无助、流离失所；还有许多儿童一无所有，既没有爱，又没有过上正常的生活；有些人则无法摆脱各种个人癖好的奴役，沉溺于吸毒，依赖救济为生，或沾染上肆虐于贫民窟的堕落习气。街头巷尾的粗暴犯罪需要我们去打击；有不少年轻的女性需要我们的帮助——她们将为人母，但对她们即将出生的孩子不知如何照料，或根本就不爱孩子。她们需要我们去关心、去引导、去教育，尽管我们祝愿她们选择自己的生活。

14. 过去的解决办法和过去的途径是认为只要政府拨款就能解决所有这些问题。但是我们业已懂得情况并非如此。况且，我们的财力还不够雄厚，我们的赤字还有待消减。我们的意志胜过金钱，而意志正是我们所需要的。我们要做出艰难的抉择：看一看我们所拥有的财力，也许要作适当的调配，使我们的决策建立在真正的需要和谨慎、安全的基础之上。然后，我们将采取最明智的做法：我们将求助于我们所拥有的、在需要时总是会不断增加的唯一资源——美国人民的善良和勇气。

15. 我现在说的是一种关心他人生活的新态度，一种能有所作为的实际行动、亲身投入的新的积极态度。我们要使各代人都参与其中，发挥老一代人的未尽之才，调动年轻一代尚未集中的精力。因为代代相传的不仅是领导职位，还有对国家事务的管理。而且，第二次世界大战后出生的一代人也已经成年。

16. 我曾谈到上千个发光点，所有那些从事有益工作的社区组织，像繁星一样遍布全国。我们将携起手、相互鼓励，不论领导还是被领导，去做出卓有成效的工作。我们将在白宫、在内阁的各个部门进行这项工作。我会帮助那些作为更亮的发光点的人员和项目，并要求本届政府的所有成员都来参与这一活动。老的观念又焕发新的活力，是因为他们并不陈旧且具有永恒的价值。履行义务、献身精神、实践承诺以及爱国主义，这些都会在人们的参与和奋斗中得到体现。

17. 在行政部门和国会之间，我们也需要达成一项新的约定。摆在我们面前的挑战需要同众议院和参议院研究解决。我们必须使联邦预算达到平衡。我们必须确保美国以团结的姿态屹立于世界，强大、安宁、财政状况良好。当然，事情不会是一帆风顺的。我们需要妥协，因为我们有过纷争不和。我们需要和谐，因为我们曾众说纷纭。

18. 因为国会在我们这个时代也发生了变化。那里出现了某种分裂。我们看到了一些冷峻的面容，听到了一些言论，但其中的争端不在于彼此的观念，而在于彼此的动机。我们两个伟大的党彼此相距过远、互不信任的时候太多了。自越南战争以来，情况即已如此。那场战争至今还在我们中间挑起分裂。但是，朋友们，那场战争始于 25 年前，而且毫无疑问，有关那场战争的诉讼时效法规早已确定下来。事实上，越南战争的最终教训是，任何大国都无法长期承受由记忆的阴影所造成的分裂。一阵清新的和风正在吹拂，原有的两党关系必须再次更新。

19. 向忠诚的反对派朋友们——对，我是说“忠诚的”和“朋友们”——我伸出了手。议长先生，我向您伸出了手。多数党领袖先生，我向您伸出了手。因为事实就是如此：这是握手言和的时代。我们不能倒拨时钟，我也不想这样做。但是议长先生，当我们的父辈还年轻时，我们的分歧只局限于国内问题上。我们也不希望时光倒流，但是多数党领袖先生，在我们的母亲还年轻时，国会和行政部门能够同心协力，并制订了我们的国家可以赖以为生的预算。让我们早日努力地进行协商，但最终我们需要得出结果。美国人民期待着行动。他们派我们到这里来，不是要我们相互斗嘴争吵，而是要我们超脱于纯粹的党派立场。我说过，"在关键问题上我们要团结一致"。朋友们，这个就是关键的问题。

20. 对全世界，我们也提出新的约定并许下新的誓言：我们将保持强大，以维护世界和平。我们"伸出的手"是不情愿的拳头。这个拳头一旦紧握将十分有力，并会产生巨大的效力。今天有些美国人在违背其意愿的情况下被扣留在异国他乡，还有些美国人下落不明。援助在这里可以得到体现，也会被人们长久铭记。善有善报。美好的信仰会像一只从不停转的螺旋，不断向前推进。

21. 伟大的民族也像伟人一样必须信守诺言。无论是签订的条约、协议，还是在大理石台阶上发表的誓言，美国人向来说话算数。我们将始终力求言辞清楚明白，因为坦率乃是一种值得赞美的东西。但微妙的言词也是有益和不可缺少的。我们要在全世界加强与盟国的关系，发展友谊，使之永远稳固的同时，将继续发展同苏联的新的密切关系。这与我们的安全和进步是一致的。有人或许会说，我们这种新型关系部分地反映了希望和力量胜过经验。然而，希望固然是美好的，保持力量和警惕也是必要的。

22. 今天，成千上万的美国人在这里感受到了那些投身于民主事业，并看到自己的希望得到实现的人们所流露出的那种可以理解的满足。然而近几天来，我的思绪却转向那些正在家里观礼的人们，我想到了一个在国旗经过身旁时会自动敬礼的老人，和一位会将战歌歌词告诉孩子们的妇女。我不想说这是多愁善感。我是说，在像今天这样的日子里，我们要牢记我们都是一个连续统一体的组成部分，都是不可避免地由各种纽带联系在一起。

23. 全国各地的孩子们都在学校观看这一典礼。对他们，我要说，谢谢你们观看民主的盛况。因为民主属于我们大家，而自由就像一只美丽的风筝，能随着和风越飞越高。对全体人民，我要说，不论你们情况如何，也不论你们身在何处，你们都是这个重要日子的一部分，你们都是我们伟大祖国生活的一部分。

24. 总统不是君主，也不是教皇。我不寻求"人的心灵之窗"。事实上，我向往的是更大的宽容，和人们对彼此的态度与生活方式不作苛求。

25. 然而，在极少数明显问题上，我们作为一个社会必须团结起来，明确地表示决不宽容。目前最突出的是毒品问题。自从第一批可卡因通过船只偷运入境，就完全可以说它是一种致命的病菌，因为它如此严重地损害了我们国家的肌体与灵魂。对此要做和要说的都很多，但请记住我的话：这个祸害必将被制止。

26. 因此，要做的事情很多。明天就要开始工作。对未来，我毫无怀疑；对前途，我毫无恐惧。因为，我们的问题虽大，但我们的心胸更大；我们的挑战虽大，但我们的决心更大。而且，如果说我们的缺点无穷无尽，上帝的爱则更是无边无垠。

27. 有人把领袖做为看做是高亢激越的戏剧和催人奋进的号角，有时确实如此。但在我看来，历史是一部鸿篇巨制，我们每天都以充满希望和富有意义的行动去书写一页。一阵清新的和风正在吹拂，一页历史正在翻动，故事展开了。今天就这样开始了新的一章，这个故事虽短小却十分庄严，它是一个团结一致、多样并存、宽宏大量的故事，是一个我们共同分享和一起撰写的故事。
28. 谢谢各位。上帝保佑你们，上帝保佑美利坚合众国。

Bill Clinton

(1946—)

比尔·克林顿

14

Bill Clinton's First Inaugural Address

Delivered 20 January, 1993, in Washington, D.C.

❑ About the Author

比尔·克林顿 (Bill Clinton, 1946—　) 原名威廉·杰斐逊·克林顿 (William Jefferson Clinton)，第 42 任美国总统（1993—2001）。他是美国第一位出生于第二次世界大战之后的总统，第三位被弹劾的总统（前两位分别是安德鲁·约翰逊和理查德·尼克松），也是仅次于西奥多·罗斯福和约翰·肯尼迪之后最年轻的美国总统，以及富兰克林·罗斯福之后连任成功的首位民主党总统。

克林顿 1946 年出生于阿肯色州霍普镇一个小店主的家庭。1964 年进入乔治敦大学主修外交专业，曾担任大学学生会主席并协助联邦参议员威廉·富布莱特工作。1968 年，克林顿获国际政治学学士学位，并获罗德奖学金赴牛津大学学习。1970 年考入耶鲁法学院，1973 年获法学博士学位，同年到阿肯色州州立大学担任教授，同时开业当律师。

1976 年，克林顿出任阿肯色州司法部长。1979 年—1981 年、1983 年—1992 年任阿肯色州州长。任州长期间，在推动州教育改革和实施经济发展计划方面取得成就，被选为美国南部经济发展政策委员会主席，兼任全美州长联席会议主席，并曾协助总统主持国家最高教育当局的工作。1990 年，克林顿被选为民主党最高委员会主席。1992 年，他击败老布什当选总统，并于 1996 年连任。1998 年 6 月，克林顿对中国进行国事访问，期间他在北京大学发表演讲，并向北大图书馆捐赠 500 多册英文书籍。2005 年 4 月克林顿出任联合国海啸救灾特使。2009 年 5 月，联合国秘书长潘基文任命他为联合国海地事务特使。

克林顿被称为新民主党人，其执政理念也被归结为第三种道路。这位能言善辩、思想新颖的“改革家”执政期间最大的成就是创造了美国 8 年的长期经济繁荣，实现了财政收支平衡和国库盈余 5 590 亿美元；并使美国高科技行业飞速发展，奠定了今日美国高科技大国的地位。所以克林顿是历史上得到最多公众肯定的总统之一。担任美国总统期间，克林顿一直深得非裔美国人、中西部和西部蓝领工人以及妇女的爱戴，他也是美国总统当中为数不多的少数族裔民权和男女平等的最坚定的支持者。克林顿以 65% 的民意支持率结束任期，创下了第二次世界大战后美国总统离任最高支持率纪录。此后，他一直进行公开演讲和人道主义工作，成立了威廉·J·克林顿基金，致力于艾滋病和全球变暖等国际问题的预防。2009 年 5 月，克林顿被授予"杜鲁门公共服务奖"，以表彰他在任总统前、任总统期间和卸任后所做的公共服务。

❑ About the Speech

1993 年 1 月 20 日，首都华盛顿天气非常晴朗，空气十分清新。上午 10 时 30 分，克林顿夫妇驱车由国宾馆抵达白宫，然后与其前任布什总统乘同一辆豪华轿车驶向国会大厦。在正午的钟声敲响时，在美国最高法院首席法官伦奎斯特主持下，克林顿手按《圣经》，宣读宪法上规定的誓言。随后，克林顿总统发表了简短的就职演说，定下了他今后任期的施政基调：变革与复兴。

克林顿宣誓就职时，美国正处于战后持续时间最长的经济黯淡期，失业率高、商业消费能力萎缩、国民士气低落，一片抱怨之声。当选总统克林顿向世人庄严宣告，这是"一个伟大的开端"，它将实现"变革"诺言，重振美国雄风。演说中所指的改革即日后克林顿力主的政府对经济进行干预，通过加快经济增长速度来减少财政赤字、扩大社会福利、缩小贫富差距的思想。他说："世界需要一个强大的美国，而造就一个强大美国的根源来自国内。"自这位年轻的总统带着一份活力与朝气踏进白宫起，他那平民化的笑容就成了美国经济欣欣向荣的代名词。在其任期内，美国经济不但保持了最长的持续增长期，而且失业率和犯罪率也明显降低；美国在航天技术、生物基因工程以及互联网领域所展示出的实力都是其他国家所无法望其项背的。

在演说中，克林顿总统提到了两个世纪以来美国的历史，表达了美国对自由和民主的向往。他的音调坚强有力、举止满怀信心，一副天生演说家的风度。整篇演讲仿佛是早来的春风，带着清新和生机，以其崭新的姿态征服了听众，他的就职演说词更被认为是演讲中的经典之作。

❑ The Speech in Full

My fellow citizens:

1. Today we celebrate the mystery of American renewal.

2. This ceremony is held in the depth of winter. But by the words we speak and the faces we show the world, we force the spring. **A spring reborn in the world's oldest democracy, that brings forth the vision and courage to reinvent America.**

3. When our founders boldly declared America's independence to the world and our purposes to the Almighty, they knew that **America, to endure, would have to change. Not change for change's sake, but change to preserve America's ideals—life, liberty, the pursuit of happiness. Though we march to the music of our time, our mission is timeless.** Each generation of Americans must define what it means to be an American.

4. On behalf of our nation, I salute my predecessor, President Bush, for his half-century of service to America. And I thank the millions of men and women whose steadfastness and sacrifice triumphed over depression, fascism and communism[1].

5. Today, a generation raised in the shadows of the Cold War **assumes new responsibilities in a world warmed by the sunshine of freedom but threatened still by ancient hatreds and new plagues.**

6. **Raised in unrivaled prosperity, we inherit an economy that is still the world's strongest, but is weakened by[2] business failures, stagnant wages, increasing inequality, and deep divisions among our own people.**

7. When George Washington first took the oath I have just sworn to uphold, news traveled slowly across the land by horseback and across the ocean by boat. Now, the sights and sounds of this ceremony are broadcast instantaneously[3] to billions around the world.

8. **Communications and commerce are global; investment is mobile; technology is almost magical; and ambition for a better life is now universal.** We earn our livelihood in America today in peaceful competition with people all across the earth.

9. Profound and powerful forces are shaking and remaking our world, and the urgent question of our time is whether we can make change our friend and not our enemy.

10. This new world has already enriched the lives of millions of Americans who are able to compete and win in it. **But when most people are working harder for less; when others cannot work at all; when the cost of health care devastates[4] families and threatens to bankrupt our enterprises, great and small; when fear of crime robs law-abiding citizens of their freedom; and when millions of poor children cannot even imagine the lives we are calling them to lead—we have not made change our friend.**

11. We know we have to face hard truths and take strong steps. But we have not done so. Instead, **we have drifted, and that drifting has eroded our resources, fractured[5] our economy, and shaken our confidence.**

12. Though our challenges are fearsome, so are our strengths. And Americans have ever been a restless, questing, hopeful people. We must bring to our task today the vision and will of those who came before us.

13. From our revolution, the Civil War, to the Great Depression to the civil rights movement[6], our people have always mustered[7] the determination to construct from these crises the pillars of our history.

14. Thomas Jefferson believed that to preserve the very foundations of our nation, we would need dramatic change from time to time[8]. Well, my fellow citizens, this is our time. Let us embrace it.

15. **Our democracy must be not only the envy of the world but the engine of our own renewal. There is nothing wrong with America that cannot be cured by what is right with America.**

16. And so today, we pledge an end to the era of deadlock[9] and drift—a new season of American renewal has begun. To renew America, we must be bold. We must do what no generation has had to do before. We must invest more in our own people, in their jobs, in their future, and at the same time cut our massive debt. And we must do so in a world in which we must compete for every opportunity. It will not be easy; it will require sacrifice. But it can be done, and done fairly, not choosing sacrifice for its own sake, but for our own sake. We must provide for our nation the way a family provides for its children.

17. Our Founders saw themselves in the light of posterity[10]. We can do no less. Anyone who has ever watched a child's eyes wander into sleep knows what posterity is. Posterity is the world to come—the world for whom we hold our ideals, from whom we have borrowed our planet, and to whom we bear sacred responsibility. **We must do what America does best: offer more opportunity to all and demand more responsibility from all.**

18. It is time to break the bad habit of expecting something for nothing, from our government or from each other. Let us all take more responsibility, not only for ourselves and our families but for our communities and our country. To renew America, we must revitalize our democracy.

19. **This beautiful capital, like every capital since the dawn of civilization, is often a place of intrigue[11] and calculation.** Powerful people maneuver[12] for position and worry endlessly about who is in and who is out, who is up and who is down, forgetting those people whose toil and sweat sends us here and pays our way.

20. Americans deserve better, and in this city today, there are people who want to do better. And so I say to all of us here, **let us resolve to reform our politics, so that power and privilege no longer shout down the voice of the people. Let us put aside personal advantage so that we can feel the pain and see the promise of America. Let us resolve to make our government a place for what Franklin Roosevelt called "bold, persistent experimentation," a government for our tomorrows, not our yesterdays. Let us give this capital back to the people to whom it belongs.**

21. To renew America, we must meet challenges abroad as well as at home. There is no longer a clear division between what is foreign and what is domestic—the world economy, the world environment, the world AIDS crisis, the world arms race—they affect us all.

22. Today, as an old order passes, the new world is more free but less stable. Communism's collapse has called forth old animosities[13] and new dangers. Clearly America must continue to lead the world we did so much to make.

23. While America rebuilds at home, we will not shrink from the challenges, nor fail to seize the opportunities, of this new world. Together with our friends and allies, we will work to shape change, lest it engulf[14] us.

24. **When our vital interests are challenged, or the will and conscience of the international community is defied[15], we will act—with peaceful diplomacy whenever possible, with force when necessary.** The brave Americans serving our nation today in the Persian Gulf, in Somalia, and wherever else they stand are testament to[16] our resolve.

25. **But our greatest strength is the power of our ideas, which are still new in many lands. Across the world, we see them embraced—and we rejoice. Our hopes, our hearts, our hands, are with those on every continent who are building democracy and freedom. Their cause is America's cause.**

26. The American people have summoned the change we celebrate today. **You have raised your voices in an unmistakable chorus. You have cast your votes in historic numbers. And you have changed the face of Congress, the presidency and the political process itself. Yes, you, my fellow Americans have forced the spring. Now, we must do the work the season demands.**

27. To that work I now turn, with all the authority of my office. I ask the Congress to join with me. But no President, no Congress, no government, can undertake this mission alone. My fellow Americans, you, too, must play your part in our renewal. I challenge a new generation of young Americans to a season of service—to act on your idealism by helping troubled children, keeping company with those in need, reconnecting our torn communities. There is so much to be done—enough, indeed, for millions of others who are still young in spirit to give of themselves in service, too.

28. In serving, we recognize a simple but powerful truth—we need each other. And we must care for one another. Today we do more than celebrate America; we rededicate ourselves to the very idea of America.

29. **An idea born in revolution and renewed through two centuries of challenge. An idea tempered by the knowledge that, but for fate, we—the**

fortunate and the unfortunate—might have been each other. An idea ennobled by the faith that our nation can summon from its myriad[17] diversity the deepest measure of unity. An idea infused with the conviction that America's long, heroic journey must go forever upward.

30. And so, my fellow Americans, at the edge of the 21st century, **let us begin with energy and hope, with faith and discipline, and let us work until our work is done.** The scripture says, "And let us not be weary in well-doing, for in due season, we shall reap, if we faint not[18]."

31. From this joyful mountaintop of celebration, we hear a call to service in the valley. We have heard the trumpets. We have changed the guard. And now, each in our way, and with God's help, we must answer the call.

32. Thank you and God bless you all. (1,620 words)

❑ Notes to the Speech

1. triumphed over depression, fascism and communism：战胜了大萧条（即 1929—1933 年的经济危机）、法西斯主义和共产主义
2. but is weakened by：该句指，从 1990 年底开始美国经济再度进入衰退时期，至 1992 年失业率高达 7.6%，贸易赤字突破 600 亿美元，美国的经济形势于是变得十分严峻。
3. instantaneously [ˌinstən'teinjəsli] *adv.* happening immediately, without any delay 立即；瞬间
4. devastate ['devəsteit] *vt.* damage something very badly or completely 毁坏
5. fracture ['fræktʃə] *vt.* damage or destroy as if by rupturing 毁坏；打破
6. civil rights movement：民权运动，指 20 世纪 50、60 年代美国黑人反对种族歧视、争取平等权利的群众运动。
7. muster ['mʌstə] *vt.* get enough courage, confidence, support etc. to do something, especially with difficulty 鼓起（勇气等）；使振作（常与 up 连用）
8. dramatic change from time to time：托马斯·杰斐逊在 1786 年谢斯起义发生后曾说："不时发生一点小小的反叛乃是一件好事，它在政治领域实有必要，正如暴风雨在自然界是必要的一样。"
9. deadlock ['dedlɔk] *n.* a situation in which no progress can be made or no advancement is possible 僵局，停滞

10. posterity [pɔs'teriti] *n.* all of the offspring of a given progenitor 子孙，后代
11. intrigue [in'tri:g] *n.* the making of secret plans to harm someone or make them lose their position of power, or a plan of this kind 阴谋，诡计
12. maneuver [mə'nu:və] *vi.* use cleverly planned and often dishonest methods to get the result that you want 用策略，耍花招
13. animosity [ˌæni'mɔsiti] *n.* a feeling of ill will arousing active hostility 仇恨
14. engulf [in'gʌlf] *vt.* completely surround or cover 吞没；席卷
15. defy [di'fai] *vt.* refuse to obey a law or rule, or refuse to do what someone in authority tells you to do 公然反抗；蔑视
16. testament to something：proving or showing very clearly that something exists or is true, strong evidence for something 证明，证据
17. myriad ['miriəd] *adj.* too numerous to be counted 无数的，种种的
18. let us not be weary in well-doing, for in due season, we shall reap, if we faint not：语出《圣经·新约全书·加拉太书》第六章第九节，原句是：“So let us not grow weary in doing what is right, for we will reap at harvest time, if we do not give up. 我们行善，不可丧志，只要坚持，终有收获。”

❑ Appreciating the Speech

在演说中，克林顿总统以清新明快的语调畅言变革 (change)，宣布自己的施政纲领 (administrative program)，陈述改革的正确性，敦促美国人实施行动 (take actions)，进行改革。他首先提出要庆祝美国的新生 (rebirth)，振奋人心 (inspiring)，为演说奠定了高昂的基调。克林顿上任时刚好是东欧剧变 (drastic changes in Eastern Europe)、苏联解体 (the Soviet collapse) 之后，所谓“后冷战时期”(post-cold war) 的开始。他说冷战结束，现在主要问题是国内经济 (domestic economy)，要“开创一个美国复兴的新时代”(a new season of American renewal)。接着克林顿指出当今时代的迫切问题 (urgent question) 是，“能否使变革成为我们的朋友，而不是敌人”(make change our friend and not our enemy)。然后列举事实，陈述改革之必要性。克林顿一上台就列举不平等现象 (inequality) 和医疗费用问题 (medical cost)，恐怖犯罪活动 (terrorist crimes) 等社会问题，庄严宣告要“结束这个僵持停顿、放任自流的时代”(the era of deadlock and drift)。以“复兴美国”为主线，从经济上 (economically)、政治上 (politically)、外交上 (diplomatically) 提出各项变革措施。他明确继承 (carry on) 罗斯福的精神，要把美国变成罗斯福称之为进行“大胆而持久试验”(bold, persistent experimentation) 的地方。同时指出，世界因旧怨新仇 (old animosity and new hatred) 而更不稳定 (less stable)，美国面临新的挑战，不会退缩不前，并以波斯湾、索马里为例，号召美国人民作出新的奉献 (rededicate)，尤其

强调了美国思想的力量 (the power of ideas)。最后，克林顿号召国民投身理想，呼吁“我们必须做这个时代要求于我们的工作”(we must do the work the season demands)。演说充满了其克服困难的决心和开创未来的勇气，言辞精彩、鼓舞人心。

从语言上看，该篇演说衔接合理、逻辑清晰、一气呵成。为了提高表达效果，克林顿总统大量使用修辞格 (figures of speech)、丰富的句子类型 (types of sentences) 并赋予其宗教色彩 (religious tone)，具有强烈的感召力 (emotional appeal)，有利于促使国人响应他的号召 (answer his call)，大力进行变革。①象征 (symbolization)。以春天的到来象征美国复兴时代的到来；以欢庆的山巅象征就职典礼这一举国庆祝的时刻；以号角象征为国效力的召唤。②对照 (antithesis)，使矛盾鲜明突出，揭示本质，给人深刻启示。第 5 段“but”构成了两个分句之间的转折关系，通过“自由的阳光”(sunshine of freedom) 和“旧仇宿怨和新的祸患的威胁”(ancient hatreds and new plagues) 构成的对比，使美国人民意识到面临的机遇和挑战。③排比 (parallelism)。如第 10 段，连用 5 个并列句“when”使观点严密透彻，列举美国面临的严酷现实，说明变革的必要性。第 29 段 4 个“an idea”体现了美国思想深邃崇高的内涵，气势磅礴动人心扉，整齐的句式与分明的节奏体现了韵律美。④头韵 (alliteration)、尾韵 (end rhythm)，读起来朗朗上口、铿锵有力。譬如“let us resolve to reform our politics, so that power and privilege no longer shout down the voice of the people.”该句中 4 个“p”排在词首，形成一字长蛇阵，读音相同，具有音韵美。再如“It is time to break the bad habit of expecting something for nothing.”该句中头韵和尾韵一起使用，首尾呼应、极富乐感，体现了语言的艺术魅力 (artistic charm)。⑤反复 (repetition)，表现越来越加剧的紧迫感。全文多次重复使用“change”、“challenge”等词，其中“change”一词被重复 11 次之多，足以感染听众，使他们认识到总统力促改革的决心和其必要性。而“threaten”只重复了 2 次，在文字上的吝惜意在使美国人相信，威胁并没有什么可怕的，国内暂时的经济困难通过变革是可以战胜的。克林顿通过对“change”的偏爱 (preference) 和对“threaten”的轻视 (contempt)，明确而强烈地表达了自己对于国内经济形势的政见和立场。此外“my fellow Americans，my fellow citizens”也被重复使用了 5 次之多，使人倍感亲切，更易赢得听众支持并接受他的一系列改革措施。⑥使用同义词 (synonym) 或概括性词 (general word)，避免枯燥，使语言活泼。用“the world's oldest democracy”指 America，强调美国是一个古老的民主国家；用“A new season of American renewal has begun”来指 our time，强调这是一个复兴美国的新时代。⑦多处选择“must”而不用其他句式，表达了面对挑战毫不畏缩的坚强决心。⑧祈使句 (imperative sentence)。第 20 段 4 个“let us”呼吁国民锐意改革、重振经济，具有鼓动性。因为要唤回国民的信心，仅靠简单的陈述事实是不够的。⑨浓郁的宗教色彩。《圣经》对美国的文化生活影响很大，引用《圣经》来为其施政纲领作阐述，更具感染力和号召力。第 30 段“我们行善，不可丧志，只要坚持，终有收获。”借助上帝的力量鼓舞美国人民重拾信心，勇于挑战困难、进行改革。

❑ Culture Links

（1）美国为何如此强大

美国是个仅仅有两百多年历史的移民国家，它却将一块大陆由部落时代变身为全球科技高地与实力高地，成长为世界超级大国。《纽约时报》专栏作家安东尼·路易斯是这样说的："美国的强大既不是由于它的军事实力，也不是它的经济实力，而是它的'思想力量'。"其国力强盛的根本动因来自社会内部。

法治传统和法治精神：美国的法治，一方面体现在一个较为健全的宪政体制，另一方面表现为美国社会深厚的法律至上传统。法治而非人治是美国的立国之本，是美国从小到大、从弱到强、保持长治久安的最根本的制度保障。美国著名政论家弗里德曼认为，美利坚民族对宪政法治的信仰是美国强大的关键。美国成功的秘密不在于华尔街，也不在于硅谷；不在于空军，也不在于海军；不在于言论自由，也不在于自由市场。真正的秘密在于长盛不衰的法治及其背后的制度。正是这种制度使得不论谁在掌权，每一个人都可以充分发展。美国真正强大的力量，在于其"所继承的良好的法律与制度体系。"

社会核心价值观保持一致性和连续性：美国人追求自由和平等。自由和平等是天赋人权，政府和他人不得侵犯。他们追求的是起点平等、机会平等，而不是结果平等；美国人始终乐观进取。他们知道适可而止、急流勇退、知足常乐；美国人崇尚公平竞争。他们提倡社会为每个人提供均等机会，鼓励大家在法律范围内积极地竞争。毋庸置疑，以"自由"为核心的价值体系是美国的立国之本。自由、民主、公民权利、三权分立、政教分离、以私有财产不可侵犯为基础的市场经济、宪法至高无上的法治等等，是美国社会中超越政治、宗教派别、阶级和种族界限、为全民所接受的核心价值体系。这套完整的思想体系保证了美国社会的凝聚力和国家的统一。

的确，美国的强大不是源于它的坚船利炮，而是源于自由、平等的理念和机会均等的民主制度，这是一切创造力的源泉。正如克林顿在演讲中所说，"我们最伟大的力量是我们思想的威力，这些思想在许多国家还是一种新生力量。看到这些思想在世界各地被接受，我们感到欢欣鼓舞。我们的希望、我们的心、我们的手，与世界各大洲正在建设民主和自由的人们是连在一起的。他们的事业也是美国的事业。"民主、自由、机遇、坚定不屈的希望成就了这个世界强国的光荣与梦想。

（2）政绩诚可贵，诚实价更高

美国人从小就受到"做人必须诚实"(people must be honest) 的教育。不能说谎、不能欺骗别人，欺骗是一种很丢脸的行为。对诚信的培养早已潜移默化地渗透到美国人生活的方方面面。同时，公民监督推行诚信的意识也很高。此外，在美国破坏诚信的代价非常高，惩处相当严厉。正是这种"教、督、罚"相结合的诚信建设体系，促进了美国诚信经济的繁荣。

在美国，无论你地位有多高、财富有多巨大，一撒谎你便失去了信誉，便没有价值。众所周知，1972年美国总统大选期间，为取得民主党内部竞选策略的情报，以共和党尼克松竞选班子的首席安全顾问为首的5人闯入位于华盛顿水门大厦的民主党全国委员会办公室，安装窃听器并偷拍有关文件。在调查中，尼克松曾一度竭力掩盖脱罪，但随后其政府里的许多人被陆续揭发，尼克松也因卷入“水门事件”而成为美国历史上首位辞职的总统。无独有偶，担任了两届美国总统的克林顿，在他的任期内，美国经济快速增长、失业人口降到历史最低点，其内政外交得心应手。但是1999年的“拉链门事件”使政绩卓越的克林顿受到国会的追究和民众的谴责，主要不是因为他和莱温斯基的暧昧关系，而是因为他作假口供妨碍司法公正，否认自己的错误构成的“撒谎”，因为“撒谎”这一行为违背了“诚实”这一美国第一精神原则。在美国，一个人若是丢失了诚信美德，他将会寸步难行，不论他是平民还是高官。幸而，克林顿后来正视自己的错误，认了错，才得到公众的谅解。

美国人遵循“诚实是最好”的方针，追求身心的全部释放，不喜欢撒一个谎然后背上一个沉甸甸的包袱。弗吉尼亚大学有一条规定，每个入学的新生都必须在杰斐逊的铜像面前宣誓，不得背叛荣誉体系，“我以我的荣誉担保，我没有说谎、欺骗和偷窃”。在平时的作业、论文或者考试中，也必须要在首页上写下一段誓言：“我以学生的名义起誓，我在这次作业（或考试）中没有给予或接受任何帮助。”在美国，诚实被认为是最重要的生活信条和准则。一位美国商人曾说：“一个人可以失去财富、失去职业、失去机会，但万万不可失去信誉。”这足以使人感到“诚信”二字那沉甸甸的分量，而这二字乃是立足社会之根本。

正如美国第3任总统杰斐逊纪念馆中他的21条语录中第一条所说，“在美国这部大书里，诚实是它的第一章，它应当成为我们这个国家的第一性格。”是的，在美国，诚实、讲真话不必被号召，更不会被压制，它早已内化为美国人性格的一部分。

❑ Questions Concerning the Speech

1. What is the implication of "winter" and "spring" in Paragraph 2?
2. Why does Clinton express his thanks to the millions of men and women?
3. What is the urgent question of the time when the address is delivered?
4. How to renew America according to Clinton?
5. Why is the beautiful capital described as "a place of intrigue and calculation"?
6. Together with whom will America work to shape change?
7. What is the greatest strength of America?
8. How could young Americans act on their idealism?

❑ Paraphrase the Following Sentences

1. But by the words we speak and the faces we show the world, we force the spring.
2. Though we march to the music of our time, our mission is timeless.
3. Powerful people maneuver for position and worry endlessly about who is in and who is out, who is up and who is down, forgetting those people whose toil and sweat sends us here and pays our way.
4. Together with our friends and allies, we will work to shape change, lest it engulf us.
5. An idea tempered by the knowledge that, but for fate, we—the fortunate and the unfortunate—might have been each other.
6. And let us not be weary in well-doing, for in due season, we shall reap, if we faint not.

❑ Questions for Discussion

1. 克林顿上台后，把重振美国经济列为其最优先和最根本的任务。请简述克林顿执政时期美国是如何“靠变革而繁荣的”？
2. 克林顿在该演讲中指出，“美国没有任何错误的东西不能被正确的东西所纠正。”对此，你是否认同？请谈谈你的看法。
3.《晏子春秋》中说：橘生淮南则为橘，橘生淮北则为枳。你认为美国式民主适应现代之中国吗？中国能否从美国的民主制度中借鉴点什么？试分析原因，并举例论证。

❑ Translation

比尔·克林顿：首任就职演讲

1993 年 1 月 20 日，华盛顿特区

同胞们：

1. 今天，我们庆祝美国复兴的奇迹。
2. 这个仪式虽在隆冬举行，然而，我们通过自己的言语和向世界展示的面貌，却促使春回大地——回到了世界上这个最古老的民主国家，并带来了重新创造美国的远见和勇气。
3. 当我国的缔造者勇敢地向世界宣布美国独立，并向上帝表明自己的目的时，他们知道，美国若要永存，就必须变革。不是为变革而变革，而是为了维护美国的理想—为了生命、自由和追求幸福而变革。尽管我们随着当今时代的节拍前进，但我们的使命永恒不变。每一代美国人，都必须明确作为一个美国人意味着什么。

4. 我的前任布什总统为美国服务了半个世纪。在此，我谨代表我们的国家向他致以崇高的敬意。我还要向千百万人民表示感谢。他们坚定不移、勇于牺牲，先后战胜了经济萧条、法西斯主义和共产主义。
5. 今天，在冷战阴影下成长起来的一代人，在世界上已肩负起新的责任。这个世界虽然沐浴着自由的阳光，但仍受到旧仇宿怨和新灾祸的威胁。
6. 我们在无与伦比的繁荣中成长，继承了仍然是世界上最强大的经济。但由于企业倒闭、工资水平停滞、不平等状况加剧、人民的分歧加深，我们的经济已经削弱。
7. 当乔治·华盛顿第一次宣读我刚才立誓要信守的誓言时，消息的传递十分缓慢，在陆地要靠马背、在海上则指望船只。而现在，这个仪式的情景和声音即刻向全球数十亿人播放。
8. 通讯和商务是全球性的；投资是流动性的；技术几乎具有魔力；要求改善生活的强烈愿望现在具有普遍性。今天，我们美国人通过同世界各地人民进行和平竞争来谋求生存。
9. 各种深远而强大的力量正在震撼和改造我们的世界。我们这个时代所面临的紧迫问题是，我们能否使变革成为我们的朋友，而不是我们的敌人。
10. 这个新世界已经使几百万能够参与竞争并且取胜的美国人过上了富裕的生活。但是，只要多数人更加拼命地工作而收入却在减少，只要还有人根本不能工作，只要医疗保健的开支仍使众多家庭不堪承受、使大大小小的企业濒临破产，只要犯罪活动造成的恐惧仍使守法公民不能自由行动，只要还有千百万贫穷儿童甚至不能想象我们呼唤他们过的那种生活，我们就尚未使变革成为我们的朋友。
11. 我们知道，我们必须面对严酷的真相，并采取有力的措施。但我们没有这样做，而是听之任之，以致侵蚀了我们的资源、破坏了我们的经济、动摇了我们的信心。
12. 虽然我们的挑战令人生畏，但我们的力量也令人生畏。美国人历来是不安现状、勇于追求和满怀希望的民族。今天，我们必须把前人的远见和意志带到我们的任务中去。
13. 从独立革命到内战、到大萧条、到民权运动，我国人民总是下定决心，从历次危机中构筑我国历史的支柱。
14. 托马斯·杰斐逊认为，为了维护我国的根基，我们需要时常进行激动人心的变革。美国同胞们，我们的时代就是变革的时代，让我们拥抱这个时代吧！
15. 我们的民主制度不仅要成为举世称羡的对象，而且要成为举国复兴的动力。美国没有任何错误的东西不能被正确的东西所纠正。
16. 因此，我们今天立下誓言，要结束这个僵持停顿、放任自流的时代。一个复兴美国的新时代已经开始。我们要复兴美国，就必须英勇无畏。我们必须做前人从未做过的事情。我们必须更多地投资于人民，投资于他们的工作和未来。与此同时，我们必须减少巨额债务。而且，在一个需要为每个机会而竞争的世界上，我们必须这样做。这不是一件轻而易举的事，它需要作出牺牲。但我们能够做到，而且会做得很好。我们不是为牺牲而牺牲，而是为了我们自己的利益。我们必须像家庭供养子女那样供养自己的国家。

17. 我国的缔造者是从子孙后代的角度来审视自己的。我们也必须这样做。任何曾经注意过孩子的双眼朦胧进入梦乡的人，都知道什么是子孙后代。后代就是未来的世界——我们为之坚持自己的理想，我们向之借用这个星球，我们对之负有神圣的责任。我们必须做美国最为拿手的事情：为所有的人提供更多的机会，要所有的人承担更多的责任。

18. 现在是破除只求向政府或别人免费索取的恶习的时候了。让我们大家不仅为自己和家庭，而且为社区和国家担负起更多的责任吧。我们要复兴美国，就必须恢复我们民主制度的活力。

19. 这个美丽的首都，就像文明的曙光出现以来的每一个首都一样，常常是搞阴谋诡计、钩心斗角之地。大人物争权夺势，随时都为官员的更替升降而烦神，却忘记了那些用辛勤和汗水把我们送到这里、并为我们承担费用的人。

20. 美国人理应得到更好的回报。在这个城市里，今天有人想把事情办得更好。因此，我要对在场的诸位说：让我们下定决心改革政治，使权力和特权的喧嚣不再压倒人民的呼声。让我们抛开个人利益，这样我们就能感受到美国的痛苦，也看到美国的希望。让我们下定决心，使政府成为富兰克林·罗斯福所说的进行“大胆而持久试验”的地方，成为一个面向未来而不是留恋过去的政府。让我们把这个首都归还给它所属的人民。

21. 我们要复兴美国，就必须迎接国内外的种种挑战。外交和内政之间已不再有明确的界线——世界经济、世界环境、世界艾滋病危机、世界军备竞赛——这一切都在影响着我们大家。

22. 今天，随着旧秩序被打破，新的世界更加自由，但又更加不稳定。共产主义的崩溃激起了旧的仇恨和新的危险。显然，美国必须继续领导这个我们曾付出巨大努力所造就的世界。

23. 我们在国内进行重建的同时，面对这个新世界的挑战不会退缩不前，也不会坐失良机。我们将同我们的朋友和盟国一起，努力进行变革，以免被变革所吞没。

24. 当我们的重要利益受到挑战，或者国际社会的意志和良知受到蔑视的时候，我们将采取行动——尽可能采用和平外交手段，必要时也会诉诸武力。今天，在波斯湾、索马里和任何其他地方为国效力的勇敢的美国人，都证明了我们的决心。

25. 但是，我们最伟大的力量是我们思想的威力，这些思想在许多国家还是一种新生力量。看到这些思想在世界各地被接受，我们十分高兴。我们的希望、我们的心、我们的手，与世界各大洲正在建设民主和自由的人们是连在一起的。他们的事业也是美国的事业。

26. 美国人民呼唤我们今天所庆祝的变革。你们异口同声地提高了自己的呼声。你们以前所未有的人数参加了投票。你们使国会、总统职务和政治进程本身全都面目一新。是的，是你们，我的美国同胞们，促使春回大地。现在，我们必须做这个时代要求于我们的工作。

27. 现在，我就运用我的全部职权投入这项工作。我请求国会同我合作。但是任何总统、任何国会、任何政府都不能单独承担这一使命。同胞们，你们也必须在国家的复兴中发挥作用。我要向新一代美国年轻人倡导一种奉献意识；按照你们的理想主义行动起来，帮助困难儿童、陪伴那些需要陪伴的人们，把我们四分五裂的社会重新联系起来。要做的事情太多——确实足以使几百万精神上依然年轻的其他人也作出贡献。

28. 在奉献的过程中，我们认识到一个简单而又强大的真理——我们相互需要，而且必须相互关心。今天，我们不仅是在庆祝美国，而且是在重新献身于美国的思想。

29. 这个思想在革命中诞生，在两个世纪的挑战中更新；这个思想经受了认识的锤炼，大家认识到，若非命运的安排，幸运者和不幸者有可能互换位置；这个思想由于一种信念而变得崇高，即我国能够从纷繁的多样性中实现最深刻的团结一致；这个思想还洋溢着一种信念，即美国漫长而英勇的旅程必将永远蓬勃向上。

30. 因此，同胞们，在即将跨入 21 世纪之际，让我们以旺盛的精力和满腔的希望，以坚定的信念和严明的纪律开始工作，直到大功告成。《圣经》说：“我们行善，不可丧志，只要坚持，终有收获。”

31. 在这个欢庆的山巅，我们听见山谷中传来了要求我们奉献的召唤。我们听到了号角声。我们已经换岗。现在，我们必须以各自的方式在上帝的佑助下响应这一召唤。

32. 谢谢各位。愿上帝保佑大家。

George W. Bush

(1946—　)

乔治·W·布什

15

George W. Bush's 9/11 Address to the Nation

Delivered 11 September, 2001, Oval Office, Washington, D.C.

❑ About the Author

乔治·W·布什 (George W. Bush, 1946 年 7 月 6 日—)，出生于美国康涅狄格州的纽黑文市，美国第 43 任总统。布什在 2001 年 1 月 20 日就职，并且在 2004 年的选举中击败民主党参选人约翰·凯利当选连任。布什 1968 年毕业于耶鲁大学，获历史学学士学位，1975 年获哈佛商学院工商管理硕士学位，并曾在得克萨斯州国民警卫队空军任飞行员。在担任总统之前，他于 1995 年至 2000 年间担任第 46 任得克萨斯州州长。布什家族很早就开始投入共和党以及美国政治。布什的父亲是曾担任第 41 任总统的乔治·赫伯特·沃克·布什，由于与父亲同样都是美国总统，因此又常被称为小布什以区别，而他父亲就被称为老布什。

小布什总统任内遭遇了 2001 年的"9·11"事件,他因此发动了一连串的"反恐战争"。2001 年 10 月，他发动了阿富汗战争，以推翻塔利班政权并铲除基地组织势力。接着他在 2003 年 3 月发动了伊拉克战争，推翻了萨达姆独裁政权。

在经过激烈的选战后，他连任总统。在任内小布什推行了 1.3 万亿元的减税计划以及对于医疗保险和社会福利体制的改革，同时也推行了社会保守主义的政策，例如禁止堕胎的法案以及反对承认同性婚姻的联邦法案提议。近年来，小布什总统任期的内外政策不时受到质疑。但对小布什的评价，还有待下一代历史学家做出结论。

在美国在线于 2005 年举办的票选活动《最伟大的美国人》中，小布什被选为美国最伟大的人物第 6 位。

❑ About the Speech

2001年9月11日，是美国人民以至全世界都不会忘记的日子，是人类文明史上的一个耻辱日。美国东部时间2001年9月11日上午（北京时间9月11日晚上）约8点40分，在两小时之内，4架美国民航客机被劫持。其中两架撞向纽约地标性建筑——世界贸易中心双子塔，这两幢摩天大楼分别被撞穿一个大洞，烈焰滔天，然后在全世界目光注视之下，相继倒塌、灰飞烟灭。第三架被劫持民航客机撞向美国首都华盛顿的国防部——五角大楼，第四架在飞抵华盛顿特区第二个目标前，被见义勇为的乘客阻止。乘客冲进驾驶舱与劫机犯搏斗，最后飞机在宾夕法尼亚州的匹兹堡东南面坠毁。

这是自日本偷袭珍珠港以来美国受到的最大规模袭击，致使近3 000人遇难。美国陷入一片恐慌，华盛顿进入紧急状态。在这一严峻的形势下，小布什总统在事发当晚（“9·11”事件发生后仅12小时），以镇定自若的元首风度和充满信心的语气，在白宫向全国人民发表演说，严厉谴责恐怖分子的罪恶行径，表达了战胜恐怖分子、捍卫自由和正义的坚定决心。

❑ The Speech in Full

Good evening.

1. **Today, our fellow citizens, our way of life, our very freedom came under attack in a series of deliberate and deadly terrorist acts.** The victims were in airplanes or in their offices: secretaries, business men and women, military and federal workers, moms and dads, friends and neighbors. Thousands of lives were suddenly ended by evil, despicable[1] acts of terror. The pictures of airplanes flying into buildings, fires burning, huge—huge structures collapsing have filled us with disbelief, terrible sadness, and a quiet, unyielding[2] anger. These acts of mass murder were intended to frighten our nation into chaos and retreat. But they have failed. Our country is strong.

2. **A great people has been moved to defend a great nation. Terrorist attacks can shake the foundations of our biggest buildings, but they cannot touch the foundation of America. These acts shatter steel, but they cannot dent[3] the steel of American resolve. America was targeted for attack because we're the brightest beacon for freedom and opportunity in the world. And no one will keep that light from shining.** Today, our nation saw evil—the very worst of human nature—and we responded with the best of America. With the daring of our rescue workers, with the caring for strangers, and neighbors who came to give blood and help in any way they could.

3. Immediately following the first attack, I implemented our government's emergency response plans. Our military is powerful, and it's prepared. Our emergency teams are working in New York City and Washington D.C. to help with local rescue efforts. Our first priority is to get help to those who have been injured, and to take every precaution to protect our citizens at home and around the world from further attacks. The functions of our government continue without interruption. Federal agencies in Washington which had to be evacuated[4] today are reopening for essential personnel tonight and will be open for business tomorrow. Our financial institutions remain strong, and the American economy will be open for business as well.

4. The search is underway for those who were behind these evil acts. I have directed the full resources of our intelligence and law enforcement communities to find those responsible and to bring them to justice. We will make no distinction between the terrorists who committed these acts and those who harbor them.

5. I appreciate so very much the members of Congress who have joined me in strongly condemning these attacks. And on behalf of the American people, I thank the many world leaders who have called to offer their condolences[5] and assistance. America and our friends and allies join with all those who want peace and security in the world, and we stand together to win the war against terrorism.

6. Tonight, I ask for your prayers for all those who grieve, for the children whose worlds have been shattered, for all whose sense of safety and security has been threatened. And I pray they will be comforted by a Power greater than any of us, spoken through the ages in *Psalm 23*:

Even though I walk through the valley of the shadow of death, I fear no evil for You are with me[6].

7. This is a day when all Americans from every walk of life unite in our resolve for justice and peace. America has stood down enemies before, and we will do so this time. None of us will ever forget this day, yet we go forward to defend freedom and all that is good and just in our world.

8. Thank you. Good night. And God bless America. (607 words)

❑ Notes to the Speech

1. despicable [dis'pikəbl] *adj.* deserving hatred and contempt 卑鄙的，可耻的
2. unyielding [ʌn'jiːldiŋ] *adj.* not giving in to persuasion, pressure, or force 固执的，坚定的，不屈的
3. dent [dent] *vt.* have a bad effect on 削弱；损害
4. evacuate [i'vækjueit] *vt.* remove someone from a place of danger to a safer place 疏散；使（从危险地点）撤离
5. condolence [kən'dəuləns] *n.* （常 *pl.*）an expression of sympathy 慰问；慰唁
6. 此句从《圣经·诗篇 23》(*The Bible · Psalm 23*) 的诗句演变而来。原句是"Even though I walk through the darkest valley, I fear no evil; for You are with me."

❑ Appreciating the Speech

布什这次简短的演说，在知名度上，未必可与我们前文介绍过的林肯、肯尼迪等的演说相比；但就文采 (literary talent) 和语调 (tone of voice) 而言，无疑是一篇有分量之作。

在演说中，布什首先对恐怖分子的卑劣行径表示谴责和愤慨 (expressed his condemnation and indignation towards the terrorists' evil acts)。他说："今天，我们的同胞、我们的生活及我们珍视的自由受到了恐怖主义分子的蓄意攻击……数千人在恐怖分子的卑劣和罪恶行径下突然间失掉了宝贵的生命。"然后，他以激昂的语调对美国人民说"恐怖主义分子的袭击可以震撼我们的建筑，但他们无法动摇我们牢固的国家基础。这些行径可以粉碎钢铁，但它们无法挫伤美国人民捍卫国家的决心 (Terrorist attacks can shake the foundations of our biggest buildings, but they cannot touch the foundation of America. These acts shatter steel, but they cannot dent the steel of American resolve.)。"接下来，他告诉美国人民政府已经开始实施紧急应对计划，将采取一切行动保卫国内及全世界美国人不再受到伤害；并宣布全力调查肇事元凶，将其绳之以法。他向内阁中与他一道声讨此次恐怖事件的成员表示感谢，并代表美国人民向对"9·11"事件表示谴责、对美国人民表示同情的国家表达感谢。最后，他引用《圣经》中的语句，"尽管我行走在死亡的阴影之谷中，但我并不惧怕邪恶，因你与我同在 (Even though I walk through the valley of the shadow of death, I fear no evil for you are with me.)"，用信仰的力量来激励美国人民战胜恐惧，击败敌人 (employed the power of religious belief to stimulate the American people to overcome fears and defeat the enemies)，奋勇"捍卫自由、捍卫世界上一切美好与正义的事物 (defend freedom and all that is good and just in our world)"。

从语言上讲，这篇演说的主要特点是对比 (antithesis)、暗喻 (metaphor) 和引用 (quotation) 的运用。如第 2 段第 2 句"Terrorist attacks can shake the foundations of our biggest buildings, but they cannot touch the foundation of America. These acts shatter steel, but they cannot dent the steel of American resolve.”，就恰到好处地使用了对比的修辞手法，表达了对美国的牢固的国家基础、对美国人民捍卫国家的钢铁般意志的坚定信心。在第 2 段中间，“...we’re the brightest beacon for freedom and opportunity in the world. And no one will keep that light from shining.”一句中，布什运用暗喻的手法，把美国比作自由与机遇的灯塔，生动、形象、贴切，表达了布什对美国的自豪之情和捍卫这一自由国度的决心。在演讲临近结尾处，布什引用的《圣经》诗篇中的句子“Even though I walk through the valley of the shadow of death, I fear no evil, for You are with me.”，用宗教的力量来增强美国人民战胜恐惧和邪恶、彻底击败恐怖主义分子的信心，这一对《圣经》语句的引用，有效地增加了语言的感染力。

❑ Culture Links

（1）国际恐怖主义

恐怖主义是实施者对非武装人员（即平民）有组织地使用暴力或以暴力相威胁，通过将一定的对象置于恐怖之中，来达到某种政治目的的行为。跟黑社会相比，恐怖主义对国家、社会的危害要大得多，它不仅有组织、有制度，更因带有政治目的导致了极端与疯狂。

国际社会中某些组织或个人对他国平民或设施有组织地采取绑架、暗杀、爆炸、空中劫持、扣押人质等恐怖手段，企求实现其政治目标或某项具体要求的主张和行动，被称为**国际恐怖主义**。国际恐怖主义事件主要是由一些极左翼和极右翼的恐怖主义团体，以及极端的民族主义、种族主义的组织和派别所组织策划的。2001 年发生在美国的“9·11”恐怖袭击事件是人类历史上迄今为止最严重的恐怖袭击事件。美国政府对此次事件的谴责和立场也受到大多数国家的同情与支持，该事件也导致了此后国际范围内的多国合作反恐行动。

国际恐怖主义的根源主要有以下几个：

① 冷战结束后，意识形态冲突让位于种族的与宗教的以文化价值为分界线的冲突。这种冲突是孕育国际恐怖主义的温床；

② 美国成为世界上唯一的帝国，它的单边主义政策引起世界其他国家，特别是弱小的不发达国家的不满与仇恨；

③ 西方文化价值与东方文化价值的冲突是造成宗教激进主义和国际恐怖主义的催化剂。

国际恐怖主义严重破坏各国的民族和睦，引发社会动荡；极大地阻碍各国的经济发展和社会进步；影响一些国家世俗政府形象，造成政局动荡、社会不安；破坏世界的和平与发展，威胁着全人类的安全。

(2) 小布什总统与单边主义

单边主义与多边、双边主义都是国际关系中用来定义外交政策行为模式的专有名词。

单边主义多指国际社会中实力地位较强的某一个国家，为了落实外交政策而忽视多数人民意愿，违反国际社会潮流、不顾他国利益、拒绝采取协商途径，凭借自己的力量我行我素的行为。

不少人认为，"9·11"事件后，小布什政府实施了单边主义政策——他们根据自己的利益和判断，依仗美国的经济实力和综合国力，在国际事务中为谋求美国的安全和私利，而不是根据国际社会的需求和意见来做有关全人类利益与安全的政策决定。他们在争取联合国的授权未果情况下，绕过联合国，以自己为主导、联合少数几个盟国，对一些他们认为是支持恐怖、独裁专制的国家采取军事行动，从而招致了一些认为"主权高于人权"的国家的批评和谴责。在不少人的头脑中，单边主义似乎只是美国的专利。但一些国家问题专家认为，单边主义并不为美国所独有。正如北京大学国际关系学院副院长贾庆国教授指出的："从某种意义上讲，所有国家在处理对外关系时都或多或少地采取单边主义的做法，美国也不例外。"中国现代国际关系研究院美国所所长傅梦孜先生认为："单边主义本来是国际体系中'主导力量'的国家，特别是像美国这样的'唯一超级大国'惯有的心理与行为偏好方式。"根据他们的观点，单边主义是国际体系中大国一贯的做法。

实际上，单边主义并不只是一个大国才可拥有的政策，小国、弱国中推行单边主义政策的也不乏先例，只是其影响较小而未引起太多关注罢了。

❑ Questions Concerning the Speech

1. What does Bush say about the 9/11 terrorists' intention?
2. What do you think is the foundation of America?
3. Why was America targeted for attacks?
4. How did the American people respond to the those terrorist attacks?
5. What does Bush say about those who were behind the evil acts?
6. Why does Bush pray together with the audience, quoting the line from Psalm 23?

❑ Paraphrase the Following Sentences

1. Today, our fellow citizens, our way of life, our very freedom came under attack in a series of deliberate and deadly terrorist acts.
2. These acts shatter steel, but they cannot dent the steel of American resolve.
3. We will make no distinction between the terrorists who committed these acts and those who harbor them.

❑ Questions for Discussion

1. 为什么美英等西方发达国家更易遭受国际恐怖主义袭击？如何防止国际恐怖主义袭击，使世界更安全？
2. 你认为美国的“自由和机遇之灯塔是世界上最明亮、最耀眼的”吗？为什么？
3. 你对美国主导的推翻伊拉克萨达姆政权的战争持什么看法？为什么？

❑ Translation

乔治·W·布什：就“9·11”事件对全国的演讲

2001 年 9 月 11 日，华盛顿特区，椭圆办公室

晚上好，

1. 今天，我们的同胞、我们的生活及我们珍视的自由受到了恐怖主义分子的蓄意攻击。许多被劫持的乘客、正在办公的工作人员都不幸遇难。他们可能是：秘书文员、商人、妇女、军方或联邦政府工作人员、孩子的父母、你们的亲朋好友或邻居。数千人在恐怖分子的卑劣和罪恶行径下突然间失掉了宝贵的生命。面对飞机撞毁、熊熊大火、楼房倒塌等图片，我们无法相信眼前的惨状，感到无比的悲哀和愤怒。恐怖分子的大范围屠戮行为旨在将我们的国家引向混乱和倒退，但他们的阴谋没有得逞。我们的国家依然强大。
2. 伟大的美国人民已被动员起来保卫自己的国家。恐怖主义分子的袭击可以震撼我们的建筑，但他们无法动摇我们牢固的国家基础。这些行径可以粉碎钢铁，但它们无法挫伤美国人民捍卫国家的决心。美国之所以成为攻击的目标，是因为我们的自由和机遇之灯塔是世界上最明亮、最耀眼的。没有人能阻止这种自由之光。今天，我们见识了人性中最肮脏的灵魂，而我们以美国人的善良回应罪恶。我们的救援人员表现出了大无畏精神，人们纷纷为陌生人及邻里贡献鲜血及爱心。
3. 在首次遭受袭击后，我下令实施了政府紧急救援计划。我们的强大的军队随时准备投入战斗。紧急行动小组正在纽约市和华府协助地方力量实施求援。我们的第一要务是抢救受伤人员，并保护国内及全世界的美国人不再受到伤害。美国政府的政务仍在正常进行，今天被迫撤出华府的联邦各部门中的重要机构今晚已恢复办公，所有部门均将于明天恢复办公。政府的经济机构仍强大有力，美国各经济部门也将正常办公。
4. 调查此次邪恶事件元凶的工作正在进行。我已下令美国所有的情报机构和执法机构全力找出肇事元凶，并将其绳之以法。胆敢包庇肇事恐怖分子的人也会被我们视为恐怖分子。

5. 我向内阁中与我一道强烈声讨此次恐怖事件的成员表示感谢，也代表美国人民向表示哀悼并给予我们帮助的其他国家的领导人表示感谢。美国、我们的盟国与友邦和全世界所有热爱和平的人将并肩战斗，与恐怖主义活动作斗争。
6. 今晚，我请求你们与我一道为在事件中受到伤害的人祈祷、为那些受伤的儿童祈祷、为那些安全感被打破的人祈祷。我祈祷他们能得到神的安抚，正如世代流传的《圣经》所书，“尽管我行走在死亡的阴影之谷中，但我并不惧怕邪恶，因你与我同在。”
7. 今天是所有美国人团结起来寻求正义与和平的日子。过去，美国击败了自己的敌人，今天的美国人也会战胜自己的敌人。每一个美国人都不会忘记今天，但我们将奋力向前、捍卫自由、捍卫世界上一切美好与正义的事物。
8. 谢谢你们。晚安。愿主保佑美利坚。

Barack Obama

(1961—　)

巴拉克·奥巴马

16

Barack Obama's First Victory Speech

Delivered 5 November, 2008, in Chicago

❑ About the Author

巴拉克·奥巴马(Barack Obama, 1961—)，1961年8月4日出生在美国夏威夷州檀香山市，父亲是来自肯尼亚的留学生，母亲是堪萨斯州人。他是第44任美国总统，也是美国历史上首位非洲裔总统。

奥巴马的童年和青少年时期分别在印尼和夏威夷度过。1991年，他以优等生荣誉从哈佛法学院毕业，获法学博士学位。奥巴马是民主党人，1996年、1998年、2002年曾先后3次当选伊利诺伊州州参议员。在2004年的国会选举中，奥巴马当选联邦参议员。

2007年2月，奥巴马正式宣布竞选总统。他在竞选中以"变革"为主题，强调结束伊拉克战争、实现能源自给、停止减税政策和普及医疗保险等，并承诺实现党派团结、在国际上重建同盟关系、恢复美国领导地位。2008年8月，他在民主党全国代表大会上获得总统候选人提名。11月4日，他在美国总统大选中获胜，当选美国第44任总统。2009年1月20日，奥巴马正式宣誓就职。2009年10月9日，挪威诺贝尔委员会将2009年诺贝尔和平奖授予奥巴马，以表彰他为加强"国际外交和人民之间合作"所做出的努力。2012年11月6日，在第57届美国总统大选中，奥巴马击败共和党候选人罗姆尼，成功连任。

❑ About the Speech

2008 年 8 月 27 日在民主党全国代表大会上，奥巴马被正式提名为该党总统候选人，并且选择了参议员乔·拜登为副总统候选人。11 月 4 日他在总统大选中获胜，击败共和党候选人麦凯恩，成功当选为美国第 44 任总统，更成为美国有史以来第一位非洲裔总统。当晚（美国当地时间 11 月 5 日零点）他在芝加哥发表题为“美国的变革”胜选感言，称美国变革的时代已经到来。他指出了美国所面临的种种严峻挑战，并激励面临挑战的美国人民坚定信心，同心同德，战胜危机。

这次演说非常有震撼力并富有强烈的感情色彩，许多观众倾听时还不禁流下了眼泪。“是的，我们可以（或我们能够做到）”也成了他的名言。

❑ The Speech in Full

Hello, Chicago.

1. **If there is anyone out there who still doubts that America is a place where all things are possible; who still wonders if the dream of our founders is alive in our time; who still questions the power of our democracy, tonight is your answer.**

2. It's the answer told by lines that stretched around schools and churches in numbers this nation has never seen; by people who waited three hours and four hours, many for the very first time in their lives, because they believed that this time must be different; that their voices could be that difference.

3. It's the answer spoken by young and old, rich and poor, Democrat and Republican, black, white, Latino, Asian, Native American, gay[1], straight[2], disabled and not disabled—Americans who sent a message to the world that we have never been just a collection of individuals or a collection of Red States and Blue States[3]: we are, and always will be, the United States of America.

4. It's the answer that led those who have been told for so long by so many to be cynical, and fearful, and doubtful of what we can achieve to put their hands on the arc of history and bend it once more toward the hope of a better day.

5. **It's been a long time coming, but tonight, because of what we did on this day, in this election, at this defining moment, change has come to America.**

6. I just received a very gracious call from Senator McCain[4]. He fought long and hard in this campaign, and he's fought even longer and harder for the country he loves. He has endured sacrifices for America that most of us cannot begin to imagine, and we are better off for the service rendered by this brave and selfless leader. I congratulate him and Governor Palin for all they have achieved, and I look forward to working with them to renew this nation's promise in the months ahead.

7. I want to thank my partner in this journey, a man who campaigned from his heart and spoke for the men and women he grew up with on the streets of Scranton and rode with on that train home to Delaware, the Vice-President-elect of the United States, Joe Biden.

8. I would not be standing here tonight without the unyielding support of my best friend for the last sixteen years, the rock of our family and the love of my life, our nation's next First Lady, Michelle Obama. Sasha and Malia, I love you both more than you can imagine, and you have earned the new puppy that's coming with us to the White House. And while she's no longer with us, I know my grandmother is watching, along with the family that made me who I am. I miss them tonight, and know that my debt to them is beyond measure...

9. To my campaign manager David Plouffe, ...my chief strategist David Axelrod, and the best campaign team ever assembled in the history of politics—you made this happen, and I am forever grateful for what you've sacrificed to get it done.

10. **But above all, I will never forget who this victory truly belongs to—it belongs to you.**

11. I was never the likeliest candidate for this office. We didn't start with much money or many endorsements[5]. Our campaign was not hatched in the halls of Washington—it began in the backyards of Des Moines and the living rooms of Concord and the front porches of Charleston.

12. It was built by working men and women who dug into what little savings they had to give five dollars and ten dollars and twenty dollars to this cause. It grew strength from the young people who rejected the myth of their generation's apathy; who left their homes and their families for jobs that offered little pay and less sleep; from the not-so-young people

who braved the bitter cold and scorching heat to knock on the doors of perfect strangers; **from the millions of Americans who volunteered, and organized, and proved that more than two centuries later, a government of the people, by the people and for the people has not perished from this Earth. This is your victory.**

13. I know you didn't do this just to win an election and I know you didn't do it for me. You did it because you understand the enormity of the task that lies ahead. For even as we celebrate tonight, we know the challenges that tomorrow will bring are the greatest of our lifetime—two wars, a planet in peril, the worst financial crisis in a century. Even as we stand here tonight, we know there are brave Americans waking up in the deserts of Iraq and the mountains of Afghanistan to risk their lives for us. There are mothers and fathers who will lie awake after their children fall asleep and wonder how they'll make the mortgage, or pay their doctor's bills, or save enough for their child's college education. There is new energy to harness and new jobs to be created; new schools to build and threats to meet and alliances to repair.

14. **The road ahead will be long. Our climb will be steep. We may not get there in one year or even one term, but America—I have never been more hopeful than I am tonight that we will get there. I promise you–we as a people will get there.**

15. There will be setbacks and false starts[6]. There are many who won't agree with every decision or policy I make as President, and we know that government can't solve every problem. But I will always be honest with you about the challenges we face. I will listen to you, especially when we disagree. And above all, I will ask you to join in the work of remaking this nation the only way it's been done in America for two-hundred and twenty-one years—block by block, brick by brick, calloused hand by calloused hand.

16. What began twenty-one months ago in the depths of winter can not end on this autumn night. This victory alone is not the change we seek—it is only the chance for us to make that change. And that cannot happen if we go back to the way things were. It cannot happen without you, without a new spirit of service, a new spirit of sacrifice.

17. **So let us** summon a new spirit of patriotism; of responsibility where each of us resolves to pitch in[7] and work harder and look after not only ourselves, but each other.

18. **Let us** remember that if this financial crisis taught us anything, it's that we cannot have a thriving Wall Street[8] while Main Street[9] suffers—in this country, we rise or fall as one nation; as one people.

19. **Let us** resist the temptation to fall back on[10] the same partisanship[11] and pettiness[12] and immaturity that has poisoned our politics for so long. **Let us** remember that it was a man from this state who first carried the banner of the Republican Party to the White House—a party founded on the values of self-reliance, individual liberty, and national unity. Those are values we all share, and while the Democratic Party has won a great victory tonight, we do so with a measure of humility and determination to heal the divides that have held back our progress. As Lincoln said to a nation far more divided than ours, "We are not enemies, but friends. Though passion may have strained it must not break our bonds of affection." And to those Americans whose support I have yet to earn—I may not have won your vote tonight, but I hear your voices, I need your help, and I will be your President too.

20. And to all those watching tonight from beyond our shores, from parliaments and palaces to those who are huddled around radios in the forgotten corners of our world—our stories are singular[13], but our destiny is shared, and a new dawn of American leadership is at hand. **To those who would tear the world down—we will defeat you. To those who seek peace and security—we support you. And to all those who have wondered if America's beacon still burns as bright—tonight we proved once more that the true strength of our nation comes not from the might of our arms or the scale of our wealth, but from the enduring power of our ideals: democracy, liberty, opportunity, and unyielding hope.**

21. That is the true genius of America—that America can change. Our union can be perfected. And what we have already achieved gives us hope for what we can and must achieve tomorrow.

22. This election had many firsts and many stories that will be told for generations. But one that's on my mind tonight is about a woman who cast her ballot in Atlanta. She's a lot like the millions of others who stood in line to make their voice heard in this election except for one thing—Ann Nixon Cooper is 106 years old.

23. She was born just a generation past slavery; a time when there were no cars on the road or planes in the sky; when someone like her couldn't vote for two reasons—because she was a woman and because of the colour of her skin.

24. And tonight, I think about all that she's seen throughout her century in America—the heartache and the hope; the struggle and the progress; the times we were told that we can't, and the people who pressed on with that American creed: **Yes we can**.

25. At a time when women's voices were silenced and their hopes dismissed, she lived to see them stand up and speak out and reach for the ballot. **Yes we can**.

26. When there was despair in the dust bowl and depression across the land, she saw a nation conquer fear itself with a New Deal, new jobs and a new sense of common purpose. **Yes we can.**

27. When the bombs fell on our harbour and tyranny threatened the world, she was there to witness a generation rise to greatness and a democracy was saved. **Yes we can**.

28. She was there for the buses in Montgomery, the hoses in Birmingham, a bridge in Selma, and a preacher from Atlanta who told a people that "We Shall Overcome." **Yes we can**.

29. A man touched down[14] on the moon, a wall came down in Berlin, a world was connected by our own science and imagination. And this year, in this election, she touched her finger to a screen, and cast her vote, because after 106 years in America, through the best of times and the darkest of hours, she knows how America can change. **Yes we can**.

30. America, we have come so far. We have seen so much. But there is so much more to do. So tonight, let us ask ourselves—if our children should live to see the next century; if my daughters should be so lucky to live as long as Ann Nixon Cooper, what change will they see? What progress will we have made?

31. **This is our chance to answer that call. This is our moment. This is our time—to put our people back to work and open doors of opportunity for our**

kids; to restore prosperity and promote the cause of peace; to reclaim the American Dream and reaffirm that fundamental truth—that out of many, we are one; that while we breathe, we hope, and where we are met with cynicism, and doubt, and those who tell us that we can't, we will respond with that timeless creed that sums up the spirit of a people: Yes We Can.

32. Thank you, God bless you, and may God Bless the United States of America. (2,006 words)

❑ Notes to the Speech

1. gay [gei] *n.* a homosexual person, esp. a man 同性恋者（尤指男同性恋者）
2. straight [streit] *n.* <informal> a heterosexual person 异性恋者
3. Red States and Blue States：红州和蓝州（共和党支持率较高的州在大选地图上用红色标示，因而“红州”指共和党，而“蓝州”则代表民主党）
4. Senator McCain：参议员麦凯恩（美国政治家，共和党总统候选人。生于 1936 年 8 月 29 日，共和党重量级人物，亚利桑那州资深联邦参议员。他曾在越南战争中出生入死，被俘并拘禁了长达五年半的时间，这使他成为美国家喻户晓的战斗英雄。）
5. endorsement [in'dɔ:smənt] *n.* public support for somebody or something（公众的）支持
6. false starts：unsuccessful beginning 不顺利的开始
7. pitch in：start working energetically 使劲地干起来
8. Wall Street：华尔街。此处指金融业或富有阶层。
9. Main Street：（一个城市的）主街。此处指普通民众。
10. fall back on sb./sth.：go to sb. for support or use sth. when in difficulty 有困难时求助于某人，依靠某事物
11. partisanship [ˌpɑ:ti'zænʃip] *n.* 党派偏见
12. pettiness ['petinis] *n.* 琐碎；小气；褊狭
13. singular ['siŋgjulə] *adj.* outstanding, remarkable 突出的；非凡的（此处意为“有特色的，不同的”）
14. touch down：(of an aircraft) land（指飞行器）着陆

❑ Appreciating the Speech

奥巴马总统的胜选演说篇幅并不长，但条理分明，内容丰富，激情澎湃，极富鼓动性和感召力，受到了美国国内外媒体和各界的一致好评。

演说一开始，他就阐明了他胜选的意义所在 (expounded the significance of his victory in the election)：这显示了民主制度的力量，这反映了美国人民要求变革的呼声（This displayed the power of democracy and reflected the American people's call for change.）。接下来他感谢家人和竞选团队给予他的支持，指出了美国目前主要面临的3大挑战：伊拉克和阿富汗战争、百年一遇的全国性金融危机以及全球环境问题。然后，他以支持他的一位百岁黑人女选民为例，回顾了美国历史上的标志性事件 (looked back on the monumental events in American history)，指明了美国的力量的源泉所在 (pointed out the source of power of the United States)，最后，他连续在7个句子（或段落）的末尾处重复7遍"Yes we can."（是的，我们能够做到）来强调美国人民非凡的创造力、美国社会的不断进步以及美国实力的强大，从而激励美国人民信心百倍地迎接挑战，战胜困难，创造更加美好的明天 (encouraged the American people to meet the challenges confidently, overcome difficulties, and create brighter future)。

从语言上看，这篇演说有如下几个特点。①排比的运用 (the use of parallelism) 多达十几处，如，"If there is anyone out there who still doubts that America is a place where all things are possible; who still wonders if the dream of our founders is alive in our time; who still questions the power of our democracy, tonight is your answer." 一句以 If 开头，以3个 who 引导的排比句居中，以 tonight is your answer 结束，表达了对美国梦和民主制度的强烈信念，给听众以深刻的震撼；又如，"It grew strength from the young people who…; from the not-so-young people who…; from the millions of Americans who volunteered, and organized, and proved that more than two centuries later, a government of the people, by the people and for the people has not perished from this Earth. This is your victory." 一句，真挚地表达了对来自各阶层民众支持的感激之情；并强调说，这在本质上是美国人们的胜利，是民主制度的胜利。②反复的使用 (the use of repetition)。最突出的例子是演说临近结束时对"Yes we can."多达7次的反复，起到了增强语势的作用，达到了鼓舞人心的效果，表达了对美国美好未来的坚定信心。③头韵法的运用 (the use of alliteration)。如"Let us resist the temptation to fall back on the same partisanship and pettiness…"和"she lived to see them stand up and speak out and reach for the ballot."两句中都用了头韵的修辞手法，增加了语言的节奏感和感染力。另外，奥巴马在本篇演讲中很少使用大词，更多的是使用普通词汇、简短词汇，这样更便于听众理解、使听众产生共鸣，也拉近了与听众的距离。

❑ Culture Links

(1)美国人的家庭观

传统的美国家庭是“核心家庭”。所谓的核心家庭是指丈夫、妻子和他们的孩子组成的家庭。今天，一般美国家庭有两到三个孩子。在某些文化的国度里，人们生活在一个大家庭里中，甚至是几代人生活在一起。而在美国，只是在极少数情况下几代人才生活在同一个屋檐下。

如果说中国人的家庭观注重不同辈分家庭成员间的等级关系，强调一家人相互依靠、父母对儿女的无微不至的关怀、儿女对父母的孝顺与服从，以及子孙满堂的天伦之乐的话，那么美国人的家庭观则突出个人的平等观念、独立发展、权利意识以及在个人独立基础上的天伦之乐。其中最突出的观念是家庭成员之间的独立平等。美国家庭一般都很民主，每一位家庭成员都有发言权。孩子们会把父母当做好朋友，而不是惧怕他们。父母和孩子分担家务。在多数情况下，孩子们在他们的卧室享有隐私权。他们在很小的时候就担负起自己管理钱财的责任。他们可能每周都会得到一些零用钱甚至打点短工。父母经常让孩子们有自己做决定的自由。学龄前儿童就开始自己选择该穿什么样的衣服或该买什么样的玩具。青年人既可以自主择业，也可以自己选择伴侣。

正如其他不同文化国度中的家庭一样，美国的家庭也面临许多问题。社会压力使越来越多的美国家庭分崩离析。现在，美国有半数以上的婚姻以离婚的方式解体。超过四分之一的美国孩子在单亲家庭中长大成人。因而，许多人认为美国的家庭陷入了困境。幸而包括美国政治家在内的各界人士已经认识到了稳固的家庭对社会发展和进步的重要性，他们一直在努力地弘扬、维护美国传统家庭观。比如，里根总统在他的就职演说中说，“家庭和工作是我们美国生活的中心，是自由人民尊严的基础”；克林顿以改革为竞选主题，其改革的依据就是恢复美国传统的价值观，其中维护、巩固传统的家庭观是一项重要内容，这是他竞选成功的重要原因之一。

在本篇演讲中，奥巴马动情地说，“如果没有米歇尔·奥巴马，这一准美国第一夫人的坚定支持，今晚我就不会站在这儿了。我们相伴走过了16个春秋，她是我们整个家庭的顶梁柱、我一生的挚爱。还有萨沙和玛利亚，我爱你们，你们姊妹俩终于可以带着你们的新宠物狗入主白宫了。我知道，就像我的其他已故亲属一样，外祖母一定也在某处注视着我……”在这里，奥巴马是以他自己的方式向美国人民强调了家庭的重要性。

(2)美国政治家的绅士风度

美国是两党政治的国家。四年一度的美国总统大选是两党推出的总统候选人之间的激烈的角逐。在各自的竞选演讲和电视辩论中，两党的总统候选人会在积极地阐述本党立场和政策的同时，质疑对方候选人的政策和观点，但他们总是遵守着一个底线，即无论在什么情况下，绝不会对对方候选人的人格进行诋毁，更不会对大选的投票结果进行质疑。在大选结果发布后，败选的一方会在第一时间坦然承认失败，并向胜选的一方表示诚挚的祝贺，而胜选的一方（当选总统）也往往会在胜选演讲中向竞选失利的一方表示敬意。当然，他也总是会在就职演讲中向前任总统表示敬意和感谢。美国政治家们深信，在美国这一法治至上的国度里，公开、公平、公正的竞争，在美国的宪法原则、联邦竞选法、竞选资金法等的规范、制约下，有着切实的保障。所以，无论哪方竞选失败，他们也毫无怨言。或许这就是"**Fair Play**"精神的体现。

请看奥巴马与麦凯恩竞选总统结果公布的当天，**2008** 年 **11** 月 **5** 日，麦凯恩和奥巴马在各自在演讲中说的话。先看麦凯恩，他在败选感言中对他的支持者说，"我的朋友们，我们已经结束了一段长途旅程。美国人已经清晰地做出了他们的选择。不久之前，我非常荣幸地打电话给奥巴马参议员，向他祝贺胜利。祝贺他当选为这个我们都热爱的国家的新一任总统……我希望所有支持我的美国人，不仅仅是要和我一起来祝贺他，同时还要向我们的新任总统表达我们良好的心愿以及我们真诚的努力……今夜，在我的心中，我比以往任何一个夜晚都更加深爱这个国家、深爱这个国家的全体国民，无论他们是投票支持了我，还是他们支持了奥巴马参议员。"而奥巴马在随后的胜选演讲中同样表达了对竞选对手麦凯恩的感谢和敬佩之情。奥巴马说："刚才，我接到了麦凯恩参议员礼貌的祝贺电话。为了此次竞选，他奋战良久、竭尽所能；为了他所深爱的美国，他曾做出了更长久、更努力的奉献。麦凯恩参议员为美国所做出的牺牲是大部分人难以想象的，他这种英勇无私的奉献改善了我们的生活。对于麦凯恩参议员和佩林州长所取得的成就，我对他们致以祝贺。在接下来的几个月里，以重振美国为目标，我期待着与他们的合作。"

其实，他们在竞选过程中的绅士风度不仅基于他们对美国公平竞争原则的信心，而且基于这样一种理念，即某一党派总统竞选人的胜利从根本上讲并不是某一政党的胜利，而是民主制度的胜利、是人民的胜利。他们知道，他们要时刻注意自己的言行，否则他们就会被人民抛弃。

❑ Questions Concerning the Speech

1. What answer does his victory in the election bring to the American people?
2. Why didn't Obama think of himself as the likeliest candidate at the beginning of the election campaign?
3. What are the challenges facing the Americans?
4. What does the crisis teach them?
5. In Obama's opinion, from what does the true strength of the United States come?
6. What example does he give to recall the history of America's past century?

❑ Paraphrase the Following Sentences

1. Our campaign was not hatched in the halls of Washington—it began in the backyards of Des Moines and the living rooms of Concord and the front porches of Charleston.
2. This victory alone is not the change we seek—it is only the chance for us to make that change.
3. …we cannot have a thriving Wall Street while Main Street suffers
4. our stories are singular, but our destiny is shared
5. When the bombs fell on our harbour and tyranny threatened the world, she was there to witness a generation rise to greatness and a democracy was saved.
6. to reclaim the American Dream and reaffirm that fundamental truth—that out of many, we are one

❑ Questions for Discussion

1. 作为第一位美国黑人总统，同时又来自于社会底层，奥巴马会改变美国的对内、对外基本政策吗？请分析并试论其原因。
2. 我国存在对某一族群或某一群体的歧视吗？如果有，请指出最普遍、最严重的一种歧视是什么，并请说明你对此问题的态度。如有可能，也请给出解决此问题的建议。
3. 从 2011 年 9 月起，在美国纽约等不少大中城市，许多人走上街头，举标语、喊口号，举行示威游行，痛斥华尔街金融大亨的贪得无厌，批评政府偏袒金融大鳄、造成社会不公、损害了广大中低收入阶层的利益。请分析美国政府是如何应对这一事件的，你认为这一事件会对美国造成何种影响。

❑ Translation

巴拉克·奥巴马：首任胜选演讲

2008 年 11 月 5 日，芝加哥

你好，芝加哥！

1. 美国是否暗藏一切皆有可能的巨大潜力？美国是否已经实现开国者锻造的美国梦？民主信仰是否具有强大力量？如果还有人对此抱以怀疑，那么今晚这里发生的一切就是答案。

2. 学校旁、教堂边，无数人都在排队投票，这一情景我们已经多年未见；3 个小时、4 个小时，他们为此而等候良久，这是很多同胞有生以来的第一次。因为他们相信，这一次，将不同以往；这一次，因为他们的呼声而有所不同。
3. 无论老少贫富，无论共和党抑或民主党，不管是黑皮肤、白种人、拉丁后裔、亚裔子孙还是本土美国人；无论性向如何，不论健康还是残疾，所有的美国人民都向全世界传递出这样一条信息：我们从来都不是红蓝阵营的政治堆砌；我们是，而且永远是，美利坚合众国。
4. 长期以来，很多人缺乏信心，对自己所能取得的成就畏首畏尾、疑心重重。如今，我们走在历史的长河里，挺起胸膛、勾勒出美好明天的光辉画卷。
5. 此情此景，等待尤长。然而，就在今晚、在这个大选的日子，在这个具有历史性意义的时刻，由于你们的付出，美国终于迎来了变革。
6. 刚刚，我接到了麦凯恩参议员礼貌得体的祝贺电话。为了此次竞选，他奋战良久、竭尽所能；为了他所深爱的美国，他曾做出了更长久、更努力的奉献。麦凯恩参议员为美国所做出的牺牲是大部分人难以想象的，他这种英勇无私的奉献改善了我们的生活。对于麦凯恩参议员和佩林州长所取得的成就，我对他们致以祝贺。在接下来的几个月里，以重振美国为目标，我期待着与他们的合作。
7. 在此，我想感谢一路陪伴我的竞选搭档，他就是我们即将上任的副总统，乔·拜登。为了让美国广大的工人阶层发出自己的声音，他毫无私心地全身心投入竞选，因为他和那些宾夕法尼亚州斯克兰顿城街头的人们一样，出生平凡，一切白手起家。
8. 如果没有米歇尔·奥巴马这一准美国第一夫人的坚定支持，今晚我就不会站在这儿了。我们相伴走过了 16 个春秋，她是我们整个家庭的顶梁柱，我一生的挚爱。还有萨沙和玛利亚，我爱你们，你们姊妹俩终于可以带着你们的新宠物狗入主白宫了。我知道，就像我的其他已故亲属一样，外祖母一定也在某处注视着我，虽然她已经不在人世。是他们造就了今天的我。今晚我很想念他们，我对他们的亏欠无以计量。
9. 我想对我的竞选经理戴维·普劳夫、首席战略师戴维·阿克塞尔罗德以及我们这个史上最佳的竞选团队说：是你们让这一切成为了现实，对于你们为此所做的牺牲和付出我永远感怀在心。
10. 然而，有一点是最重要的，那就是我永远都不会忘记，真正拥有这个胜利的是你们，你们所有人！
11. 对于入主白宫，我从来都不是最热候选人。竞选伊始，我们的资金并不充裕，获得的支持也不多。我们的竞选班子并非始于华府，而是一路从艾奥瓦州的得梅因酒店后院、辗转北卡罗来纳州的康克酒店客房，后来会首在西弗吉尼亚州查尔斯顿酒店的主厅……
12. 我们的胜利来自于广大工薪阶级，正是他们从仅有的微薄存款里掏出 5 美元、10 美元或者 20 美元来支持我们的竞选。我们的力量来自于摘下冷漠面罩的年轻一代，来自于夜以继日奋力工作以维持生计的下层百姓，来自于冒着严寒酷暑、户户敲门宣传的团队中流砥柱，更来自于成千上万的大选志愿者。他们用出色的奉献精神和组织能力证明了一个民有、民治、民享的政府在两百年后仍然保持着生命力。这就是你们的胜利！

13. 我明白，你们所做的这些，并不仅仅是为了赢得这次竞选，也不单单只是为了我本人。你们之所以这么做，是因为你们懂得前方任务的艰巨。即使我们今晚沉浸于庆祝的喜悦之中，我们也深知明天将会面临的将是我们这辈子最为艰巨的挑战：两场战争、濒临危险的地球和百年一遇的金融危机；即使今晚我们安然站在此处，我们也深知那些深陷伊拉克沙漠和阿富汗山区的英勇美国战士，是为了我们而冒着生命危险。还有那些孩子早已熟睡、自己却辗转反侧的人父人母，他们夜不能寐，想着如何还清房贷、如何支付医药费以及给孩子存下大学经费。我们要掌握新能源、创造就业岗位、建造新校舍，正视存在的威胁，并修复与盟友的关系。
14. 前方的道路很漫长，我们将步履维艰。我们也许无法在一年内，甚至是（我的）一个任期内，达成我们的目标。但是，今晚，我比任何时候都对此更有信心。我承诺，我们所有人将作为一个整体顺利地到达目的地。
15. 我们将不可避免地遭遇许多挫折，也许开头并不会一帆风顺。我们需要弄明白一点，那就是政府无法解决所有的问题，也许有很多人会不同意我上台执政后制定的政策。不过，我将坦诚地接受各方的批评，直面我们的挑战。我将倾听你们的意见，尤其是不同的政见。总之，我邀请各位一同投入到国家的建设中来，用我们勤劳的双手堆砌建设这个国家所需的砖瓦。正是这一方式，使美国在 221 年的建国道路上不断前行。
16. 我在 21 个月前的深冬开始为竞选做出的努力并不会在今晚画上句号。我们所追求的并不是这场选举的胜利，这仅仅是为我们提供了一个做出变革的机会。如果回到过去的老路，我们将无法做出任何改变。当然，如果没有你们，一切都无法发生。
17. 所以，让我们一同唤醒自己的爱国心，唤醒为国效力的责任感，我们将一道披星戴月，披荆斩棘向前行进，我们需要照顾的不再只有我们自己，而是每一个人。
18. 让我们记住，如果说这次金融危机给予了我们什么教训的话，那就是：如果大众受苦受难，华尔街就不可能繁花似锦。我们必须携手与共、共同经历这个国家的荣辱兴衰。
19. 长期以来，两党隔阂以及不成熟的狭隘主义造成了我们现在的失败政策，所以让我们一同抵制住这种倾向，避免回到那条老路。请记住，这个国家有一个民主党人将第一次手扛民主和共和两党旗帜迈向白宫。充满自信、崇尚个人自由、维护国家团结将是我们共同追求的价值观。尽管民主党在今晚取得了压倒性的胜利，但是我们将继续带着谦卑前行，愈合这个国家因分裂而受到的创伤。社会的分裂曾经阻碍我们国家前行的脚步。正如林肯总统在 1861 年反国家分裂的演说中所说“我们不是敌人，而是朋友。我们决不能成为敌人。尽管目前的情绪有些紧张，但决不能容许它使我们之间的亲密情感纽带破裂。”我要告诉那些没有将选票投给我的朋友，也许我没有赢得你们的选票，但我将聆听你们的声音，我需要你们的帮助，因为我同样将成为你们的总统。

20. 我要告诉那些在美国大陆以外关注今晚选举的人们，也许你们在一个被世界遗忘的角落通过收音机了解今晚的选举，尽管我们的国情不一样，但是我们的命运是紧紧联系在一起的。一个全新的美国领导层即将呼之欲出。我要告诉那些试图破坏这个世界的人们，我们将打败你们！我要告诉那些追求和平和安全的人们，我们将全力支持你们！我要告诉那些对美国的未来持怀疑态度的人们，今晚，我们再次证明了一个事实，那就是这个国家拥有强大的力量。这并不是因为我们拥有众多的武器和财富。民主、自由、机遇、坚定不屈的希望才是这个国家保持强大的持久力量！

21. 美国强大的真谛在于它能够做出改变。我们的国家可以变得更加完美。我们过去所达到的成就让我们看到了前进的希望。

22. 本届选举创造了多项历史之最，有许多故事将代代相传。但此时此刻，我脑海中想起的是一名来自亚特兰大的选民。这位名叫安妮·尼克松·库珀的女性和千千万万的选民一样，静静地站在投票队伍之中，投出自己的选票，表达自己的声音。不过，与众不同的是，她已经 106 岁高龄了。

23. 在她出生的年代，奴隶制刚刚过去一代人的时间，公路上没有汽车、天空中没有飞机。像她一样的人仅仅因为肤色和性别就被挡在参与投票的大门之外。

24. 今晚，我由此联想到了她一个世纪以来，在美国见证的一切：困苦与希望，奋斗与进步。那是一个让人无能为力的年代，但人们必须不断告诉自己美国的伟大信条：“是的，我们可以！”

25. 曾经，女性无法表达自己的意见，她们的希望成为幻影。如今，她终于见证了这一幕，和她一样有着悲惨遭遇的人们成功地投出了自己的选票。是的，我们可以！

26. 当整个美国大陆都笼罩在经济大萧条的绝望之中时，她见证了一个国家战胜自身恐惧，重新崛起。罗斯福总统推行的“新政”不仅给美国带来了新的就业机会，更给美国人民带来了共同的价值观。是的，我们可以！

27. 当敌人的炮弹投向我们的港口，当世界被暴政所威胁，她见证了一个崛起的民族，民主重获新生。是的，我们可以！

28. 她目睹了发生在蒙哥马利巴士上、伯明翰的高压水龙头下、塞尔玛大桥上的种族歧视暴行……而后，来自亚特兰大的民权先驱告诉人们，“我们可以战胜这一切”。是的，我们可以！

29. 而后，人类登月，柏林墙倒塌，世界重新集结在科学和想象力的号角下。现在，在这场选举中，她终于用自己的指尖触碰到投票屏幕，郑重地投下选票。饱经 106 年的沧桑变化，穿越岁月的风云变迁，她知道美国能作出怎样的改变。是的，我们可以！

30. 美国，我们风雨兼程，一路走来。我们经历了太多，但前方仍有许多梦想等待着我们去实现。今晚，让我们大声地问自己，我们的孩子是否还能看到下一个世纪；我可爱的女儿是否能和安妮·尼克松·库珀一样幸运，享受漫长的人生？他们将看到怎样的变革？我们将取得怎样的进步？

31. 这是我们给出答案的机会。这是属于我们的时刻。这是我们的时代：让人们有事可做；为我们的孩子打开机遇之门；推动世界和平与繁荣；再次锻造美国梦，重申这一不可动摇的事实——虽然我们每个人不尽相同，但我们是一个整体。只要我们呼吸尚存，希望就永不磨灭。我们将用那历经时间考验的不朽信条掷地有声地直面质疑：“是的，我们可以！”

32. 谢谢！上帝保佑你们，保佑美利坚合众国！

附　录

1

The Mayflower Compact (Modern Version)

(With Comments)

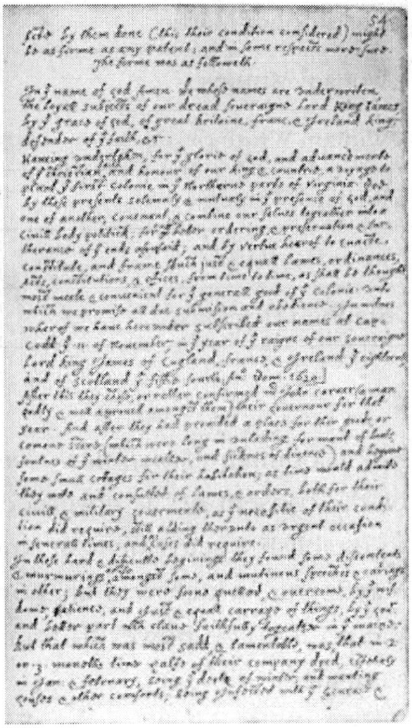

In the name of God, Amen. We, whose names are underwritten, the loyal subjects of our dread Sovereign Lord King James, by the Grace of God, of Great Britain, France, and Ireland, King, defender of the Faith, etc. having undertaken, for the Glory of God, and advancements of the Christian faith and honor of our King and Country, a voyage to plant the first colony in the Northern parts of Virginia, do by these presents, solemnly and mutually, in the presence of God, and one another, covenant and combine ourselves together into a civil body politic; for our better ordering, and preservation and furtherance of the ends aforesaid; and by virtue hereof to enact, constitute, and frame, such just and equal laws, ordinances, acts, constitutions, and offices, from time to time, as shall be thought most meet and convenient for the general good of the colony; unto which we promise all due submission and obedience.

In witness whereof we have hereunto subscribed our names at Cape Cod the 11th of November, in the year of the reign of our Sovereign Lord King James, of England, France, and Ireland, the eighteenth, and of Scotland the fifty-fourth, 1620.

John Carver	Edward Tilley	Degory Priest
William Bradford	John Tilley	Thomas Williams
Edward Winslow	Francis Cooke	Gilbert Winslow
William Brewster	Thomas Rogers	Edmund Margeson
Issac Allerton	Thomas Tinker	Peter Browne
Myles Standish	John Rigdale	Richard Britteridge
John Alden	Edward Fuller	George Soule
Samuel Fuller	John Turner	Richard Clarke
Christopher Martin	Francis Eaton	Richard Gardiner
William Mullins	James Chilton	John Allerton
William White	John Crackston	Thomas English
Richard Warren	John Billington	Edward Dotey
John Howland	Moses Fletcher	Edward Leister
Stephen Hopkins	John Goodman	

(Comment: *Mayflower Compact*, first colonial agreement that formed a government by the consent of the governed, was signed in 1620 by Pilgrims, English people hoping to establish a settlement in North America. The agreement was completed on the ship Mayflower, which was anchored off the coast of Massachusetts. The compact gave the settlers the power to frame and enact laws for the general good of the planned settlement.

In the whole history of human civilization, the significance of *Mayflower Compact* can almost rival that of the *Magna Charta*（《大宪章》）of Great Britain, *United States Declaration of Independence*, and France's *Declaration of the Rights of Man and of the Citizen*（《人权宣言》）. The development of the United States has been based on this short political covenant. And such words in it as "faith", "laws", "just", "equal" have become the founding principles of this new and promising country.

Translation

五月花号公约

以上帝的名义，阿门。

我们，下面的签名人，作为伟大的詹姆斯一世的忠顺臣民，为了给上帝增光，发扬基督教的信仰和我们祖国和君主的荣誉，特着手在弗吉尼亚北部这片新开拓的海岸建立第一个殖民地。我们在上帝的面前，彼此以庄严的面貌出现，现约定将我们全体组成公民政治体，以使我们能更好地生存下来并在我们之间创造良好的秩序。为了殖民地的公众利益，我们将根据这项契约颁布我们应当忠实遵守的公正平等的法律、法令和命令，并视需要而任命我们应当服从的行政官员。

据此于公元 **1620** 年 **11** 月 **11** 日，于英格兰、法兰西、爱尔兰第 **18** 世国王暨苏格兰第 **54** 世国王詹姆斯陛下在位之年，我们在科德角签名如下。

签名（略）

2

Declaration of Independence

(With Comments)

In Congress, July 4, 1776

The unanimous Declaration of the thirteen united States of America

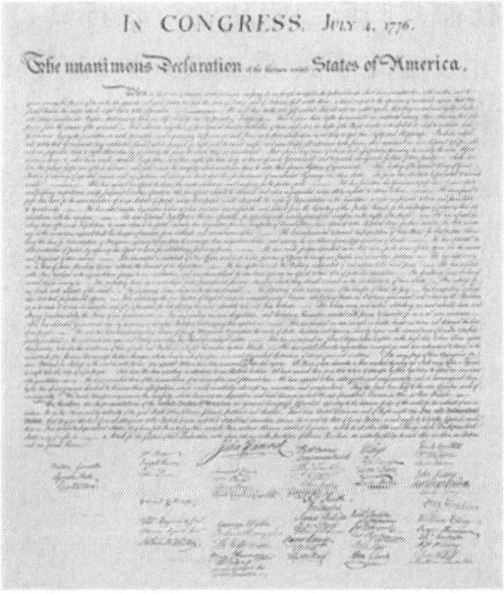
IN CONGRESS. JULY 4, 1776.

The unanimous Declaration of the ... States of America.

When in the Course of human events it becomes necessary for one people to dissolve the political bands which have connected them with another and to assume among the powers of the earth, the separate and equal station to which the Laws of Nature and of Nature's God entitle them, a decent respect to the opinions of mankind requires that they should declare the causes which impel them to the separation.

(Comment: *This part serves as* ***Introduction****, which asserts as a matter of Natural Law the ability of a people to assume political independence; acknowledges that the grounds for such independence must be reasonable, and therefore explicable, and ought to be explained.*)

We hold these truths to be self-evident, that all men are created equal, that they are endowed by their Creator with certain unalienable Rights, that among these are Life, Liberty and the pursuit of Happiness. —That to secure these rights, Governments are instituted among Men, deriving their just powers from the consent of the governed, —That whenever any Form of Government becomes destructive of these ends, it is the Right of the People to alter or to abolish it, and to institute new Government, laying its foundation on such principles and organizing its powers in such form, as to them shall seem most likely to effect their Safety and Happiness. Prudence, indeed, will dictate that Governments long established should not be changed for light and transient causes; and accordingly all experience hath shewn that mankind are more disposed to suffer, while evils are sufferable than to right themselves by abolishing the forms to which they are accustomed. But when a long train of abuses and usurpations, pursuing invariably the same Object evinces a design to reduce them under absolute Despotism, it is their right, it is their duty, to throw off such Government, and to provide new Guards for their future security.

(**Comment:** *This part serves as* ***Preamble****, which outlines a general philosophy of government that justifies revolution when government harms natural rights.*)

Such has been the patient sufferance of these Colonies; and such is now the necessity which constrains them to alter their former Systems of Government. The history of the present King of Great Britain is a history of repeated injuries and usurpations, all having in direct object the establishment of an absolute Tyranny over these States. To prove this, let Facts be submitted to a candid world.

He has refused his Assent to Laws, the most wholesome and necessary for the public good.

He has forbidden his Governors to pass Laws of immediate and pressing importance, unless suspended in their operation till his Assent should be obtained; and when so suspended, he has utterly neglected to attend to them.

He has refused to pass other Laws for the accommodation of large districts of people, unless those people would relinquish the right of Representation in the Legislature, a right inestimable to them and formidable to tyrants only.

He has called together legislative bodies at places unusual, uncomfortable, and distant from the depository of their Public Records, for the sole purpose of fatiguing them into compliance with his measures.

He has dissolved Representative Houses repeatedly, for opposing with manly firmness his invasions on the rights of the people.

He has refused for a long time, after such dissolutions, to cause others to be elected, whereby the Legislative Powers, incapable of Annihilation, have returned to the People at large for their exercise; the State remaining in the mean time exposed to all the dangers of invasion from without, and convulsions within.

He has endeavored to prevent the population of these States; for that purpose obstructing the Laws for Naturalization of Foreigners; refusing to pass others to encourage their migrations hither, and raising the conditions of new Appropriations of Lands.

He has obstructed the Administration of Justice by refusing his Assent to Laws for establishing Judiciary Powers.

He has made Judges dependent on his Will alone for the tenure of their offices, and the amount an payment of their salaries.

He has erected a multitude of New Offices, and sent hither swarms of Officers to harass our people and eat out their substance.

He has kept among us, in times of peace, Standing Armies without the Consent of our legislatures.

He has affected to render the Military independent of and superior to the Civil Power.

He has combined with others to subject us to a jurisdiction foreign to our constitution, and unacknowledged by our laws; giving his Assent to their Acts of pretended Legislation:

For quartering large bodies of armed troops among us:

For protecting them, by a mock Trial from punishment for any Murders which they should commit on the Inhabitants of these States:

For cutting off our Trade with all parts of the world:

For imposing Taxes on us without our Consent:

For depriving us in many cases, of the benefit of Trial by Jury:

For transporting us beyond Seas to be tried for pretended offences:

For abolishing the free System of English Laws in a neighbouring Province, establishing therein an Arbitrary government, and enlarging its Boundaries so as to render it at once an example and fit instrument for introducing the same absolute rule into these Colonies

For taking away our Charters, abolishing our most valuable Laws and altering fundamentally the Forms of our Governments:

For suspending our own Legislatures, and declaring themselves invested with power to legislate for us in all cases whatsoever.

He has abdicated Government here, by declaring us out of his Protection and waging War against us.

He has plundered our seas, ravaged our Coasts burnt our towns, and destroyed the lives of our people.

He is at this time transporting large Armies of foreign Mercenaries to compleat the works of death, desolation, and tyranny, already begun with circumstances of Cruelty & Perfidy scarcely paralleled in the most barbarous ages, and totally unworthy the Head of a civilized nation.

He has constrained our fellow Citizens taken Captive on the high Seas to bear Arms against their Country, to become the executioners of their friends and Brethren, or to fall themselves by their Hands.

He has excited domestic insurrections amongst us, and has endeavored to bring on the inhabitants of our frontiers, the merciless Indian Savages whose known rule of warfare, is an undistinguished destruction of all ages, sexes and conditions.

In every stage of these Oppressions We have Petitioned for Redress in the most humble terms: Our repeated Petitions have been answered only by repeated injury. A Prince, whose character is thus marked by every act which may define a Tyrant, is unfit to be the ruler of a free people.

(**Comment:** *This part is* ***indictment.*** *It is a bill of particulars documenting the king's "repeated injuries and usurpations" of the Americans' rights and liberties.*)

Nor have We been wanting in attentions to our British brethren. We have warned them from time to time of attempts by their legislature to extend an unwarrantable jurisdiction over us. We have reminded them of the circumstances of our emigration and settlement here. We have appealed to their native justice and magnanimity, and we have conjured them by the ties of our common kindred. to disavow these usurpations, which would inevitably interrupt our connections and correspondence. They too have been deaf to the voice of justice and of consanguinity. We must, therefore, acquiesce in the necessity, which denounces our Separation, and hold them, as we hold the rest of mankind, Enemies in War, in Peace Friends.

(**Comment:** *This part is* ***denunciation****, which essentially finished the case for independence. The conditions that justified revolution have been shown.*)

We, therefore, the Representatives of the United States of America, in General Congress, Assembled, appealing to the Supreme Judge of the world for the rectitude of our intentions, do, in the Name, and by Authority of the good People of these Colonies, solemnly publish and declare, That these United Colonies are, and of Right ought to be Free and Independent States, that they are Absolved from all Allegiance to the British Crown, and that all political connection between them and the State of Great Britain, is and ought to be totally dissolved; and that as Free and Independent States, they have full Power to levy War, conclude Peace contract Alliances, establish Commerce, and to do all other Acts and Things which Independent States may of right do. —And for the support of this Declaration, with a firm reliance on the protection of Divine Providence, we mutually pledge to each other our Lives, our Fortunes and our sacred Honor.

(**Comment:** *This part serves as* ***conclusion.*** *The signers assert that there exist conditions under which people must change their government, that the British have produced such conditions, and by necessity the colonies must throw off political ties with the British Crown and become independent states. The conclusion contains, at its core, the Lee Resolution that had been passed on July 2.*)

—John Hancock

New Hampshire:

Josiah Bartlett, William Whipple, Matthew Thornton

Massachusetts:

John Hancock, Samuel Adams, John Adams, Robert Treat Paine, Elbridge Gerry

Rhode Island:

Stephen Hopkins, William Ellery

Connecticut:

Roger Sherman, Samuel Huntington, William Williams, Oliver Wolcott

New York:

William Floyd, Philip Livingston, Francis Lewis, Lewis Morris

New Jersey:

Richard Stockton, John Witherspoon, Francis Hopkinson, John Hart, Abraham Clark

Pennsylvania:

Robert Morris, Benjamin Rush, Benjamin Franklin, John Morton, George Clymer, James Smith, George Taylor, James Wilson, George Ross

Delaware:

Caesar Rodney, George Read, Thomas McKean

Maryland:

Samuel Chase, William Paca, Thomas Stone, Charles Carroll of Carrollton

Virginia:

George Wythe, Richard Henry Lee, Thomas Jefferson, Benjamin Harrison, Thomas Nelson, Jr., Francis Lightfoot Lee, Carter Braxton

North Carolina:

William Hooper, Joseph Hewes, John Penn

South Carolina:

Edward Rutledge, Thomas Heyward, Jr., Thomas Lynch, Jr., Arthur Middleton

Georgia:

Button Gwinnett, Lyman Hall, George Walton

(**Comment:** *This part is* ***signatures****. The first and most famous signature on the engrossed copy was that of John Hancock, President of the Continental Congress. Two future presidents, Thomas Jefferson and John Adams, were among the signatories. Edward Rutledge (age 26), was the youngest signer, and Benjamin Franklin (age 70) was the oldest signer. The fifty-six signers of the Declaration represented the new states (from north to south).*)

(**Comment on the whole document:** The ***Declaration of Independence*** was a statement adopted by the Continental Congress on July 4, 1776, which announced that the thirteen American colonies, then at war with Great Britain, regarded themselves as independent states, and no longer a part of the British Empire. It transformed the colonists' struggle with Great Britain from a defense of their rights as Englishmen to a revolution aimed at overthrowing the existing form of government. It did not establish a structure of government and should not be confused with either the Articles of Confederation or the Constitution of the United States. For the American colonists, the declaration was an announcement to the rest of the world that the colonies were independent from Great Britain; it also provided a rationale for this action. The goal was to solidify internal support for their struggle and to encourage external assistance from European powers such as France.

The *Declaration of Independence*'s eloquent rhetoric and political significance rank it as one of the greatest documents in world history. The sentence "We hold these truths to be self-evident, that all men are created equal, that they are endowed by their Creator with certain unalienable Rights, that among these are Life, Liberty and the pursuit of Happiness." has been called "one of the best-known sentences in the English language". And ever since its publishment, the *Declaration of Independence* has inspired work for the rights of marginalized people throughout the world.)

Translation

独立宣言

大陆会议（1776 年 7 月 4 日）美利坚合众国 13 个州一致通过的独立宣言

[**注：**独立宣言之本文可分为 5 个章节：序文、前言、控诉、谴责以及总结。（独立宣言本文中并没有这 5 个章节的标题。）]

序文

在有关人类事务的发展过程中，当一个民族必须解除其和另一个民族之间的政治联系并在世界各国之间依照自然法则和上帝的意旨、接受独立和平等的地位时，出于对人类舆论的尊重，必须把他们不得不独立的原因予以宣布。

前言

我们认为下面这些真理是不证自明的：人人生而平等，造物者赋予他们若干不可剥夺的权利，其中包括生命权、自由权和追求幸福的权利。为了保障这些权利，人类才在他们之间建立政府，而政府之正当权力，是经被治理者的同意而产生的。当任何形式的政府对这些目标具破坏作用时，人民便有权改变或废除它，以建立一个新的政府。新政府所依据的原则和组织其权利的方式，务使人民认为唯有这样才最有可能使他们获得安全和幸福。若真要审慎地来说，成立多年的政府是不应当由于无关紧要的和一时的原因而予以更换的。过去的一切经验都说明，任何苦难，只要尚能忍受，人类还是情愿忍受，也不想为申冤而废除他们久已习惯了的政府形式。然而，当始终追求同一目标的一系列滥用职权和强取豪夺的行为表明政府企图把人民置于专制暴政之下时，人民就有权力也有义务去推翻这样的政府，并为其未来的安全提供新的保障。

控诉

这就是这些殖民地过去忍受苦难的经过，也是他们现在不得不改变政府制度的原因。当今大不列颠王国的历史，就是屡屡伤害和掠夺这些殖民地的历史，其直接目标就是要在各州之上建立一个独裁暴政。为了证明上述句句属实，现将事实公之于世，让公正的世人作出评判。

他拒绝批准对公众利益最有益、最必需的法律。

他禁止他的殖民总督批准刻不容缓、极端重要的法律，或者就先行搁置这些法律直至征得他的同意；而这些法律被搁置以后，他又完全置之不理。

他拒绝批准便利广大地区人民的其他的法律，除非这些地区的人民情愿放弃自己在立法机构中的代表权；而代表权对人民是无比珍贵的，只有暴君才畏惧它。

他把各州的立法委员召集到一个异乎寻常、极不舒适而又远离他们的档案库的地方去开会，其目的无非是使他们疲惫不堪，被迫就范。

他一再解散各州的众议院，因为后者坚决反对他侵犯人民的权利。

他在解散众议院之后，又长期拒绝另选他人，于是这项不可剥夺的立法权便归由普通人民来行使，致使在这其间各州仍处于外敌入侵和内部骚乱的种种危险之中。

他力图阻止各州增加人口。为此目的，他阻挠外国人入籍法的通过，拒绝批准其他鼓励移民的法律，并提高分配新土地的条件。

他拒绝批准建立司法权力的法律，以阻挠司法的执行。

他迫使法官为了保住任期、薪金的数额和支付而置于他个人意志的支配之下。

他滥设新官署，委派大批官员到这里骚扰我们的人民，吞噬他们的财物。

他在和平时期，未经我们立法机构同意，就在我们中间维持其常备军。

他施加影响，使军队独立于文官政权之外、并凌驾于文官政权之上。

他同他人勾结，把我们置于一种既不符合我们的法规也未经我们法律承认的管辖之下，而且还批准他们炮制的各种伪法案，以便任其在我们中间驻扎大批武装部队；不论这些人对我们各州居民犯下何等严重的谋杀罪，他可用假审判来庇护他们，让他们逍遥法外；他可以切断我们同世界各地的贸易；未经我们同意便向我们强行征税；在许多案件中剥夺我们享有陪审制的权益；以莫须有的罪名把我们押送海外受审；他在一个邻省废除了英国法律的自由制度，在那里建立专制政府、扩大其疆域，使其立即成为一个样板和合适的工具，以便向这里各殖民地推行同样的专制统治；他取消我们的许多特许状，废除我们最珍贵的法律并从根本上改变我们各州政府的形式；他终止我们立法机构行使权力，宣称他们自己拥有在任何情况下为我们制定法律的权力。

他们放弃设在这里的政府，宣称我们已不属他们保护之列，并向我们发动战争。

他在我们的海域里大肆掠夺，蹂躏我们的沿海地区、烧毁我们的城镇、残害我们人民的生命。

他此时正在运送大批外国雇佣兵，来从事其制造死亡、荒凉和暴政的勾当，其残忍与卑劣从一开始就连最野蛮的时代也难以相比，他已完全不配当一个文明国家的元首。

他强迫我们在公海被他们俘虏的同胞拿起武器反对自己的国家，使他们成为残杀自己亲友的刽子手，或使他们死于自己亲友的手下。

他在我们中间煽动内乱，并竭力挑唆残酷无情的印第安蛮子来对付我们边疆的居民。而众所周知，印第安人作战的准则是不分男女老幼、是非曲直，格杀勿论。

在遭受这些压迫的每一阶段，我们都曾以最谦卑的言辞吁请予以纠正。而我们一次又一次的情愿，却只是被报以一次又一次的伤害。

一个君主，其品格被他的每一个只有暴君才做得出的行为所暴露时，就不配君临自由的人民。

谴责

我们并不是没有想到我们英国的弟兄。他们的立法机关想把无理的管辖权扩展到我们这里来，我们时常把这个企图通知他们。我们也曾把我们移民来这里和在这里定居的情况告诉他们。我们曾恳求他们天生的正义感和雅量，念在同种同宗的分上，弃绝这些掠夺行为，因为这些掠夺行为难免会使我们之间的关系和来往中断。可他们对这种正义和同宗的呼声也同样充耳不闻。因此，我们不得不宣布脱离他们，以对待世界上其他民族的态度对待他们：同我交战者，就是敌人；同我和好者，即为朋友。

总结

因此我们这些在大陆会议上集会的美利坚合众国的代表们，以各殖民地善良人民的名义、并经他们授权，向世界最高裁判者申诉，说明我们的严正意向，同时郑重宣布：

我们这些联合起来的殖民地现在是，而且按公理也应该是，独立自由的国家；我们对英国王室效忠的全部义务、我们与大不列颠王国之间一切政治联系全部断绝，而且必须断绝。作为一个独立自由的国家，我们完全有权宣战、缔合、结盟、通商和采取独立国家有权采取的一切行动。为了支持这篇宣言，我们坚决信赖上帝的庇佑，以我们的生命、我们的财产和我们神圣的名誉，彼此宣誓。

签名（略）

3

The Constitution of the United States of America

(With Approriate Interpretation for Every Section)

March 4, 1789

Preamble

We the people of the United States, in order to form a more perfect union, establish justice, insure domestic tranquility, provide for the common defense, promote the general welfare, and secure the blessings of liberty to ourselves and our posterity, do ordain and establish this Constitution for the United States of America.

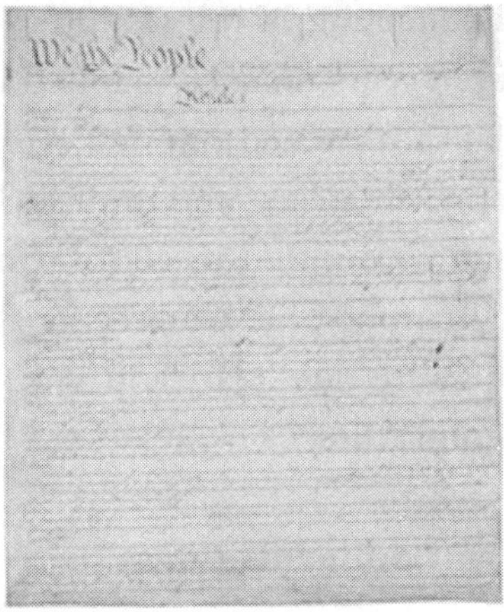

Article I

Section 1. All legislative powers herein granted shall be vested in a Congress of the United States, which shall consist of a Senate and House of Representatives.

(**Comment:** *Congress controls all power to write legislation, and has two chambers—the House of Representatives and the Senate.*)

Section 2. The House of Representatives shall be composed of members chosen every second year by the people of the several states, and the electors in each state shall have the qualifications requisite for electors of the most numerous branch of the state legislature.

(**Comment:** *The house is directly elected by the people, and its members serve two-year terms.*)

No person shall be a Representative who shall not have attained to the age of twenty five years, and been seven years a citizen of the United States, and who shall not, when elected, be an inhabitant of that state in which he shall be chosen.

(**Comment:** *Members of the House of Representatives must be at least 25 years old, a citizen of the United States for at least seven years, and live in the state that elect them to the House.*)

Representatives and direct taxes shall be apportioned among the several states which may be included within this union, according to their respective numbers, which shall be determined by adding to the whole number of free persons, including those bound to service for a term of years, and excluding Indians not taxed, three fifths of all other Persons. The actual Enumeration shall be made within three years after the first meeting of the Congress of the United States, and within every subsequent term of ten years, in such manner as they shall by law direct. The number of Representatives shall not exceed one for every thirty thousand, but each state shall have at least one Representative; and until such enumeration shall be made, the state of New Hampshire shall be entitled to choose three, Massachusetts eight, Rhode Island and Providence Plantations one, Connecticut five, New York six, New Jersey four, Pennsylvania eight, Delaware one, Maryland six, Virginia ten, North Carolina five, South Carolina five, and Georgia three.

(**Comment:** *House seats are assigned according to a census conducted every ten years, initially using a formula that counted African American slaves as three-fifths of a person and excluded Native Americans altogether. The 14th Amendment abolished the rule counting African Americans as three-fifths of a person, but it did not end the exclusion of Native Americans. Native Americans' citizenship rights were gradually extended in the late 19th an 20th centuries.*)

When vacancies happen in the Representation from any state, the executive authority thereof shall issue writs of election to fill such vacancies.

The House of Representatives shall choose their speaker and other officers; and shall have the sole power of impeachment.

(**Comment:** *The House manages itself and has the power to impeach senior government officials.*)

Section 3. The Senate of the United States shall be composed of two Senators from each state, chosen by the legislature thereof, for six years; and each Senator shall have one vote.

(**Comment:** *Each state has two senators, and they serve six-year terms.*)

Immediately after they shall be assembled in consequence of the first election, they shall be divided as equally as may be into three classes. The seats of the Senators of the first class shall be vacated at the expiration of the second year, of the second class at the expiration of the fourth year, and the third class at the expiration of the sixth year, so that one third may be chosen every second year; and if vacancies happen by resignation, or otherwise, during the recess of the legislature of any state, the executive thereof may make temporary appointments until the next meeting of the legislature, which shall then fill such vacancies.

(**Comment:** *One-third of the Senate faces election at a time.*)

No person shall be a Senator who shall not have attained to the age of thirty years, and been nine years a citizen of the United States and who shall not, when elected, be an inhabitant of that state for which he shall be chosen.

(**Comment:** *Senators must be at least 30 years old, a citizen of the United States for at least nine years, and live in the state that elects them to the Senate.*)

The Vice-President of the United States shall be President of the Senate, but shall have no vote, unless they be equally divided.

(**Comment:** *The Vice-President presides over the Senate but can cast a vote only in case of a tie.*)

The Senate shall choose their other officers, and also a President pro tempore, in the absence of the Vice-President, or when he shall exercise the office of President of the United States.

(**Comment:** *The Senate is usually presided over by a temporary leader, the president pro tempore, who fills in for the Vice-President of the United States.*)

The Senate shall have the sole power to try all impeachments. When sitting for that purpose, they shall be on oath or affirmation. When the President of the United States is tried, the Chief Justice shall preside: And no person shall be convicted without the concurrence of two thirds of the members present.

(**Comment:** *The Senate tries impeachment cases against senior federal officials after the House has voted to impeach. A conviction requires the support of two-thirds of the Senate members present.*)

Judgment in cases of impeachment shall not extend further than to removal from office, and disqualification to hold and enjoy any office of honor, trust or profit under the United States: but the party convicted shall nevertheless be liable and subject to indictment, trial, judgment and punishment, according to law.

(**Comment:** *Any convicted of impeachable offenses can be removed from office and can be barred from serving in other senior government posts. The convicted person can also be tried in the courts.*)

Section 4. The times, places and manner of holding elections for Senators and Representatives, shall be prescribed in each state by the legislature thereof; but the Congress may at any time by law make or alter such regulations, except as to the places of choosing Senators.

The Congress shall assemble at least once in every year, and such meeting shall be on the first Monday in December, unless they shall by law appoint a different day.

Section 5. Each House shall be the judge of the elections, returns and qualifications of its own members, and a majority of each shall constitute a quorum to do business; but a smaller number may adjourn from day to day, and may be authorized to compel the attendance of absent members, in such manner, and under such penalties as each House may provide.

(**Comment:** *The House and the Senate each monitor the elections of their own members. The chambers cannot take official action unless a majority of members are present.*)

Each House may determine the rules of its proceedings, punish its members for disorderly behavior, and, with the concurrence of two thirds, expel a member.

(**Comment:** *The House and the Senate discipline their own members.*)

Each House shall keep a journal of its proceedings, and from time to time publish the same, excepting such parts as may in their judgment require secrecy; and the yeas and nays of the members of either House on any question shall, at the desire of one fifth of those present, be entered on the journal.

(**Comment:** *Congress must maintain a public record of its work except in matters that it decides should be kept secret.*)

Neither House, during the session of Congress, shall, without the consent of the other, adjourn for more than three days, nor to any other place than that in which the two Houses shall be sitting.

Section 6. The Senators and Representatives shall receive a compensation for their services, to be ascertained by law, and paid out of the treasury of the United States. They shall in all cases, except treason, felony and breach of the peace, be privileged from arrest during their attendance at the session of their respective Houses, and in going to and returning from the same; and for any speech or debate in either House, they shall not be questioned in any other place.

(**Comment:** *Congress makes a law that sets the salaries of senators and representatives.*)

No Senator or Representative shall, during the time for which he was elected, be appointed to any civil office under the authority of the United States, which shall have been created, or the emoluments whereof shall have been increased during such time; and no person holding any office under the United States, shall be a member of either House during his continuance in office.

(**Comment:** *Unlike most parliamentary systems, members of the House and Senate cannot hold other government offices, including positions in the president's cabinet.*)

Section 7. All bills for raising revenue shall originate in the House of Representatives; but the Senate may propose or concur with amendments as on other Bills.

(**Comment:** *Bills to impose taxes originate in the House. This provision is not always followed in practice.*)

Every bill which shall have passed the House of Representatives and the Senate, shall, before it become a law, be presented to the President of the United States; if he approve he shall sign it, but if not he shall return it, with his objections to that House in which it shall have originated, who shall enter the objections at large on their journal, and proceed to reconsider it. If after such reconsideration two thirds of that House shall agree to pass the bill, it shall be sent, together with the objections, to the other House, by which it shall likewise be reconsidered, and if approved by two thirds of that House, it shall become a law. But in all such cases the votes of both Houses shall be determined by yeas and nays, and the names of the persons voting for and against the bill shall be entered on the journal of each House respectively. If any bill shall not be returned by the President within ten days (Sundays excepted) after it shall have been presented to him, the same shall be a law, in like manner as if he had signed it, unless the Congress by their adjournment prevent its return, in which case it shall not be a law.

Every order, resolution, or vote to which the concurrence of the Senate and House of Representatives may be necessary (except on a question of adjournment) shall be presented to the President of the United States; and before the same shall take effect, shall be approved by him, or being disapproved by him, shall be repassed by two thirds of the Senate and House of Representatives, according to the rules and limitations prescribed in the case of a bill.

(**Comment:** *After a bill passes both the House and the Senate, the president has ten days to decide whether to sign it into law or veto it. If the president does nothing,* *the bill becomes law automatically, unless Congress is not in session. If congress is out of session and ten days lapse after Congress has submitted a bill to the president, then it is automatically vetoed. Congress can pass a law over a president's veto through a two-thirds vote of each chamber.*)

Section 8. The Congress shall have power to lay and collect taxes, duties, imposts and excises, to pay the debts and provide for the common defense and general welfare of the United States; but all duties, imposts and excises shall be uniform throughout the United States;

To borrow money on the credit of the United States;

To regulate commerce with foreign nations, and among the several states, and with the Indian tribes;

To establish a uniform rule of naturalization, and uniform laws on the subject of bankruptcies throughout the United States;

To coin money, regulate the value thereof, and of foreign coin, and fix the standard of weights and measures;

To provide for the punishment of counterfeiting the securities and current coin of the United States;

To establish post offices and post roads;

To promote the progress of science and useful arts, by securing for limited times to authors and inventors the exclusive right to their respective writings and discoveries;

To constitute tribunals inferior to the Supreme Court;

To define and punish piracies and felonies committed on the high seas, and offenses against the law of nations;

To declare war, grant letters of marque and reprisal, and make rules concerning captures on land and water;

To raise and support armies, but no appropriation of money to that use shall be for a longer term than two years;

To provide and maintain a navy;

To make rules for the government and regulation of the land and naval forces;

To provide for calling forth the militia to execute the laws of the union, suppress insurrections and repel invasions;

To provide for organizing, arming, and disciplining, the militia, and for governing such part of them as may be employed in the service of the United States, reserving to the states respectively, the appointment of the officers, and the authority of training the militia according to the discipline prescribed by Congress;

To exercise exclusive legislation in all cases whatsoever, over such District (not exceeding ten miles square) as may, by cession of particular states, and the acceptance of Congress, become the seat of the government of the United States, and to exercise like authority over all places purchased by the consent of the legislature of the state in which the same shall be, for the erection of forts, magazines, arsenals, dockyards, and other needful buildings;

To make all laws which shall be necessary and proper for carrying into execution the foregoing powers, and all other powers vested by this Constitution in the government of the United States, or in any department or officer thereof.

(**Comment:** *Congress has broad authority, including the powers to impose taxes, maintain a military, declare war, manage a postal system, create a judicial system, and borrow money. In addition, Congress has sweeping power to enact laws to provide for the general welfare of the country, and to pass any law it regards as necessary to carry out its other duties.*)

Section 9. The migration or importation of such persons as any of the states now existing shall think proper to admit, shall not be prohibited by the Congress prior to the year one thousand eight hundred and eight, but a tax or duty may be imposed on such importation, not exceeding ten dollars for each person.

The privilege of the writ of habeas corpus shall not be suspended, unless when in cases of rebellion or invasion the public safety may require it.

(**Comment:** *Citizens cannot be arrested or jailed arbitrarily except in extreme circumstances.*)

No bill of attainder or ex post facto Law shall be passed.

(**Comment:** *Congress cannot pass a law that declares a person guilty of a crime or that makes an action in the past illegal.*)

No capitation, or other direct, tax shall be laid, unless in proportion to the census or enumeration herein before directed to be taken.

(Comment: ***Congress cannot impose direct taxes except in proportion to population. The 16th Amendment superseded this clause, but only as it pertains to income tax.*****)**

No tax or duty shall be laid on articles exported from any state.

No preference shall be given by any regulation of commerce or revenue to the ports of one state over those of another: nor shall vessels bound to, or from, one state, be obliged to enter, clear or pay duties in another.

(Comment: ***Congress cannot create laws that arbitrarily favor the ports of some states over others.*****)**

No money shall be drawn from the treasury, but in consequence of appropriations made by law; and a regular statement and account of receipts and expenditures of all public money shall be published from time to time.

(Comment: ***The government can only spend money if Congress has approved the expenditure by law, and the government must maintain public records of all revenues and spending.*****)**

No title of nobility shall be granted by the United States: and no person holding any office of profit or trust under them, shall, without the consent of the Congress, accept of any present, emolument, office, or title, of any kind whatever, from any king, prince, or foreign state.

(Comment: ***The United States cannot name a king or other royalty, and US officials cannot accept payments or royal titles from other countries without congressional approval.*****)**

Section 10. No state shall enter into any treaty, alliance, or confederation; grant letters of marque and reprisal; coin money; emit bills of credit; make anything but gold and silver coin a tender in payment of debts; pass any bill of attainder, ex post facto law, or law impairing the obligation of contracts, or grant any title of nobility.

No state shall, without the consent of the Congress, lay any imposts or duties on imports or exports, except what may be absolutely necessary for executing its inspection laws: and the net produce of all duties and imposts, laid by any state on imports or exports, shall be for the use of the treasury of the United States; and all such laws shall be subject to the revision and control of the Congress.

No state shall, without the consent of Congress, lay any duty of tonnage, keep troops, or ships of war in time of peace, enter into any agreement or compact with another state, or with a foreign power, or engage in war, unless actually invaded, or in such imminent danger as will not admit of delay.

(**Comment:** *Congress has powers over the states in many areas. The states are barred from encroaching on most congressional duties, including the issuing of money, entering into alliances with other countries, and imposing duties on imports from other countries.*)

Article Ⅱ

Section 1. The executive power shall be vested in a President of the United States of America. He shall hold his office during the term of four years, and, together with the Vice-President, chosen for the same term, be elected, as follows:

Each state shall appoint, in such manner as the Legislature thereof may direct, a number of electors, equal to the whole number of Senators and Representatives to which the State may be entitled in the Congress: but no Senator or Representative, or person holding an office of trust or profit under the United States, shall be appointed an elector.

(**Comment:** *The President ensures that the nation's laws are carried out and enforced. The President serves a four-year term, and is formally elected by electors of the Electoral College. Originally the state legislatures chose the electors, but since the 1820s they have been chosen through direct elections.*)

The electors shall meet in their respective states, and vote by ballot for two persons, of whom one at least shall not be an inhabitant of the same state with themselves. And they shall make a list of all the persons voted for, and of the number of votes for each; which list they shall sign and certify, and transmit sealed to the seat of the government of the United States, directed to the President of the Senate. The President of the Senate shall, in the presence of the Senate and House of Representatives, open all the certificates, and the votes shall then be counted. The person having the greatest number of votes shall be the President, if such number be a majority of the whole number of electors appointed; and if there be more than one who have such majority, and have an equal number of votes, then the House of Representatives shall immediately choose by ballot one of them for President; and if no person have a majority, then from the five highest on the list the said House shall in like manner choose the President. But in choosing the President, the votes shall be taken by States, the representation from each state having one vote; A quorum for this purpose shall consist of a member or members from two thirds of the states, and a majority of all the states shall be necessary to a choice. In every case, after the choice of the President, the person having the greatest number of votes of the electors shall be the Vice-President. But if there should remain two or more who have equal votes, the Senate shall choose from them by ballot the Vice-President.

(**Comment:** *Congress formally counts the presidential election ballots from electoral college. If no presidential candidate receives a majority of vote in the electoral college, the House chooses the President. Originally the second place winner in the electoral college became the Vice-President, with ties decided in the Senate. This section was amended by the 12th Amendment, which specified that the Vice-President be chosen on a separate ballot.*)

The Congress may determine the time of choosing the electors, and the day on which they shall give their votes; which day shall be the same throughout the United States.

No person except a natural born citizen, or a citizen of the United States, at the time of the adoption of this Constitution, shall be eligible to the office of President; neither shall any person be eligible to that office who shall not have attained to the age of thirty five years, and been fourteen Years a resident within the United States.

(**Comment:** *The President must be at least 35 years old, a United States citizen born in the United States, and a resident of the country for at least 14 years.*)

In case of the removal of the President from office, or of his death, resignation, or inability to discharge the powers and duties of the said office, the same shall devolve on the Vice-President, and the Congress may by law provide for the case of removal, death, resignation or inability, both of the President and Vice-President, declaring what officer shall then act as President, and such officer shall act accordingly, until the disability be removed, or a President shall be elected.

(**Comment:** *This section was amended by the 25th Amendment. If the President dies, resigns, or becomes unable to carry out the responsibilities of the job, the Vice-President steps in. If there is no President or Vice-President, Congress has the power to appoint someone to fill the position. Currently the line of succession after the Vice-President is (1) the Speaker of the House, (2) the President pro tempore of the Senate, and (3) a sequence of cabinet officials.*)

The President shall, at stated times, receive for his services, a compensation, which shall neither be increased nor diminished during the period for which he shall have been elected, and he shall not receive within that period any other emolument from the United States, or any of them.

(**Comment:** *Congress sets the President's pay rate, and the rate cannot be changed once the President takes office. The President cannot accept other payments from the federal or state governments.*)

Before he enter on the execution of his office, he shall take the following oath or affirmation:—"I do solemnly swear (or affirm) that I will faithfully execute the office of President of the United States, and will to the best of my ability, preserve, protect and defend the Constitution of the United States."

(**Comment:** *On inauguration day the President takes an oath of office, traditionally administered by the chief justice of the United States.*)

Section 2. The President shall be commander in chief of the Army and Navy of the United States, and of the militia of the several states, when called into the actual service of the United States; he may require the opinion, in writing, of the principal officer in each of the executive departments, upon any subject relating to the duties of their respective offices, and he shall have power to grant reprieves and pardons for offenses against the United States, except in cases of impeachment.

(**Comment:** *The President has wide authority in the executive branch. These* *powers include serving as Commander-in-Chief of the military, supervisory responsibility for executive branch departments, and the power to grant pardons in criminal cases.*)

He shall have power, by and with the advice and consent of the Senate, to make treaties, provided two thirds of the Senators present concur; and he shall nominate, and by and with the advice and consent of the Senate, shall appoint ambassadors, other public ministers and consuls, judges of the Supreme Court, and all other officers of the United States, whose appointments are not herein otherwise provided for, and which shall be established by law: but the Congress may by law vest the appointment of such inferior officers, as they think proper, in the President alone, in the courts of law, or in the heads of departments.

(**Comment:** *The Senate acts as a check on some presidential powers. The President makes treaties with other countries, but they take effect only if two-thirds of the Senate approves. The President's nominations of ambassadors, federal judges, cabinet members, and other top government officials require the approval of a majority of the Senate.*)

The President shall have power to fill up all vacancies that may happen during the recess of the Senate, by granting commissions which shall expire at the end of their next session.

(**Comment:** *The President can make appointments without Senate approval if Congress is not in session. These so-called recess appointments expire at the end of the next congressional term.*)

Section 3. He shall from time to time give to the Congress information of the state of the union, and recommend to their consideration such measures as he shall judge necessary and expedient; he may, on extraordinary occasions, convene both Houses, or either of them, and in case of disagreement between them, with respect to the time of adjournment, he may adjourn them to such time as he shall think proper; he shall receive ambassadors and other public ministers; he shall take care that the laws be faithfully executed, and shall commission all the officers of the United States.

(**Comment:** *The President must periodically issue a State of the Union Message, usually a speech delivered in person, in which the President explains the condition of the country and offers legislative suggestions. The President can also call a joint session of Congress, or call a session of either of the houses separately. The President may decide when Congress should adjourn for a recess, although presidents rarely do so.*)

Section 4. The President, Vice-President and all civil officers of the United States, shall be removed from office on impeachment for, and conviction of, treason, bribery, or other high crimes and misdemeanors.

(**Comment:** *The president, Vice-President, and other top officials can be removed from office if they commit serious offenses.*)

Article Ⅲ

Section 1. The judicial power of the United States, shall be vested in one Supreme Court, and in such inferior courts as the Congress may from time to time ordain and establish. The judges, both of the supreme and inferior courts, shall hold their offices during good behaviour, and shall, at stated times, receive for their services, a compensation, which shall not be diminished during their continuance in office.

(**Comment:** *The Supreme Court has some administrative control over the legal system, but Congress decides the number of courts that are necessary and many other important issues. Supreme Court justices and other federal judges hold their appointments for life unless they violate significant laws. Their salary cannot be reduced while they are serving on the Court.*)

Section 2. The judicial power shall extend to all cases, in law and equity, arising under this Constitution, the laws of the United States, and treaties made, or which shall be made, under their authority; —to all cases affecting ambassadors, other public ministers and consuls; —to all cases of admiralty and maritime jurisdiction; —to controversies to which the United States shall be a party; —to controversies between two or more states; —between a state and citizens of another state; —between citizens of different states; —between citizens of the same state claiming lands under grants of different states, and between a state, or the citizens thereof, and foreign states, citizens or subjects.

(**Comment:** *The Supreme Court has jurisdiction in seven types of cases: (1) cases raising issues involving the Constitution, federal law, or treaties; (2) cases affecting ambassadors; (3) maritime cases; (4) controversies in which the United States is a party; (5) controversies in which two or more states are parties; (6) controversies involving residents of different states; and (7) controversies in which residents of the same state make a claim on land in another state.*)

In all cases affecting ambassadors, other public ministers and consuls, and those in which a state shall be party, the Supreme Court shall have original jurisdiction. In all the other cases before mentioned, the Supreme Court shall have appellate jurisdiction, both as to law and fact, with such exceptions, and under such regulations as the Congress shall make.

(**Comment:** *Only in cases involving ambassadors, or if a state is a party, does the Supreme Court have original jurisdiction to conduct a trial to determine the facts of a case and issue a judgement. The Supreme Court hears only appeals in all other types of cases. Congress can limit the Court's appellate jurisdiction.*)

The trial of all crimes, except in cases of impeachment, shall be by jury; and such trial shall be held in the state where the said crimes shall have been committed; but when not committed within any state, the trial shall be at such place or places as the Congress may by law have directed.

(**Comment:** *Americans have a right to a jury trial in significant cases, and the trial must be held in the state where the crime is alleged to have occurred. Congress can enact laws to handle the rare case that involve offenses occurring outside of the states.*)

Section 3. Treason against the United States, shall consist only in levying war against them, or in adhering to their enemies, giving them aid and comfort. No person shall be convicted of treason unless on the testimony of two witnesses to the same overt act, or on confession in open court.

(**Comment:** *Congress can only define a few types of offenses as treason. A person accused of treason can only be convicted if there are two witnesses to the crime, or if the person confesses in court.*)

The Congress shall have power to declare the punishment of treason, but no attainder of treason shall work corruption of blood, or forfeiture except during the life of the person attainted.

(**Comment:** *Congress can impose punishments and can confiscate property from those convicted of treason. The heirs of the convicted person retain a right to inherit any estate, however.*)

Article Ⅳ

Section 1. Full faith and credit shall be given in each state to the public acts, records, and judicial proceedings of every other state. And the Congress may by general laws prescribe the manner in which such acts, records, and proceedings shall be proved, and the effect thereof.

(**Comment:** *States must accept most laws and legal decisions made in other states.*)

Section 2. The citizens of each state shall be entitled to all privileges and immunities of citizens in the several states.

(**Comment:** *The states must offer most fundamental legal rights to both residents and nonresidents of the state.*)

A person charged in any state with treason, felony, or other crime, who shall flee from justice, and be found in another state, shall on demand of the executive authority of the state from which he fled, be delivered up, to be removed to the state having jurisdiction of the crime.

(**Comment:** *People accused of serious crimes cannot take refuge in other states.*)

No person held to service or labor in one state, under the laws thereof, escaping into another, shall, in consequence of any law or regulation therein, be discharged from such service or labor, but shall be delivered up on claim of the party to whom such service or labor may be due.

(**Comment:** *The Fugitive Slave Clause barred slaves from passing laws that freed* *escaped slaves and required that such slaves be returned to their owners. The 13th Amendment, which abolished slavery, made this clause obsolete.*)

Section 3. New states may be admitted by the Congress into this union; but no new states shall be formed or erected within the jurisdiction of any other state; nor any state be formed by the junction of two or more states, or parts of states, without the consent of the legislatures of the states concerned as well as of the Congress.

(**Comment:** *Congress controls the admission of new states. Congress and the legislatures of the states involved must approve the merger of two states or the creation of a new state within the boundaries of an existing state.*)

The Congress shall have power to dispose of and make all needful rules and regulations respecting the territory or other property belonging to the United States; and nothing in this Constitution shall be so construed as to prejudice any claims of the United States, or of any particular state.

(**Comment:** *The government has the right to use federal buildings, lands, and property in almost any way it sees fit.*)

Section 4. The United States shall guarantee to every state in this union a republican form of government, and shall protect each of them against invasion; and on application of the legislature, or of the executive (when the legislature cannot be convened) against domestic violence.

(**Comment:** *The federal government has an obligation to protect the political and physical integrity of the states. The federal government must take responsibility for stopping invasions and, if the states ask, to squelch domestic unrest.*)

Article V

The Congress, whenever two thirds of both houses shall deem it necessary, shall propose amendments to this Constitution, or, on the application of the legislatures of two thirds of the several states, shall call a convention for proposing amendments, which, in either case, shall be valid to all intents and purposes, as part of this

Constitution, when ratified by the legislatures of three fourths of the several states, or by conventions in three fourths thereof, as the one or the other mode of ratification may be proposed by the Congress; provided that no amendment which may be made prior to the year one thousand eight hundred and eight shall in any manner affect the first and fourth clauses in the ninth section of the first article; and that no state, without its consent, shall be deprived of its equal suffrage in the Senate.

(**Comment:** *Both the states and Congress can propose amendments to the Constitution. It takes two-thirds of the states to call a constitutional convention to propose amendments, which must then be approved by state legislatures in three-quarters of the states. Congress can propose amendments to the Constitution if two-thirds of the members in both chambers vote to support the amendment. After Congress proposes an amendment, it then requires approval by three-quarters of the state legislatures, or three-quarters of special state conventions, whichever congress specifies.*)

Article Ⅵ

All debts contracted and engagements entered into, before the adoption of this Constitution, shall be as valid against the United States under this Constitution, as under the Confederation.

This Constitution, and the laws of the United States which shall be made in pursuance thereof; and all treaties made, or which shall be made, under the authority of the United States, shall be the supreme law of the land; and the judges in every state shall be bound thereby, anything in the Constitution or laws of any State to the contrary notwithstanding.

(**Comment:** *All laws in the United States—federal, state, and, local—must be consistent with the Constitution. All judges must hold the US Constitution above all other law.*)

The Senators and Representatives before mentioned, and the members of the several state legislatures, and all executive and judicial officers, both of the United States and of the several states, shall be bound by oath or affirmation, to support this Constitution; but no religious test shall ever be required as a qualification to any office or public trust under the United States.

(**Comment:** *Members of Congress, the state legislatures, state and federal judges, and state and federal executive officials must agree to support the Constitution. This clause was intended to bind all government officials, including those at the state level, to support the Constitution and federal laws.*)

Article Ⅶ

The ratification of the conventions of nine states, shall be sufficient for the establishment of this Constitution between the states so ratifying the same.

(**Comment:** *Only 9 of the 13 states were needed to approve the Constitution. New Hampshire became the ninth on June 21, 1788.*)

Done in convention by the unanimous consent of the states present the seventeenth day of September in the year of our Lord one thousand seven hundred and eighty seven and of the independence of the United States of America the twelfth. In witness whereof, we have hereunto subscribed our Names,

G. Washington—Presidt. and deputy from Virginia

New Hampshire: John Langdon, Nicholas Gilman

Massachusetts: Nathaniel Gorham, Rufus King

Connecticut: Wm: Saml. Johnson, Roger Sherman

New York: Alexander Hamilton

New Jersey: Wil: Livingston, David Brearly, Wm. Paterson, Jona: Dayton

Pennsylvania: B. Franklin, Thomas Mifflin, Robt. Morris, Geo. Clymer, Thos. FitzSimons, Jared Ingersoll, James Wilson, Gouv Morris

Delaware: Geo: Read, Gunning Bedford jun, John Dickinson, Richard Bassett, Jaco: Broom

Maryland: James McHenry, Dan of St Thos. Jenifer, Danl Carroll

Virginia: John Blair, James Madison Jr.

North Carolina: Wm. Blount, Richd. Dobbs Spaight, Hu Williamson

South Carolina: J. Rutledge, Charles Cotesworth Pinckney, Charles Pinckney, Pierce Butler

Georgia: William Few, Abr Baldwin

Translation

美国宪法

序言

我们美利坚合众国的人民，为了组织一个更完善的联邦，树立正义，保障国内的安宁，建立共同的国防，增进全民福利和确保我们自己及我们后代能安享自由带来的幸福，乃为美利坚合众国制定和确立这一部宪法。

第一条

第一款　本宪法所规定的立法权，全部属于合众国的国会，国会由一个参议院和一个众议院组成。

第二款　众议院应由各州人民每两年选举一次之议员组成，各州选举人应具有该州州议会中人数最多之一院的选举人所需之资格。凡年龄未满二十五岁，或取得合众国公民资格未满七年，或于某州当选而并非该州居民者，均不得任众议员。众议员人数及直接税税额，应按联邦所辖各州的人口数目比例分配，此项人口数目的计算法，应在全体自由人民——包括订有契约的短期仆役，但不包括未被课税的印第安人——数目之外，再加上所有其他人口之五分之三。实际人口调查，应于合众国国会第一次会议后三年内举行，并于其后每十年举行一次，其调查方法另以法律规定之。众议员的数目，不得超过每三万人口有众议员一人，但每州至少应有众议员一人；在举行人口调查以前，各州得按照下列数目选举众议员：新罕布什尔三人、马萨诸塞八人、罗德岛及普罗维登斯垦殖区一人、康涅狄格五人、纽约州六人、新泽西四人、宾夕法尼亚八人、特拉华一人、马里兰六人、弗吉尼亚十人、北卡罗来纳五人、南卡罗来纳五人、佐治亚三人。任何一州的众议员有缺额时，该州的行政长官应颁布选举令、选出众议员以补充缺额。众议院应选举该院议长及其他官员；只有众议院具有提出弹劾案的权力。

第三款　合众国的参议院由每州的州议会选举两名参议员组成。参议员的任期为六年，每名参议员有一票表决权。参议员于第一次选举后举行会议之时，应当立即尽量均等地分成三组。第一组参议员的任期，到第二年年终时届满，第二组到第四年年终时届满，第三组到第六年年终时届满，以使每两年有三分之一的参议员改选；如果在某州州议会休会期间，有参议员因辞职或其他原因出缺，该州的行政长官得任命临时参议员，等到州议会下次集会时，再予选举补缺。凡年龄未满三十岁，或取得合众国公民资格未满九年，或于某州当选而并非该州居民者，均不得任参议员。合众国副总统应为参议院议长，除非在投票票数相等时，议长无投票权。参议院应选举该院的其他官员，在副总统缺席或执行合众国总统职务时，还应选举临时议长。所有弹劾案，只有参议院有权审理。在开庭审理弹劾案时，参议员们均应宣誓或誓愿。如受审者为合众国总统，则应由最高法院首席大法官担任主席；在未得出席的参议员的三分之二同意时，任何人不得被判有罪。弹劾案的判决，不得超过免职及取消其担任合众国政府任何有荣誉、有责任或有俸给的职位之资格；但被判处者仍须服从另据法律所作之控诉、审讯、判决及惩罚。

第四款　各州州议会应规定本州参议员及众议员之选举时间、地点及程序；但国会得随时以法律制定或变更此种规定，唯有选举议员的地点不在此例。国会应至少每年集会一次，开会日期应为十二月的第一个星期一，除非他们通过法律来指定另一个日期。

第五款　参众两院应各自审查本院的选举、选举结果报告和本院议员的资格，每院议员过半数即构成可以议事的法定人数；不足法定人数时，可以一天推一天地延期开会，并有权依照该议院规定的程序和罚则，强迫缺席的议员出席。参众两院各自规定本院的议事规则，处罚本院扰乱秩序的议员，并且得以三分之二的同意，开除本院的议员。参众两院应各自保存一份议事记录，并经常公布，唯各该院认为应保守秘密之部分除外；两院议员对于每一问题之赞成或反对，如有五分之一出席议员请求，则应记载于议事记录内。在国会开会期间，任一议院未得别院同意，不得休会超过三日，亦不得迁往非两院开会的其他地点。

第六款　参议员与众议员得因其服务而获报酬，报酬的多寡由法律定之，并由合众国国库支付。两院议员除犯叛国罪、重罪以及扰乱治安罪外，在出席各该院会议及往返各该院途中，有不受逮捕之特权；两院议员在议院内所发表之演说及辩论，在其他场合不受质询。参议员或众议员不得在其当选任期内担任合众国政府任何新添设的职位，或在其任期内支取因新职位而增添的俸给；在合众国政府供职的人，不得在其任职期间担任国会议员。

第七款　有关征税的所有法案应在众议院中提出；但参议院得以处理其他法案的方式，以修正案提出建议或表示同意。经众议院和参议院通过的法案，在正式成为法律之前，须呈送合众国总统。总统如批准，便须签署；如不批准，即应连同他的异议把它退还给原来提出该案的议院，该议院应将异议详细记入议事记录，然后进行复议。倘若在复议之后，该议院议员的三分之二仍然同意通过该法案，该院即应将该法案连同异议书送交另一院，由其同样予以复议，若此另一院亦以三分之二的多数通过，该法案即成为法律。但遇有这样的情形时，两院的表决均应以赞同或反对来定，而赞同和反对该法案的议员的姓名，均应由两院分别记载于各该院的议事记录之内。如总统接到法案后十日之内（星期日除外），不将之退还，该法案即等于曾由总统签署一样，成为法律。除非因国会休会而使该法案不能退还，在此种情况下，该法案才不得成为法律。任何命令、决议或表决（有关休会问题者除外），凡须由参议院及众议院予以同意者，均应呈送合众国总统；经其批准之后，方始生效，如总统不予批准，则参众两院可依照对于通过法案所规定的各种规则和限制，各以三分之二的多数，再行通过。

第八款　国会有权规定并征收税金、捐税、关税和其他赋税，用以偿付国债并为合众国的共同防御和全民福利提供经费；但是各种捐税、关税和其他赋税，在合众国内应划一征收；以合众国的信用举债；管理与外国的、州与州间的，以及对印第安部落的贸易；制定在合众国内一致适用的归化条例，和有关破产的一致适用的法律；铸造货币，调议其价值，并厘定外币价值，以及制定度量衡的标准；制定对伪造合众国证券和货币的惩罚条例；设立邮政局及建造驿路；为促进科学和实用技艺的进步，对作家和发明家的著作和发明，在一定期限内给予专利权的保障；设置最高法院以下的各级法院；界定并惩罚海盗罪、在公海所犯的重罪和违背国际公法的罪行；宣战，对民用船只颁发捕押敌船及采取报复行动的特许证，制定在陆地和海面虏获战利品的规则；募集和维持陆军，但每次拨付该项费用的款项，其有效期不得超过两年；配备和保持海军；制定有关管理和控制陆海军队的各种条例；制定召集民兵的条例，以便执行联邦法律，镇压叛乱和击退侵略；规定民兵的组织、装备和训练，以及民兵为合众国服务时的管理办法，但各州保留其军官任命权，和依照国会规定的条例训练其民团的权力；对于由某州让与而由国会承受，用以充当合众国政府所在地的地区（不逾十平方英里），握有对其一切事务的全部立法权；对于经州议会同意，向州政府购得，用以建筑要塞、弹药库、兵工厂、船坞和其他必要建筑物的地方，也握有同样的权力；——并且为了行使上述各项权力，以及行使本宪法赋予合众国政府或其各部门或其官员的种种权力，制定一切必要的和适当的法律。

第九款　对于现有任何一州所认为的应准其移民或入境的人，在1808年以前，国会不得加以禁止，但可以对入境者课税，唯以每人不超过十美元为限。不得中止人身保护令所保障的特权，唯在叛乱或受到侵犯的情况下，出于公共安全的必要时不在此限。不得通过任何褫夺公权的法案或者追溯既往的法律。除非按本宪法所规定的人口调查或统计之比例，不得征收任何人口税或其他直接税。对各州输出之货物，不得课税。任何有关商务或纳税的条例，均不得赋予某一州的港口以优惠待遇；亦不得强迫任何开往或来自某一州的船只，驶入或驶出另一州、或向另一州纳税。除了依照法律的规定拨款之外，不得自国库中提出任何款项；一切公款收支的报告和账目，应经常公布。合众国不得颁发任何贵族爵位：凡是在合众国政府担任有俸给或有责任之职务者，未经国会许可，不得接受任何国王、王子或外国的任何礼物、薪酬、职务或爵位。

第十款　各州不得缔结任何条约、结盟或组织邦联；不得对民用船只颁发捕押敌船及采取报复行动之特许证；不得铸造货币；不得发行纸币；不得指定金银币以外的物品作为偿还债务的法定货币；不得通过任何褫夺公权的法案、追溯既往的法律和损害契约义务的法律；也不得颁发任何贵族爵位。未经国会同意，各州不得对进口货物或出口货物征收任何税款；但为了执行该州的检查法律而有绝对的必要时，不在此限；任何州对于进出口货物所征的税，其净收益应归合众国国库使用；所有这一类的检查法律，国会对之有修正和监督之权。未经国会同意，各州不得征收船舶吨位税，不得在和平时期保持军队和军舰，不得和另外一州或国缔结任何协定或契约，除非实际遭受入侵，或者遇到刻不容缓的危急情形时，不得从事战争。

第二条

第一款　行政权力赋予美利坚合众国总统。总统任期四年，总统和具有同样任期的副总统，应照下列手续选举：每个州应依照该州州议会所规定之手续，指定选举人若干名，其人数应与该州在国会之参议员及众议员之总数相等；但参议员、众议员及任何在合众国政府担任有责任及有俸给之职务的人，均不得被指定为选举人。各选举人应于其本身所属的州内集会，每人投票选举二人，其中至少应有一人不属本州居民。选举人应开列全体被选人名单，注明每人所得票数；他们还应签名作证明，并将封印后的名单送至合众国政府所在地交与参议院议长。参议院议长应于参众两院全体议员之前，开拆所有来件，然后计算票数。得票最多者，如其所得票数超过全体选举人的半数，即当选为总统；如同时不止一人得票过半数，但又得同等票数，则众议院应立即投票表决，选举其中一人为总统；如无人得票过半数，则众议院应自得票最多之前五名中用同样方法选举总统。但依此法选举总统时，应以州为单位，每州之代表共有一票；如全国三分之二的州各有一名或多名众议员出席，即构成选举总统的法定人数；当选总统者需获全部州的过半数票。在每次这样的选举中，于总统选出后，其获得选举人所投票数最多者，即为副总统。但如有二人或二人以上得票相等时，则应由参议院投票表决，选举其中一人为副总统。国会决定各州选出选举人的时期以及他们投票的日子；投票日期全国一律。只有出生时为合众国公民，或在本宪法实施时已为合众国公民者，可被选为总统； 凡年龄未满三十五岁，或居住合众国境内未满十四年者，不得被选为总统。如遇总统被免职，或因死亡、辞职或丧失能力而不能执行其权力及职务时，总统职权应由副总统执行之。国会得以法律规定，在总统及副总统均被免职，或死亡、辞职或丧失能力时，由何人代理总统职务，该人应即遵此行事，至总统能力恢复，或新总统被选出时为止。总统得因其服务而在规定的时间内接受俸给，在其任期之内，俸金数额不得增加或减低，他亦不得在此任期内，自合众国政府和任何州政府接受其他报酬。在他就职之前，他应宣誓或誓愿如下：“我郑重宣誓（或誓言），我必忠诚地执行合众国总统的职务，并尽我最大的能力，维持、保护和捍卫合众国宪法。”

第二款　总统为合众国陆海军的总司令，并在各州民团奉召为合众国执行任务的担任统帅；他可以要求每个行政部门的主管官员提出有关他们职务的任何事件的书面意见，除了弹劾案之外，他有权对于违犯合众国法律者颁赐缓刑和特赦。总统有权缔订条约，但须争取参议院的意见和同意，并须出席的参议员中三分之二的人赞成；他有权提名，并于取得参议院的意见和同意后，任命大使、公使及领事、最高法院的法官，以及一切其他在本宪法中未经明定、但以后将依法律的规定而设置之合众国官员；国会可以制定法律，酌情把这些较低级官员的任命权，授予总统本人、授予法院、或授予各行政部门的首长。在参议院休会期间，如遇有职位出缺，总统有权任命官员补充缺额，任期于参议院下届会议结束时终结。

第三款　总统应经常向国会报告联邦的情况，并向国会提出他认为必要和适当的措施，供其考虑；在特殊情况下，他得召集两院或其中一院开会，并得于两院对于休会时间意见不一致时，命令两院休会到他认为适当的时期为止；他应接见大使和公使；他应注意使法律切实执行，并任命所有合众国的军官。

第四款　合众国总统、副总统及其他所有文官，因叛国、贿赂或其他重罪和轻罪，被弹劾而判罪者，均应免职。

第三条

第一款　合众国的司法权属于一个最高法院以及由国会随时下令设立的低级法院。最高法院和低级法院的法官，如果尽忠职守，应继续任职，并按期接受俸给作为其服务之报酬；在其继续任职期间，该项俸给不得削减。

第二款　司法权适用的范围，应包括在本宪法、合众国法律、和合众国已订的及将订的条约之下发生的一切涉及普通法及衡平法的案件；一切有关大使、公使及领事的案件；一切有关海上裁判权及海事裁判权的案件；合众国为当事一方的诉讼；州与州之间的诉讼，州与另一州的公民之间的诉讼，一州公民与另一州公民之间的诉讼，同州公民之间为不同之州所让与之土地而争执的诉讼，以及一州或其公民与外国政府、公民或其属民之间的诉讼。在一切有关大使、公使、领事以及州为当事一方的案件中，最高法院有最初审理权。在上述所有其他案件中，最高法院有关于法律和事实的受理上诉权，但由国会规定为例外及另有处理条例者，不在此限。对一切罪行的审判，除了弹劾案以外，均应由陪审团裁定，并且该审判应在罪案发生的州内举行；但如罪案发生地点并不在任何一州之内，该项审判应在国会按法律指定之地点或几个地点举行。

第三款　只有对合众国发动战争，或投向它的敌人，予敌人以协助及方便者，方构成叛国罪。无论何人，如非经由两个证人证明他的公然叛国行为，或经由本人在公开法庭认罪者，均不得被判叛国罪。国会有权宣布对于叛国罪的惩处，但因叛国罪而被褫夺公权者，其后人之继承权不受影响，叛国者之财产亦只能在其本人生存期间被没收。

第四条

第一款　各州对其他各州的公共法案、记录、和司法程序，应给予完全的信赖和尊重。国会得制定一般法律，用以规定这种法案、记录、和司法程序如何证明以及具有何等效力。

第二款　每个州的公民应享受各州公民所有之一切特权及豁免。凡在任何一州被控犯有叛国罪、重罪或其他罪行者，逃出法外而在另一州被缉获时，该州应即依照该罪犯所逃出之州的行政当局之请求，将该罪犯交出，以便移交至该犯罪案件有管辖权之州。凡根据一州之法律应在该州服役或服劳役者逃往另一州时，不得因另一州之任何法律或条例解除其服役或劳役，而应依照有权要求该项服役或劳役之当事一方的要求把人交出。

第三款　国会得准许新州加入联邦；如无有关各州之州议会及国会之同意，不得于任何州之管辖区域内建立新州；亦不得合并两州或数州、或数州之一部分而成立新州。国会有权处置合众国之属地及其他产业，并制定有关这些属地及产业的一切必要的法规和章则；本宪法中任何条文，不得作有损于合众国或任何一州之权利的解释。

第四款　合众国保证联邦中的每一州皆为共和政体，保障它们不受外来的侵略；并且根据各州州议会或行政部门(当州议会不能召集时)的请求，平定其内部的暴乱。

第五条

举凡两院议员各以三分之二的多数认为必要时，国会应提出对本宪法的修正案；或者，当现有诸州三分之二的州议会提出请求时，国会应召集修宪大会；以上两种修正案，如经诸州四分之三的州议会或四分之三的州修宪大会批准时，即成为本宪法之一部分而发生全部效力，至于采用那一种批准方式，则由国会议决；但 1808 年以前可能制定之修正案，在任何情形下，不得影响本宪法第一条第九款之第一、第四两项；任何一州，没有它的同意，不得被剥夺它在参议院中的平等投票权。

第六条

合众国政府于本宪法被批准之前所积欠之债务及所签订之条约，于本宪法通过后，具有和在邦联政府时同等的效力。本宪法及依本宪法所制定之合众国法律；以及合众国已经缔结及将要缔结的一切条约，皆为全国之最高法律；每个州的法官都应受其约束，任何一州宪法或法律中的任何内容与之抵触时，均不得有违这一规定。前述之参议员及众议员，各州州议会议员，合众国政府及各州政府之一切行政及司法官员，均应宣誓或誓愿拥护本宪法；但合众国政府之任何职位或公职，均不得以任何宗教标准作为任职的必要条件。

第七条

本宪法经过九个州的制宪大会批准后，即在批准本宪法的各州之间开始生效。

本宪法于公元 1791 年，即美利坚合众国独立后第 12 年的 9 月 17 日，经出席制宪会议的各州在会上一致同意后制定。我们谨在此签名作证。

签名（略）

4

Amendments to the Constitution

(With Approriate Interpretation for Every Section)

ARTICLES IN ADDITION TO, AND AMENDMENTS OF, THE CONSTITUTION OF THE UNITED STATES OF AMERICA, PROPOSED BY CONGRESS, AND RATIFIED BY THE LEGISLATURES OF THE SEVERAL STATES, PURSUANT TO THE FIFTH ARTICLE OF THE ORIGINAL CONSTITUTION.

(**Comment:** *The first ten amendments were ratified on December 15, 1791, and form what is known as the* Bill of Rights.)

Amendment I **(Key Words:** Freedoms, Petitions, Assembly)

Congress shall make no law respecting an establishment of religion, or prohibiting the free exercise thereof; or abridging the freedom of speech, or of the press; or the right of the people peaceably to assemble, and to petition the Government for a redress of grievances.

(**Comment:** *The government cannot create or inhibit religion, ban most types of speech, restrict the press, stop people from gathering peacefully, or bar citizens from asking the government for reform.*)

Amendment Ⅱ (Key Words: Right to bear arms)

A well regulated Militia, being necessary to the security of a free State, the right of the people to keep and bear Arms, shall not be infringed.

(**Comment:** *It is not clear if under this amendment the federal government can ban firearms, but government at all levels can impose restrictions on their ownership and use.*)

Amendment Ⅲ (Key Words: Quartering of soldiers)

No Soldier shall, in time of peace be quartered in any house, without the consent of the Owner, nor in time of war, but in a manner to be prescribed by law.

(**Comment:** *Under the British rule, American colonists were forced to feed and house British soldiers deployed to help enforce colonial tax laws. The colonists resented this practice, and so banned it with this amendment. This amendment has been basically irrelevant since the end of the American Revolution.*)

Amendment Ⅳ (Key Words: Search and arrest)

The right of the people to be secure in their persons, houses, papers, and effects, against unreasonable searches and seizures, shall not be violated, and no Warrants shall issue, but upon probable cause, supported by Oath or affirmation, and particularly describing the place to be searched, and the persons or things to be seized.

(**Comment:** *The police and other government officials cannot conduct searches of private property unless they have reason to believe a crime has been committed. In most cases, police can conduct a search of a person's home only after they get a written search warrant from a judge, detailing where they will search and what they expect to find.*)

Amendment Ⅴ (Key Words: Rights in criminal cases)

No person shall be held to answer for a capital, or otherwise infamous crime, unless on a presentment or indictment of a Grand Jury, except in cases arising in the land or naval forces, or in the Militia, when in actual service in time of War or public danger; nor shall any person be subject for the same offence to be twice put in jeopardy of life or limb; nor shall be compelled in any criminal case to be a witness against himself, nor be deprived of life, liberty, or property, without due process of law; nor shall private property be taken for public use, without just compensation.

(**Comment:** *People can only be prosecuted for serious federal crimes after a grand jury issues an indictment (accusation). If acquitted, a person cannot be tried for the same crime again. No one can be forced to provide self-incriminating testimony. Legal proceedings must be fair. If the government takes private property, it must usually provide reasonable payment or other compensation.*)

Amendment Ⅵ (Key Words: Right to a fair trial**)**

In all criminal prosecutions, the accused shall enjoy the right to a speedy and public trial, by an impartial jury of the State and district wherein the crime shall have been committed, which district shall have been previously ascertained by law, and to be informed of the nature and cause of the accusation; to be confronted with the witnesses against him; to have compulsory process for obtaining witnesses in his favor, and to have the Assistance of Counsel for his defence.

(*Comment: People accused of crimes have a right to a public trial soon after they are arrested, and in federal and state cases they have a right to have a jury decide their guilt or innocence. The government must tell the accused individuals what crime they are charged with and give them a chance to confront witnesses testifying against them. Those accused also have a right to subpoena / compel supporting witnesses to testify in court and to have a lawyer assist in their legal defense.*)

Amendment Ⅶ (Key Words: Rights in civil cases**)**

In Suits at common law, where the value in controversy shall exceed twenty dollars, the right of trial by jury shall be preserved, and no fact tried by a jury, shall be otherwise reexamined in any Court of the United States, than according to the rules of the common law.

(**Comment:** *Parties involved in some types of federal civil / noncriminal cases have a right to a jury trial.*)

Amendment Ⅷ (Key Words:= Bail, fines, punishment**)**

Excessive bail shall not be required, nor excessive fines imposed, nor cruel and unusual punishments inflicted.

(**Comment:** *The court must allow most criminal defendants out of jail before their trial if the defendants put up a reasonable bail, a financial guarantee that they will come to the trial. If a person is convicted of a crime, the government cannot impose unreasonable fines or inflict inhumane punishments.*)

Amendment Ⅸ (Key Words: Rights retained by the people)

The enumeration in the Constitution, of certain rights, shall not be construed to deny or disparage others retained by the people.

(**Comment:** *The fact that the Constitution lists certain rights for American citizens does not mean that these are the only rights that Americans have.*)

Amendment X (Key Words: States' rights)

The powers not delegated to the United States by the Constitution, nor prohibited by it to the States, are reserved to the States respectively, or to the people.

(**Comment:** *The states retain all powers not forbidden under the Constitution and not otherwise delegated to the federal government. This amendment has been read narrowly, generally in favor of the federal government.*)

Amendment Ⅺ (Ratified February 7, 1795) **(Key Words:** Lawsuits against states)

The Judicial power of the United States shall not be construed to extend to any suit in law or equity, commenced or prosecuted against one of the United States by Citizens of another State, or by Citizens or Subjects of any Foreign State.

(**Comment:** *State governments have immunity from some types of suits in federal courts.*)

Amendment Ⅻ (Ratified July 27, 1804) **(Key Words:** Presidential elections)

The Electors shall meet in their respective states, and vote by ballot for President and Vice-President, one of whom, at least, shall not be an inhabitant of the same state with themselves; they shall name in their ballots the person voted for as President, and in distinct ballots the person voted for as Vice-President, and they shall make distinct lists of all persons voted for as President, and of all persons voted for as Vice-President, and of the number of votes for each, which lists they shall sign and certify, and transmit sealed to the seat of the government of the United States, directed to the President of the Senate; —The President of the Senate shall, in the presence of the Senate and House of Representatives, open all the certificates and the votes shall then be counted; —The person having the greatest number of votes for President, shall be the President, if such number be a majority of the whole number of Electors appointed; and if no person have such majority, then from the persons having the highest numbers not exceeding three on the list of those voted for as President, the House of Representatives shall choose immediately, by ballot, the President. But in choosing the President, the votes shall be taken by states, the representation from each state having one vote; a quorum for this purpose shall consist of a member or members from two-thirds of the states, and a majority of all the states shall be necessary to a choice. And if the House of Representatives shall not choose a President whenever the right of choice shall devolve upon them, before the fourth day of March next following, then the Vice-President shall act as President, as in the case of the death or other constitutional disability of the President. (See Note 14)—The person having the greatest number of votes as Vice-President, shall be the Vice-President, if such number be a majority of the whole number of Electors appointed, and if no person have a majority, then from the two highest numbers on the list, the Senate shall choose the Vice-President; a quorum for the purpose shall consist of two-thirds of the whole number of Senators, and a majority of the whole number shall be necessary to a choice. But no person constitutionally ineligible to the office of President shall be eligible to that of Vice-President of the United States.

(**Comment:** *If no presidential candidate wins a majority in the electoral college, then the House of Representatives, voting by state, chooses the President, and the Senate chooses the Vice-President.*)

Amendment XIII (Ratified December 6, 1865) (**Key Words:** Abolition of slavery)

Section 1. Neither slavery nor involuntary servitude, except as a punishment for crime whereof the party shall have been duly convicted, shall exist within the United States, or any place subject to their jurisdiction.

Section 2. Congress shall have power to enforce this article by appropriate legislation.

(**Comment:** *Slavery and peonage are illegal.*)

Amendment XIV (Ratified July 9, 1868) (**Key Words:** Civil rights)

Section 1. All persons born or naturalized in the United States, and subject to the jurisdiction thereof, are citizens of the United States and of the State wherein they reside. No State shall make or enforce any law which shall abridge the privileges or immunities of citizens of the United States; nor shall any State deprive any person of life, liberty, or property, without due process of law; nor deny to any person within its jurisdiction the equal protection of the laws.

(**Comment:** *Anyone born or naturalized in the United States is a citizen. All citizens are entitled to due process (basic fairness), according to the Constitution and the* Bill of Rights. *Laws must be enacted and enforced in a way that treats people equally.*)

Section 2. Representatives shall be apportioned among the several States according to their respective numbers, counting the whole number of persons in each State, excluding Indians not taxed. But when the right to vote at any election for the choice of electors for President and Vice-President of the United States, Representatives in Congress, the Executive and Judicial officers of a State, or the members of the Legislature thereof, is denied to any of the male inhabitants of such State, being twenty-one years of age, (See Note 15) and citizens of the United States, or in any way abridged, except for participation in rebellion, or other crime, the basis of representation therein shall be reduced in the proportion which the number of such male citizens shall bear to the whole number of male citizens twenty-one years of age in such State.

(**Comment:** *If a state bars adult men from voting, the state's congressional representation is reduced proportionately. Historically, this section has had very little effect.*)

Section 3. No person shall be a Senator or Representative in Congress, or elector of President and Vice-President, or hold any office, civil or military, under the United States, or under any State, who, having previously taken an oath, as a member of

Congress, or as an officer of the United States, or as a member of any State legislature, or as an executive or judicial officer of any State, to support the Constitution of the United States, shall have engaged in insurrection or rebellion against the same, or given aid or comfort to the enemies thereof. But Congress may by a vote of two-thirds of each House, remove such disability.

(**Comment:** *Those who pledged their loyalty to the Confederacy in the Civil War were barred from serving in Congress, unless two-thirds of Congress agreed to waive the restriction for an individual.*)

Section 4. The validity of the public debt of the United States, authorized by law, including debts incurred for payment of pensions and bounties for services in suppressing insurrection or rebellion, shall not be questioned. But neither the United States nor any State shall assume or pay any debt or obligation incurred in aid of insurrection or rebellion against the United States, or any claim for the loss or emancipation of any slave; but all such debts, obligations and claims shall be held illegal and void.

(**Comment:** *Debts incurred by the Confederacy during the Civil War were declared invalid and noncollectable from the states and the federal government.*)

Section 5. The Congress shall have power to enforce, by appropriate legislation, the provisions of this article.

Amendment XV (Ratified February 3, 1870) (**Key Words:** Black suffrage)

Section 1. The right of citizens of the United States to vote shall not be denied or abridged by the United States or by any State on account of race, color, or previous condition of servitude.

Section 2. The Congress shall have power to enforce this article by appropriate legislation.

(**Comment:** *Neither state governments nor the federal government can stop people from voting because of their race or because they were once slaves. This amendment was enforced briefly in the 1870s, and after that not until 1960s and later.*)

Amendment XVI (Ratified February 3, 1913) (**Key Words:** Income taxes)

The Congress shall have power to lay and collect taxes on incomes, from whatever source derived, without apportionment among the several States, and without regard to any census or enumeration.

(**Comment:** *Congress can impose an income tax, and it need not be tied to variances in state population.*)

Amendment XVII (Ratified April 8, 1913) (**Key Words:** Senatorial elections)

The Senate of the United States shall be composed of two Senators from each State, elected by the people thereof, for six years; and each Senator shall have one vote. The electors in each State shall have the qualifications requisite for electors of the most numerous branch of the State legislatures.

When vacancies happen in the representation of any State in the Senate, the executive authority of such State shall issue writs of election to fill such vacancies: Provided, That the legislature of any State may empower the executive thereof to make temporary appointments until the people fill the vacancies by election as the legislature may direct.

This amendment shall not be so construed as to affect the election or term of any Senator chosen before it becomes valid as part of the Constitution.

(**Comment:** *Voters in each state elect two members to the United States Senate. Previously Article 1, Section 3, gave this power to state legislatures. When there is a vacancy in a state Senate delegation, the state governor can appoint a replacement until an election can be held to fill the position.*)

Amendment XVIII (Ratified January 16, 1919) (**Key Words:** Prohibition of liquor)

Section 1. After one year from the ratification of this article the manufacture, sale, or transportation of intoxicating liquors within, the importation thereof into, or the exportation thereof from the United States and all territory subject to the jurisdiction thereof for beverage purposes is hereby prohibited.

Section 2. The Congress and the several States shall have concurrent power to enforce this article by appropriate legislation.

Section 3. This article shall be inoperative unless it shall have been ratified as an amendment to the Constitution by the legislatures of the several States, as provided in the Constitution, within seven years from the date of the submission hereof to the States by the Congress.

(**Comment:** *This was the ban on alcohol known as Prohibition, which was repealed in 1933.*)

Amendment XIX (Ratified August 18, 1920) (**Key Words:** Women's suffrage)

The right of citizens of the United States to vote shall not be denied or abridged by the United States or by any State on account of sex.

Congress shall have power to enforce this article by appropriate legislation.

(**Comment:** *Women have the right to vote.*)

Amendment XX (Ratified January 23, 1933) (**Key Words:** Terms of office)

Section 1. The terms of the President and Vice-President shall end at noon on the 20th day of January, and the terms of Senators and Representatives at noon on the 3d day of January, of the years in which such terms would have ended if this article had not been ratified; and the terms of their successors shall then begin.

(**Comment:** *The terms of the President and Vice-President begin on January 20 each year following presidential elections. Members of Congress assume office on January 3 after their election.*)

Section 2. The Congress shall assemble at least once in every year, and such meeting shall begin at noon on the 3d day of January, unless they shall by law appoint a different day.

(**Comment:** *Congressional sessions begin on January 3 unless Congress decides otherwise.*)

Section 3. If, at the time fixed for the beginning of the term of the President, the President elect shall have died, the Vice-President elect shall become President. If a

President shall not have been chosen before the time fixed for the beginning of his term, or if the President elect shall have failed to qualify, then the Vice-President elect shall act as President until a President shall have qualified; and the Congress may by law provide for the case wherein neither a President elect nor a Vice-President elect shall have qualified, declaring who shall then act as President, or the manner in which one who is to act shall be selected, and such person shall act accordingly until a President or Vice-President shall have qualified.

(**Comment:** *If a newly elected President dies before taking office, the newly elected Vice-President assumes the office. If no President has been chosen when the new presidential term is set to begin, the newly elected Vice-President becomes acting President until the President is chosen. If neither the President nor the Vice-President has been chosen when the President's term is set to begin, Congress can determine who becomes acting President.*)

Section 4. The Congress may by law provide for the case of the death of any of the persons from whom the House of Representatives may choose a President whenever the right of choice shall have devolved upon them, and for the case of the death of any of the persons from whom the Senate may choose a Vice-President whenever the right of choice shall have devolved upon them.

(**Comment:** *Congress can pass a law to determine the line of presidential succession after the Vice-President. Currently the office goes to the Speaker of the House, followed by the President pro tempore of the Senate, and then a sequence of cabinet officials.*)

Section 5. Sections 1 and 2 shall take effect on the 15th day of October following the ratification of this article.

Section 6. This article shall be inoperative unless it shall have been ratified as an amendment to the Constitution by the legislatures of three-fourths of the several States within seven years from the date of its submission.

Amendment XXI (Ratified December 5, 1933) (**Key Words:** Repeal of Prohibition)

Section 1. The eighteenth article of amendment to the Constitution of the United States is hereby repealed.

Section 2. The transportation or importation into any State, Territory, or possession of the United States for delivery or use therein of intoxicating liquors, in violation of the laws thereof, is hereby prohibited.

Section 3. This article shall be inoperative unless it shall have been ratified as an amendment to the Constitution by conventions in the several States, as provided in the Constitution, within seven years from the date of the submission hereof to the States by the Congress.

(**Comment:** *The ban on alcohol known as Prohibition was repealed, but states retain the right to regulate alcohol.*)

Amendment XXII (Ratified February 27,1951) (**Key Words:** Term Limits for the Presidency)

Section 1. No person shall be elected to the office of the President more than twice, and no person who has held the office of President, or acted as President, for more than two years of a term to which some other person was elected President shall be elected to the office of the President more than once. But this article shall not apply to any person holding the office of President when this article was proposed by the Congress, and shall not prevent any person who may be holding the office of President, or acting as President, during the term within which this article becomes operative from holding the office of President or acting as President during the remainder of such term.

Section 2. This article shall be inoperative unless it shall have been ratified as an amendment to the Constitution by the legislatures of three-fourths of the several states within seven years from the date of its submission to the states by the Congress.

(**Comment:** *Nobody can be elected to more than two terms as President. This amendment was passed in reaction to Franklin D. Roosevelt's four terms.*)

Amendment XXIII (Ratified March 29, 1961) (**Key Words:** Washington, D.C., suffrage)

Section 1. The District constituting the seat of government of the United States shall appoint in such manner as the Congress may direct:

A number of electors of President and Vice-President equal to the whole number of Senators and Representatives in Congress to which the District would be entitled if it were a state, but in no event more than the least populous state; they shall be in addition to those appointed by the states, but they shall be considered, for the purposes of the election of President and Vice-President, to be electors appointed by a state; and they shall meet in the District and perform such duties as provided by the twelfth article of amendment.

Section 2. The Congress shall have power to enforce this article by appropriate legislation.

(**Comment:** *Residents of Washington, D.C. can vote in presidential elections.*)

Amendment XXIV (Ratified January 23,1964) (**Key Words:** Abolition of poll taxes)

Section 1. The right of citizens of the United States to vote in any primary or other election for President or Vice-President, for electors for President or Vice-President, or for Senator or Representative in Congress, shall not be denied or abridged by the United States or any state by reason of failure to pay any poll tax or other tax.

Section 2. The Congress shall have power to enforce this article by appropriate legislation.

(**Comment:** *Nobody can be barred from voting because they have not paid a poll tax, a special tax on voters used historically in the South to prevent African Americans from participating in elections.*)

Amendment XXV (Ratified February 10,1967) (**Key Words:** Presidential succession)

Section 1. In case of the removal of the President from office or of his death or resignation, the Vice-President shall become President.

(**Comment:** *If the President resigns, the Vice-President takes over.*)

Section 2. Whenever there is a vacancy in the office of the Vice-President, the President shall nominate a Vice-President who shall take office upon confirmation by a majority vote of both Houses of Congress.

(**Comment:** *If there is no Vice-President, the President can appoint a replacement, subject to the approval of a majority of both Houses of Congress.*)

Section 3. Whenever the President transmits to the President pro tempore of the Senate and the Speaker of the House of Representatives his written declaration that he is unable to discharge the powers and duties of his office, and until he transmits to them a written declaration to the contrary, such powers and duties shall be discharged by the Vice-President as Acting President.

(**Comment:** *The Vice-President takes over the presidency if the President notifies congressional leaders that he or she is unable to continue in office.*)

Section 4. Whenever the Vice-President and a majority of either the principal officers of the executive departments or of such other body as Congress may by law provide, transmit to the President pro tempore of the Senate and the Speaker of the House of Representatives their written declaration that the President is unable to discharge the powers and duties of his office, the Vice-President shall immediately assume the powers and duties of the office as Acting President.

Thereafter, when the President transmits to the President pro tempore of the Senate and the Speaker of the House of Representatives his written declaration that no inability exists, he shall resume the powers and duties of his office unless the Vice-President and a majority of either the principal officers of the executive department or of such other body as Congress may by law provide, transmit within four days to the President pro tempore of the Senate and the Speaker of the House of Representatives their written declaration that the President is unable to discharge the powers and duties of his office. Thereupon Congress shall decide the issue, assembling within forty-eight hours for that purpose if not in session. If the Congress, within twenty-one days after receipt of the latter written declaration, or, if Congress is not in session, within twenty-one days after Congress is required to assemble, determines by two-thirds vote of both Houses that the President is unable to discharge the powers and duties of his office, the Vice-President shall continue to discharge the same as Acting President; otherwise, the President shall resume the powers and duties of his office.

(**Comment:** *The Vice-President and a majority of cabinet members can strip the*

President of power if they certify to congressional leaders that he or she has become incapable of doing the job. The President regains power by notifying congressional leaders that he or she is fit to work. If the Vice-President and a majority of the cabinet continue to maintain that the President cannot serve, the President retains his or her power unless two-thirds of each House of Congress vote that he or she is unfit.)

Amendment XXVI ((Ratified July 1, 1971) (**Key Words:** 18-year-old suffrage)

Section 1. The right of citizens of the United States, who are 18 years of age or older, to vote, shall not be denied or abridged by the United States or any state on account of age.

Section 2. The Congress shall have the power to enforce this article by appropriate legislation.

(**Comment:** *The minimum voting age in all federal, state, and local elections in the United States is 18.*)

Amendment XXVII (Ratified May 7, 1992) (**Key Words:** Congressional pay raises)

No law varying the compensation for the services of the Senators and Representatives shall take effect until an election of Representatives shall have intervened.

(**Comment:** *Congressional pay rates cannot be changed until an intervening House of Representatives election has occurred.*)

Translation

美国宪法修正案

（前十条修正案于 1791 年 12 月 15 日批准，被称为《权利法案》。）

修正案 [一]

国会不得制定关于下列事项的法律：确立国教或禁止信教自由，剥夺言论自由或出版自由；剥夺人民和平集会和向政府诉冤请愿的权利。

修正案［二］

管理良好的民兵是保障自由州的安全之所必需，此人民持有和携带武器的权利不得侵犯。

修正案［三］

士兵在和平时期，未经房主许可不得驻扎于任何民房；在战争时期，除依法律规定的方式外亦不得进驻民房。

修正案［四］

人民保护其人身、住房、文件和财物不受无理搜查扣押的权利不得侵犯；除非有合理的根据认为有罪，以宣誓或郑重声明保证，并详细开列应予搜查的地点、应予扣押的人或物，不得颁发搜查和扣押证。

修正案［五］

非经大陪审团提出报告或起诉，任何人不受死罪或其他重罪的惩罚，唯在战时国家危急时期发生在陆、海军中或正在服役的民兵中的案件不在此限。任何人不得因同一犯罪行为而两次遭受生命或身体伤残的危害；不得在任何刑事案件中被迫自证其罪；未经正当法律程序，不得剥夺任何人的生命、自由或财产；非有恰当补偿，不得将私有财产充作公用。

修正案［六］

在一切刑事诉讼中，被告应享受下列权利：由犯罪行为发生地的州或地区的公正陪审团予以迅速和公开的审判，该地区应事先已由法律确定；获知控告的性质和原因；同原告证人对质；以强制程序取得有利于自己的证据；取得律师帮助为其辩护。

修正案［七］

在习惯法诉讼中，争执价额超过 20 美元，由陪审团审判的权利应予保护；案情事实经陪审团审定后，除非依照习惯法的规则，合众国的任何法院不得再行审理。

修正案［八］

不得索取过多的保释金，不得处以过重的罚金，或施加残酷的、非常的刑罚。

修正案［九］

本宪法对某些权利的列举不得被解释为否定或轻视由人民保有的其他权利。

修正案［十］

宪法未授予合众国、也未禁止各州行使的权力，分别由各州或由人民保留。

修正案［十一］（1795 年 2 月 7 日批准）

合众国司法权，不得被解释为可扩大适用受理另一州公民或任何外国公民或国民对合众国一州提出的或起诉的任何法律或衡平法的诉讼。

修正案［十二］（1804 年 7 月 27 日批准）

选举人应在各自州内集会，投票选举总统和副总统。所选的总统和副总统至少应有 1 人不是选举人本州的居民；选举人应在选票上写明被选为总统之人的姓名，并在另一选票上写明被选为副总统之人的姓名。选举人须将所有被选为总统及副总统的人分别开列名单，写明每人所得票数，在名单上签名作证，封印后送至合众国政府所在地，呈交参议院议长。参议院议长在参议院和众议院全体议员面前开拆所有证明书，然后计算票数。获得总统选票最多的人，如所得票数超过选举人总数之半，即当选为总统。如无人获得这种过半数票，众议院应立即从被选为总统之人的名单中得票最多者（不超过 3 人）中投票选举其中一人为总统。但选举总统时应以州为单位计票。每州代表有一票表决权。以此种方式选举总统的法定人数为全国 2/3 的州各有 1 名或数名众议员出席，选出总统需要所有州的过半数票。如选举总统的权力转移给众议院而该院在次年 3 月 4 日前尚未选出总统，则副总统应按总统死亡或宪法规定的其他有关总统丧失任职能力的条款代行总统职务。获得副总统选票最多者，如所得票数超过选举人总数之半，即当选为副总统。如无人获得过半数票，则参议院应从名单上得票最多的 2 人中选举 1 人为副总统。以此种方式选举副总统的法定人数为参议员总数的 2/3，选出副总统需要参议员总数的过半数票。但依宪法无资格当选为合众国总统的人不得当选为合众国副总统。

修正案[十三]（1865 年 12 月 6 日批准）

第一款　在合众国境内或属合众国管辖的任何地方，不准有奴隶制或强制劳役的存在，但唯用于业经定罪的罪犯作为惩罚者不在此限。

第二款　国会有权以适当立法实施本条规定。

修正案[十四]（1868 年 7 月 9 日批准）

第一款　在合众国出生或归化合众国并受合众国管辖的人，均为合众国和他所居住的州的公民。无论何州均不得制定或实施任何剥夺合众国公民的特权或豁免权的法律；无论何州未经正当法律程序不得剥夺任何人的生命、自由或财产；亦不得拒绝给予在其管辖下的任何人以同等的法律保护。

第二款　众议员名额应按各州人口总数的比例分配，但不纳税的印第安人除外。各州年满 21 岁且为合众国公民的男性居民，除因参加叛乱或犯其他罪行者外，其选举合众国总统与副总统选举人、国会为议员、州行政和司法官员或州议会议员的权利被取消或剥夺时，该州众议员人数应按上述男性公民的人数同该州年满 21 岁的男性公民总人数的比例予以削减。

第三款　无论何人，凡先前曾以国会议员、合众国官员、州议会议员或州行政或司法官员，宣誓拥护合众国宪法，而又参与反对合众国的暴乱或谋叛，或给予合众国敌人以帮助或庇护者，不得为国会参议员或众议员、总统和副总统选举人，或在合众国或任何一州任文职、军职官员。但国会可以每院 2/3 的票数取消此项限制。

第四款　经法律认可的合众国公债，包括因支付平定暴乱或叛乱有功人员的养老金和奖金而产生的债务，其效力不得怀疑。但合众国或任何一州都不得承担或偿付因资助对合众国作乱或谋叛而产生的任何债务或义务，或因丧失或解放任何奴隶而提出的任何赔偿要求；所有此类债务、义务和要求均应被认为是非法和无效的。

第五款　国会有权以适当立法实施本条各项规定。

修正案［十五］（1870年2月3日批准）

第一款　合众国或任何一州不得因种族、肤色或以前的奴隶身份而否认或剥夺合众国公民的选举权。

第二款　国会有权以适当立法实施本条规定。

修正案［十六］（1913年2月3日批准）

国会有权对任何来源的收入规定并征收所得税；所得税收入不按比例分配于各州，也不必考虑任何人口普查或统计。

修正案［十七］（1913年4月8日批准）

合众国参议院由每州人民选出2名参议员组成，参议员任期6年，各有一票表决权。各州选举人应具备州议会中人数最多一院的选举人所必需的资格。

任何一州在参议院的议席出现缺额时，该州行政当局应发布选举令以填补此项缺额；但任何一州州议会在人民按照州议会指示进行选举补足缺额以前，可授权行政长官做出临时任命。

本修正案对于本条作为合众国宪法一部分被批准生效前当选的任何参议员的选举或任期不发生影响。

修正案［十八］（1919年1月16日批准）

第一款　从本条批准起一年以后，禁止在合众国及其管辖下的一切领土内酿造、出售和运送致醉酒类，并且不准此种酒类输入或输出合众国及其管辖下的一切领土。

第二款　国会和各州都有权以适当立法实施本条规定。

第三款　本条除非在国会送达各州之日起7年内经各州州议会按照宪法规定批准为宪法修正案，不得发生效力。

修正案［十九］（1920年8月18日批准）

合众国或任何一州不得因性别而否认或剥夺合众国公民的选举权。

国会有权以适当立法实施本条规定。

修正案［二十］（1933年1月23日批准）

第一款　如果本条尚未获批准，总统和副总统的任期应于原定任期届满之年1月20日正午终止，参议员和众议员的任期应于原定任期届满之年1月3日正午终止；其继任人的任期即在此时开始。

第二款　国会每年至少开会一次。开会日期除以法律另行规定外，应于1月3日正午开始。

第三款　如当选总统在规定的任期开始之前已死亡，当选副总统应成为总统。如在规定的总统任期开始以前总统尚未选出，或当选总统不符合资格，则当选副总统应代行总统职权直到有一名符合资格的总统为止；如遇当选总统和当选副总统均不符合资格的情况，国会可以法律规定代理总统人选或选择代理总统的方式，此人即可依法代行总统职务，直至有一名符合资格的总统或副总统为止。

第四款　当选总统的权利转移到众议院，而可被该院选为总统的人中有人死亡；或选举副总统的权利转移到参议院，而可被该院选为副总统的人中有人死亡时，国会得以法律对此种情况做出规定。

第五款　第一款与第二款应在本条批准后之10月15日起生效。

第六款　本条如在国会送达各州之日起7年内，未经3/4的州议会批准为《宪法修正案》，将不发生效力。

修正案［二十一］（1933年12月5日批准）

第一款　美利坚合众国宪法修正案第18条现予废除。

第二款　在合众国各州、各领地或属地内为交付或使用致醉酒类而进行的运送或输入，如违反有关法律，应予禁止。

第三款　本条除非在国会送达各州之日起7年内经各州制宪会议按照宪法规定批准为宪法修正案，不发生效力。

修正案［二十二］（1951年2月27日批准）

第一款　无论何人不得当选总统职务两次以上；无论何人在他人任期内担任总统职务或代理总统超过两年者，不得当选担任总统职务一次以上。但本条不适用于在国会提出本条时正在担任总统职务的任何人；也不妨碍在本条开始生效的总统任期内可能担任总统职务或代理总统的任何人在此任期结束以前担任总统职务或代理总统。

第二款　本条除非在国会将其提交各州之日起7年内由3 / 4州议会批准为宪法修正案，不发生效力。

修正案［二十三］（1961年3月29日）

第一款　合众国政府所在的特区，应按国会所指定的方式选派若干名总统和副总统的选举人，为此目的，该特区应被视为一个州，选举人数量应相当于它有权选举的参议员和众议员人数的总和，但不得超过人数最少的州的选举人人数；以上选举人是在各州所选派的选举人之外所增添的，但是为了选举总统和副总统，应被视为由一个州所选派的选举人。他们应在特区集会，并依照宪法修正案第12条的规定履行其职责。

第二款　国会有权以适当立法实施本条规定。

修正案［二十四］（1964年1月23日批准）

第一款　合众国或任何一州不得以未交人头税或其他税款为理由，否认或剥夺合众国公民在总统或副总统、总统或副总统选举人或参议员、众议员的任何初选或其他选举中的选举权。

第二款　国会有权以适当立法实施本条规定。

修正案［二十五］（1967年2月10日批准）

第一款　如果总统免职、死亡或辞职，副总统应成为总统。

第二款　副总统职位出现空缺时，总统应提名一位副总统，经由国会两院都以过半数票批准后就职。

第三款　如总统向参议院临时议长及众议院议长递交书面声明，宣称他无能力履行其权力与职责，则其权力与职责应由副总统作为代理总统来履行，直至他提出相反的书面声明为止。

第四款　如副总统以及各行政部门或国会依法设立的此种其他机构的多数主要官员，向参议院临时议长和众议院议长递交关于总统无能力履行其权力与职责的书面声明，则副总统应作为代理总统立即承担以上权力与职责。

此后，当总统向参议院临时议长和众议院议长递交他丧失能力情况并不存在的书面声明时，除非副总统以及各行政部门或国会依法设立的此种其他机构的多数主要官员在4日内向参议院临时议长和众议院议长递交总统无能力履行其权力与职责的书面声明，总统应恢复其权力与职责。国会应对此作出裁决。如在休会期间，应在48小时内为此目的召集会议。如果国会收到后一书面声明21天之内，或处在休会期间被要求召集会议以后的21天之内，以两院的2/3票数决定总统不能履行其权力与职责，副总统应继续作为代理总统履行上述权力与职责；否则，总统应恢复其权力与职责。

修正案[二十六]（1971年7月1日批准）

第一款　合众国或任何一州不得因年龄而否认或剥夺已满18岁或18岁以上的合众国公民的选举权。

第二款　国会有权以适当立法实施本条规定。

修正案[二十七]（1992年5月7日批准）

新一届众议员选出之前，任何有关改变参议员和众议员的任职报酬的法律，均不得生效。

5

Barack Obama's Second Victory Speech

Delivered 7 November, 2012, in Chicago

❑ About the Speech

2012 年 11 月 6 日，让美国人民既期待又纠结、交织着希望与绝望的 2012 年美国总统大选尘埃落定，现任总统、民主党候选人奥巴马击败共和党挑战者罗姆尼，成功连任。其实在大选当天，尽管选票还没有统计完毕，但已经确定奥巴马获得了 303 张选举人票，超过获胜所需票数，而最后一个州佛罗里达州的票数最终于 10 日清点完毕，奥巴马赢得该州 29 张选举人票。换言之，奥巴马以总数 332 张选票赢得大选，远超其对手共和党总统候选人罗姆尼的 206 张选举人票。

当地时间 7 日凌晨，奥巴马发表胜选演讲。在胜选演讲中，奥巴马感谢支持者，感谢副总统拜登，感谢 20 年来携手的妻子米歇尔，感谢他的女儿。他也对罗姆尼展开的激烈竞选活动表示赞赏。他表示，将与罗姆尼就“推动国家向前发展”的方式进行讨论。同时，奥巴马呼吁人们坚定信念、努力工作，并发扬美国精神。他在演讲中表示，美国能前进是因为每一个美国人的共同努力，但美国还没有迎来最好的时代。另外他还呼吁美国人民在选举后保持团结，并承诺将给美国人民带来“更美好的未来”。此外，**从语言上来讲，**这篇演讲很突出的特点是排比的大量运用，突出演讲主题，同时使演讲慷慨激昂，极具感染力和鼓动性。

奥巴马的成功连任，不仅代表着奥巴马成为第二次世界大战结束以来第二名赢得连任的民主党籍总统，也改写了过去 70 年失业率高于 7.4% 时白宫必定易主的历史。

❑ The Speech in Full

Thank you so much.

Tonight, more than 200 years after a former colony won the right to determine its own destiny, the task of perfecting our union moves forward.

It moves forward because of you. It moves forward because you reaffirmed the spirit that has triumphed over war and depression, the spirit that has lifted this country from the depths of despair to the great heights of hope, the belief that while each of us will pursue our own individual dreams, we are an American family and we rise or fall together as one nation and as one people.

Tonight, in this election, you, the American people, reminded us that while our road has been hard, while our journey has been long, we have picked ourselves up, we have fought our way back, and we know in our hearts that for the United States of America the best is yet to come.

I want to thank every American who participated in this election, whether you voted for the very first time or waited in line for a very long time. By the way, we have to fix that. Whether you pounded the pavement or picked up the phone, whether you held an Obama sign or a Romney sign, you made your voice heard and you made a difference.

I just spoke with Gov. Romney and I congratulated him and Paul Ryan on a hard-fought campaign. We may have battled fiercely, but it's only because we love this country deeply and we care so strongly about its future. From George to Lenore to their son Mitt, the Romney family has chosen to give back to America through public service and that is the legacy that we honor and applaud tonight. In the weeks ahead, I also look forward to sitting down with Gov. Romney to talk about where we can work together to move this country forward.

I want to thank my friend and partner of the last four years, America's happy warrior, the best vice president anybody could ever hope for, Joe Biden.

And I wouldn't be the man I am today without the woman who agreed to marry me 20 years ago. Let me say this publicly: Michelle, I have never loved you more. I have never been prouder to watch the rest of America fall in love with you, too, as our nation's first lady. Sasha and Malia, before our very eyes you're growing up to become two strong, smart beautiful young women, just like your mom. And I'm so proud of you guys. But I will say that for now one dog's probably enough.

To the best campaign team and volunteers in the history of politics. The best. The best ever. Some of you were new this time around, and some of you have been at my side since the very beginning. But all of you are family. No matter what you do or where you go from here, you will carry the memory of the history we made together and you will have the lifelong appreciation of a grateful president. Thank you for believing all the way, through every hill, through every valley. You lifted me up the whole way and I will always be grateful for everything that you've done and all the incredible work that you put in.

I know that political campaigns can sometimes seem small, even silly. And that provides plenty of fodder for the cynics that tell us that politics is nothing more than a contest of egos or the domain of special interests. But if you ever get the chance to talk to folks who turned out at our rallies and crowded along a rope line in a high school gym, or saw folks working late in a campaign office in some tiny county far away from home, you'll discover something else.

You'll hear the determination in the voice of a young field organizer who's working his way through college and wants to make sure every child has that same opportunity. You'll hear the pride in the voice of a volunteer who's going door to door because her brother was finally hired when the local auto plant added another shift. You'll hear the deep patriotism in the voice of a military spouse who's working the phones late at night to make sure that no one who fights for this country ever has to fight for a job or a roof over their head when they come home.

That's why we do this. That's what politics can be. That's why elections matter. It's not small, it's big. It's important. Democracy in a nation of 300 million can be noisy and messy and complicated. We have our own opinions. Each of us has deeply held beliefs. And when we go through tough times, when we make big decisions as a country, it necessarily stirs passions, stirs up controversy.

That won't change after tonight, and it shouldn't. These arguments we have are a mark of our liberty. We can never forget that as we speak people in distant nations are risking their lives right now just for a chance to argue about the issues that matter, the chance to cast their ballots like we did today.

But despite all our differences, most of us share certain hopes for America's future. We want our kids to grow up in a country where they have access to the best schools and the best teachers. A country that lives up to its legacy as the global leader in technology and discovery and innovation, with all the good jobs and new businesses that follow.

We want our children to live in an America that isn't burdened by debt, that isn't weakened by inequality, that isn't threatened by the destructive power of a warming planet. We want to pass on a country that's safe and respected and admired around the world, a nation that is defended by the strongest military on earth and the best troops this—this world has ever known. But also a country that moves with confidence beyond this time of war, to shape a peace that is built on the promise of freedom and dignity for every human being.

We believe in a generous America, in a compassionate America, in a tolerant America, open to the dreams of an immigrant's daughter who studies in our schools and pledges to our flag. To the young boy on the south side of Chicago who sees a life beyond the nearest street corner. To the furniture worker's child in North Carolina who wants to become a doctor or a scientist, an engineer or an entrepreneur, a diplomat or even a President—that's the future we hope for. That's the vision we share. That's where we need to go—forward. That's where we need to go.

Now, we will disagree, sometimes fiercely, about how to get there. As it has for more than two centuries, progress will come in fits and starts. It's not always a straight line. It's not always a smooth path.

By itself, the recognition that we have common hopes and dreams won't end all the gridlock or solve all our problems or substitute for the painstaking work of building consensus and making the difficult compromises needed to move this country forward. But that common bond is where we must begin.

Our economy is recovering. A decade of war is ending. A long campaign is now over. And whether I earned your vote or not, I have listened to you, I have learned from you, and you've made me a better President. And with your stories and your struggles, I return to the White House more determined and more inspired than ever about the work there is to do and the future that lies ahead.

Tonight you voted for action, not politics as usual. You elected us to focus on your jobs, not ours. And in the coming weeks and months, I am looking forward to reaching out and working with leaders of both parties to meet the challenges we can only solve together. Reducing our deficit. Reforming our tax code. Fixing our immigration system. Freeing ourselves from foreign oil. We've got more work to do.

But that doesn't mean your work is done. The role of citizen in our democracy does not end with your vote. America's never been about what can be done for us. It's about what can be done by us together through the hard and frustrating, but necessary work of self-government. That's the principle we were founded on.

This country has more wealth than any nation, but that's not what makes us rich. We have the most powerful military in history, but that's not what makes us strong. Our university, our culture are all the envy of the world, but that's not what keeps the world coming to our shores.

What makes America exceptional are the bonds that hold together the most diverse nation on earth. The belief that our destiny is shared; that this country only works when we accept certain obligations to one another and to future generations. The freedom which so many Americans have fought for and died for come with responsibilities as well as rights. And among those are love and charity and duty and patriotism. That's what makes America great.

I am hopeful tonight because I've seen the spirit at work in America. I've seen it in the family business whose owners would rather cut their own pay than lay off their neighbors, and in the workers who would rather cut back their hours than see a friend lose a job. I've seen it in the soldiers who reenlist after losing a limb and in those SEALs who charged up the stairs into darkness and danger because they knew there was a buddy behind them watching their back.

I've seen it on the shores of New Jersey and New York, where leaders from every party and level of government have swept aside their differences to help a community rebuild from the wreckage of a terrible storm. And I saw just the other day, in Mentor, Ohio, where a father told the story of his 8-year-old daughter, whose long battle with leukemia nearly cost their family everything had it not been for health care reform passing just a few months before the insurance company was about to stop paying for her care.

I had an opportunity to not just talk to the father, but meet this incredible daughter of his. And when he spoke to the crowd listening to that father's story, every parent in that room had tears in their eyes, because we knew that little girl could be our own. And I know that every American wants her future to be just as bright. That's who we are. That's the country I'm so proud to lead as your President.

And tonight, despite all the hardship we've been through, despite all the frustrations of Washington, I've never been more hopeful about our future. I have never been more hopeful about America. And I ask you to sustain that hope. I'm not talking about blind optimism, the kind of hope that just ignores the enormity of the tasks ahead or the roadblocks that stand in our path. I'm not talking about the wishful idealism that allows us to just sit on the sidelines or shirk from a fight.

I have always believed that hope is that stubborn thing inside us that insists, despite all the evidence to the contrary, that something better awaits us so long as we have the courage to keep reaching, to keep working, to keep fighting.

America, I believe we can build on the progress we've made and continue to fight for new jobs and new opportunity and new security for the middle class. I believe we can keep the promise of our founders, the idea that if you're willing to work hard, it doesn't matter who you are or where you come from or what you look like or where you love. It doesn't matter whether you're black or white or Hispanic or Asian or Native American or young or old or rich or poor, able, disabled, gay or straight, you can make it here in America if you're willing to try.

I believe we can seize this future together because we are not as divided as our politics suggests. We're not as cynical as the pundits believe. We are greater than the sum of our individual ambitions, and we remain more than a collection of red states and blue states. We are and forever will be the United States of America.

And together with your help and God's grace we will continue our journey forward and remind the world just why it is that we live in the greatest nation on Earth.

Thank you, America. God bless you. God bless these United States.

❑ Translation

巴拉克·奥巴马连任胜选演讲

2012 年 11 月 7 日，芝加哥

非常感谢大家。

今夜，在当年的殖民地赢得了决定自己命运的权利 200 多年以后，让美利坚合众国更加完美的任务又向前推进了一步。

这一进程是因为你们而向前推进的，因为你们再次确认了那种使美国胜利克服了战争和萧条的精神，那种使美国摆脱绝望的深渊并走向希望的最高点的精神，以及那种虽然我们每个人都在追求自己的个人梦想、但我们同属一个美国大家庭、并作为一个国家和民族共同进退的信仰。

今夜，在此次选举中，你们这些美国人民提醒我们，虽然我们的道路一直艰难，虽然我们的旅程一直漫长，但我们已经让自己振作起来，我们已经发起反击。我们在自己内心深处知道，对美利坚合众国来说，最美好的一切属于未来。

我想感谢所有参加此次选举的美国人，无论你是首次参加选举还是为投票曾长时间排队等候。顺便说一句，我们需要解决这些问题。无论你是到投票站投票还是发传真投票，无论你选的是奥巴马还是罗姆尼，你都让别人听到了自己的声音，你都让美国因你而不同。

我要对罗姆尼州长说几句话，我对他和保罗·莱恩在这次竞争激烈的选举中的表现表示祝贺。我们可能争夺得很激烈，但这仅仅是因为我们深爱着这个国家以及我们如此强烈地关心着它的未来。从乔治到勒诺到他们的儿子米特，罗姆尼家族选择了通过公共服务来回报美国，那是一种我们今夜表示敬重和赞许的遗产。我期待着今后几周能与罗姆尼州长坐下来讨论一下我们可以从何处着手一起努力将美国推向前进。

我想对我在过去四年中的朋友和伙伴表示感谢。他就是美国的快乐战士、无出其右的最佳副总统乔·拜登。

如果不是那位 20 年前同意嫁给我的女性，我不会成为今天的我。请让我公开说出下面这段话：米歇尔，我对你的爱无以复加，我无比骄傲地看到其他美国人也爱上了你这位我们国家的第一夫人。萨沙和玛利亚，在我们所有人的见证下你们正成长为两个坚强、聪明和美丽的年轻女性，就像你们的妈妈一样。我十分以你们为荣。不过我要说的是，眼下家里养一条狗或许已经够了。

在这个有史以来的最佳竞选团队和有史以来的最佳志愿者队伍中，你们有些人是这次新加入进来的，有些人则一开始就在我身边。但你们所有人都属于一个大家庭。无论你的工作是什么，无论你从哪里来，你们都将获得我们共同创造的历史记忆，你们都将被一位充满感激之情的总统终生感激。感谢你们始终充满信心，无论是在高峰还是在低谷。你们鼓舞着我走完整个选举过程，我对你们所做的每件事、你们所做的每项不可思议的工作将一直充满感激。

我知道政治角力有时会显得小家子气甚至愚蠢。它为愤世嫉俗者提供了足够的口实，他们告诉我们政治不过是自负者之间的竞争，是特殊利益集团的地盘。但如果你曾经有机会与参加我们集会的那些人以及高中体育馆内挤在隔离绳外的那些人攀谈，或者看到那些在远离家乡的偏远小县的竞选办公室内加班工作的人，你会发现一些别的东西。

你将从一位年轻的活动现场组织者的声音里听到他的决心，他边在大学里学习边从事助选工作，他希望确保每个孩子都能拥有同样的机会。你将从一位志愿者的声音里听到她的骄傲，她挨门挨户地动员选民是因为她哥哥终因当地一家汽车制造厂增加了一个班次而有了工作。你将从一对军人夫妇的声音里听到深深的爱国情怀。他们深夜时还在接听选举电话，以确保那些曾经为这个国家作战的人不会在返回家园时还要为得到一份工作或栖身之所而苦苦争斗。

正因为如此，我们要进行选举。这是政治所能够实现的。正因为如此，选举很重要。这不是小事，而是大事，是至关重要的事。在一个有三亿人口的国家实行民主制度可能嘈杂不堪、一团混乱、情况复杂。我们有自己的观点。我们每个人都有自己深信的信仰。当我们经历艰难时期，当我们作为一个国家作出重大决定时，这必然会激发热情，也必然会引发争议。

今晚过后，这都不会改变，也不应该改变。我们进行的这些争论恰恰体现了我们的自由。我们永远不应忘记，就在我们讲话之际，遥远国度的人们现在正冒着生命危险，仅仅是为了获得一个能够对重要问题进行争论、像我们今天这样投票的机会。

不过，尽管我们存在这样那样的分歧，我们大多数人都对美国的未来有着某些共同的希望。我们希望我们的孩子成长的国家能够让他们上最好的学校、接受最好老师的教导。一个无愧于全球技术、探索和创新领袖光辉历史的国家，倘能如此，各种好工作和新企业将随之而来。

我们希望我们的孩子能够生活在一个没有债务之累、没有不公之苦、没有全球变暖带来的破坏之虞的美国。我们希望留给后代一个安全、受到全球尊重和赞赏的国家，一个由全球有史以来最强大的军事力量和最好的部队保卫的国家，一个满怀信心走过战争、在人人享有自由和尊严的承诺之上构建和平的国家。

我们坚信一个慷慨的美国、一个富有同情心的美国、一个宽容的美国。美国向一位移民的女儿的梦想打开了大门，让她有机会在我们的学校学习、对着我们的国旗宣誓；美国向芝加哥南部地区的一个小男孩打开了大门，让有机会他看到一个最近街角以外的远大人生；美国向北卡罗来纳州的一位家具工人的孩子打开了大门，让他有机会实现自己当医生或科学家、工程师或企业家、外交官甚至是总统的梦想。这是我们希望的未来。这是我们共同的憧憬。这是我们奔赴的方向、前进的方向。这是我们需要实现的目标。

现在，我们对如何实现这一目标存在分歧，有时分歧还很严重。正如两个多世纪以来一样，进展的取得将是断断续续的，并非总是一条直线，并非总能一帆风顺。

承认我们拥有共同的希望和梦想，仅凭这一点不会结束所有的僵局，或解决我们所有的问题，或代替推动这个国家向前所需的达成共识和作出艰难让步的辛苦努力。不过，这一共同的纽带是我们必须开始的地方。

我们的经济正在好转。长达 10 年的战争即将结束。一场漫长的竞选现已落幕。无论我是否赢得了你们的选票，我一直在倾听你们的故事、向你们学习、是你们使我成为一位更好的总统。听过你们的故事和困难经历，我在重返白宫时对今后需要做的工作和未来将怀着比以往更坚定的决心和更大的热情。

今晚你们把票投给了行动，而不是像以往那样投给了政治。你们选举我们来专注于你们的工作，而不是我们的工作。在未来的几周和几个月内，我将期待与两党领袖接触并合作，以便面对我们团结一致才能解决的问题：减少赤字，改革税法，修改移民制度，摆脱对外国石油的依赖。我们还有更多工作要做。

但这并不意味着你们的工作就此结束。民主国家公民的角色并不随着投票完结而结束。美国看重的从来都不是能够为我们个人做些什么，而是我们团结一致通过自治这一艰难、令人倍感挫折但必要的工作能够实现什么。这正是我们的立国之本。

美国的财富多于世界上任何其他国家，但真正让我们富有的并非金钱；我们拥有有史以来最强大的军力，但真正让我们充满力量的并非军队；我们的大学和文化为全世界所艳羡，但美国真正吸引各国人踏上这片土地的魅力也不在于此。

真正让美国与众不同的，是将这个地球上最多元化的国家的人民团结在一起的那些纽带；是我们共命运的信念，是只有当我们肩负某些对彼此以及对后代的责任美国才能走下去的信念；是无数的美国人前赴后继为之奋斗的自由——它既赋予了我们权利，也给我们带来了责任，其中就包括爱、慈善、义务和爱国。正是这些让美国变得伟大。

今晚，我满怀希望，因为我已经看到美国精神正在得以发扬。我看到有些家族企业，所有者宁可减少自己的薪酬也不愿让邻居丢掉工作；我看到有些工人宁愿缩减自己的工时也不愿看到朋友没有活干；我看到有些士兵在失去一条腿或胳膊之后又选择再次入伍；我看到海豹突击队员不避危险冲上楼梯、冲入黑暗，因为他们知道有一个兄弟在做他的后盾。

在新泽西和纽约的海岸，我也看到了美国精神。每一个政党和各级政府的领导者都摒弃分歧，为在骇人风暴过后的废墟上重建社区各尽己力。就在不久前的一天，在俄亥俄的门托，我看到一位父亲在讲述他 8 岁女儿的故事。这个女孩与白血病进行了长期的斗争，如果不是因为几个月前通过的医改法案，保险公司就会停止支付医疗费用，他们的家庭就将失去一切。

我曾有机会与这位父亲攀谈。不仅如此，我还见到了他的女儿，这个非常了不起的小姑娘。当这位父亲向倾听他的故事的人讲述时，每一位在场的父母眼里都含着泪水，因为我们知道，我们自己的孩子也有可能遇到这种状况。而且我知道，每一位美国人都希望这位小女孩的未来能像所有人的未来一样光明。这就是美国人，这就是美国。我为自己能够成为这个国家的总统、带领这个国家前行感到无比光荣。

今晚，尽管我们遭遇了很多困难，尽管华盛顿有诸多不尽如人意之处，我仍从未像现在这样对未来充满希望。我从未像现在这样对美国充满希望。我请大家也保持这样的希望。我所说的并非盲目的乐观主义，不是那种看不到眼前的任务有多么艰巨、看不到前行的路上有什么样的障碍的希望；我所说的并非作壁上观或是临战退缩的一厢情愿的理想主义。

我一直相信，所谓希望就是我们内心倔强地坚持的力量。相信不管有多少相反的证据，都要相信有更好的东西在等着我们，只要我们有勇气不断前行、不懈工作、不停战斗。

国民们，我相信我们有能力在已经取得的进步的基础上再进一步，继续为了给中产阶级创造新的工作、新的机遇、新的保障而战斗。我相信我们有能力信守开国者们许下的诺言，信守这样一种理念，那就是不管你是谁，不管你来自哪里，不管你长相如何，不管你爱着哪个地方，你所需要做的就是努力工作。不管你的肤色是黑是白，不管你是拉美裔、亚裔还是美国原住民，不管你年轻还是年老，富有还是贫穷，身体健全或是残障，同性恋还是异性恋，只要你愿意努力，就能够在美国大有作为。

我相信我们有能力共同把握住这样的未来，因为美国人民并不像政界认为的那么分歧严重。美国人民不像某些饱学之士所认为的那样愤世嫉俗。美国的抱负并不是每一个美国人的抱负的简单汇总，美国也不是红州和蓝州的简单联合。我们是美利坚合众国，我们将永远是美利坚合众国。

有你们的帮助，有上帝的仁慈，我们将继续携手前行，让全世界知道我们生活在全球最伟大国度的原因到底是什么。

谢谢你们，国民们。上帝保佑你们，上帝保佑美国。

6

The End of a Long Journey —John McCain's Concession Speech

Delivered 5 November, 2008, in Phoenix, Arizona

□ About the Author

约翰·西德尼·麦凯恩三世（John Sidney McCain Ⅲ，1936 年 8 月—　），美国政治家、共和党重量级人物，亚利桑那州资深参议员，属于共和党内的“温和派”。

麦凯恩出生于巴拿马运河区域一个著名的海军世家。父亲小约翰·西德尼·麦凯恩（John Sidney McCain Jr.）和祖父老约翰·西德尼·麦凯恩（John Sidney McCain Sr.）皆获得美国海军上将军衔。麦凯恩在维吉尼亚州的亚历山德里亚圣公会中学和安那波利斯的美国海军学院接受教育。他曾担任海军的飞行员赴越南作战。1967 年 10 月，麦凯恩驾驶的 A-4 天鹰攻击机被越南人民军的对空导弹击落，他在战俘营里受尽折磨，却不肯因自己的父亲是海军上将而为越南人做宣传以享受提前释放的待遇，因而被拘禁长达五年半的时间，这也使他成为全国知名人物。

获释回国后，命运坎坷的麦凯恩进军政坛。他于 1982 年当选亚利桑那州第一选区的联邦众议员，并在 1986 年当选该州联邦参议员。1997 年，《时代》周刊把麦凯恩列为美国最有影响的 25 个人之一。麦凯恩在 2000 年总统大选中曾经角逐共和党的提名，但败给了得州州长乔治·沃克·布什。2007 年 2 月他宣布参加 2008 年的美国总统选举，并在初选中迅速击败党内对手成为共和党总统候选人，却最终在与民主党的巴拉克·奥巴马的对决中落败，再次与总统职位擦肩而过。

❑ About the Speech

2008 年 11 月 5 日，美国大选日。数千名共和党支持者从菲尼克斯市各处汇聚到巴尔的摩酒店草坪前，原打算隆重庆祝麦凯恩胜选。集会开场以英国著名音乐人埃尔顿·约翰的歌曲《我仍在坚持》为背景音乐，支持者穿戴印有“胜利 2008”字样的 T 恤衫或徽章，情绪高昂。在得知麦凯恩获胜无望后，他们的脸上显露出难以掩饰的失望，许多女性支持者眼中甚至含着泪水。面对这些神情落寞的支持者，72 岁的麦凯恩发表了这篇败选演讲。

在演说中，麦凯恩首先祝贺民主党候选人奥巴马，对他的能力和毅力表达了自己的敬意。麦凯恩称这次总统选举具有“历史性”意义。他说，一个世纪前，前总统西奥多·罗斯福邀请非裔美国教育家布克·华盛顿赴白宫共进晚餐，招致强烈反对。如今，美国诞生首位非洲裔总统，足以证明这种残酷、可怕的偏见已不复存在。麦凯恩说，美国人民作出了选择，这不仅是奥巴马个人取得的胜利，也是美国人民取得的胜利。他呼吁全体美国人抛弃政见分歧，共同支持在选举中获胜的奥巴马。

在谈到自己的竞选失败时，麦凯恩说：“当然我们今天会有失落，虽然我们会感到遗憾，但是，这是我一个人的失败，不是你们的。”他称自己因能为美国人民服务而感到荣幸。随后，他对家人、朋友、竞选搭档佩林、竞选团队和支持者表达了诚挚的感谢。演讲的最后，麦凯恩不无动情地说：“今天，我是我所热爱的这个国家的最高职位的候选人；今夜，我依然是她的一位仆人。在我心中，我比以往任何一个夜晚都更加深爱这个国家，深爱这个国家的国民，无论他们是支持我，还是支持奥巴马。”“我祝福我曾经的对手、未来的总统成功。我呼吁所有的美国人，不要对目前的困难沮丧。美国人绝不放弃，我们绝不投降！我们绝不逃避历史，我们创造历史！”——这样的败选演讲，对于悲情英雄麦凯恩来说，确实就是虽败犹荣。或许这样说更为恰当：在美国的政治竞选中，成也英雄，败也英雄。

❑ The Speech in Full

MCCAIN: Thank you. Thank you, my friends. Thank you for coming here on this beautiful Arizona evening.

My friends, we have—we have come to the end of a long journey. The American people have spoken, and they have spoken clearly.

A little while ago, I had the honor of calling Senator Barack Obama to congratulate him.

Please. To congratulate him on being elected the next President of the country that we both love.

In a contest as long and difficult as this campaign has been, his success alone commands my respect for his ability and perseverance. But that he managed to do so by inspiring the hopes of so many millions of Americans who had once wrongly believed that they had little at stake or little influence in the election of an American President is something I deeply admire and commend him for achieving.

This is an historic election, and I recognize the special significance it has for African-Americans and for the special pride that must be theirs tonight.

I've always believed that America offers opportunities to all who have the industry and will to seize it. Senator Obama believes that, too.

But we both recognize that, though we have come a long way from the old injustices that once stained our nation's reputation and denied some Americans the full blessings of American citizenship, the memory of them still had the power to wound.

A century ago, President Theodore Roosevelt's invitation of Booker T. Washington to dine... at the White House was taken as an outrage in many quarters.

America today is a world away from the cruel and frightful bigotry of that time. There is no better evidence of this than the election of an African-American to the presidency of the United States.

Let there be no reason now...

Let there be no reason now for any American to fail to cherish their citizenship in this, the greatest nation on Earth.

Senator Obama has achieved a great thing for himself and for his country. I applaud him for it, and offer him my sincere sympathy that his beloved grandmother did not live to see this day. Though our faith assures us she is at rest in the presence of her creator and so very proud of the good man she helped raise.

Senator Obama and I have had and argued our differences, and he has prevailed. No doubt many of those differences remain.

These are difficult times for our country. And I pledge to him tonight to do all in my power to help him lead us through the many challenges we face.

I urge all Americans...

I urge all Americans who supported me to join me in not just congratulating him, but offering our next President our good will and earnest effort to find ways to come together to find the necessary compromises to bridge our differences and help restore our prosperity, defend our security in a dangerous world, and leave our children and grandchildren a stronger, better country than we inherited.

Whatever our differences, we are fellow Americans. And please believe me when I say no association has ever meant more to me than that.

It is natural. It's natural, tonight, to feel some disappointment. But tomorrow, we must move beyond it and work together to get our country moving again.

We fought—we fought as hard as we could. And though we feel short, the failure is mine, not yours.

I am so... I am so deeply grateful to all of you for the great honor of your support and for all you have done for me. I wish the outcome had been different, my friends.

The road was a difficult one from the outset, but your support and friendship never wavered. I cannot adequately express how deeply indebted I am to you.

I'm especially grateful to my wife, Cindy, my children, my dear mother...(APPLAUSE) ... my dear mother and all my family, and to the many old and dear friends who have stood by my side through the many ups and downs of this long campaign.

I have always been a fortunate man, and never more so for the love and encouragement you have given me.

You know, campaigns are often harder on a candidate's family than on the candidate, and that's been true in this campaign.

All I can offer in compensation is my love and gratitude and the promise of more peaceful years ahead.

I am also—I am also, of course, very thankful to Governor Sarah Palin, one of the best campaigners I've ever seen...

... one of the best campaigners I have ever seen, and an impressive new voice in our party for reform and the principles that have always been our greatest strength...

... her husband Todd and their five beautiful children...

... for their tireless dedication to our cause, and the courage and grace they showed in the rough and tumble of a presidential campaign.

We can all look forward with great interest to her future service to Alaska, the Republican Party and our country.

To all my campaign comrades, from Rick Davis and Steve Schmidt and Mark Salter, to every last volunteer who fought so hard and valiantly, month after month, in what at times seemed to be the most challenged campaign in modern times, thank you so much. A lost election will never mean more to me than the privilege of your faith and friendship.

I don't know—I don't know what more we could have done to try to win this election. I'll leave that to others to determine. Every candidate makes mistakes, and I'm sure I made my share of them. But I won't spend a moment of the future regretting what might have been.

This campaign was and will remain the great honor of my life, and my heart is filled with nothing but gratitude for the experience and to the American people for giving me a fair hearing before deciding that Senator Obama and my old friend Senator Joe Biden should have the honor of leading us for the next four years.

I would not—I would not be an American worthy of the name should I regret a fate that has allowed me the extraordinary privilege of serving this country for a half a century.

Today, I was a candidate for the highest office in the country I love so much. And tonight, I remain her servant. That is blessing enough for anyone, and I thank the people of Arizona for it.

Tonight—tonight, more than any night, I hold in my heart nothing but love for this country and for all its citizens, whether they supported me or Senator Obama—whether they supported me or Senator Obama.

I wish Godspeed to the man who was my former opponent and will be my President. And I call on all Americans, as I have often in this campaign, to not despair of our present difficulties, but to believe, always, in the promise and greatness of America, because nothing is inevitable here.

Americans never quit. We never surrender.

We never hide from history. We make history.

Thank you, and God bless you, and God bless America. Thank you all very much.

❑ Translation

胜得光明，败得伟大！

——约翰·麦凯恩败选演讲

2008 年 11 月 5 日，亚利桑那州菲尼克斯

感谢各位。非常感谢你们，我的朋友们。感谢你们在这样一个美丽的亚利桑那州之夜，来到这里。

我的朋友们，我们已经，已经走完了这次漫长的旅程。美国人民已经作出了他们的选择，清晰地作出了他们的选择。

就在刚才，我非常荣幸地给奥巴马参议员打电话，向他表示祝贺。

（大家请冷静下来）祝贺他当选为这个我们都深爱的国家的新一任总统。

在这场如此漫长、如此艰辛的竞选活动中，他的成功赢得了我对他能力和毅力的尊敬。但是更让我钦佩和赞赏的是，他激起了数千万美国人民的希望。他们原本错误地以为他们自己在选举中所发挥的作用有限。

这是一次历史性的选举，我承认它对非洲裔美国人的重要性，今晚的荣耀必定属于他们。

我一直相信，美国为所有勤奋并愿意抓住机会的人提供了机会。奥巴马参议员也相信这一点。

但我们都意识到，尽管我们已经远离了以前的不公正，但这些不公正曾玷污了这个国家的名誉，剥夺了一些美国人作为美国公民应该享有的权益，伤痛的记忆依然存在。

一个世纪以前，西奥多·罗斯福总统邀请布克·华盛顿在白宫共进晚餐，这曾引起了许多人的愤怒。

但今天的美国已经远离了那个时代残忍以及可怕的顽固。再也没有比一位非洲裔美国人当选美国总统更能证明这一点了。

我们要让所有的美国人都没有理由不珍视他们的国民身份，珍视这个地球上最伟大国家的国民身份。

奥巴马参议员实现了他个人的伟大目标，同时也实现了这个国家的目标。我为他鼓掌喝彩，同时也对他敬爱的外祖母没有活着看到这一天而表示真挚的同情。但我们的信念告诉我们，她一定是在上帝那里安息，她一定非常骄傲自己抚养了那么好的一个人。

奥巴马参议员与我曾就许多分歧进行过争论，但他最终获胜了。毫无疑问许多分歧仍然继续存在。

我们的国家正处在困难时期。我今晚向他承诺，将尽我的全力帮助他带领我们共同迎接目前面临的许多挑战。

我呼吁所有美国人，我敦促所有支持我的美国人，不仅仅是要和我一起来祝贺他，同时还要向我们的新任总统表达我们良好的心愿以及最真诚的努力。找到必要的妥协，能让我们一起化解分歧。帮助重新恢复我们的繁荣，在这个危险的世界中捍卫我们的安全，给我们的子孙创造一个比我们当初继承的更强大、更美好的国家。

无论我们存在何种分歧，我们都是美国人。请相信我，对我而言，这比什么都重要。

自然地，今夜大家会感到失望。但明天，我们必须摆脱失望，共同奋斗使我们的国家继续前行。

我们努力了，我们尽了我们最大的努力，虽然没有达成目标。但那是我个人的失败，不是你们的失败。

对于有幸获得你们的支持，以及你们为我所做的一切，我表示最深挚的感谢。我的朋友们，我也希望结果不是这样的。

这条道路从一开始就充满艰辛，但你们的支持与友爱从来没有动摇，我实在找不出任何合适的词语来表达我对你们的感谢。

我要特别感谢我的妻子辛迪、我的孩子们、我亲爱的母亲、我所有的家人，以及许多老朋友们，在这场跌宕起伏的漫长竞选中始终在旁支持我。

我一直都是一个幸运的人，再没有比得到你们给我的爱和鼓励更幸运的了。

大家知道，竞选对于候选人的家人往往比对候选人本身更为艰难。在这次的竞选过程中同样如此。

我所能补偿的，就是我的爱和感激，以及承诺今后平静的岁月。

当然，我也非常感谢莎拉·佩林州长，她是我见过的最好的搭档之一。她为共和党的改革以及我们强大的信条带来了新的声音。

我还要感谢她的丈夫托迪以及他们 5 个美丽的孩子，在竞选的坎坷路途中所付出的不倦的努力、勇气和优雅。

我们所有人都期待她未来更好地为阿拉斯加州服务，为共和党以及我们的国家服务。

感谢我所有的竞选伙伴，迪克·戴维斯、斯蒂汶·斯米德特、马克·萨尔特，以及努力不懈及勇敢的志愿者们，一个月又一个月，这应该是现代最有挑战性的竞选，非常感谢你们。和你们的信任以及友情相比，这场失败了的选举根本算不了什么。

我不知道，我不知道我们还要多做些什么才能赢得这场选举。还是将让别人去决定吧。每位候选人都会犯错误，我相信我也犯了不少错误，但我未来绝对不会对此感到有一丝的遗憾。

这场选举过去和将来都会是我生命中的巨大荣幸，我的心中充满了对这种经历的感谢。美国人民在选择奥巴马参议员以及我的老朋友拜登参议员来领导美国的下一个 4 年之前，给了我一个倾听的公平机会。

如果我后悔命运让我为这个国家服务 50 年，我就不配是美国人。

今天，我是我所热爱的这个国家的最高职位的一位候选人，今夜，我依然是她的仆人。对任何人来说，这都是无上的荣幸。为此，我要谢谢亚利桑那州的民众。

今夜，相比以往任何一个夜晚，我的内心更加充满对这个国家和人民的热爱，无论他们是支持我，还是支持奥巴马参议员。

我祝福我曾经的对手、未来的总统成功。我呼吁所有的美国人，正如我在竞选中经常说的那样，不要对现在的困难沮丧，而是永远相信美国的前景和伟大，因为在这里，没有什么事情是必然的。

美国人绝不放弃，我们绝不投降！我们绝不逃避历史，我们创造历史！

谢谢。愿上帝保佑你们，愿上帝保佑美国。非常感谢你们。

参考文献

安东尼·刘易斯．批评官员的尺度：《纽约时报》诉警察局长沙利文案 [M]. 北京大学出版社，2011

蔡永良，董剑桥．英语国家社会与文化（美国篇）[M]. 苏州：苏州大学出版社，2008

崔永禄，孙毅兵．20 世纪美国最佳演说精选（一）[M]. 天津：南开大学出版社，2010

李树德，冯奇．英语修辞简明教程 [M]. 上海：复旦大学出版社，2011

邹颉．美国的精神——美国现代政界领袖演讲精选 [M]. 北京：中国经济出版社，2009

戴安娜·拉维奇．美国读本（修订本）[M]. 北京：国际文化出版公司，2005

郝澎．美国历史重大事件及著名人物 [M]. 海口：南海出版公司，2007

刘再复．阅读美国 [M] 福州：福建教育出版社，2009

孙毅兵，卞建华．美国总统演讲集萃 [M]. 天津：天津科学技术出版社，2005

王波．美国历史与文化选读 [M]. 北京：北京大学出版社，2004

王建华．美国总统就职演说精选 [M]. 南昌：江西人民出版社，2008

肖福寿．美国总统就职演说赏析（1789—2005）[M]. 上海：上海大学出版社，2009

徐翰林．感动一个国家的文字 [M]. 哈尔滨：哈尔滨出版社，2004

袁明．美国文化与社会十五讲 [M]. 北京：北京大学出版社，2007

袁贺，谈火生．美国历届总统就职演说全集 [M]. 北京：经济日报出版社，2007

詹姆斯·M·麦克菲尔．总统的力量：从殖民地到超级大国 [M]. 北京：中国友谊出版公司，2007

张千帆．自由的魂魄所在——美国宪法与政府体制 [M]. 北京：中国社会科学出版社，2000

朱永涛．美国价值观 [M]. 北京：外语教学与研究出版社，2002

张立平．林登·约翰逊与民权法案 [J]. 美国研究，1996,(2)

资中筠．从美国总统就职演说看美国的变与不变 [J]. 美国研究 , 2005,(2)

陈冬梅，辛柯．从就职演说探讨演说词的修辞风格 [J]. 西北工业大学学报（社会科学版），2006,(3): 68-71

http:// www. americanrhetoric.com

http://en.wikipedia.org/wiki

http://myloc.gov/Exhibitions

http://www. the freelibrary.com

http://www.dcpages.com/

http://www.ldoceonline.com/

图书在版编目（CIP）数据

美国总统演讲名篇赏析：英文/徐中川主编. —北京：中国人民大学出版社，2013.1
高级实用英语系列教材
ISBN 978-7-300-17015-2

Ⅰ. ①美… Ⅱ. ①徐… Ⅲ. ①英语–语言读物 ②演讲–美国–选集 Ⅳ. ①H319.4：I

中国版本图书馆 CIP 数据核字（2013）第 015231 号

高级实用英语系列教材
美国总统演讲名篇赏析
Appreciating Excellent Speeches by the US Presidents
主　编　徐中川（中国海洋大学）
编　委　邹姗姗（中国海洋大学）
　　　　孙广峰（中国海洋大学）
　　　　乔发光（山东大学）
　　　　冯延群（上海海洋大学）
　　　　李玉香（同济大学）
Meiguo Zongtong Yanjiang Mingpian Shangxi

出版发行	中国人民大学出版社		
社　　址	北京中关村大街31号	邮政编码	100080
电　　话	010–62511242（总编室）		010–62511770（质管部）
	010–82501766（邮购部）		010–62514148（门市部）
	010–62515195（发行公司）		010–62515275（盗版举报）
网　　址	http://www.crup.com.cn		
	http://www.ttrnet.com（人大教研网）		
经　　销	新华书店		
印　　刷	北京鑫丰华彩印有限公司		
规　　格	185 mm × 240 mm　16 开本	版　　次	2013 年 2 月第 1 版
印　　张	23.25	印　　次	2018 年 1 月第 2 次印刷
字　　数	515 000	定　　价	42.00 元（附赠光盘）

中国人民大学出版社外语出版分社读者信息反馈表

尊敬的读者：

感谢您购买和使用中国人民大学出版社外语出版分社的 ______________ 一书，我们希望通过这张小小的反馈卡来获得您更多的建议和意见，以改进我们的工作，加强我们双方的沟通和联系。我们期待着能为更多的读者提供更多的好书。

请您填妥下表后，寄回或传真回复我们，对您的支持我们不胜感激！

1. 您是从何种途径得知本书的：
   □书店　□网上　□报纸杂志　□朋友推荐
2. 您为什么决定购买本书：
   □工作需要　□学习参考　□对本书主题感兴趣　□随便翻翻
3. 您对本书内容的评价是：
   □很好　□好　□一般　□差　□很差
4. 您在阅读本书的过程中有没有发现明显的专业及编校错误，如果有，它们是：
   ____
   ____
   ____
5. 您对哪些专业的图书信息比较感兴趣：
   ____
   ____
   ____

6. 如果方便，请提供您的个人信息，以便于我们和您联系（您的个人资料我们将严格保密）：

您供职的单位：______________________________

您教授的课程（教师填写）：______________________________

您的通信地址：______________________________

您的电子邮箱：______________________________

请联系我们：贾乐凯　黄婷　程子殊　于真妮　鞠方安

电话：010–62515580，62512737，62513265，62515037，62515576

传真：010-62514961

E-mail：jialk@crup.com.cn　huangt@crup.com.cn　chengzsh@crup.com.cn

yuzn@crup.com.cn　jufa@crup.com.cn

通信地址：北京市海淀区中关村大街甲 59 号文化大厦 15 层　邮编：100872

中国人民大学出版社外语出版分社